W9-ASH-293

SOCIAL GROUP WORK

Other books by HARLEIGH B. TRECKER

Social Work Administration: Principles and Practices
Education for Social Work Administration *(with Frank Z. Glick and John C.*
        Kidneigh)
Group Services in Public Welfare
Citizen Boards at Work: New Challenges to Effective Action

AVPT
HV
45
.T7
1972

SOCIAL GROUP WORK

Principles and Practices

HARLEIGH B. TRECKER

University Professor of Social Work
School of Social Work
The University of Connecticut

Thoroughly Rewritten, Updated and Expanded

ASSOCIATION PRESS • NEW YORK

SOCIAL GROUP WORK

Copyright © 1972, 1955 by Harleigh B. Trecker

Association Press, 291 Broadway, New York, N.Y. 10007
All rights reserved. No part of this publication may be reprinted, reproduced, transmitted, stored in a retrieval system, or otherwise utilized, in any form or by any
means, electronic or mechanical, including photocopying or recording, now existing
or hereinafter invented, without the prior written permission of the publisher.

Second Printing 1975

Library of Congress Cataloging in Publication Data

Trecker, Harleigh Bradley, 1911–
    Social group work, principles and practices.

    Bibliography: p.
    1. Social group work.
HV45.T7   1972   361.4   70-189012
ISBN 0-8096-1846-X

International Standard Book Number: 0-8096-1846-X
Library of Congress Catalog Card Number: 70-189012

Printed in the United States of America

to my grandson James Harleigh Trecker
with love

Contents

8. Evaluation of Social Group Work   202

9. Basic Principles of Social Group Work   221

Part II: Social Group Work Practice—Selected Records, Documents, and Teaching Aids

Figures

Introduction

SOCIAL GROUP WORK: PRINCIPLES AND PRACTICES is a book for those persons in social work and related fields who wish to learn about one of the major methods in social work practice. I have tried to make it a broad, useful and generally comprehensive book for the student of social group work and the teacher. The theoretical material in Part I is followed by Part II which contains historical and contemporary documents and cases for teaching purposes. In addition the extensive bibliography of selected readings is aimed at putting in the hands of the reader as complete a book as is possible.

For several decades I have worked and taught in this challenging area of social work. I have seen social group work grow in scope and importance as its usefulness has been proven again and again. The small group is a vital means for helping people to grow, to relate to one another, and to find their place in society. Many workers in the human services field have the opportunity to help people become participating group members. To do so they must understand the process of helping people *through* and in groups.

In 1948 I published *Social Group Work: Principles and Practices,* one of the first textbooks in group work. In 1955 this book was revised and enlarged and during the intervening years it has gone through a number of printings. Many letters received from users of the book from around the world indicate that it has been useful. Hence, the basic material in the early book has been reproduced here with appropriate rewriting and updating. In addition, a considerable amount of new material has been added to make the book more useful. Yet, the basic focus of the book has not changed. It is an introduction to social group work as it has developed and is being practiced in community agency settings.

For whom is the book intended? It is intended to be an introduction for all persons who are learning to work with groups and to everyone now doing so who wishes to learn more about this important activity. It should be of help to undergraduate and graduate students, to beginning workers, both

13

professional and volunteer, and perhaps to some experienced workers who are interested in a thorough review of social group work.

The book is set up as an introductory text which hopefully will be useful to faculty members and students who wish to pursue a logical course of study. Part I: Method and Principles is essentially theoretical material. In the first chapter social group work is defined and its development is outlined. The community agency as a setting for social group work is considered in Chapter 2. Chapter 3 is focused on the small group—understanding and working with the small group. Chapter 4 deals with role and responsibility of the group worker and is in a sense a key chapter. The basic process of program development is reviewed in Chapter 5. Working with individuals in the group is the theme of Chapter 6. In Chapter 7 new material on social group work in a variety of special settings is presented. Evaluation of social group work is the substance of Chapter 8. Basic principles are offered in Chapter 9. The above chapters contain ten figures, or diagrams, as visual aids. All of the figures have been used in connection with teaching. As visual aids these figures may help students to understand better the points that they illustrate.

The material in Part II: Selected Records, Documents, and Teaching Aids has been organized to provide a selection of teaching and study material so that users will have handy in one volume many items that should be helpful in the teaching and learning of group work. Special references, definitions, cases, documents, teaching tools, and new approaches to group work in special settings have been chosen for their potential usefulness to new and experienced workers. These selections may encourage readers to create their own file of helpful aids for further study and continuing education.

One of the striking changes over the years has been the extensive use that is being made of social group work in a wide variety of settings. Always a major method in neighborhood and community centers and in work with children and youth, now social group work is used in public welfare, mental health, corrections, child welfare, schools, hospitals and clinics, senior centers, and the like.

In recent years there have been many articles on social group work written for the professional periodicals. Hundreds of articles have been read and researched in the preparation of this book and much interesting and helpful material has been selected for inclusion. The lengthy bibliography of selected readings at the end of the book is given as a help to students. An effort has been made to provide both a contemporary and historical array of contributions to the literature of social group work. Every effort has been made to make the bibliography up to date, but at the same time the historically classic writings of some group work pioneers have been included for those who wish to trace group work progress. It is to be hoped that the bibliography will be useful to many readers. This is also the goal of the complete index provided.

Over the years many people have helped in the preparation of this book. Faculty members from other schools of social work have sent their outlines and bibliographies to me. Agency workers have given time and material especially in the area of illustrative material. My colleagues and students at the University of Connecticut School of Social Work have been most generous and gracious in the help they have given to me. I am especially indebted to Norman Goroff and Albert Alissi, associate professors at the University of Connecticut School of Social Work. They have given me much material and have provided me with hours of stimulating conferences. Louise C. Johnson, assistant professor at the School of Social Work, University of Iowa, has been exceedingly helpful in sharing material with me. Joseph Montgomery, Director of Social Services, General Hospital, University of Iowa, and Janice Baumback have permitted me to use material. I am grateful to them. James T. Jones, Program Director, Adult Social Services, Department of Social Services, State of Michigan; Gladys V. Bolling, Chief, Social Work Service, Veterans Administration Hospital, Pittsburgh, Pa., Carolyn Thomas, associate professor, Boston College Graduate School of Social Work; Jack C. Sternbach, associate professor, School of Social Work, University of Pennsylvania, have been kind in granting me permission to use selected material.

Mrs. Jean Tetu and her staff in the Library at the University of Connecticut School of Social Work have been so helpful for so many years that I can never thank them enough. Miss Thelma Caruso has done her usual outstanding job of preparing the manuscript for publication. This is the third book that she has typed for me and I am quite fortunate to have her services.

As always, my wife Audrey R. Trecker has been of never-ending help, support, and encouragement to me in this entire project. My sons Jerrold and James and my daughters-in-law Janice and Barbara have been a source of sustainment during the long years of work. My grandson, James Harleigh, has provided inspiration when energy seemed to flag. The book is dedicated to him with love and hope for his future and the futures of all of the little ones like him.

HARLEIGH B. TRECKER

West Hartford, Connecticut

PART I

METHOD AND PRINCIPLES

1

Social Group Work—
Definition and Development

In this book we are considering the question: What does the social worker who works primarily with groups need to know and understand about these groups in order to work with them effectively? We are interested in helping new workers and those who are studying social group work to develop an approach to working with groups and a point of view about them that will ultimately lead to deeper knowledge, insight and skill. For experienced workers we hope to present a systematic review of the group work method which will be helpful to them as they assess their accomplishments. We also want to locate and make explicit the principles which underlie professional skill in social group work. Furthermore, we wish to look ahead and cite some of the future goals of group work development.

Social group work is one method in the profession of social work. The other methods are social casework, community organization work, and social work administration. All are important and all are interrelated.

What Is Social Group Work?

When we speak of social group work as a *method* we mean an orderly, systematic, planned way of working with people in groups. A method is a conscious procedure, a designed means of achieving a goal. In its outer aspects, a method is a way of doing something, but underneath the doing we always discover an integrated arrangement of knowledge, understanding, and principles.

Occasionally some persons tend to identify social group work with a specific kind of social work or community agency. Social group work is, however, not an agency but one way of carrying out all or part of the function of many agencies. As indicated by Vinter:

Specialized use of group procedures is now to be found across a broad range of health, welfare, and educational agencies: anti-poverty organizations, child guidance clinics, school social services, juvenile courts and delinquency control programs, mental hospitals and correctional institutions, public welfare agencies, youth development and recreational programs, and others. Group work is a mode of serving individuals within and through small face-to-face groups in order to induce desired changes among the client participants. This mode of practice cannot adequately be distinguished from other helping processes, particularly those in the profession of social work, by reference to types of clientele served, to the organizational contexts of service, or to the general service goals set for clients. The essential difference lies in the primary—but not exclusive—reliance on the multi-person group session rather than on the interview as the basic form of intervention.[1]

Other persons tend to describe social group work as a type of activity program. Actually, social group work is not an activity, but a way of working with people who may engage in many different activities. And still others declare that social group work refers to a specific kind of group—a small club group, for example. This is, unfortuately, limiting because social group work refers to a way of work with many different kinds of groups. Lippitt says:

My use of the term "group work" is a generic rather than a specialized one. I refer to all contexts in which professional practitioners use their professional values and skills to help a group develop and function for such diverse purposes as the social-emotional growth of group members, the development of task competence of group members, facilitation of the individual productivity of group members, and the growth of the *group* as a *group* toward such objectives as competence in collective achievement or facilitation of group productivity, committee decision-making and so on.[2]

Over the years distinguished scholars have contributed much to the definition and development of social group work. In the 1950's Grace Coyle said:

Social group work, like casework, community organization, administration, and research, is now recognized as a basic aspect of social work practice. Its distinct characteristics lie in the fact that group work is used in social relationships within group experience as a means to individual growth and development, and that the group worker is concerned in developing social responsibility and active citizenship for the improvement of democratic society.[3]

About the same time Gertrude Wilson and Gladys Ryland elaborated on this theme when they said:

In the enabling method, the members are helped to learn new ideas, develop new skills, change attitudes and deepen their personalities through participation in a social process wherein they make decisions and take the social action necessary to accomplish the purposes of the group. It is the *quality* of group experience that is the basis for differentiating among the methods. This quality arises out of the relationship between the members and between the members and the worker who affects the interacting process. And the relationship of the worker to the members (and hence, the role he fulfills) stems directly from his philosophy and purposes of the auspice with which he is identified and from which he receives his functional sanction. . . . We therefore see social group work as a process and a method through which group life is affected by a worker who consciously directs the interacting process toward the accomplishment of goals which in our country are conceived in a democratic frame of reference.[4]

In more recent years other distinguished scholars have taken up these themes and have defined social group work with precision and clarity. Konopka puts it this way:

Social group work is a method of social work which helps individuals to enhance their social functioning through purposeful group experiences and to cope more effectively with their personal, group, or community problems.[5]

In a superb article in the *Encyclopedia of Social Work* Vinter states:

Group work is a way of serving individuals within and through small face-to-face groups in order to bring about changes among the client participants. This method of practice recognizes the potency of social forces that are generated within small groups and seeks to marshal them in the interest of client change. The composition, development, and processes of the groups are deliberately guided by the practitioner toward achieving his service goals for the clients. Intervention in the experience of the group is the primary means for effecting change, although practitioners engage in many other activities with or on behalf of their clients in addition to conducting group sessions. The group is viewed as a small social system whose influence can be managed to develop client abilities, to modify self-images and perspectives, to resolve conflicts, and to inculcate new patterns of behavior.[6]

Northern observes: "Social work practice uses the small group as both the context and means through which its members support and modify their attitudes, interpersonal relationships, and abilities to cope effectively with their environment."[7]

Esterson makes a real contribution when he distinguishes between social group work and recreation. He writes:

It is generally believed that recreation, group activity and group experience all contribute to the satisfaction of some psychological needs. Recreation and group activity provide opportunity for self-expression, recognition and belonging. Similarly, the hunger for cooperation and competition may be satisfied through team or group games. The recreation leader who does not employ the group work method is mainly concerned with providing recreational activities and programs without conscious and direct concern for the social adjustment or growth of the individual. Whatever adjustment or growth occurs is spontaneous. In contrast to recreation, group work is a method by which the group worker enables various types of groups to function in such a way that group interaction and program activities contribute to the growth of the individual, and the achievement of desirable social goals. The social group worker is seen as primarily an enabler in the group process. By use of his understanding of group and individual needs, he establishes relationships through which he seeks to develop the potentialities of the group to accomplish its purposes and he aids individual members of the group to find satisfying and socially productive experiences. The group worker must be aware of cultural factors and social forces as they affect and are affected by the group, and he is concerned with helping the group to bring about changes in community or cultural patterns as they relate to the group needs and interests.[8]

If we are to present a clear definition of social group work we must recognize that many factors are involved: agencies, groups, workers, programs, and underlying purposes. However, since a method, to mean anything, must be used by a worker, perhaps the heart of the definition should be what the worker does and how it is done.

In the brief paragraphs which follow, an attempt is made to define social group work in operational terms:

Social group work is a method in social work through which individuals in many groups in a variety of community agency settings are helped by a worker who guides their interaction in program activities so that they may relate themselves to others and experience growth opportunities in accordance with their needs and capacities to the end of individual, group, and community development.

In social group work, the group itself is utilized by the individual with the help of the worker as a primary means of personality growth, change, and development. The worker is interested in helping to bring about individual growth and social development for the group as a whole and for the community as a result of guided group interaction.

In Figure 1 an attempt is made to define and analyze social group work schematically to show its composition, setting, methodology, and ultimate purposes. In studying the figure the reader should first read the upper portion I through V, following the arrows across the page. Then he should read the material vertically, Roman I to Arabic 1, Roman II to Arabic 2, and so on.

In 1959 the Curriculum Study of the Council on Social Work Education summarized generalizations on social group work method, process, and goals, on which a substantial degree of acceptance was evident:

1. Social group work is a method of rendering service to persons, through providing experience in groups. Development of the person towards his individual potential, improvement of relationship and social functioning competencies, and social action are recognized as purposes of social group work. The worker functions within a framework of ethical social work values.

FIGURE 1

An Analysis of Social Group Work

I	II	III	IV	V
Social group work is a method	through which individuals in many groups in a variety of community agency settings	are helped by a worker who guides their interaction in program activities	so that they may relate themselves to other people and experience growth opportunities in accordance with their needs and capacities	to the end of individual, group, and community development
1. *Made up of* knowledge understanding principles skills	2. *Including* the individual in the group in the agency in the community setting	3. *Through* relationship based on acceptance individualizing the group helping the group to determine objectives and programs stimulation and guidance organization and procedures use of resources	4. *Such as* participation belonging decision making responsibility achievement self-motivation adjustment to others	5. *Objective* change in behavior of individuals and groups in terms of democratic goals and community development

2. Social group work is a generic method which can be used in different settings.

3. The method includes conscious use of worker-member relationships, relationships among members, and of group activity. The worker simultaneously uses relationships with individual members and the group as a whole. He works as an enabler with both, helping members and the group to use their capacities and strengths. He uses himself differently in accordance with specific objectives and his assessment of members' needs, interests, and capacities.

4. Social group work is often used in conjunction with other social work service methods, and with other disciplines. It is sometimes used predominantly, and sometimes as one method in more inclusive treatment plans. It is used in short-term as well as long-term programs.

5. Goal selection, decision-making, program development, acceptance of and internalization of appropriate controls, creative utilization of conflicts, are recognized as some of the components of social group work process.[9]

It has become increasingly evident that in social group work the focus of the worker is always on the individual *in the group*. Group work can be carried on in a wide variety of settings. Group work has the tripartite purpose of individual growth, group growth, and community change. In group work the group itself is a major tool for individual development. Group work requires a special kind of worker who accents the helping process. The worker is viewed as a "helping person" whose job it is to help people discover and utilize individual, group, agency, and community strengths for the well-being of all persons involved.

The use of the word "help" in referring to the role of group worker is deliberate. In group work, individuals and groups are helped by the worker to attain certain ends. The worker is a "helping person" or an "enabler" rather than a "group leader." What kind of help does the worker give to the group? How does he give it? These are fundamental questions which need considerable exploration. Social group work is not only a matter of *what* the worker does, but also a matter of *how* the worker does it and *why* he does it that way. Truly, the key to social group work is the worker.

Groups may need help in coming together. They may need help in developing a form of organization. They may need help in deciding standards and qualifications for membership. Most groups need help with program development and in dealing with conflict. Groups may need help in understanding and accepting their own limitations. They may need help in learning how to utilize the agency and community setting. The group worker always gives help with certain purposes in mind. He wants to help groups solve problems themselves rather than work out the answers and hand them over to the groups. He is interested in seeing to it that groups are helped to a greater independence and self-reliance even though he recognizes that this takes considerable time.

The Need for, and the Importance of, Social Group Work Today

Inasmuch as the major and basic problems of our times continue to be those of human relationships, it can be stated with certainty and conviction that any professional service which endeavors to help people learn how to get along with others is not only important but essential. The community, through its wide recognition of social group work, has said that it does not wish to leave the availability of such services to chance. As the Family Service Association of America pointed out: "One of the most serious psychological problems of today is the lack of opportunity for persons in large cities and overcrowded suburbs to interact with each other in meaningful ways. In recent years, social work and other professions have become increasingly concerned about the mental health implications of the social isolation of large segments of the population and have attempted to find means of bringing people into more intimate personal contact with each other. Groups of various kinds have been established with the purpose of reducing the general emotional impoverishment of people and of meeting the particular social and psychological needs of certain individuals. Many kinds of groups—educational, avocational, recreational, and therapeutic—have been sponsored by social agencies, clinics, hospitals, churches, and schools; each has its place in the community's network of services." [10]

Society needs the services of social group work today for a variety of reasons. In the first place, the swift and ever-increasing advances in the physical sciences and technology have put the means of total destruction at the fingertips of nations around the globe. The people of the world must somehow discover one another and learn to live together if they are to avoid instant obliteration. The interdependence of people in the modern, shrinking world is perhaps their outstanding characteristic. Unless we find ways of working together on the community level, we can scarcely expect to achieve much success on a worldwide basis.

Although we recognize the need to understand one another and the need to get along, we see also that life each day becomes more complex. The growth of large cities and larger metropolitan areas, the development of giant industries, the increase in the size and centralization of government, all tend to make it difficult for the individual person to feel that he is a part of significant enterprises. As Maliver said, "Our population grows, yet there is less intimacy between human beings, less family life, fewer opportunities to share emotional experiences. People are more likely to assimilate a set of emotional values from what they see on television than by relating to people they know and feel close to." [11] As life becomes more complex, social adjustment needs also increase in complexity. The evidence of individual emotional breakdown is enormous. The impersonal nature of many life situations, especially in the realm of work, makes it difficult for persons to establish meaningful group relationships.

As a major primary group the family has changed in size, organization, and function. Social group work cannot take the place of the family group, but it can provide something in the way of a substitute for experiences which were once an accepted part of home life.

The speed, the tension, the pace of modern life make it difficult for some people to relax. Opportunities for social creativity are limited. There has been a vast increase in the amount of leisure time; witness the five-day week now giving way to the four-day week in some industries, witness the lengthening of the vacation allowances, and earlier retirement. But individuals are often ill prepared to put their additional leisure to work for their own growth or for the general welfare.

The problems of the modern community must be solved by group and intergroup effort. No other way is possible if we believe that the ultimate controls of human destiny must rest in the hands of the people rather than in the hands of the state. To develop individuals who are socially responsible is an exceedingly important task at any moment in history; it is more important than ever today. The skills of democratic living are developed slowly through actual firsthand, practical experiences. As citizens we must know how to participate with our neighbors in the affairs of government; somehow we must be helped to learn what is involved in citizen participation and social responsibility.

There can be little doubt that much of the confusion, indecision, and alienation present today grows out of individual inability to know where to take hold of society's problems. Many people want earnestly to work for a world of peace; they want to do something about the needs of others, especially those who are without work, food, shelter, and medical care. They want to help government become more creative and responsive to the needs of people. But alone they can do little. They must work in harmony with other people. The group worker may think he is "just working with a group of children or youth or adults." Actually, he is providing opportunities that are not only individually important but basic to the preparation of people who must learn how to assume responsibilities in a world that will grow more, rather than less, complex. The group worker is a key figure in the enrichment of the social environment. René Jules Dubos puts it:

Each person has a wide range of innate potentialities that remain untapped. Whether physical or mental, these potentialities can become expressed only to the extent that circumstances are favorable to their existential manifestation. Society thus plays a large role in the unfolding and development of man's nature. One can take it for granted that the latent potentialities of human beings have a better chance to become actualized when the social environment is sufficiently diversified to provide a variety of stimulating experiences, especially for the young. As more persons find the opportunity to express their biological endowment under diversified conditions, society becomes richer in experiences and civilization continues to unfold. In contrast, if the surrounding and ways of life are highly stereotyped, the only components of man's nature that flourish are those adapted to the narrow edge of prevailing conditions.[12]

The National Commission for Social Work Careers said:

Social work's business is to help people bring about healthy change within themselves and in society. The goal is to foster productive interaction between man and his world. The job requires a social worker to understand and use knowledge of human behavior and relationships, the social trends and problems affecting human lives, and the structure and dyamics of social organizations and society. An experience common to all is that group interaction can be a catalyst for change within the group member, and that progress—or lack of it—of the group affects its members. For social workers who work with groups, the central concern is to insure that what happens has positive meaning both to the individual member and to the group. In America today, the population increase, mass urbanization, and rapid growth of technology and industrialization have increasing impact upon the lives of people. Most of our citizens enjoy the fruits of material and technical progress, but few escape its dehumanizing effects. The principal need of the adolescent—to lay firm grip on an identity which will enable him to grow into adulthood securely—has become increasingly difficult. The adult struggles against becoming a cipher. The older adult must deal with the particular problems of aging in a rapidly changing world. Cutting across all age groups, anachronistic aspects of our society—poverty, racial discrimination, inadequate provisions for housing, education and health—contrast painfully with our long held goals of the good life for all. In such a world people need each other, need the support of relationships with others as they cope with day-to-day problems. Some need help in learning how to give and take, how to develop and use relationships. Many need help in dealing with the "systems" which confront citizens of our mass society in their roles as consumers, users of health and welfare services, taxpayers, tenants or homeowners, and many others. Those who struggle with extraordinary problems resulting from physical or mental illness, extreme deprivation, or antisocial behavior, often need social work services in a group as part of their rehabilitation. The social worker who works with groups whether in a program of prevention or one of rehabilitation, is in a unique position to help people meet their individual and collective needs.[13]

The Purposes of Social Group Work

What are the general purposes of social group work? What do individuals get out of group experiences provided by social group work programs? To be sure, the broad over-all objectives of any of the social work methods are similar to the objectives of the social work profession as a whole. Smalley puts it:

The underlying purpose of all social work effort is to release human power in individuals for personal fulfillment and social good, and to release social power for the creation of the kinds of society, social institutions, and social policy which make self-realization most possible for all men. Two values which are primary in such a purpose are respect for the worth and dignity of every individual and concern that he have the opportunity to realize his potential as an individually fulfilled, socially contributive person.[14]

Community agencies, however, do have specialized objectives, and workers must have some notion of the purposes they wish to accomplish with their groups. In general, group workers are interested in furthering the social adjustment of the individual and in developing the social consciousness of the group. They believe that personality development and growth come from mutually satisfying experiences had by people. Berelson and Steiner declare:

> The group strongly influences the behavior of its members by providing them with support, reinforcement, security, encouragement, protection, rationale, rationalization, etc. . . . When an individual is genuinely attached to a group, and in close and continuous contact with it, his group-anchored behaviors and beliefs are extremely resistant to change; and in such circumstances the group can exercise firm "control" over him.[15]

Group workers seek to provide opportunities for planned group experiences that are needed by all people. It is an objective of group work to help individuals develop their capacity to participate intelligently in the groups and communities of which they are a part. Group workers believe that it is important that individuals be given a chance to belong, to gain acceptance from other persons, and to feel secure in relation to others. Group work also functions in another way: It provides experiences that are relaxing and that give individuals a chance to create, to share, and to express themselves.

In 1962 the Practice Commission of the Group Work Section of the National Association of Social Workers stated:

> Social group work is that part of social work in which the primary medium of practice is the group, served for the purpose of effecting the social functioning of its members. To this end the social group worker focuses simultaneously on the functioning of individual members and the development of the group as an entity within the social situation.

In their discussion of what social group work does for people they said:

> Group experience is used in social group work for helping people in a number of ways including 1) helping group members to learn to participate actively in group life as experience in developing a sense of responsibility for active citizenship, 2) helping individuals develop their growth potential and achieve enrichment of life through collective experience and interpersonal exchange, 3) helping individuals find social associations or peer relations necessary for strengthening self-awareness and social belonging, or for personal support through particular stress periods, or to extend the range of social relationships, or to assist the individual to prepare for and adapt to new situations, 4) helping individuals maintain a satisfactory level of social functioning

especially when it is in danger due to personal or social circumstances, 5) helping by providing corrective experiences where there has been social breakdown or marked distress in the social situation.[16]

Somers offers a four-part statement of purpose when she writes:

Through the purposeful use of selected group experiences, social group workers (1) assist in implementing the normal growth and continuing development of individuals within our society; (2) assist in supplementing lacks and deprivations in social experience and functioning of individuals and groups; (3) assist in modifying, correcting, and preventing individual and social breakdown and deterioration; and (4) assist in aiding individuals and groups to fulfill their motivations and capacities for contributing to their society.[17]

In a recent discussion of the purposes of social group work Alissi observes that ". . . group experiences can be used to achieve the following purposes: 1) *Corrective*—to provide restorative or remedial experiences in instances where there has been social or personal dysfunction or breakdown of individuals or within social situations; 2) *Preventive*—to prevent personal and social breakdown where there is danger of deterioration; 3) *Normal Growth and Development*—to facilitate the normal growth and development processes of individual members particularly during certain stressful periods in the life cycle; 4) *Personal Enhancement*—to achieve a greater measure of self-fulfillment and personal enhancement through meaningful and stimulating interpersonal relations; 5) *Citizen Responsibility and Participation*—to inculcate democratic values among group members as they are helped to become responsibly involved as individuals and members of groups, as active participants in society." [18]

Since the community provides group work service by supporting the agencies, what does the community get from social group work? Social work programs are always determined by social need, by community understanding and acceptance of the need, and by community support and sanction. Social group work enriches community life when individuals learn how to take responsibility for their own behavior and how to become participating members of society. Persons who have had satisfying group relationships become socially mature and learn how to respond to the demands of cooperative working relationships so paramount in modern-day living.

Tropp emphasizes the unique centrality of social group work in social work practice when he writes:

Group work is, in effect, the primary social work practice in a position to meet people at the point of average functioning, and the primary one with the structure and method to undertake this task. For optimum social functioning, group experiences must be provided that are challenging rather than protected, demanding rather than permissive, and externally oriented rather than self-oriented. These experiences should provide participants with the widest possible spectrum of social realities comparable to the demands of society at large. The testing of individuals against the demands of organized society is the real business of group work. For this testing ground it is not enough to speak of "interaction" and "relationships" which may be only of the one-to-one variety. It is in the acting out of the drama of the individual against society, through society, and for society that group work finds its natural place. This drama is composed of a series of external challenges and necessities through which the individual is put to the test through the organized group. The pull of external necessity is a compelling force that represents the maximum social challenge. Further, outer necessity has the greatest potential for making the individuals feel necessary to society. In this need to be needed is the root of the problem of alienation. The quality of engagement in a common-goal group meets the basic requirement for feeling necessary. There is much reason to believe that the conflict and engagement process makes an important contribution to the development of full ego identity.[19]

Social Work and Social Group Work

Over the years the profession of social work has developed certain insights which have proved to be helpful in the rendering of services to individuals, groups, and communities. In defining social work we see it as a helping process designed to aid the individual, group, or community in attitude and behavior change within a particular social situation. Social service begins at the point of first contact and is coextensive with the entire period of the helping relationship between the worker and the unit served. The aim of social work is to facilitate the social functioning of the individual, the group, or the community. Social group work is thus one part of the social work whole with a distinct way of helping individuals in groups based upon and growing out of the knowledge, understanding, and skill that is generic to all social work practice.

Modern social work is based upon a number of important assumptions. To a certain extent these assumptions represent a theory of human behavior and a theory of social change. While some persons might disagree with the particular wording of these underlying assumptions, they are offered here as a kind of general platform from which professional social workers move out to provide services.

Social work is based upon certain assumptions and convictions regarding people. These convictions become basic values which underlie every action taken by the worker. For example, in social work the worth and dignity of every human being is central and all-pervasive. Furthermore, it is assumed that people can and do change in their behavior when they are given the right help at the right time and in the correct amount. Furthermore, it is known that people who need help will respond better when help is given early before needs and problems become too great. Social work assumes also that all behavior is purposeful and that while the purpose may not always be consciously recognized, behavior represents the individual's striving to meet needs which are important to him. It is also assumed that the family is the most influential force in the development of personality, and that early life experiences are of tremendous importance in shaping the behavior patterns of the individual.

Modern social work assumes that most problems of people are complex, interwoven, and embedded in the total life situation, they include elements of depth, duration, width, and range. The human personality is a highly complex mechanism consisting of inner forces constantly being shaped by outer forces.

The primary change agent in the social work process is the social worker who with his insight, understanding, self-awareness, and skill enables or helps persons to change. The social worker's chief tool is the relationship of acceptance, understanding, love, integrity, and warmth which he creates with the individual in need of help. In social work the worker's own needs are kept under control and every effort is made to strive for an objective, scientific, yet human approach. Of increasing importance to the social worker are his collaborative or teamwork skills because more and more the social worker must expect to work with other specialists in the realm of community services so as to muster, rally, and utilize more fully all of the resources that are available.

Social work assumes that behavior change comes from within and must be motivated by the individual's desire to change. Furthermore, basic behavior changes come slowly, take time, and the individual must become engaged or involved in the change process. He must participate in the experience, otherwise no real change is likely to take place. This means that the social worker and the individual, group, or community must establish a working relationship which produces a new design for motivation and change.

Basic to all of social work is the principle of study and diagnosis. This means that the social worker must study the individual, the group, or the community and understand the behavior and motivations present in the situation. The worker must endeavor to analyze with care and with diligence the possible factors that enter into each situation.

The principle of individualization means that each person, group, or community is different and each situation is different. Therefore, social work plans must be individualized and must be designed to meet the needs of a given person, group, or community at a given time.

It is important to realize that the social work process, the same as the educational process, must have clearly defined objectives and must have a clearly defined focus. Actually, social work is a step-by-step process and changes in individuals, groups, and communities come about in stages rather than in dramatic or sudden ways. When the worker draws up in his mind precisely what he wants to have happen in terms of clearly defined objectives he is able to measure and evaluate the success of his efforts.

Before change can come about it is necessary for the person and the social worker to become related in an effective professional way. This is true for the group, and the community as well. In every case the social worker must exercise a conscious, controlled use of himself and through his warmth, acceptance, and understanding he will strive to create a bond of feeling which will help the individual to understand the basis for going on with the work.

The principle of participation means that the social worker and the individual, group, or community must become engaged, involved, or seen as working together. Participation engages, motivates, and mobilizes the individual, group, or community for change. Since there is no real change it is important that the social work process be looked upon as a participatory process.

As a matter of principle, modern social workers are increasingly accepting the fact that they must use all of the resources available in behalf of the persons they are serving. This means that they will work with other agencies and other services in order to create the most favorable climate for change.

The principle of continuous evaluation means that the social worker seeks constantly to check up on his own work to determine the extent to which he is effective. It means, too, that the social worker avoids rigidity and maintains a degree of flexibility so that methods can be modified as circumstances require.

Social group work is thus one part of a methodological whole that is called social work. Social group work is based upon the values and principles of social work practice. At the same time it is a separate and distinct way of helping individuals in groups to attain satisfying relationships. It makes a contribution to the whole of social work; yet it stands alone as well. It cannot be said that social casework, social group work, community organization work, or administration are any more or less important in the social work whole. All are needed and all are related.

Social Group Work Based on the Fact of Group Life

Social group workers recognize and place significance on the fact of group life. From infancy onward, each person is a member of groups in ever-widening circles. Group associations become multiplied, and effective living depends upon the ability of the individual to live, work, and play in diverse groups. The establishment of satisfying group relationships in the family and outside of the family is something everyone must accomplish and re-accomplish throughout all of life. The need for group experience is basic and universal. Thompson and Kahn put it this way:

We know that we cannot carry on life in isolation from our fellows, and that it is the quality of the relationships we make with other people that so much of our happiness and success depends on. Through these relationships we either meet, or fail to meet, most of our basic needs. They are not only central to our intimate, personal lives, but they also affect every activity in which we have contact with other people, at home, at work, and at play.[20]

No matter what philosophy of human needs one may tend to develop and follow, it is a central concept of social group work that all people need a variety of group experiences. Their needs for group experience tend to parallel the various kinds of group adjustments all people must make. The small, intimate, cohesive friendship group affords an opportunity for individual development and personal satisfaction. Larger, less cohesive groups supply the means of integrating the individual with a wider range of experiences. Social group workers thus seek to provide group experiences on several levels.

Social group workers know that individuals can be helped to grow and change in personality and attitudes through experiences with other people in the setting of community agencies. Personality growth is enhanced in those groups which have workers appropriately skilled in the process of utilizing group interaction. Group workers know that persons not only develop *in* groups but *through* groups, also. Our closest and most intimate associates with whom we have reciprocal status and acceptance are the powerful influences on the formation of our attitudes, habits, and patterns of response. Since social group work is fundamentally concerned with the development of the individual, group workers believe this goal can be better accomplished through the deliberate formation of groups and the conscious enrollment of groups already in existence.

The dynamic forces of group life, those qualities which when understood and guided make groups influential, are the relationships between people and their interactions with one another. Social group workers are increasingly aware of the fact that structure and organization within a group have little to do with the actual influence of the group on the individual. Rather, the emotional quality and tone that individuals bring to, and take from, group experiences are most significant. How people feel about the group is of signal importance. Acceptance and rejection are phenomena not limited to the one-to-one relationship. Persons are accepted in and by groups and are likewise, at times, rejected. Without a reasonable degree of mutual acceptance, group life is not satisfying. Acceptance comes about through interaction or the reciprocal interplay of feelings, attitudes, and desires expressed in the group setting.

Like all other social work, social group work has roots in the democratic value system. Democratic behavior is learned behavior which depends upon two parallel and equally vital factors: individuals must be helped to understand what democracy really means, and the same individuals must be given an opportunity for practice in democratic living. The only way that individuals can develop habits of cooperation is through the conscious practice of the democratic process.

The method called social group work is operating to its fullest extent when it makes possible the release of individual capacities and the growth of healthy personalities. There is no room for rigid, predetermined standards and imposed program in which the individual is subordinate to the activity. The social group work method calls for a maximum amount of flexibility and adaptability in terms of individual needs and interests. There is ample evidence that through group experiences individuals acquire skills and other abilities of a like nature. These are important because through such acquisitions the individual grows and develops greater maturity. It has been well stated that social group work is primarily a means to an end, and that end is the development of persons.

Community Agency Settings

Social group work is practiced in a variety of community agencies. As was recently pointed out, "Group services are found in neighborhood centers, hospitals; agencies and institutions working with children, adolescents, or the aging; in public welfare programs, and in other community service agencies. Both voluntary and governmental agencies make use of social group work method and techniques to carry out their functions. Many of the agencies are national and international in scope, thus some jobs involve interesting travel opportunities to work and live in various settings of the country and other parts of the world." [21]

Some would classify the agency settings into "primary" or "traditional" and "secondary" or "host." Primary settings, where social group work is the major method used, include the neighborhood and community centers, the youth serving agencies, recreational centers, senior centers, churches, and the like. Secondary settings, where social group work is practiced but not necessarily as the major method used, include public schools, hospitals, clinics, welfare departments, both public assistance and child welfare, probation departments and correctional institutions, mental health centers, family service agencies, antipoverty agencies, homes for the aged and so on. In a brilliantly edited volume, Schwartz and his colleagues describe group work practice in nine settings. [22]

Over the years community agencies under governmental or voluntary auspices have been organized to help people meet their needs. People need economic security, health services, recreational and cultural services, and they need help in dealing with personal problems. The problems that arise out of unsatisfactory relationships between the individual and his environment are well known. Children, youth, and adults have needs that can best be met by the organized efforts of community agencies. The group worker is usually a part of one of these agencies. He represents the agency; his work is made possible in large part by the agency, which provides facilities, finances, and support. The worker's general objectives are in large measure determined by the agency's expressions of purpose and function. The group worker must become a part of the agency and the agency must determine the qualifications that make the worker competent to help it fulfill its stated purposes.

The agency, the worker, and the group are needed to carry on the practice of social group work. All must meet standards of adequacy. The agency must state its purposes in terms of the social needs of individuals and must have convictions relative to the importance of these needs. Also, it must stand for something in the community and must have the support of the community. It must have workers sufficiently well prepared to accomplish its objectives. In addition, it must consciously develop a method of selecting and forming groups with which it believes it is competent to work. It must be so organized and administered as to encourage widespread participation by all persons who are a part of it.

In Summary: The Social Group Work Whole

By now we have seen that social group work as a method in social work has many aspects and many parts. To sum it up, it can be said that social group work calls for the unified working together of individuals in groups in community agencies committed to defined objectives and helped toward the attainment of these objectives by a worker who works in a certain way. The kind of agency, the kind of group, the kind of worker, and especially, the relatedness of the three make up the group work whole.

This idea of the social group work *whole* is illustrated in the accompanying Figure 2. Here we picture the individual in the very center of the diagram because the individual is always the central focus of all social work effort. It should be noted, however, that the individual is a part of the group and is in a relationship of interaction with other group members. Closer scrutiny of the figure will reveal that the central large circle, representing the group, is overlapped by the three other large circles of the community, the agency, and the worker. In additions, all these circles are connected and are a part of the larger democratic society and culture. The radiating arrows point to the fact that the forces of society and culture are constantly brought to bear upon the community, the worker, and the agency. Furthermore, the group itself is influenced by its community and agency setting and by the group worker who works with it.

Social group work always calls for a worker from outside the group. This worker comes with certain skills based on his understanding of persons and his interest in them as individuals. Group work implies that there will be a group possessing some degree of likeness, present or potential, in the shape of mutual interests, similarity of age, like vocation or occupation, or proximity of neighborhood. It implies that this group will be small enough to give every member an opportunity to participate actively and enjoy the results of group effort with every other member and with the worker. Group work also suggests that the group and the worker will engage themselves in

FIGURE 2

The Social Group Work Whole

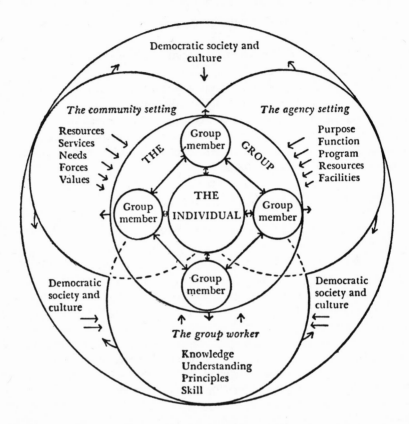

program activities which may be social, recreational, educational or interest focused. Group work assumes that the individual will develop a variety of skills leading him toward a better social adjustment and an unfolding personality.

The group worker is, of course, of tremendous importance in social group work. He should bring to his work a background of knowledge and experience and a mature personality. He works as a helping person to enable the members of the group to make choices and to carry out their own decisions. The group worker wants the group to become as self-directing and self-governing as possible, and wants the control of the group to rest primarily in the hands of the members. He works with them to this end, and thus it is necessary that he give direction and guidance to the thinking and feeling and the other kinds of interaction that are taking place. The group worker is also interested in helping the group to participate with other groups as a part of the total agency and the larger community. The ultimate product of the group work experience will be the development of individuals and groups able to take an increasingly active part in the important affairs of community living.

In a brilliant summing up, Konopka has outlined the essential parts of the social group method as follows:

1. The function of the social group worker is a helping or enabling function: This means that his goal is to help the members of the group and the group as a whole to move toward greater independence and capacity for self-help.

2. In determining his way of helping, the group worker uses the scientific method; fact-finding (observation), analyzing, diagnosis in relation to the individual, the group, and the social environment.

3. The group work method includes the worker forming purposeful relationships to group members and the group: This includes a conscious focusing on the needs of the members, on the purpose of the group as expressed by the members, as expected by the sponsoring agency and as implied in the members' behavior. It is differentiated from a casual unfocused relationship.

4. One of the main tools in achieving such a relationship is the conscious use of self. This includes self-knowledge and discipline in relationships without the loss of warmth and spontaneity.

5. There should be acceptance of people without accepting all their behavior: This involves the capacity for "empathy" as well as the incorporation of societal demands. It is the part of the method that is most closely intertwined with a high flexibility and abundance of warmth in the social group worker as well as identification with values and knowledge.

6. Starting where the group is: The capacity to let groups develop from their own point of departure, of capacity, without immediately imposing outside demands.

7. The constructive use of limitations: Limitations must be used judiciously in relation to individual and group needs and agency function. The forms will vary greatly. The group worker will mainly use himself, program materials, interaction of the group and awakening of insight in the group members.

8. Individualization: It is one of the specifics of the group work method that the individual is not lost in the whole, but that he is helped to feel as a unique person who can contribute to the whole.

9. Use of the interacting process: The capacity to help balance the group, to allow for conflict when necessary and to prevent it when harmful; the help given to the isolate not only through individual attention by the group worker alone, but also by relating him to other members.

10. The understanding and conscious use of non-verbal as well as verbal material: I especially put non-verbal material first, since the group worker deals a great deal with this, especially in work with children. His capacity to use program materials, which do not demand verbal expression and yet are helpful, should be very wide. [23]

NOTES

1. Robert D. Vinter, "An Approach to Group Work Practice" in Robert D. Vinter (editor), *Readings in Group Work Practice* (Ann Arbor, Michigan: Campus Publications, 1967), p. 1.

2. Ronald Lippitt, "Unplanned Maintenance and Planned Change in the Group Work Process," in *Social Work Practice, 1962* (Published for the National Conference on Social Welfare by Columbia University Press, New York, 1962), p. 76.

3. Grace L. Coyle, "Social Group Work," *Social Work Yearbook, 1954* (New York: American Association of Social Workers, 1954), p. 480.

4. Gertrude Wilson and Gladys Ryland, *Social Group Work Practice* (Boston: Houghton Mifflin, 1949), p. 61.

5. Gisela Konopka, *Social Group Work: A Helping Process* (Englewood Cliffs, N.J.: Prentice-Hall, Inc., 1963), p. 29.

6. Robert D. Vinter, "Social Group Work," *Encyclopedia of Social Work* (New York: National Association of Social Workers, 1965), p. 715.

7. Helen Northen, *Social Work with Groups* (New York: Columbia University Press, 1969), p. 13.

8. Harold Esterson, "Differential Approach in Social Group Work" (New York: Manhattanville Community Center, 1962, mimeographed).

9. Marjorie Murphy, *The Social Group Work Method in Social Work Education,* Vol. XI, Curriculum Study (Council on Social Work Education, New York, 1959), p. 78.

10. *Group Treatment in Family Service Agencies* (New York: Family Service Association of America, 1964), p. 11.

11. Bruce L. Maliver, "Encounter Groups Up Against the Wall," *New York Times Magazine,* January 3, 1971, p. 5.

12. René Jules Dubos, "Man Adapting: His Limitations and Potentialities" in Walter R. Ewald, Jr. (editor), *Environment for Man—The Next Fifty Years* (Bloomington, Indiana: Indiana University Press, 1967), p. 19.

13. *Social Work with Groups.* Brochure published by National Commission for Social Work Careers, 2 Park Avenue, New York, N.Y. Undated. P. 1.

14. Ruth E. Smalley, *Theory for Social Work Practice* (New York: Columbia University Press, 1967), p. 1.

15. Bernard Berelson and Gary A. Steiner, *Human Behavior: An Inventory of Scientific Findings* (New York: Harcourt, Brace and World, Inc., 1964), p. 337.

16. Practice Commission, Group Work Section, National Association of Social Workers, New York, N.Y., 1962.

17. Mary Louise Somers, "Helping Through Social Group Work" in *Potentials for Service Through Group Work in Public Welfare* (Chicago: American Public Welfare Association, 1962), pp. 3–4.

18. Albert S. Alissi, "Establishing Patterns of Intervention in Group Work Practice," *Journal of Jewish Communal Service,* Summer 1970, pp. 315–316.

19. Emanuel Tropp, *A Humanistic Foundation for Group Work Practice* (New York: Selected Academic Readings—a Division of Associated Educational Services Corporation, 1969), p. 17A.

20. Sheila Thompson and J. H. Kahn, *The Group Process as a Helping Technique* (Oxford: Pergamon Press, 1970), pp. 29–30.

21. *Social Work with Groups, op. cit.*

22. William Schwartz and Serapio R. Zalba, *The Practice of Group Work* (New York: Columbia University Press, 1970).

23. Gisela Konopka, "The Generic and the Specific in Group Work Practice" in Harleigh B. Trecker (editor), *Group Work in the Psychiatric Setting* (New York: Whiteside, 1956).

2

The Agency—
Setting for Social Group Work

Social group work calls for a worker, a group, and a community service agency—all working together to accomplish agreed-upon purposes. The extent to which the worker has an understanding of the agency and the community will sharply influence what he does with the group. Likewise, the agency's purpose and philosophy will inevitably exert an influence upon the worker and the group. Since the group worker is rarely a free-lance worker or private practitioner, his skill is exercised as a representative of an agency which operates in a given community because the community wants the service and accepts the agency as a proper means of carrying it out. The initial question the group worker must ask and answer is: What is this agency, of which I am a part, trying to accomplish in this community with these groups of people? Without an answer to this question the group worker can scarcely proceed to an understanding of his group and his role within it.

Community Service Agencies

Modern society has many community service agencies that have been established over the years to meet the needs of people. Some of these agencies are called "private" or "voluntary" in that they are operated under legal charters granted to individuals and groups who sponsor the programs and provide financial resources through contributions and fees. The other broad category of agencies is "public" or "governmental" in that they are established, operated, and funded by a unit of government. No matter what their sponsorship these agencies are instruments for service and millions of people have come to depend upon them.

Community service agencies may be organized on the basis of age groups served, such as children, youth, adults, or the aged. Or they may be organized around the community needs they plan to meet, such as family and child welfare social services, recreational and cultural services, neighborhood development, economic and employment services, housing, health, education, social welfare, mental health, environmental protection, and the like. Some agencies provide only one service; others provide many and are known as "multiservice" centers. Some agencies use a variety of methods and processes in carrying out their work. Others concentrate on one primary method such as social group work.

All of these agencies are instruments of the people. They represent the organized efforts of groups of people to meet specific human needs which arise out of social conditions. Obviously, the community service agency is a nonprofit institution which can only operate if it has the sanction and support of the people it serves. It meets specific, recognizable, visible needs that are agreed upon as important by a substantial number of persons.

Agency Settings in Which Social Group Work Method Is Used

Social group work is the major method used by many agencies. These agencies are sometimes called "primary" or "traditional" settings for the practice of social group work. To "type" or "classify" these agencies in any rigid pattern has proved to be difficult if not impossible. Some are called "youth serving agencies" but many so designated work with adults and children, too. Some are called "leisure-time" agencies but this is by no means representative of their mission if one thinks of it as being the filling of leisure time. Some are called "informal education" agencies and this may be partially correct as to their function. Some are called "social work" or "social service" agencies because of their primary identification with the professional methods of social work. Apart from what the agency may be called, most of them are known by a name and it is these names that are frequently associated with social group work.

If one were to look at a directory of agency services in a middle-sized or large city he would stand a very good chance of finding such listings as follows: settlements and neighborhood centers which were started in this country in 1886; Young Men's Christian Association which began in Boston in 1851; Young Women's Christian Association, 1858; Boys' Clubs of America, 1906; Jewish Community Centers, 1954; Girl Scouts of the U.S.A., 1912; Boy Scouts of America, 1910; Camp Fire Girls, 1910; Catholic Youth Organization, 1930; Young Men's-Young Women's Hebrew Association, 1874; Girls Clubs of America, 1945; American Red Cross Youth Services; 4-H Clubs beginning in the early 1900's; community recreation centers; church center programs; and camps.

An agency's decision to employ the social group work method depends upon what it conceives its function to be and whether or not it believes that social group work can contribute to the fulfillment of that function. The authorization of the agency, whether it be voluntary or governmental, is not a basic criterion; nor is the age of the persons the agency hopes to serve nor the kind of activities it hopes to foster. What are some of the basic characteristics of these community service agencies where social group work is practiced? Though each agency is different, and rightfully so, there are many similarities:

1. All of these agencies have as their fundamental objective *the individual and social development of persons as a means of working toward a society that will be increasingly democratic, humane, and just.* The kinds of attitudes that these agencies hope to be instrumental in helping individuals to develop are variously expressed. Some accent citizen participation; others stress socialization and cooperation; religious motivation and dynamic are the foci of some agencies; still others emphasize emotional health and maturity. The central focus of the agency is upon the person and his development as a means of fostering genuine community living.

2. These agencies work with people who *voluntarily* choose to align themselves with the agency and participate because they wish to do so. Though there is a difference in the degree of participation, ranging from those who do so on only a temporary basis to those who actually become agency members, the agency service is offered without pressure or compulsion.

3. These agencies work with persons *in groups*. The group is the chief unit of service and the primary means through which people identify themselves with the agency. There are differences between groups, but every agency places emphasis on group participation as a basic avenue for individual growth.

4. These agencies work with groups in an *informal* manner. The relationships between group members and group workers are deliberately developed in an atmosphere of planned informality as contrasted with prescribed or rigid arrangements.

5. These agencies provide services to groups and through groups in that portion of their time that is more apt to be "leisure time" than "work time." That is, most group work is done during the time when the individual is free from economic pursuits or other required activities.

6. These agencies usually have *dual personnel* consisting of both paid workers and volunteer workers. In fact, the prominent agencies employing the social group work method make extensive use of volunteers and these volunteers have made significant contributions to the programs.

There are differences as well as similarities between the many agencies employing the group work method. Although some persons might question the validity of the need for what seems to be a large number of different agencies, there is nothing inherently undesirable in the fact of difference. The community is better served when there is a variety of agencies with clearly defined purposes. However, if agencies duplicate one another or compete for clientele or deploy their forces unwisely, there is evidence of a problem in community social welfare organization that reflects a lack of understanding and a failure to plan together. If agencies are understood in their differences as well as their likenesses, such conflicts are less likely to occur. Prominent differences between agencies center around: the specific focus of their objectives; the choice of constituency as to age, sex, and background; the degree to which the individual must identify himself with the agency, which ranges from merely receiving services to joining and becoming a member; areas of program content which are made possible by facilities, budget and staff; and general day-to-day operating policies.

Newer Agency Settings for Social Group Work

In recent years a considerable number of new agency settings have begun to use social group work as one of their methods of giving service. Sometimes they are called "secondary" or "nontraditional" or "host" settings. Apart from what they are called, these agencies have found that social group work can make a major contribution to the lives of the people they serve. In the field of health, hospitals, clinics, and convalescent homes are using the group worker as a member of the treatment team. Residential treatment centers for emotionally disturbed children are also using group work. The field of education as represented by the public schools is still another relatively new setting. In some housing projects group work has become a prominent part of tenant services and relations. In correctional institutions, adult and juvenile, group work has made a contribution. In the field of the family service agency much use is being made of groups. Children's institutions and institutions for older persons also have discovered the value of group services. In work with the physically and mentally handicapped and in the antipoverty programs some use has been made of group work. In public welfare, both public assistance and child welfare, group work has come to take its place as a prominent method. In Chapter 7 we will discuss some of these new settings in detail.

The Importance of Understanding the Agency

Before a group worker can understand what he is trying to accomplish with his group, he must first understand what the agency is trying to do. The group, the worker, and the agency constitute parts of a whole that must be seen as interrelated. The new worker especially needs to have a clear grasp of what being part of agency means. He must also understand the function of the agency.

The dictionary definition of *function* is "the natural and proper activity of anything." When agencies state their function it usually appears thus: "It is our function to provide this kind of service to these groups to the attainment of these goals." The elements that make up function, then, are purpose, program, policy, method, and constituency. Function in its broadest aspect includes consideration of what the agency is trying to do, the persons with whom it chooses to do it, and how it elects to operate with these persons to the ends stated. It is not only desirable but basically essential for all agencies to be clear on their function. As the number of agencies increases and as interagency relationships become more and more complex, it will be necessary to devote a larger share of time to acquainting new workers with the specific role of the agency with which they are associated.

The agency should have a clear statement of purpose in addition to and in elaboration of that which is stated in the legal charter. This statement of purpose should be developed out of a study of the needs of the community. The purpose should be used to interpret the work of the agency to those who participate, volunteers, staff, board members and the community. The statement should be shared with other agencies in the community so they will know about the goals and what the agency is trying to do. The statement of purpose should be used as a basis for formulating specific goals for divisions, departments, and groups in the agency. The statement of purpose should be used for making periodic evaluations of program and it should be periodically reviewed and revised as circumstances change.

Agency function should be regarded as a positive tool which the worker can use in his work with groups. By defining the situation the agency helps the group and the worker to a clearer conception of the reason for their being there and what each can expect of the other. When the agency limits its scope and concentrates its efforts sharply on realistic objectives, frustrations are less apt to occur, and tangible results are more easily measured. But agency function must be thought of as dynamic as well as specific. In a changing community situation agencies must be especially alert to keep abreast of rapidly changing circumstances. Determination of function and redetermination of function are parts of a continuing process in which the total agency is involved in relation to other agencies.

What are some of the factors that agencies must study to determine or redefine their function? The central factor is, of course, community need. An effective agency has defined the geographic area within which it will work and render service. It endeavors to understand basic physical, social, and cultural facts about its area and to use such information in planning its work. This means that the agency is constantly collecting and analyzing basic factual data on the geographic area it serves. Such facts as population, occupation, income, housing, and the like are used in program planning. The agency also studies major trends in community life and tries to anticipate or forecast major changes. The agency regularly reviews its goals and objectives in the light of changes in the community. The agency is familiar with the work of similar and allied community service agencies such as schools, churches, and the like. In addition, it has defined the basic social problems of the community which it will endeavor to help solve through working with other agencies. The modern agency is an active participant with appropriate community planning groups. In addition, it cooperates with other agencies on specific program activities and makes use of community facilities and resources. It has worked out policies and procedures for the making of referrals to other agencies and for the receiving of referrals from them.

When an agency says clearly what it is trying to do, it inevitably declares what it is *not* trying to do. Definition of function always carries with it limitations. Consequently, when workers discuss with groups the function of the agency, it is important for them to point out everything that is inherent in the situation. Groups must be helped to see, understand, and accept both the opportunities and the limits implied in the agency purpose and setting. As a representative of the agency, the group worker is constantly called upon to interpret and reinterpret agency function and his own job in relation to it. Without the understanding that emerges from such a process, it is doubtful whether groups can relate satisfactorily to the agency for any very long time.

An effective agency has made decisions regarding the clientele with whom it will endeavor to work. It seeks to understand the people with whom it works and it endeavors to help these people become related to the agency as a whole. A written statement describing the clientele the agency intends to serve in terms of age, sex, program activities, and the like is helpful to have. Such statements should be known by the community. In addition, the agency should have written policies and procedures regarding how people may use, join, or take part in the programs offered. It is of course essential that the agency have basic identifying information on each individual with whom it works and it should keep statistical information on service achievements. There should be a planned procedure for admission, reception, or intake of new clientele designed to help persons understand the agency and the agency to understand the individual.

What does the agency offer to the groups that choose to become a part of it? (1) The agency offers a general over-all conception of purpose which the group is invited to subscribe to in whole or in part. As Middleman puts it in her pioneer discussion of non-verbal content in group work:

Within the field of social work, and in group work in particular, the purposeful use of non-verbal content would follow two main directions, determined primarily by the underlying purpose for which the sponsoring agency has placed the group worker into a communicating relationship with the group. One broad purpose would include those activities which aim at encouraging socialization, fun and relaxation, pleasurable group experiences, creative use of leisure, democratic group processes, increased social responsibility, and actions geared toward the overall social good. A second broad purpose that would give direction to the non-verbal activities is aimed at the growth and development of the individual, the rehabilitation of those who suffer from social, emotional, and physical ills as well as intellectual lacks. In this second focus, the development of the group as a group may be absent or, more often, may take a secondary place in the worker's focus. His primary set is toward serving individuals through their participation in a group under his direction so that their social, emotional, or physical functioning as individuals is enhanced. It is most important that the worker is eminently clear in his over-all objectives and that his program choices are, in fact, conducive to the goals he is pursuing.[1]

(2) The agency offers facilities and program opportunities which it believes to be valuable and in keeping with high standards. (3) It offers the support and acceptance of the wider community, which automatically carry with them status value for the particular group or groups. (4) It offers workers who are prepared to be of help to groups and without whom professional service is not possible. (5) It offers values, beliefs, and a philosophy of life that reflect the wisdom that comes from long experience. (6) It offers a controlled environmental situation in which groups have an opportunity to be partners in significant community undertakings. (7) It offers a way of work that has been tested; thus, common mistakes of group organization and method may be avoided. (8) Most important, it offers people opportunities for growth. As Klein puts it so well:

Social work through group process is a means of helping people to grow, develop, and maximize their full potentials. The method is useful in enabling people to self-realization, identity, and birth of a real self. These objectives are reachable through meeting the basic needs for validation, favorable response, support, and above all closeness. Groups can be systems of mutual aid and through group process, people can learn to enable others and, in so doing can also find themselves. These seem to me to be the functions of most group service agencies.[2]

(9) In our impersonal society the agency offers the individual the opportunity to belong to something, to be a member of a body that is a dynamic part of the community. Frey and Meyer accent the importance of the membership concept and of belonging when they write:

The membership concept is one which provides . . . uniquely in group service agencies an excellent way of actualizing some of social work's most precious values and beliefs. A member is one of the persons who compose a society, community or party; a member is a part of a whole. This vitality of interconnection and sharing in the life of the whole, is an asset to group work services which unfortunately has not been fully appreciated either philosophically or practically. Its dignity has not been explicitly nurtured so that the process of joining an agency has been treated as an event of little significance for both the joiner and the joined. An absence of exploration into a request to join, demeans the agency program as well as the applicant, for it seems to say that the agency offers nothing of value to impart to the applicant. The applicant would not have the good sense to want to join the agency if he knew what it, as a social service, was set up to do for him. When a casual approach to the period of application is replaced by a carefully, thoughtfully planned one, the exploration of the meaning of joining can be the beginning of a rich association between the member and the social workers in the agency. A frank recognition of the aspects of joining a social agency which are different from joining a social organization is an obligation of the agency toward its members which is not only philosophically sound but also eminently sensible and necessary to the growth-producing experiences which are the concern of social work.[3]

It should be pointed out that the agency setting inevitably limits the group. Here it should be observed that for some groups *any* rules or limits might be too much, and we are well aware of groups that require a long period of preparation before they can successfully relate their efforts to other groups in the community agency setting. The factor of agency purpose is a first limit to which the group must give consideration. If the purposes of the group are opposed to the purposes of the agency, there cannot be any basis for service. Because agencies work with many different groups, there are necessary limits on the use of the various facilities. The amount of time that the agency can allow a group and the hours of the day that may be devoted to a given group in a certain facility must be scheduled. Conditions of health and safety are additional limitations.

The agency must also make decisions regarding the size of the group in an optimum sense, setting both minimum and maximum numbers. Frequently, the agency must decide on admission policies for individuals who seek to become a part of groups and cannot permit the group to be an agent of exclusion if it is to be part of an organization that is open to all. The payment of fees and charges is another factor that must be understood by the group. Required standards for workers, whether they be paid or volunteer, are more and more a part of good agency practice. Accepted standards of conduct or behavior are rightfully sought by agencies that serve not only as hosts but as representatives of community-approved social standards.

Agency Policies on Groups, Grouping, and Group Formation

Agency grouping policies and practices call for study by new workers. The groups with which agencies work are the service units, the means, the vehicles through which help and service are given to individuals. The group is simultaneously an instrument of individual growth and tool of personality development. The agencies specializing in work with groups must have an ever-expanding knowledge of groups, group life, group influence, and group behavior.

Every agency has to be selective at the point of intake. It cannot work with all of the groups in the community, nor can it adequately provide sound group experiences for all of the individuals there. The limits of space, staff, group loads, and budget are always present when we look beneath the surface of agency life. Furthermore, as has been pointed out, there are many different agencies which carry a portion of the community service program and competition between agencies for the recruitment of groups is undesirable. To complicate matters still further, all persons have need for a variety of group experiences and it is doubtful whether any agency can meet these needs completely. In addition to this fact, it is known that certain kinds of groups are more influential at the point of both personality development and the achievement of agency purpose. Thus, the grouping question is a basic one if agency service is to be soundly organized.

When an agency begins to study the grouping question, at least four areas of concern are readily apparent. a) Should the agency continue to work with the ongoing groups already within its program? b) Should the agency accept into service already-formed groups that exist in the neighborhood and seek admission to the agency? c) Should the agency recruit already-formed groups that have no affiliation with any agency but would seem to profit from one? d) Should the agency deliberately attempt to form special groups made up of individuals already within the agency or community but seemingly without group affiliations?

Strictly speaking the community service agency cannot "form" groups. It can, however, present individuals with the opportunities and conditions under which they may so relate themselves to one another that a group does take shape. The actual emergence of the group is up to the persons, themselves. If the need for such a group does not exist, the group will never form, though there may be "fits and starts" in the direction of formation. Some of the questions agencies must ask when they set out to form groups are: What persons are we attempting to reach? For whom are we endeavoring to provide opportunities? What needs are we trying to meet and what is the evidence that these needs exist? How will the groups that we propose to help form relate to our conception of agency purpose? What is the optimum size for such groups? In what manner should we present the opportunity to these groups so that they will be attracted to us and wish to become affiliated with us?

When already-formed groups come to the agency and seek alignment with it, other questions must be asked and answered. How did the group come into being? What purposes does it serve in the lives of its members? What does the group seem to want from the agency? What can the agency provide for the group, and what can the group give to the agency? How long has the group existed, and where is it in terms of social development? Can the agency accept this group, and can the group accept the agency? What is the future outlook for this group? How long will it endure as a group?

Many questions come up when the agency reviews its group load in an attempt to determine whether or not it should continue to work with certain groups: Do the members of this group want to continue as a group? What are they getting out of their experiences together? Can the agency help them to realize more fully their goals and help them to meet their needs? How much have the individuals grown as a result of this association?

Should the group be encouraged to continue, or should it be helped to conclude its organized life? Should some of the individuals be helped into membership with other groups from which they may conceivably realize a new and richer experience?

Questions such as these point up the major factors that an agency interested in improving its grouping practices must consider. Ultimately agencies must fashion a sound policy on grouping by analyzing four basic factors.

1. The first factor is *agency purpose*. Though agency purposes range from general to very specific, each agency must show how work with a certain kind of group helps the agency to achieve its purpose in the community and how the decision not to work with other groups can be justified on like grounds. In this connection there will be natural variation between agencies, especially with respect to agency maturity and availability of staff. A new agency may conceivably elect to work with a very different segment of group life than do the established agencies because it seeks to meet some of the needs of the unserved population. An agency relying largely on volunteer workers would naturally limit itself to work with groups that can be helped through the efforts of a less specialized staff. Tropp accents the importance of *group* purpose within the agency framework when he writes, "The purpose of a group—why it is formed—is the principal element to be defined. It may be that the agency's idea of the group's purpose and the group's idea of its purpose are not identical; but at the point at which they meet, in effect a definition of the group's operations purpose can be found. If a group leader has not thought clearly about purpose, he will find himself drifting with the group into irrelevant, unproductive, and meaningless areas, into confusing situations and shaky operational patterns. . . . Having determined the purpose for which the group has been organized, the worker can clarify its function—what the group members are supposed to do to carry out that purpose. . . . Once the worker knows what a group is supposed to be doing, he can think clearly about structure—how the group will do it." [4]

2. The second factor that needs study is the *community situation*. The geographic location of the agency, the scattering and concentration of the population, the age distribution of residents, the degree of mobility and transiency, and the extent of homogeneity have bearing on the formation of groups. In a community that contains a large percentage of older citizens, the agency may decide to concentrate on groupings designed to meet their needs. If people move into and out of the community at a rapid rate, it is doubtful whether that agency should try to build permanent long-term groups. If there are many agencies in the community, choice must be made as to which groups need service and are not receiving it.

3. The third factor that enters into sound decisions at the point of groups is *agency resources*. The availability of staff, facilities, equipment, space, and time are conditioning elements of ever-present significance. Agency

finances and fee-charging policies enter into every decision, though the extent to which they are major determinants will vary with each agency.

4. The fourth factor, and the most important of all, is our *general knowledge of groups* and their influence on individuals. The small cohesive group may be an absolute necessity for the development of certain personality characteristics, whereas the larger and less cohesive group may make a desirable contribution in another direction. This will be discussed in greater detail in Chapter 3, "The Group—Understanding It and Working With It."

Summary

Before starting to work with a group, the worker should know and understand many things about the agency setting in which he is engaged. It is the responsibility of the agency, through supervision and administration, to acquaint all workers with these areas of knowledge:

1. The worker should have an understanding of the purpose and function of the agency and should agree to work within it, accepting its changing and evolving nature.

2. The worker should have knowledge of the way in which the agency helps groups to form and of the way in which it accepts groups into a relationship with it. Conditions of group affiliation with the agency must be clearly understood if the worker is to interpret properly the agency to the group and the group to the agency.

3. The worker should have knowledge of the general constituency that the agency is set up to serve as it is defined in terms of age, sex, geographic location, interests, and needs.

4. The worker should have an understanding of internal operating policies, especially as they relate to fees, hours, scheduling, sharing facilities with other groups, records required, and regulations regarding work with groups that may be carried on away from the agency.

5. The worker needs to know his relationship to other workers on the staff and the kind of supervision he may expect to receive.

6. It is important that the worker know the way in which individuals who seek to affiliate with a group may be helped to establish an effective relationship with that group.

7. The conditions or criteria by which groups are to be evaluated by the agency should be understood from the beginning of the worker's relationship with the agency.

To obtain the knowledge and understanding outlined here will take time. It will take conscious effort on the part of the worker and will develop gradually throughout the early phases of the worker's association with the agency.

NOTES

1. Ruth R. Middleman, *The Non-Verbal Method in Working with Groups* (New York: Association Press, 1968), pp. 89–90.
2. Alan F. Klein, *Social Work Through Group Process* (School of Social Welfare, State University of New York at Albany, 1971), p. 163.
3. Louise A. Frey and Marguerite Meyer, "Exploration and Working Agreement in Two Social Work Methods" in Saul Bernstein (editor), *Explorations in Group Work* (Boston: Boston University School of Social Work, 1965), p. 5.
4. Emanuel Tropp, *A Humanistic Foundation for Group Work Practice* (New York: Selected Academic Readings—a Division of Associated Educational Services Corporation, 1964), p. 50.

3

The Group—
Understanding It and Working With It

Groups, like individuals, are different. Thus, the group worker must have both general knowledge about different kinds of groups and special understanding of the particular group he is working with at any given time.

Since social group work is a method of working with individuals in *groups* it is common for the worker to start out with the group and through working with it come to know the individual member and his needs. The group thus assumes a primary role in aiding individuals to grow and change with the help of the worker.

The worker will need to know the ways in which the particular group he is working with is similar to other groups; in addition he will need to know how it differs from other groups. The worker should know the general contributions group experience can make to individuals, and he should study his group sufficiently to understand what belonging to it means to the group members.

Group work has few, if any, techniques that are universally applicable, because each group is different and each situation is different. Workers must individualize each group and continuously study and analyze where each group is in terms of broad stages of development.

There is much to understand about groups and how to work with them. Some of this material will be discussed in this chapter.

The Small Group as an Instrument for Social Development

What is meant by the term "group"? A classic definition of the term was put forth some forty years ago by the eminent sociologist Eubank. He defined a group as "two or more persons in a relationship of psychic interaction, whose relationship with one another may be abstracted and distinguished from their relationships with all others so that they must be thought of as an entity." [1] Many years later, Bogardus defined "social group" in these terms: "A social group which is the framework within which personalities develop and mature, or also become disorganized, may be thought of as a number of persons who have some common loyalty, and who participate in common activities, and who are stimulating to each other . . . a social group consists of human beings in inter-stimulation." [2]

Lewin stressed the dynamic wholeness of the group when he said, "It is widely recognized that a group is more than, or more exactly different from, the sum of its members. It has its own structure, its own goals and its own relations to other groups. The essence of the group is not the similarity or dissimilarity of its members but their interdependence. A group can be characterized as a dynamical whole, that means that a change in the state of any subpart changes the state of any other subpart. The degree of interdependence of the subparts of members of the group varies all the way from a loose mass to a compact unit. It depends among other factors upon the size, organization, and the intimacy of the group." [3] Lewin went on to emphasize the tremendous power of the group to influence personality development when he said, "The social climate in which a child lives is for the child as important as the air it breathes. The group to which a child belongs is the ground on which he stands. His relation to this group and his status in it are the most important factors for his feeling of security and insecurity. No wonder that the group the person is a part of, and the culture in which he lives, determine to a very high degree his behavior and his character." [4]

The kinds of groups Lewin seems to be talking about are unusually called "primary groups." When the sociologist Cooley first wrote about these groups he said:

By primary groups I mean those categorized by intimate face-to-face association and cooperation. They are primary in several senses, but chiefly in that they are fundamental in forming the social nature and ideals of the individual. The result of intimate association, psychologically, is a certain fusion of individuality in a common whole, so that one's very self, for many purposes at least, is the common life and purpose of the group. Perhaps the simplest way of describing this wholeness is by saying it is a "we"; it involves the sort of sympathy and mutual identification for which "we" is the natural expression. One lives in the feeling of the whole and finds the chief means of his will in that feeling. . . .The most important spheres of this intimate association and cooperation—though by no means the only ones—are the family, the play-group of children, and the neighborhood or community group of elders. These are practically universal, belonging to all times and stages of development, and are accordingly a chief basis of what is universal in human nature and human ideals. . . . Primary groups are primary in the sense that they give the individual his earliest and completest experience of social unity, and also in the sense that they do not change in the same degree as more elaborate relations, but form a comparatively permanent source out of which the latter are ever springing. . . .[5]

At a later time, Firth wrote about primary groups:

These are small-scale units—families, work groups, neighborhood groups, play groups—the members of which are in close personal contact in daily life. Such groups are primary in the sense of being the smallest type of cooperative unit in society, the bricks from which the community fabric is built. To some extent they may also be regarded as primary in the ontogenetic sense, in that they include those groups in which the growing personality of each child develops as a member of the community. Such primary groups are socially vital. They offer many types of personal satisfaction—in opportunities of feeling secure amid group support, of exercising power over others, of showing skill and petty inventiveness in adapting things to immediate group needs, in getting gratifications of a moral kind, through the display of love and self-sacrifice. They are essential also for cooperation in economic and other fields. Upon the simplest primary groups are built others of a more complex and formal character, though no very clear-cut line can be drawn. Even when an element of organization has been applied to them, such groups still preserve most of their spontaneous, personal character.[6]

What Groups Contribute to Individuals

From countless sources in both laboratory and field settings social science research reveals the profound influence of the small group upon the individual and his behavior. Berelson and Steiner define the small group:

By this term is meant an aggregate of people, from two up to an unspecified but not too large number, who associate together in face-to-face relations over an extended period of time, who differentiate themselves in some regard from others around them, who are mutually aware of their membership in the group, and whose personal relations are taken as an end in itself. It is impossible to specify a strict upper limit on the size of the informal group, except for the limitation imposed by the requirement that all members be able to engage in direct personal relations at one time—which means, roughly, an upper limit of around fifteen to twenty. If the aggregate gets much larger than that, it begins to lose some of the quality of a small group or, indeed, begins to break up into small subgroups . . . the term covers a number of different kinds of small groups . . . we can identify (1) the autonomous group, e.g., a circle of close friends built on free choice and voluntary association; (2) the institutionalized small group, e.g., the family; (3) the small group within a large organization, often called a mediating group because of its linking position between the individual and the organization, e.g., the work group in a factory or office, a group of soldiers (buddies) in the army; and (4) the problem solving group, e.g., a committee with a task to perform. Taken as a whole, these categories come down to two broad types—those small groups with specific tasks to do and those, like the family, with more diffuse purposes. Another way to look at them is to think of those groups mainly oriented to the task (such as a work group), those mainly oriented to social and emotional satisfactions (such as a bridge club), and those oriented to achieving roughly equivalent amounts of each objective (such as some voluntary associations involving charitable activities). As the definition quickly suggests, a society is full of small groups, and everyone spends a good deal of his life in them. In sum, the essential elements in the definition are: small size, personal relations, some duration, identification of the members with the group and hence, some solidarity, differentiation from others, genuine goals, common symbols and autonomy in setting up procedures.[7]

These small groups make major contributions to the individual and his behavior. First, the small group provides the person with the opportunity to develop his skills as a participating member of society. As Falck put it:

The small group is probably the single most effective portrayer of the degree of effective social functioning available. Nowhere do the individual's ego resources become as clearly evident as when he interacts in a small group. Conflict, competition, cooperation, the use of power, prestige, the discharge of role expectations—all come to life in the small group. Nor is it only the worker's perception but also the members' perception of self and of each other around these dimensions that become apparent. The small group is a situation where a person can try out his strengths, perceive his weaknesses, see progress and regression, evaluate what is effective and ineffective in social intercourse.[8]

Second, the way in which individuals learn, the speed of their learning, the retention of learned material, and the way in which they solve problems are definitely influenced by small groups to which they belong and in which they participate. Furthermore, the more involvement or participation the more learning there is. Third, the small group influences the individual's formation of attitudes and tends to be decisive in the development of norms of response to situations. Norms of response are standard, uniform, predictable behavior reactions that tend to become fixed and to be repeated by the individual when he encounters like circumstances. Even after long periods of time have elapsed the norms are operative. As put by Berelson and Steiner, "The small group strongly influences the behavior of its members by setting and/or enforcing standards (norms) for proper behavior by its members—including standards for a variety of situations not directly involved in the activities of the group itself. The more stable and cohesive the group is, and the more attached the members to it, the more influential it is in setting standards for their behavior." [9] Fourth, small group experience operates to change an individual's values, level of aspiration and striving. Individual goal setting is highly dependent upon group standards. The attainment of these goals is likewise related to the extent to which the whole group moves toward them. Berelson and Steiner claim, "The more people associate with one another under conditions of equality, the more they come to share values and norms and the more they come to like one another. In other words, small groups rest on shared values and contacts." [10] Fifth, small group experience operates to modify the individual's habits of living, working, and otherwise carrying on life's pursuits. To a great extent the way in which individuals work is determined by the dominant groups to which they belong and which tend to be pattern-setting. Sixth, small group experience has a powerful influence upon the individual's perception of himself and his role in a given situation. The acquisition of self-insight and self-understanding is definitely furthered by group influence. Seventh, small groups tend to provide psychological support for individuals and help them to express themselves. The reinforcement and support that a group gives to an individual are especially noticeable when the individual is called upon to accept and adapt to a change in his life situation. Eighth, small groups always tend to influence the choices that individuals make when they are in situations where alternatives are presented. Since choices are fundamental to an individual's value system, or "principles," the group is of tremendous importance in this area. Ninth, small groups affect an individual's speed, accuracy and productivity in the work situation. In fact, productivity itself is to a great extent determined by a group formula. Tenth, small groups have a strong effect upon an individual's susceptibility to fear, frustration, and his recovery from them is hastened because of the security-giving function of the small group. Eleventh, small groups tend to place limits on the individual's drive for power and his need to be controlling. Groups help individuals work out the inevitable conflicts between their authority and dependency needs.

While the eleven illustrations of group influence which are given above are generally known and regarded as true, it is equally true that *not every group* operates in these ways to influence the individual. There are numerous aspects of the *group situation* itself that are influential. Thus, if the goal of social group work is to help to produce a certain kind of behavior on the part of the individual, then the group situation itself is important. In other words, the worker must endeavor to create a group situation in which the following elements are present. First, the *atmosphere,* or *climate,* in which the group exists and which the group itself creates is of major importance. When efforts are made to provide an atmosphere that is essentially cooperative in character, the members of the group tend to work cooperatively and constructively. When individuals get enough real acceptance, understanding, and love, they tend to respond in accepting and cooperating ways. Second, the *degree of cohesion* that exists in a group tends to influence the extent to which the group controls member behavior. In fact, the greater the degree of cohesiveness in the group, the more powerful is the group as a force for behavior change. Without sufficient cohesiveness, or relationship between the members, the group may lack focus and will, therefore, function less vitally in the lives of the members. As Northen puts it, "A cohesive group does not just develop. A group's cohesiveness is enhanced if the leader's participation contributes to the group's maintenance and further development. The cohesiveness of a group is demonstrably influenced by its leadership. The social worker, as the technical leader of the group, influences cohesion through the way he uses his professional knowledge, tools, and skills in his work with individuals and the group system." [11] Third, the presence of *democratic leadership* influences the effectiveness of the group. Individuals tend to respond and flourish when they are encouraged to participate and share in the planning and work of the group. When the leaders of groups set up a stimulating situation and induce free, spontaneous problem-solving participation, those groups become dynamic and vital. Fourth, the *structural and functional systems* of groups make for wide variation in the effectiveness of those groups. When these systems are fixed, inflexible, and rigid, they tend to hinder, if not block, the processes of communication that are essential if interaction is to be full and participation meaningful and creative. In his pioneer research on gang groups Thrasher observed, "Each gang as a whole, and other types of social groups as well, may be conceived of as possessing an action pattern. Every person in the group performs his characteristic functions with reference to others or to put it another way, fills the individual niche that previous experience in the gang has determined for him. Lacking the group, personality . . . would not exist. The action pattern of a group tends to become fixed and automatic in the habits of its members; it may persist long after the formal organization of the group has changed. Yet the action pattern which characterizes each group can hardly be thought of as rigid and static; for it must be constantly changing to accommodate losses and additions of personnel, changes in its members due to growth and increasing experience, and other changes within and without the gang." [12] Fifth, the extent to which group members participate in the *determination of group goals* is a powerful regulator of their energy output in working to attain those goals. The only goals that individuals fully understand are those that they have helped to formulate, and the only goals toward which they will work wholeheartedly are those that *they* have decided are important. Sixth, the *decision-making process* in group life is the most powerful of several dynamics. When members have a voice in making the decisions of the group, they are involved in a most significant way. When they do not have such a voice, their degree of involvement is likely to be slight, and the group has less meaning and little influence over their behavior. The above points are but a few of the significant findings that are coming out as social scientists continue to explore the depths of group life and influences.

Understanding Group Differences

The new group worker soon learns that there are many different kinds of groups in community service agencies. There are clubs, classes, special interest groups, teams, councils, and others. Some groups have been together for a long time and others have a comparatively brief history. Some groups are seemingly set up to exist permanently, and others are short-term in intent. Some groups are small, consisting of six, eight, ten, or twelve members; other groups are large, ranging up to and in excess of fifty members. Some groups are highly organized with much structure and procedure; others are rather loosely put together and appear to be informal as to organization. Some groups appear to have a very specific program, whereas the programs of other groups are fairly general.

Tropp makes a distinctive contribution when he classifies groups in five categories:

A. The *work crew or team* is a group that has a common goal, but essentially does not engage in common decision-making. Common action is required to achieve the goal but the members play specific roles at the assignment and command of a leader, with emphasis on skill. Efficiency, achievement or victory is paramount, and consent may be either a luxury or a hindrance or, at best, an optional technique. This category includes work units, military units, and athletic teams. B. The *class* is a group whose members have similar goals but not a common goal. Although there may be common actions, they are not essential to the group function, except when the skill needs the group for instructional purposes, such as a dramatic or discussion group. The discussion group, where the purpose is education rather than action, is not a common-goal group. In the class, the members come to seek knowledge or instruction, and the decisions are essentially made by the instructor. Examples of the class are language, art, ballet, and the like. C. The *play group* is a combination of individuals seeking personal pleasure through recreation. Although it may take the organized form of a team or an interest group, requiring common action, it rarely requires group decision. Examples of play groups are golf, swimming, music-listening. D. The *mutual interest group,* generally referred to as the voluntary association, may be organized to pursue social, cultural, protective, political, or other interest. Its very base is its common goal. In our society, it generally pursues this goal through the method of common decision and action. It has essential tasks to perform but is distinguished from the work crew by virtue of having shared authority similar to the body politic. It is not essentially pleasure-oriented, expression-oriented or learning-oriented (although it may offer one or more of these values). It is mutual interest-oriented, other-oriented, common good-oriented. E. The *treatment group* is organized to provide therapy, rehabilitation or correction. These functions are carried out through such techniques as group psychotherapy, group counseling, group education, or group recreation. In the first three categories the individuals have similar goals but usually do not have a common goal. In the fourth, a common goal may exist, but group decisions are generally not essential, although they may be used at times by the therapist as a treatment technique.[13]

When one studies the small group in session he watches for the kind of *interaction* that is taking place. As Shepherd points out, "A commonly used variable in the study of small groups is *interaction*. As a construct, interaction may refer to the process of acting and reacting which takes place between people meeting together in a small group. It is abstract and complex because it includes what is manifestly and subliminally communicated between people, what is intended and what is expressed, how messages are interpreted, and the like. As a concept, interaction may refer to the overt expressions of persons meeting together in a small group, specifically to the words and gestures which are used and their apparent meaning both to the communicator and to the interpreter." [14] In their writing about interaction, Berelson and Steiner say, "This is a generic term for the exchange of meanings between people. Usually interaction is direct communication—mainly talking and listening, often writing and reading—but it can also include gestures, glances, nods or shakes of the head, pats on the back, frowns, caresses or slaps, and any other way in which meanings can be transmitted from one person to another and back again: the simultaneous effect is usually central. Simply being present in a small group and being taken into account involves interaction too. The term is somewhat awkward, but some single word is required to cover all the various ways in which people can and do express themselves in face-to-face meetings: 'interaction' refers to communication in its broadest sense." [15]

Perhaps one of the most important aspects of really understanding a group is to get some measure of the *degree of cohesiveness* that exists among the members. Shepherd says, *"Cohesion* refers to this quality of a group which includes individual pride, commitment, meaning, as well as the group's stick-togetherness, ability to weather crises, and ability to maintain itself over time. *Productivity* refers to the group's ability to work effectively and successfully, and to the willingness of members to do their jobs, no matter how onerous. Cohesion and productivity, as implied above, are related in complex ways. In some cases, cohesion and productivity are directly related—the higher the cohesion of a group, the higher its productivity." [16] In her writings Northen observes, "Group cohesiveness . . . refers to the forces which bind members of a group to each other and to the group. It has been found that the more cohesive the group, the greater its influence on its members. To the extent that a group is highly attractive to its members, it has the ability to produce changes in attitudes, opinions and behavior. With the increase in influence, the pressures toward conformity also increase. In groups of high cohesiveness, the members may disagree with each other, but they also tend to find solutions to problems and conflicts more quickly. There tends to be greater satisfaction with the group and higher morale, less internal friction, and greater capacity to survive the loss of some of its members. In general, the more cohesive the group, the more satisfying it is to its members." [17]

What Does the Group Mean to the Individual?

Most people can think back and remember the very real meaning that belonging to a certain group had for them. This is so because *belonging is essentially an emotional experience.* Persons who really belong to a group develop an inner feeling of warmth, pride, sharing, devotion, affection, and respect with reference to the others and to the purpose of the group. Belonging means to be a part of something—a real part of it—and this feeling comes as a result of definite experiences with people. It is true that not all persons want to belong to a group, and not all who do belong reach the same depth of intensity in their relationship. Thus, there may be various degrees of belonging and ever-present change in the quality of the connectedness. Some persons may become members of a group without a very clear notion of what they are joining or why they wish to join. With them there may be a period of time wherein they do not *belong* in a psychological sense and must be helped into this relationship by the skill and understanding of the group worker and the group members. As they experience the feeling of belonging, they acquire the language of the group, and a shift from "my" and "mine" to "we" and "ours" in their conversation is observable.

It is evident that the same group can mean many different things to different members. To some members being a part of the group seems to be all-important. They are devoted to it and they participate enthusiastically. Other members seem to be less interested and do not allow themselves to become so deeply involved. The nature of the individual's past experience with groups determines his present needs. The individual always responds to contemporary group experience on the basis of behavior patterns that have been built up as a result of past experience. Each person establishes the kind of relationship with the group that is most satisfying to him at the time. Differences in age, sex, background, employment, and the like are always operating as the individual voluntarily affiliates with the group.

A senior citizens group may provide opportunity for a newcomer to gain companionship and friends. Another member may use the same group to pursue a hobby or develop a skill. A third person may see the same group as an avenue for participating in community service projects. Furthermore, these individuals' usages are interrelated, and the group may have a combination of meanings for them at any one time. In addition, as individuals change and as the group itself changes, it can be expected that there will be variations in the functional utility of the group to the members. The variety of uses that an individual may make of a group are illustrated in Figure 3.

Characteristics of the Group Work Group

It is increasingly evident that the method of social group work can be used in whole or in part with many groups in the community agency setting when the groups are deliberately designed to meet the recognized needs of individuals and when they are so constituted that the members take a maximum amount of responsibility for their own affairs. Social group work is not only a matter of the type of group being served; the objectives and intent of the worker and the agency are important factors as well. The start-

FIGURE 3

*Ways in Which Children, Youth, and Adults May Use Social Group
Work Experiences*

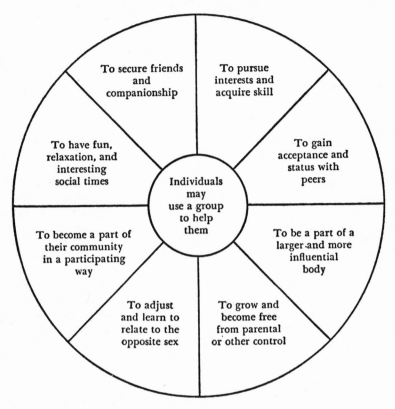

ing point for the agency may be to form a team or a science group with
only a slight degree of organization. Such a group may seem to be the
best suited to the needs and interests of the individuals at that time. In
this instance, the group work method may be utilized only in part in the
early stages of work. Later on changes in the group will call for a more
complete application of the method. The early efforts of the worker may
be directed toward helping the members of the team or the science group
to become a group in a psychological sense so that they can take more responsibility for their own affairs. If it is the purpose of the agency and the
worker to help the group become self-operative, the group work method is
being used.

In his thoughtful writing Schwartz has pointed out that the group work
group has certain characteristics which must be understood:

The first problem is to specify some of the salient characteristics of the small-
group system which helps create the social climate within which the worker

functions. First, the group is an enterprise in mutual aid, an allegiance of individuals who need each other, in varying degrees, to work on certain common problems. The important fact is that this is a helping system in which the clients need each other as well as the worker. This need to use each other, to create not one but many helping relationships, is a vital ingredient of the group process and constitutes a common need over and above the specific tasks for which the group has formed. Second, the group is a system of relationships which, in its own unique way, represents a special case of the general relationship between individuals and their society. The present group is, in other words, but one of the many associational forms through which its members interact with social values, social objectives, and social resources. More specifically, the cultural climate of the group is drawn from three major sources: generalized social attitudes about what is good and bad, right and wrong, worthy and unworthy, permeate the group and form a part of its culture. The agency in which the group is imbedded has drawn from the general culture its own characteristic and unique constellation of approved attitudes and behaviors. The group itself, by the nature of its central problem, by the activities in which it engages, and by the particular personalities it brings together, creates its own conditions for success and failure. Finally, the group is . . . an organic whole: its nature cannot be discerned by analyzing the separate characteristics of each component but by viewing the group organism as a complex of moving, interdependent, human beings, each acting out his changing relationship to society in his present interaction with others engaged in a similar enterprise. In this framework the worker is more concerned with what the member does and feels in the present situation than with what the member is. Further, the demands of society can be understood more clearly as they present themselves to the group member in the immediate situation than in abstract, holistic terms like "democratic responsibility" or "social maturity." It is, in fact, this very partialized and focused character of the present enterprise that make helping and being helped possible and manageable. The implications for the worker himself are that his ability to help is expressed in action and that this action is limited, as in any functional system, to certain areas in which he has some control. He acts to help others act and the emphasis on new ways of moving, of interacting, is more realistic and productive than the concern with total being, with discrete characteristics, and with totalistic conceptions of change.[18]

Thus, the group work group is best identified by its general characteristics rather than by its specific form or type. For example, the group should be small enough to enable the members to know one another intimately and to have a part in the functioning of the group. It should be small enough to allow the worker to know and understand the members as individuals. But "How small?" is a question that can only be answered in situational terms. It may be impossible for some persons new to a community to become real participants in a group of four or five persons who know one another well, but these newcomers can effect a good participating relationship with a group of fifteen to twenty members. On the other hand, some individuals would be overwhelmed by such a large group and would need to have their threshold experiences with much smaller groups. A further complication, which makes size alone an inadequate criterion, is the fact that workers differ a great deal. Workers with advanced professional preparation and experience may be skillful enough to do a highly individualized job with a large group. Other workers may find it impossible to work individually with more than a few persons at one time. Another general characteristic of the group work group is that there must be some bond that will hold the members together for at least a minimum amount of time. This bond, or degree of cohesiveness, may be interest in a certain activity; it may be the desire to learn something new and different; it may be a personal wish and need to be with one another. It could be the desire to do something about solving a social problem or the wish to explore some unknown area of human experience. Whatever it may be, the group must have a reasonable expectancy of remaining together for a sufficient period of time to achieve its objectives. In addition the group work group must have at least a minimum degree of organization, formal or informal, so that the members have a way of agreeing on objectives, sharing the duties, and assuming the responsibility for group decisions. If the members want and are willing and able to take their share of responsibility for the group, it is a group work group. Furthermore, the group work group must have some way of selecting and admitting members to the group, so that social controls can emerge and the group can take responsibility for its own conduct. This admission process must be worked out in cooperation with the agency and in keeping with the agency's policies. Groups must have boundaries that are known to the members. Finally, the group work group must be able and willing to accept the agency and the worker and to establish a cooperating relationship with them. By these natural processes of affiliation the group gives support and implementation to the agency's larger objectives. It is "agency" in the sense that it voluntarily subscribes to the tenets of the agency. This does not imply that it must meet within the actual physical setting of the agency. In fact, it may meet some distance away as a part of agency extension efforts, but it meets under the auspices and sponsorship of the agency.

These general characteristics of the group in social group work are interrelated. Taken as a composite rather than separately, they imply that the group work method is itself flexible and capable of modification. The nature of the group and the situation in which the worker finds it determine to a great extent the specific application of the various elements in the group work method. As Tropp points out:

The social group work method aims at the full utilization of forces in group life to bring about social growth in the individual members. It is in the process known as group-goal-achieving that these forces are at their maximum, the members being most fully engaged with each other and with the group as a whole. This process involves common decision and common action toward the accomplishment of common goals, shared by the members for the group as a whole. In the course of guiding this process, the group worker uses a variety of group experiences and program media, including social action, community service, and cultural, educational, social, and athletic activities. The group is involved in discussion and decision-making about the specific goals it wishes to achieve. It may also find itself in the course of its life, discussing general matters of concern to its members or specific matters dealing with the problems of individuals, but these discussions will have arisen naturally out of the work the group has cut out for itself and the relationships that ensue. An example of the group work process in action is a ward council of patients in a hospital who meet to discuss the conditions in which they are living and to make recommendations to the hospital for specific improvements in policies and programs. The group work method thus includes, in addition to goal-achieving by the group, the dimensions of group recreation, group education, and group counseling but any of these methods can be used separately.[19]

The Group as a Developing Unit

The well-known concept of individual differences has application to groups as well as individuals. The group is made up of individuals, each one of whom is different. Furthermore, the group consists of individuals *in relation to* one another. Granted the great complexity of individual personality, what does it mean when a number of individuals come together in a group? Obviously, groups are highly complicated mechanisms or organisms which grow and change because the individuals in the group are constantly changing.

The casual observer watching a group at work or play in a group work setting can see many of the surface characteristics of the group. For example, it is possible to see the number of members, to surmise their chronological age, and to note appearances. We can get a picture of the physical setting in which the group is meeting and can sense the adaptation that the group has made to that setting. We may observe the positions of the members and their reactions to one another. Of course, we can see what the group is doing in the way of activity. Although these items are interesting and may provide us with preliminary leads for further study, they do not tell us very much about the group.

More important, though more difficult to understand, are the dynamic characteristics of groups. These underlying factors of group development are revealed to the worker only as he consciously studies the group and works with the members. It is necessary to search for the different reasons why certain individual members seem to want the group. What use are they making of the group, and to what extent do they participate in the affairs of the group? What does the individual say about the group and how does he otherwise show his attitude toward it? The worker should watch for the differences in acceptance and status accorded individual members by their contemporaries. Some members are central and important in the life of the group; others seem peripheral and less important. Some individuals have a limited capacity for relating to others and need help in developing satisfying relations. To become accepted, individuals must adapt themselves to the climate of the group and conform to group patterns.

When an individual really belongs to a group he accepts the *purpose* of the group, interprets it, works for it. There is a commitment to the ideals and aspirations of the group. True, the member may seek modification in the purpose of the group as circumstances change and new needs arise. Such changes, however, grow out of the work of the group, and each individual has a voice in the refocusing of the purpose. The person who belongs accepts and carries responsibility in behalf of the group according to his abilities and strengths. He makes an investment in energy. In addition, belonging requires the member to accept ways of work agreed upon by the group. Here, again, he may strive for modification in the methodology of the group but does so openly and in concert with others.

As the individual becomes more and more a part of the group, he tends to help others to experience a similar relationship; he wants to help others to belong because of what belonging means to him. Later, he may adopt a critically evaluative attitude toward his group and what it does. This change makes for alertness and helps keep the group growing in effectiveness. Thus, the person who belongs has a *function* to perform, a *role* to fulfill and a growing understanding of his place in the group.

Often this process is slow. Usually individuals go through steps or stages in their identification with their group and their agency. It is necessary for the group worker constantly to apply what is known about the ways in which individuals may be helped to achieve this relationship of genuine belonging.

The study of individuals in relation to one another is a prerequisite to understanding the group. The quality of interpersonal relations among group members constitutes the bond that holds the group together. Out of this bond grows interaction and communication. As Northen describes it:

Social interaction is a term for the dynamic interplay of forces in which contact between persons results in a modification of the attitudes and behavior of the participants. Communication, both verbal and nonverbal, is basic to interaction. There is a structure to communication in that each group carries on its communication through certain agreed-upon channels, but it is a process, too, of exchanging meanings and making common meanings. Interpersonal communication is a complex social process through which information, feelings, attitudes, and other messages are transmitted, received, and interpreted: it is the very essence of a social system. Communication consists of the verbal, explicit, and intentional transmission of messages between people. It consists also of all the non-verbal processes by which persons influence one another. As a person transmits messages to others, he learns about the feelings, thoughts, hopes, and values of others. As members of a group exchange feelings and thoughts, there is a reciprocal and cyclical influence of members on each other. The sender of a message intends, consciously or not, to influence the receiver some way. The receiver needs to perceive and assess the overt and covert meaning and to respond to the message in an appropriate way. People vary in their ability to send clear messages and in their ability to interpret messages accurately.[20]

As the worker studies and analyzes the interaction patterns and communication content of the group, he is helped to discover the group's conception of its purpose and objectives since the goals of the group, as defined by the group itself, are of tremendous importance. Groups have ways of admitting and accepting new members and ways of excluding or expelling members who do not meet the standards of the group. Every group has a degree of consciousness of kind which may range from mild to strong. The spirit, unity, and morale of the group are among the intangible items which must be *felt* to be understood. In addition, the type and form of group organization and the procedure followed in making and implementing decisions are basic to understanding the group.

The presence of subgroups or cliques of members frequently exerts a powerful influence on the group as a whole. The relation of the group to other groups in the agency and community is an important area of understanding, inasmuch as some members of the group may be involved in overlapping relationships among several groups. Workers are also interested in ascertaining the developmental trend of the group, to judge whether it is growing stronger or tending to disintegrate. These processes of integration and disintegration can be understood only if they are studied over a period of time.

A systematic outline for studying the group in social group work must necessarily involve a large number of questions. The guide for studying the group which is offered in Part II of this book is designed to give the worker suggested questions from which he may prepare his own analytical instrument.

Stages of Group Development

When the group worker sees the group as a continuously developing dynamic organism rather than a static, fixed unit, it makes a real difference in the way he works with that group. This difference is based upon a fundamental principle of social group work: namely, that *the worker should start with the group at its current level of development and work with it at a rate of speed in harmony with the wishes and ability of the group.* The questions that arise as a result of this principle are: How do we know where a group is in its development? How do we know what a group is ready to undertake? How do we know when a group is ready to move? Garland and his associates point out:

Practitioners of social group work are continually faced with the question of group development. Virtually from the moment members enter the front door of an agency, the group worker begins his assessment of "where the group is." With whatever means he has at hand, he tries to evaluate the core problem with which members are struggling, their needs and capabilities as individuals and as aggregates and their state of readiness for the acceptance of particular forms of service from the agency. Once having considered where the group or individual is, however, workers tend to devote little attention to a systematic examination of "where they go" and studies of ongoing practice with a particular group rarely include a methodical investigation of the steps in the group's evolution.[21]

When one goes away from a group and then returns to it at a later time changes can be quickly noted. The members may be different, the program activities may be more complicated, leadership roles may have changed. The group has developed new ways of work and new forms of organization. Sarri and Galinsky point out:

> The concept of group development is based on a number of assumptions. . . . (1) The group is a potent influence system and can be used as an efficient vehicle for individual change. (2) The group is not an end in itself. The aim of social group work is to maximize the potentials of the group for individual change rather than to create an enduring small social system. (3) Group development can be controlled and influenced by the worker's actions. (4) There is no one optimal way in which groups develop.[22]

Experienced group workers can recall the general developmental stages through which groups may move. In the beginning, the so-called groups may seem to behave more like an assemblage of individuals than like a group. This is to be expected for, as Bennis observes, "Groups, like other highly complicated organisms, need time to develop. They need a gestation period to develop interaction, trust, communication, and commitment. No one should expect an easy maturity in groups any more than in young children." [23] Many times when a group assembles for the first time their beginning stage might better be called "pre-group" rather than group. There is the expectation that the individuals will become a group in time, but, at the moment, group consciousness may be very low. The worker can next sense the emergence of a wish on the part of the individuals to become a group, and he sees the beginning of group feeling as it develops. Later the group may develop a strong sense of group feeling. With some groups this feeling of oneness ebbs and flows, depending upon the conditions and circumstances surrounding the group. After a period of time, some groups enter a decline and ultimately choose to disassociate. To work with a group on a sound basis, the worker must study it continuously. Every time the worker enters into the life of a group, he is making a conscious or unconscious assessment of the group's stage of development and of the kind of responsibility it is ready to assume. In Figure 4 we show six stages of group development as a continuum from the beginning stage to the ending stage.

FIGURE 4

Stages of Group Development

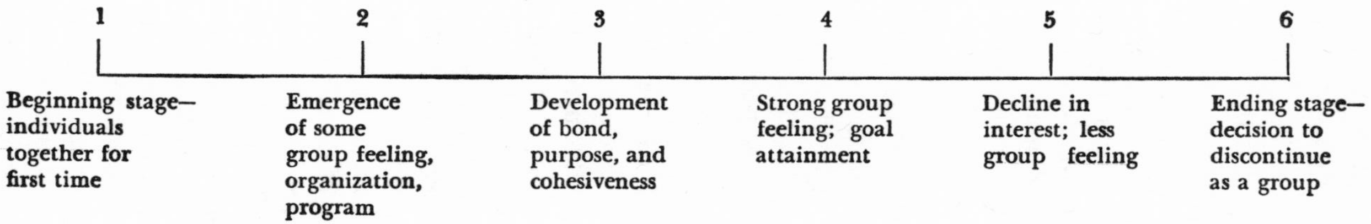

1	2	3	4	5	6
Beginning stage—individuals together for first time	Emergence of some group feeling, organization, program	Development of bond, purpose, and cohesiveness	Strong group feeling; goal attainment	Decline in interest; less group feeling	Ending stage—decision to discontinue as a group

What should the group worker look for in trying to get a measure of the group's development? What tools does he have to help in obtaining information which, when utilized, will lead to wise judgments? The only way in which the group worker can determine the stage of development of the group is to study the behavior of the members individually and collectively. The worker's role will vary with the stage of development of the group, and similarly the kinds of program experience that the group can handle will differ in relation to their emerging status as a group.

How do individuals behave in the "pre-group" or beginning stages of their association with one another? Though there will be variation among groups and individuals, it is probable the worker will observe some of the following behaviors. When the group is just getting started, there may be a lack of participation and enthusiasm on the part of the members, or there may be considerable indecision as to goals and program possibilities. The members may not know one another's names; in fact, the group may not be certain as to just who does belong. New groups will frequently express an interest in finding out about the agency and the worker and may ask questions either directly or indirectly. They may expect the worker to take all the responsibility for the work of the group, or, on the other hand, they may be very unwilling to allow the worker to do anything for them lest they obligate themselves.

In the beginning, it is possible that group members will show insecurity and nervousness, especially if it is their first experience as a group. Doubt and insecurity as to just what is expected of them or just what they are to do show up in random activity, hyperactivity, or extreme conservatism. Now and then, one or two individuals will dominate the group in its early stages and other individuals may be very much on the periphery of the group. At times, individual members will vie with one another for attention and will endeavor to move ahead of other members in getting the attention of the worker.

What does such behavior mean to the worker in terms of his role with the group in the early stages of development? In the first place, the worker will try to help the members become more at ease by replying to their questions and showing friendly interest in whatever the group wishes to discuss or do. It may be that individuals will need to learn about one another, and that the worker will help them to get better acquainted. The worker will ask himself why these persons are here as a group, and whether they show enough capacity and interest to become a group. He may help the group to understand its own potentialities and likewise help it to discover limitations and that they may stand in the way of successful group program.

The kinds of program experience enjoyed by the group in this early phase of existence will help it to determine what it wants to do in future meetings. Songs, games, and refreshments are common tools for the "breaking of the ice" and for helping the development of group feeling. Because the group has not taken shape in any definite way, the worker will take more responsibility for program but will concentrate on short-term activities that allow for a maximum amount of individual participation. By helping the group to become familiar with agency and community facilities and by encouraging members to talk about their experiences in other groups, it is possible to discover interests and lines of future direction for the group to follow.

After the individuals have been together for several meetings, the signs of group development become more pronounced. These developmental stages through which groups pass are always transitory phases in the process of maturing. Each developmental stage is interwoven with the others in a multitude of ways. Consequently, the exact moment at which an aggregation of individuals become a *group* in a psychological sense is seldom sharp and clear. The usual signs of group development include such things as more prompt and constant attendance by members, decision on a definite time and meeting place, development of formal organization, and a willingness on the part of members to take responsibility for the work of the group.

The worker will begin to hear members talking about "our" group, and will observe an accent on "we" and "us" in their conversation. Anxiety declines, and the members become more at ease in relation to one another and to the worker. There may be a desire for a name or for symbolic devices of identification. On the whole, the response of members is more enthusiastic and the range of participation wider. Certain individuals will take leadership responsibility, and others will reveal talents that can be used by the group. The group may wish for a more complex program than they have had before and may be willing to expand their relations with other groups in the agency.

During this stage of the group's development the role of the worker becomes modified. More than ever, the worker must be alert to what is happening in the group and encourage its members to take responsibility. He will guard against too rapid progression because he realizes that it is unwise for groups to take on more than they are prepared to handle successfully. During this period, programs of longer duration and more involved organization may be encouraged. The initial successful experiences of the group should be recognized as providing the foundation for larger things. The worker will be especially helpful in working with the leadership that has grown out of the group, but at the same time he will watch for individuals on the outside and endeavor to draw them into the affairs of the group. It is important to point out that groups rarely develop in an absolutely straight line, or forward motion. They have periods of retrogression, or "slump," and the worker must study these periods in the light of a longer sequence. Sometimes the group will "slow down" soon after a very significant program. The members seem to have reached a level of accomplishment, and they "slack off," seeming to rest until ready to move again.

A third developmental stage arrives when the group gives evidence of stability and maturity. Group members maintain a high average attendance.

The group seems to have reached an optimum working size which enables it to accomplish its purposes. There is a maximum amount of participation according to the capabilities of the members, and the group may desire to identify with some other groups or test itself out in cooperative events with other groups. The role of the group worker shifts again during this period. More responsibility can be carried by the group. The group sets its own goals and develops programs that result in sustained movement toward the achievement of objectives.

When a worker begins his work with a group, it may be at any of the stages already mentioned. The worker must find out at which stage the group is, because in this way he can enable the members to move ahead. Group experience that is either too demanding or too limiting is not fully satisfying to the members. When the group begins to show signs of readiness to move ahead, the worker should help the members realize their wishes for different and more demanding experiences. When group members begin to express desires to correct inadequacies and improve their work, they have reached an advanced point in their development. Programs that may have been self-centered shift in emphasis to the larger community and agency concerns. Specialized interests may be revealed, and there may be an interest in a variety of small group activities within the larger group. Here the worker is called upon to use his knowledge of agency and community resources. His role becomes that of an interpreter to the group, especially in regard to future possibilities. Evaluation occupies a larger share of time as the group becomes confident of its capacities.

Despite highly satisfactory experiences, groups sometimes reach a period in their natural life when interest diminishes and decline is noticeable. The group seems to be completing its work. Attendance falls off; members withdraw and become related to other groups. The group may include some individuals who have a strong need to have the group continue. They work hard to preserve the group and try to retain members who are ready to leave for other experiences.

This is a period which calls for careful thinking and analysis on the part of the worker. If such natural declines are misunderstood by the worker and interpreted as failure on his part or on the part of the group, serious conflicts may arise. The group and the worker may feel guilty and become hostile to one another or to the agency. The agency may make the mistake of trying to hold the group together when actually it should operate as a helpful agent for the proper closing of the group which has fulfilled its function in the lives of the members. By arranging satisfying terminal experiences with groups it is possible to make the conclusion of group life a prologue for further group experience. Those members who wish to continue may be helped to form a new group. Others may be helped to become members of ongoing groups. Some may be referred to special interest activities that the worker suggests. It is very important that the worker interpret to the group what is happening during the period of change which ultimately results in a major modification of group life.

Group Organization and Structure

As the worker comes to know his group and the needs of the individual members he helps the group to develop a form of organization and structure that will be useful to the group in arriving at goals. It is important to stress the point that good organization and structure grow out of *process* and are not simply imposed upon the group by the worker or the agency. The processes that are going on with the group have been specified by a number of authors. Alissi, for example, summarizes some key concepts regarding group processes inherent in small face-to-face groups as follows:

Group Formation—All groups in the process of formation must establish goals, determine membership, and develop some kind of structural arrangement. To the extent that these are appropriately interrelated the group can become a significant force in facilitating the social functioning of its members. . . . *Structure and Interpersonal Relations*—Groups, in the process of getting things done, get "structured," usually in terms of power, communication, personal attractions, and the like. Some kind of ranking procedure occurs in which status and role expectations are defined, relative to the distribution of rights and obligations. . . . *Group Control*—Groups establish a variety of ways of exercising authority and control over members. Controls established in a patriarchal, matriarchal, or democratic system, or in any of the variable combinations will have different implications on individual members, subgroups and the family as a whole. The nature of the control system will have an impact on how its members move in the wider social environment as well. . . . *Group Emotion*—Individual emotions have occupied considerable attention in therapy. Concepts such as cohesion, morale, social climate, and contagion have been found to be useful for describing group emotion. . . . *Group Communication and Deliberation*—Groups develop verbal and non-verbal forms of communication which convey meaning with varying degrees of effectiveness. . . . *Group Value System*—Beliefs, values, and norms develop in groups which, in concert, sort out and regulate preferences concerning individual and group behavior.[24]

Among all of these processes the one which the group worker can influence the most is that of organization. Out of his experience with many groups he should be able to select certain criteria which can be applied to the organizing process. For example, when a group is properly organized the communication system within the group, both vertical and horizontal, should function well. Also, a good structure provides for a steady flow of interaction and a maximum amount of participation on the part of the members. Satisfactory structure and organization make for an orderly grouping of tasks or duties which must be performed by group members. In addition, it clarifies the roles and responsibilities that individuals will be expected to carry. Flexibility is another criterion of structure and organization which needs to be remembered. As the group grows in maturity it may need another kind of structure to facilitate its work. Most important is the necessity for keeping structure as simple as possible.

In his discussion of group structure Tropp says:

Common decisions require joint authority; and it is at the location of the seat of authority, power and control that the basic structure of the group can be determined. The following are the characteristics of authority necessary for the operation of the common goal group: 1. The group has the authority to act in its own behalf for its stated goals. 2. The authority is shared by all the members. 3. The group itself decides who shall direct its efforts . . . and what method shall be used. It is not dependent upon a non-membership source to direct its affairs. 4. The accomplishment of a specific plan for achieving the group's purpose requires the group's consent to that plan. 5. The authority to decide for itself is inherent in the function of the group. Although it may receive this authority by delegation or sanction, and although there may be limits to its extent, the authority is genuine and not a technique that may be offered or removed by a higher authority which is really directing the group's affairs. 6. The group may, in turn, delegate this authority or part of it to a group-selected leader or subgroup, but this delegated power is subject to controls from the entire group. 7. The structure of group achievement consists of group deliberation, decision and action around the specifics of what, when, how, who, and even why. 8. The decision may be reached by unanimity, either spontaneous or negotiated, or by a smaller portion of the group yielding to a larger portion. 9. Whether a decision is reached by consensus or majority, the entire group is committed by its purpose to accept the decision and to engage in the action decided. 10. The ability of the group to decide for itself is limited by age and illness. (In law, there are classifications of minor status and incompetent status, which establish non-responsibility for actions. These are also recognized in group work so that the group worker plays a more authoritative role in these circumstances. Yet this purpose would still be to help groups to grow toward responsible decisions for their own group life.) In fact, all common-goal service groups in agencies are really laboratory groups or groups-in-training for the larger society. The provision of a professional agent is aimed at helping the group to learn how to use its power of decision in the most effective and responsible manner.[25]

Getting Started With the Group

The group worker does many things in the early stages of the group to help the individuals begin to feel that they are a part of something larger than themselves. The worker offers the warmth of his welcome and shares with the group members general identifying information about himself. If members are not known to one another he assists in introductions, but he avoids probing. He arranges the setting so it will be as informal, open, and free as possible. He understands that people may feel strange, nervous, insecure, and even frightened when they come to a group for the first time.

He helps them to relax often through the use of simple refreshments. He does not try for a long meeting the first time the group is together. In the next chapter attention will be given to the role of the worker in the life of the group.

NOTES

1. Earl Eubank, *The Concepts of Sociology* (Boston: Heath, 1932), p. 163.
2. Emory S. Bogardus, *Sociology* (New York: Macmillan, 1949), p. 4.
3. Kurt Lewin, *Resolving Social Conflict* (New York: Harper, 1948), p. 84.
4. *Ibid.*, p. 82.
5. Charles H. Cooley, "Primary Groups" in A. Paul Hare, Edgar F. Borgatta, and Robert F. Bales (editors), *Small Groups: Studies in Social Interaction* (New York: Alfred A. Knopf, 1966, Revised Edition), pp. 15–19.
6. Raymond Firth, *Elements of Social Organization* (Boston: Beacon Press, 1963), pp. 43–44.
7. Bernard Berelson and Gary A. Steiner, *Human Behavior: An Inventory of Scientific Findings* (New York: Harcourt, Brace and World, Inc., 1964), pp. 325–326.
8. Hans S. Falck, "Social Group Work and Planned Change" in *Social Work Practice, 1964* (Published for the National Conference on Social Welfare by Columbia University Press, New York, 1964), p. 210.
9. Berelson and Steiner, *op. cit.*, p. 331.
10. *Ibid.*, p. 327.
11. Helen Northen, *Social Work with Groups* (New York: Columbia University Press, 1969), p. 47.
12. Frederic M. Thrasher, "The Gang" in A. Paul Hare, Edgar F. Borgatta and Robert F. Bales (editors), *Small Groups: Studies in Social Interaction* (New York: Alfred A. Knopf, 1966), p. 40.
13. Emanuel Tropp, *A Humanistic Foundation for Group Work Practice* (New York: Selected Academic Readings—a Division of Associated Educational Services Corporation, 1969), pp. 7A, 8A.
14. Clovis R. Shepherd, *Small Groups: Some Sociological Perspectives* (San Francisco: Chandler Publishing Company, 1964), p. 22.
15. Berelson and Steiner, *op. cit.*, p. 326.
16. Shepherd, *op. cit.*, p. 88.
17. Northen, *op. cit.*, pp. 45–46.
18. William Schwartz, "The Social Worker in the Group" in *The Social Welfare Forum, 1961* (Published for the National Conference on Social Welfare by Columbia University Press, New York, 1961), pp. 158–159.
19. Tropp, *op. cit.*, pp. 7D–8D.
20. Northen, *op. cit.*, pp. 17–18.
21. James A. Garland, Hubert E. Jones, Ralph L. Kolodny, "A Model for Stages of Development in Social Work Groups" in Saul Bernstein (editor), *Explorations in Group Work* (Boston: Boston University School of Social Work, 1965), p. 15.
22. Rosemary C. Sarri and Maeda J. Galinsky, "A Conceptual Framework for Group Development" in Robert D. Vinter (editor), *Readings in Group Work Practice* (Ann Arbor, Campus Publications, 1967), p. 73.
23. Warren G. Bennis, "Post Bureaucratic Leadership" in Donald N. Michael (editor), *The Future Society* (Transaction Books published by Aldine Publishing Company, 1970), p. 42.
24. Albert S. Alissi, "Social Work with Families in Group-Service Agencies: An Overview," *The Family Coordinator, Journal of Education, Counseling and Services,* October 1969, pp. 398–399.
25. Tropp, *op. cit.*, pp. 8A–9A.

4

The Group Worker—
Roles and Responsibilities

In the first three chapters we have looked at the definitions of group work, the agency setting where group work is practiced, and the group as a unit of service. In this chapter we want to look at the group worker in terms of his roles and responsibilities. In a very real sense this chapter is the keystone of the book. There can be little disagreement with the statement that the key to effective group work lies with the worker. The worker, as a representative of the agency, is responsible for the provision of guidance and help for the group. The way in which the worker works is a distinguishing characteristic of social group work. Northen points out:

> The social worker participates in the group system to influence the ways in which members work toward facing and solving their problems—those of the individuals, the internal system of the group, and the wider environment. The social worker uses his knowledge and skills to support the group in its current functioning or to change toward some more desired state. One way that systems are influenced is through modification of the system itself or one or more of its component parts. The worker acts with such intent as: provision of psychological support to an individual, subgroup, or a total system; improvement of channels and modes of communication; clarification of attitudes, behavior, and situations; or provision of opportunities for the development of competencies essential to effective functioning. Systems are influenced also through modifications in the environment, brought about by the use of agency and community resources, referrals, the development of new or improved policies or services, or collaboration with others in behalf of individuals in the group system.[1]

The Role of the Worker and Factors That Influence It

In any and all work situations, it is necessary for the worker to clarify and make explicit the role he is to fulfill. In addition, he must be clear about the roles to be carried by others in the work situation. Group worker and group member roles are thus extremely important, for as Hill says, "One principle of group work . . . is that for a group to achieve its objectives, the members need to have some understanding of the roles they must execute." [2]

In writing about the concept of role Slater says:

We might define role as a more or less coherent and unified system of items of interpersonal behavior. With even this minimal definition it becomes apparent that role performance in the small group situation will have both consequences which are important to the functioning of the group in which the role is performed, and personal consequences of importance to the individual who performs it. Similarly, an individual may be motivated to perform a role both by specific inducements offered by the group and by more general needs operating within the individual himself.[3]

Baumgartel elaborates when he writes:

We can think of society as a social system, a network of patterned relationships among people, much as we think of the organization chart for a company or a military unit. These patterned relationships involve roles. As sociologists have pointed out, there are many cleavages in society. People are involved in different occupations; people differ with regard to age and sex; people belong to different social classes and ethnic groups; people exist at different levels in the hierarchies of wealth, power, and prestige. Each of these points, so to speak, in the social system or the network of interpersonal relations is a role. The role concept is abstracted from the concrete behavior of the people in particular points in the social system, and can be thought of in two ways. On the one hand, we can think of the regularities in the behavior of, say factory foremen and abstract out of the behavior of many foremen the particular manner of acting in this role. These regularities in behavior are also accompanied by regularities in the ways of thinking and feeling about other people as referring to the expectations other people have about the way a particular kind of person should behave, how students think a professor should behave, for example.[4]

Maas considers role with these words:

Social role may be defined as the institutionalized group expectations as to the behavior, attitudes, and other attributes for the occupant of a given position in a social system. Different societies foster variants of familial, economic, governmental, educational, religious, and other need-meeting social institutions. To ensure the adequate functioning and evolution of these institutions expectations evolve for individuals who participate in various roles in subsystems of these institutions. Expectations vary according to the position the individual occupies in a family, a work situation, or a school. For example, expectations for the student, the teacher, and for the administrator are different. Also, of course, in different subcultures and strata of a society, expectations for the positions of father, mother, older son, six-year-old daughter, grandfather, and mother's brother may vary widely. In effect, persons occupying a given position are expected to fulfill, within a range, their group's slowly changing expectations for this position. Socialization and acculturation are processes aimed at internalizing, for new members, the attitudes required for adequate role performance in the groups a society currently sanctions and encompasses. Individuals in any society, over their life-span, are expected to be members of a number of institutionalized groups. Normally, balances are reached between the changing expectations of a group and the changing values and capacities of individuals.[5]

In social group work the role of the worker is essentially "enabling" or "helping." Out of his wish to help groups have a growth experience the worker adopts a posture of facilitating rather than dominating, interpreting rather than declaring, and assisting rather than leading. As Tine has pointed out so tellingly:

The worker's role must contain certain ingredients that add to the attractiveness of the member's life. 1. Warmth and genuine interest in the member as an individual. 2. Ability to listen to the member's life history and views. 3. Genuine interest in the activity that has meaning for the member. 4. Imagination and creativity in discovering and bringing into fruition new and engaging activities and ideas. 5. Efficiency in matter-of-fact handling of the details of agency schedules, procedures, and processes.[6]

Of course, the worker's role will vary with different groups. Because groups and the situations within which they operate are so different, the worker should first seek to understand the group and the circumstances surrounding it before attempting to define specific aspects of his role with it. The primary considerations, or factors, that underlie differences in the roles of workers are: 1) the community setting; 2) the agency function and scope; 3) agency facilities and program; 4) the kind of group with which he is working; 5) the interests, needs, abilities, and limitations of individual members; 6) the skill and competence of the worker; and 7) the amount of help the group wants and its willingness to accept help from the worker. These factors are operating in every group situation. The extent to which the worker consciously studies them separately and in relation to one another will be influential at the point of role determination.

Therefore, it is difficult, if not impossible, to describe the worker's role as consisting of concrete techniques that can be applied with unvarying regularity to all group situations. When workers ask for quick answers to such questions as What do I do now? they overlook the fact that study and analysis of the situation must precede the actual decision. With some groups the worker helps by carrying a great deal of responsibility because the groups are newly formed and unfamiliar with ways of working together. He may refrain from carrying responsibility for the same group at a later time in its development. With one group the worker helps by making a definite attempt to encourage the group to participate with other groups in carrying out some large undertaking. Here he assumes that the group is ready for such a step and sees the step as contributing to the group's basic experience in the agency.

A predominant factor that must be thoroughly understood by the worker is that he is always a representative of the agency. He is not a member of the group but rather a professional worker who has the responsibility of helping the group use the agency to fulfill all or part of its needs. His skill as a group worker is always put into practice within the accepted policies and procedures of the agency. What he does with the group will depend upon the basic method of work in which the agency believes. Consequently, it is of the utmost importance that workers interpret their role with the group relatively early so that the group members may know what to expect from them. They should interpret the agency to the group and let the group know how the worker conceives of his task as a representative of the agency.

Another factor of major importance is that the worker is there to fulfill a *professional* role. Zander and his colleagues pointed out:

. . . A person's profession specifies his role. In its most general sense a role is a set of behaviors which an individual is expected to perform. The more restricted meaning we have given the term is that a professional role includes a limited set of behaviors concerning for example, task functions, responsibility relations, and normative relationships which are expected of an individual by relevant others.[7]

Characteristics of Professional Role Behavior

What does the group worker do as he fulfills his professional role? What are the characteristics of his behavior? To this writer the worker is demonstrating his professional role when he acts in the following manner:

1. The professional role of the worker is shown when he strives for objectivity and seeks and uses factual material in his work. This is another way of saying that the professional person seeks to make use of *knowledge* and *understanding* as a basis for his skill, and that knowledge and understanding replace unconsidered judgment and unfounded opinion.

2. The group worker is fulfilling his professional obligation when he works purposefully and planfully and knows what his role is and what he is endeavoring to accomplish. In other words, his *purpose* becomes so much a part of him that his every action is governed by the consideration of whether or not the step he takes will lead him toward his professional goal.

3. The group worker is behaving professionally when he exercises conscious self-discipline or control over himself at all times. He keeps his own needs out of the situation in so far as possible. He is sensitive to others;

in fact, professional behavior has been described as "sensitivity stepped up to the nth degree." Obviously, this kind of person works in the public interest and wants to contribute to man's well-being. In short, his professional integrity is based on the concept that public interest is above self-interest.

4. The professional role of the worker is strengthened as he seeks constantly to develop a sound professional philosophy based on maturing values. He seeks diligently to formulate for himself the convictions by which he lives and which become the basis for choices or decisions, especially in matters of principle.

When a group of workers are behaving professionally and are carrying forward their professional role responsibilities in harmony with basic social work principles certain things stand out. First, in an atmosphere of positive professional relationships, a feeling of mutual respect, trust, and confidence with one another is evident. This is a *feeling* tone or quality of organizational life which is difficult to describe and hard to measure, but it is there.

Second, when positive professional relationships prevail, people are warm, friendly, relaxed, open, free, and frank with one another. There is an atmosphere that is summed up by the words "respect for human beings and for human values."

Third, persons who enjoy positive professional relationships are in *communication* with one another. There is a good deal of planful talking, sharing, and evaluating and the staff works *together* rather than at cross purposes.

Fourth, under conditions of good working relationships, persons behave responsibly toward one another. Such people can be counted on to do their work and to complete their assignments because they regard their assignments as intimately related to the success of the total enterprise.

Fifth, when positive professional relationships exist, pride in the quality of the work done becomes evident. Standards are set high, and there is a general tendency on the part of persons who are well related to each other to seek for an even higher standard of performance as they go along.

Sixth, under conditions of positive professional relationships, group workers are convinced of the worthwhileness of the purpose of the agency and of what they are doing together.

Different Groups Require Different Things from Workers

Anyone who has worked with groups for any length of time realizes that different groups require different things from workers. For example, there is a difference between doing social group work with children and youth and doing it with adults. The age of group members is an important differential. Another prominent difference among groups is the length of time during which the groups are to remain together. Short-term groups call for a different application of group work skills than do long-term groups. The size of the group is an additional variable, requiring a modification of method especially when the group is made up of a large number of members. When groups are of the council type, made up of representatives of other groups, they are much different from single-interest groups. When groups consist of handicapped or ill persons their needs require different kinds of help from the worker. Age, time, size, composition, and function are thus important differentials. The differential approach of the worker implies that he will accept the importance of working with each group individually and will endeavor to understand its unique aspects.

When workers study the difference between work with children's groups and work with adult groups, they are struck with the need to understand developmental age as a factor in group work. Children are energetic, seemingly tireless, growing, and enthusiastic about their group affairs. They tend to be less selective than do adults, who are limited in energy and less inclined to all-out identification with groups. Children, whose powers of self-expression, communication, and reasoning are developing, spend a considerable amount of time in motor activity, whereas adult groups have better language articulation and spend more time in verbalization, thinking together and working out problems. Children and youth, because of their shorter life-span, have limited environmental experience to utilize and need a variety of experiences to broaden their outlook. At the same time, children's groups tend to be more flexible, liberal, and less influenced by preconceptions than are adult groups, which may be judgmental, less flexible, and more rigid in outlook.

Interactions between members of the younger age group are less complex, even impulsive, direct, uninhibited, and simple. With adult groups the process of interaction is complex, subtle, at times sophisticated and remote. Younger age groups need help in learning how to control their impulses and how to focus their energy. They may be extremely harsh in dealing with contemporaries who overstep the bounds of group propriety. Adult groups, on the other hand, may have developed ways of self-discipline in keeping with the level of their emotional maturity and in keeping with a more mature philosophy of life. Insofar as program content is concerned, the younger age groups usually desire a range of activities; they face program with anticipation and may be expansive as to the extent of their ideas and hopes. Adult groups, on the other hand, often express time pressures and seem to get more satisfaction from a slower program pace. They may spend time in reminiscing and reliving experiences and may be more interested in problem situations that call for mental effort. The goals of the group work process with adult groups are more likely to be in terms of society and its betterment than in terms of individual growth so prominent in group work's purpose for younger groups. Persons are adults longer than they are children or youth. Adults are considerably more influential than are children. Social group work with adult groups is different because of the basic social factors that characterize their age range and life situations.

The size of the group is a variable that requires different approaches from the worker. Some would assume that group work method has little application to the large open groups. Such is not the case. Many groups are large. Some agencies create or sponsor large groups in the belief that people need to learn how to function in large as well as small groups. A prominent form of group organization is the open lounge or center for youth or older adults. In creating these large-scale group forms agencies have tended to meet the needs of both groups for "a place of their own." They place accent on free choice of activities, self-government in terms of rules and regulations, and spontaneous groupings that emerge around particular interests.

Workers with large groups frequently discover that the large group actually consists of a number of smaller groups. To understand and work with the large group they have to understand the subgroups in it. In carrying out a program the large group often creates a smaller executive committee consisting of officers and committee chairman. Some individuals therefore have a small group experience plus an opportunity to be part of the larger whole. With skillful rotating of assignments, it becomes possible for many members to take responsibility for the affairs of the large unit. In the carrying out of large-scale events it is possible to exercise judgment in facility usage so that a variety of small group activities can be provided simultaneously with the large event, thus giving members a chance to form small groups around their interests. A large forum group can allocate a portion of its time to small discussion groups following the main presentation. In planning a large dance, refreshments and intermission activities can allow small groups to congregate. Recreational activities for small-group participation can be interspersed throughout the main event.

In work with large-scale groups, quite often several workers share in the responsibility. These workers may be from the same agency, or they may be from different agencies. It is their responsibility to correlate their efforts so that a consistent approach will result. Frequent meetings of the workers themselves will increase the amount of individualization that can be accomplished as different workers work with the same individuals in a variety of activities.

It may be that the large-scale group has been created primarily as an introductory experience and that from the large group the agency will make available a number of smaller groups for continuing program purposes. When small groups grow out of large groups, it is important to make certain that enough staff workers are provided so that the additional groups will be satisfying.

In a highly mobile society many groups exist for relatively short periods of time. Some communities are transient, with the population remaining for a limited period time and then moving to new and perhaps more permanent locations. Some agency settings are by nature short-term. Summer camps, to which persons go for periods of from one to several weeks, are an example of this kind of setting. Many hospital-based groups are short-term, as are groups of military personnel on leave.

The period of time during which the worker expects the group to exist is an important factor in the extent to which the group work method can be utilized. When groups are planned to be short-term, modifications in the group work method will be required. Some short-term groups have a definite time span that is determined in advance by mutual consent of the agency and the group. For example, a two-week camp period is fixed as to starting and terminating dates. Or a special activity group, such as a dramatics group, may organize for the specific purpose of presenting a play and then disband. Other short-term groups have, in addition to the limited-time factor, changing composition of membership. Members come and go, but none remain longer than a few months.

In groups of this kind the members have far less opportunity to become well acquainted with one another. The worker has less chance to know the group on an intimate basis, and the processes of interaction between members and worker are definitely curtailed. The goals of the group must be established in realistic relation to the time factor and must be within the reach of the group. Activities which call for long-term planning and continuity are inappropriate because the group does not intend to remain together long enough to complete a complex program. The worker is thus called upon to exercise his skill in helping the group to achieve a sharp focus on purpose and program so that it will be possible for it to accomplish its aims in the limited time available. Structure has to be kept very simple, and the creation of many deliberate committees, which take time to get under way, is naturally inadvisable. Usually in groups of this kind the leadership that arises within the group is functional in that certain members have skills, talents, and capabilities that can be expressed in behalf of the group's immediate needs and interests. Because personality growth requires both time and active participation on the part of the individual, it is doubtful whether the short-term group can ever meet fully the objectives of social group work. It is possible, however, for groups of this kind to become excellent introductory experiences for the individual who may later be in a position in which he can affiliate with a group on a more permanent basis.

Developing a Relationship With the Group

The group worker helps individuals in groups to discover, create, and maintain relationships with other individuals that can be increasingly satisfying, constructive, and personally productive. The ability to get along with other people, to understand them, and to cooperate with them in experiences of various kinds is basic to good social adjustment. Before he can help others to develop relationships that will lead to socialization, the worker must first create a positive relationship between himself and the group.

The helping relationships is a basic part of all of social work:

In individual treatment the relationship between the caseworker and the client is the chief dynamic for effecting change. It is the medium through which the client gains emotional release and support, incorporates new concepts about himself, and acquires increased awareness of his attitudes and behavior. The quality of the relationship, which is characterized by understanding, acceptance, and encouragement, makes it possible for the troubled person to express both his self-doubts, conflicts, weaknesses, and failures and his hopes and aspirations. Through the interaction with the caseworker, the client gains new perspective on his problems and greater confidence in his capacity to find solutions to them. In group treatment the significant relationships are inevitably more intricate than in the one-to-one interview because of the complex inter-personal situation. These relationships occur between each member and the therapist and among the members; in addition, each individual also relates to subgroupings and to the group as a whole. A major therapeutic element in group treatment is the availability of other group members to serve in the role of helper.[8]

In group work the concept of relationship refers to the bond of feeling that exists between the worker and the group and among group members themselves. Relationships consist primarily of emotional responses which ebb and flow as human behavior calls forth different reactions. There are differences in the intensity and duration of the emotional response as situations change and as needs arise. Relationship is thus a psychological concept or state of mind among persons. It is also a tool or means of creating a response from the group. An effective working relationship between the worker and group takes time to develop. It grows and changes as they go through certain experiences together. From his first meeting with the group and throughout all subsequent meetings, the group worker should be constantly concerned about his working relationship with the group. Northen observes:

The nature and quality of the social worker's relationship with individuals, subgroups, and the group as a whole has an important effect on each member's use of the group and on the development of the group itself. The use of relationship is of primary importance in motivating members to discover and develop their capacities, to have self-esteem, and to accept and use the contribution of the social worker.[9]

Perhaps the greatest single element in the beginning stages of work with a group is the worker's ability to accept the group as it is, with both strengths and limitations, positives and negatives. When the worker is able to listen to the group and accept the group's early ambitions and ideas, he controls his tendency to convert the group to his ideas or his way of doing things. Goroff emphasizes the "partnership" quality of the relationship:

Each person in the partnership brings his assets and liabilities, his capacities and needs, his ability to give help and take help, his unique personality, his knowledge and skills and places them at the disposal of the group. Thus, the social group worker must give up his desire to control either the process in the group or the individuals for some goals he has developed in favor of developing a *mutually acceptable* working agreement with the members of the group that will establish the framework for the group members and the social worker to enter into the relationship.[10]

To accept the group truly, the worker must accept the feelings of the group members. These feelings may bear upon themselves, or upon the worker or upon the agency. Group members may have feelings about other groups or about previous workers. By being accepting, the worker helps the group to accept him and the help he has to give as a representative of the agency.

In the beginning the worker should place emphasis on warmth and friendliness rather than on group organization or planning. Acceptance is shown by listening to group members and by giving undivided attention to what they say. The worker wants to become acquainted with the members of the group, but he must avoid probing or questioning which may be misinterpreted.

When the group and the worker come together for the first time, they have many questions about each other, though seldom are these questions expressed in a direct verbal manner. How does the group feel about the worker? What do the members talk about among themselves before or after the meeting when the worker is out of hearing range? If we could listen in on their conversations, we might overhear questions such as these: What is he like? How strict will he be? What does he think of us? Can he help us do the things we want to do? How does he compare with our previous worker? Does he have a sense of humor?

Similarly, the new worker has unanswered questions about himself in relation to the group: Will the group members like me, accept me, respond to me? What will this group be like in behavior and attitudes? Do I know enough or have enough skill to work with them effectively? Can I do as well as the former worker did with them? What does the agency expect me to do with this group? Will I find people in the group who can take responsibility for some of the duties incidental to group programs? Will the group present problems which will be difficult for me to understand?

Questions such as these are present in the minds of both the worker and group members at the time of the first meeting. And first meetings are very important, for as Hartford indicates, "It is through the social group worker's activity that the climate of the group is set. The worker's acceptance of all members, his interventions to provide an opportunity for comfortable participation by all members, his respect for all members, set the pattern. At the same time, his limitations on acting-out, hostile, and aggressive behavior help members to know that they will be protected from themselves and from each other. This should be equally true for children's clubs, adult committees, teen-age councils, activity groups, classes, or any type of group." [11]

Every new situation has unknowns in it. Unknowns are always threatening in the realm of personal relationships, for none of us can become secure in regard to others until knowledge about one another replaces lack of knowledge or misconceptions. So, in a sense, before a satisfactory relationship can come about between the worker and the group, each must learn about the other. The area of unknowns must be decreased, and the preliminary overtures of worker toward group and of group toward worker will be designed to this end.

The desire on the part of the worker to create a working relationship based on mutual acceptance is furthered when the worker thinks through the characteristics of an effective worker-group relationship. When the worker knows the nature of an effective relationship from the standpoint of qualitative aspects, he is better able to control consciously his part in the two-way process of creating it. The setting up of an effective working relationship is not an end in itself but rather a means toward helping the group members themselves get along better and have the best possible experience in the agency. It is assumed that when the worker has been able to relate himself successfully to the group, he will then use that relationship to further the adjustment of individuals and the progress of the group as a whole.

The characteristics of a desirable worker-group relationship are primarily emotional, or "feeling," items. The worker wants to feel warm, friendly, and relaxed toward group members, and he wants the group to feel the same way about him. Even though coldness, tension, and some hostility may greet the new worker initially, he will accept it and try to locate the reasons that underlie it. The worker wants to be open, free, and frank with the group and tries to develop similar responses from them toward him. In the beginning, the atmosphere may be secretive, inhibited, or evasive until the group feels secure toward the worker. Though the worker may encounter a negative response at the outset, he recognizes that an effective relationship must ultimately be positive, and therefore he encourages the expression of interests by all group members.

After the first few meetings with a group, the worker should begin to feel the development of a positive working relationship. Fundamentally, it is a matter of the response of members toward the worker and toward one another. Though the amount of time required will differ with individuals and groups, the beginning can frequently be felt during the early meetings. Workers can observe the group relax and rid itself of tensions; the development of freedom and spontaneity can be sensed. The participation of members increases, and the candor of member conversation indicates the degree to which the worker is getting acceptance. When the group becomes able to accept some of the limits imposed on it by the agency and the worker, this is additional evidence that a desirable relationship is emerging. Individual ability to disagree with the worker and to question the agency represents a growing security between the group and the worker. Steady attendance of the group and prompt arrival of members at meetings show how members feel toward one another and toward the worker. Later, when groups are willing to grow and to admit new members, it would seem that they have reached a new degree of inner security. These are but a few of the indications that progress is being made in the realm of relationship. To be sure, progress will not be entirely forward. There will be times when the relationship seems to retrogress, and then will once again move forward.

The Skills of the Group Worker

Social group work is a method in the profession of social work through which individuals in community agency groups are helped by a worker to relate themselves to others and to experience growth opportunities that are in accordance with their needs and capacities. Method means the purposeful use of insights and understandings based upon a body of knowledge and principles. Skill is the worker's capacity to apply knowledge and understanding to a given situation. Every worker must have skill in working as a part of an agency and community setting. He must know the agency and the community and must also possess a growing awareness of himself as well as the group. In her classic definition of skill Robinson said:

Skill implies first of all an activity, an ability to perform, and while it rests on knowledge, it is clearly distinguishable from knowledge. . . .The skillful way of working . . . develops out of some relationship between the workman and material in which he works. . . . His understanding of his material and his capacity to work with it instead of against it, to utilize and not do violence to its essential nature, determine his ability to develop skill in his handling of the process. Skill might be defined, then, as the capacity to set in motion and control a process of change in specific material in such a way that the change which takes place in the material is effective with the greatest degree of consideration for and utilization of the quality and capacity of the material.[12]

The group worker's skills are most evident while he is actually engaged in a helping capacity with the group. Hartford says:

There is an underlying assumption . . . that social group work as a method of social work practice entails *deliberate* activity on the part of the worker to bring about change or growth of the group members in and through group experience. Whether this growth and change be developmental, that is, progression to higher levels of socialization, value formulation, and ego functioning, or whether it be correctional of dysfunction in intrapersonal, interpersonal, social situational relationships or in values, the social group worker takes appropriate, deliberate action, based on his assessment of the needs of group members within the context of the group, the agency and the social situation, through his professional leadership role with the group.[13]

In her discussion of how to identify and teach the skill component in social group work Pernell observes:

There are two types of interrelated skills which the student must acquire. We distinguish these as the procedure skills and interactional skills. The first group is comprised of the steps in a methodological, knowledgeable procedure of giving help; the identification of the professional purpose, study, diagnosis, selection of goals, treatment, and reporting. The interactional skills are those behavior responses appropriate to individual and group need, within the purposes of the social group work service. These we identify . . . as accepting, relating, and enabling, and supporting, limiting, guiding, alleviating, and interpreting. . . . The procedural skills are primarily intellectual accomplishments, while the interactional skills demand the additional play of emotions—the use of self. The teaching of the second type of skill, however, is also approached on an intellectual level relying on the student's capacity to experience change in feeling and subsequent response through an intellectual approach.[14]

A listing of the skills of the group worker would include the following items:

1. *Skill in Establishing Purposeful Relationships*
   A. The group worker must be skillful in gaining the acceptance of the group and in relating himself to the group on a positive professional basis.
   B. The group worker must be skillful in helping individuals in the group to accept one another and to join with the group in common pursuits.
2. *Skill in Analyzing the Group Situation*
   A. The group worker must be skillful in judging the developmental level of the group to determine what the level is, what the group needs, how quickly the group can be expected to move. This calls for skill in direct observation of groups as a basis for analysis and judgment.
   B. The group worker must be skillful in helping the group to express ideas, work out objectives, clarify immediate goals, and see both its potentialities and limitations as a group.
3. *Skill in Participation with the Group*
   A. The group worker must be skillful in determining, interpreting, assuming, and modifying his own role with the group.
   B. The group worker must be skillful in helping group members to participate, to locate leadership among themselves, and to take responsibility for their own activities.
4. *Skill in Dealing with Group Feeling*
   A. The group worker must be skillful in controlling his own feelings

about the group and must study each new situation with a high degree of objectivity.

B. The group worker must be skillful in helping groups to release their own feelings, both positive and negative. He must be skillful in helping groups to analyze situations as a part of the working-through of group or intergroup conflicts.

5. *Skill in Program Development*

A. The group worker must be skillful in guiding group thinking so that interests and needs will be revealed and understood.

B. The group worker must be skillful in helping groups to develop programs which they want as a means through which their needs may be met.

6. *Skill in Using Agency and Community Resources*

A. The group worker must be skillful in locating and then acquainting the group with various helpful resources which can be utilized by them for program purposes.

B. The group worker must be skillful in helping certain individual members to make use of specialized services by means of referral when they have needs which cannot be met within the group.

7. *Skill in Evaluation*

A. The group worker must have skill in recording the developmental processes that are going on as he works with the group.

B. The group worker must be skillful in using his records and in helping the group to review its experiences as a means of improvement.

To summarize, it may be said that professional group work skill represents the worker's conscious application of knowledge, understanding, and principles in working with individuals and groups in defined situations in such a way that change takes place in the behavior of the individuals and the group.

The Worker Helps the Group

When we study what group workers have done in their efforts with groups, we discover numerous points at which groups need the help of skilled workers. The worker helps the group to determine its objectives, purposes and goals. He helps the group gain in understanding of the agency purpose and what it can contribute to the attainment of these goals. As Northen declares, "In a group, the purpose is a composite of the expressed purposes for the group held by the social worker and the expressed purposes of the members of the group. Purpose is a dynamic concept, not a static one. The desires and needs brought into the group by members become blended together through social interaction and develop into a group purpose." [15] The group worker helps this to come about.

In addition, the worker helps the group to develop group feeling and consciousness of itself. Perhaps he helps the group to understand its own capacities and limitations so that it will make decisions in keeping with its level of development. He may help the group to recognize internal problems which present a block to the full realization of its wishes and may help it to locate resources and means of solving these problems. He frequently helps the group to perfect its form of organization and then helps chosen leaders to understand and perform their duties. He is called upon to help groups develop standards of performance and various means of social control. He may help the group by providing the access to needed resources in the agency or in the community, and at times he may assist it by providing instruction in a subject matter area. He may be called upon to help the group understand other groups which differ, then proceed to aid in developing cooperative intergroup relationships. In addition to these group-directed efforts, the worker helps individuals to gain acceptance and establish responsible relations with the members of the group.

The *way* in which the worker gives help to the group is all-important. As Hartford puts it, "The social group worker, in providing service, gives simultaneous attention to the group process, and to the functioning of the individual members. He draws upon knowledge and skill in understanding and affecting group processes as well as knowledge and skill in working with individuals within the group. This dual focus is a particular characteristic of social group work practice. The social group worker may organize the group or may intervene in an already existing group in such a way that the group experience will provide a helping milieu for the individual members in accordance with their social needs." [16]

The quality of the group worker's helping is influenced by what he brings to the group situation in the way of experience, knowledge, understanding, and skill. He brings his deep interest in people and his ability to accept the group as it is, and he brings thought, awareness, and insight rather than material things because he is there to do things with the group rather than for the group. Falck puts forth the "hypothesis . . . that all participants in a group are members of the group—the worker included. Workers need to speak to their clients—especially, but not only, to their youthful ones—as to the aims of the agency, of the group, of the client, as judged and understood by the worker. Thus, the worker's ideas do and should become apparent. Too much hinges on social workers, educators, ministers, and others who from some distance and as outsiders promote an essentially valueless, orientationless neutrality with which both long ago and recently we thought we could best achieve our aims. A social worker is not only an outside intervener or 'enabler.' He is a methodologist, he is a philosopher, he is an actionist, and not only in Washington but in his group whether at a settlement, Jewish Center, hospital, or mental health clinic. One way or another he speaks out from within the group as to healthy and unhealthy behavior, effective and ineffective ways of living, good and bad goals, actions leading to good or poor social functioning. He must get *into* the group, be part of it, 'suffer' it." [17]

The group worker wants group members to develop their capacity to work together and achieve things as a result of their own efforts. Naturally, the worker brings all his past experience to the group. He has been a member of groups and has worked with other groups and from this experience has learned how groups respond and how they ask for help. He therefore has some understanding of groups and of what they need and seek. In addition to bringing skill in helping group members to discuss their affairs, the worker brings a willingness to listen to groups as they express their feelings, and he encourages such expression because only in this way can he become fully acquainted with the group.

It is important to point out that the group worker brings his willingness to help the group without setting up obligations in return. Though, like all other persons, he has a need to be important and appreciated, he gets these satisfactions from groups other than those with which he works.

A basic contribution of the group worker is his faith in the ability of the group to make wise decisions and judgments when given opportunities to make their own plans. He contributes also his knowledge of agency and community resources and considers it his job to be familiar with helpful aids for the group should special needs arise. He brings a sense of timing and a knowledge of group readiness because it is important that he recognize the moment at which a group is ready to move forward. His skill in planning is made available to the group so that it can wisely anticipate what is involved in developing a satisfying program. He brings his sense of values, he symbolizes social maturity but accepts the fact that groups cannot take over such qualities except as they experience growth opportunities.

Sometimes workers have been known to discuss how "they handled a group" or how "they handled a certain individual." It is important to emphasize that the essence of professional work lies in *the way in which you handle yourself as a worker* rather than in the way in which you handle somebody else. The conscious and controlled use of oneself is basic to the worker's role as a helping person. All workers—in fact, all individuals—have prejudices, blind spots, and biases in their personalities. We all have likes and dislikes, personal preferences as to activities and associates; we have our own needs for group experiences, self-expression, and other forms of ego-gratification. That we know this and accept it as natural enables us to develop our self-awareness and our capacity for self-control. To be sure, the worker must get satisfaction from his work with the group, but he does not exploit the group for the satisfaction of personality needs, which should be met in other ways. In talking about group work with emotionally troubled children Maier points out:

It is the group worker's professional skills that move the client—emotionally troubled, "delinquent," or socially inadequate to respond to his efforts to help expand their ego functioning. The worker attempts neither to change nor to do away with emotional disturbance and delinquent behavior per se. Rather, he introduces social experiences that will make it easier for the client to develop beyond his ineffective coping or delinquent behavior.[18]

There are a number of points at which the worker must consciously understand himself and control his own feelings. Some workers may have quite arbitrary standards of success which they unconsciously force upon a group and then tend to drive it toward achievements quite beyond its ability. The worker's need to make rapid progress may result in excess "doing for" the group when it would be far better for it to move more slowly and do things its own way. Sometimes strong program interests which reflect an unusual amount of technical skill on the part of the worker become the main program focus for the group. Instead of developing its own program, the group takes over the worker's program.

There is a natural tendency on the part of some workers who are adept at social organization to presume that all groups need a large amount of organizational machinery. These groups become overorganized, and their experience may consist of a frustrating series of meetings largely devoted to mechanics rather than to social activities. The worker is most likely to need deep insight in the way in which he accepts or fails to accept certain individuals. Some members are well adjusted and easily assume a responsible place in the life of the group. Others are less able to participate and need time and attention from the worker. As Alston [19] points out, the worker must become able to accept all members with equal understanding and warmth and share his time and attention with them as needs arise.

The group worker must, therefore, have considerable understanding of human behavior and of how to use himself appropriately. Pernell declares:

The use of himself in appropriate ways involves a skill which is three-faceted and made up of empathic response, creative response, and learned response to the situation which confronts him. . . . By "empathy" is meant the ability to project one's self imaginatively into the thinking and feeling of another person in order to understand what the nature of the experience is for him. This capacity seems to be a function of a flexible (as versus rigid) emotional character, where enough warmth has been generated through personal experience to come through into communication with others. By "creativity," we mean the ability to respond to interpersonal demands with flexibility, spontaneity, and imagination, which produces a new reality to be experienced by the other. [Pernell then cites Foote and Cottrell:] "The idea of creativity is commonly associated with artistic and intellectual activities. We define it here as any demonstrative capacity for innovations in behavior or real reconstruction of any aspect of the social environment. It involves the ability to develop fresh perspectives from which to view all accepted routines and to make novel combinations of ideas and objects and so define new goals, and dolling up old ones with fresh meaning, and inventing means for their realization. In interpersonal relations, it is the ability to invest or improvise new roles or alternative lines of action in problematic situations, and to promote such behavior in others. Among other things, it seems to involve curiosity, self-confidence, something of the venturesomeness and risk-taking tendencies of the explorer, a flexible mind with the kind of freedom which permits the orientation of spontaneous play." [20]

Pernell concludes that "these two abilities—empathy and creativity—which enable the individual to have a heightened awareness of another and to introduce him to new experience, are largely in the intuitive realm, and form the basis of the 'art' of social work practice. In helping the student develop skill as a social group work practitioner, we cannot give these abilities but we do take some responsibility for their development." [21]

The group worker must understand not only the individual in the group but also his own behavior. He must have an understanding of the dynamics of group relationships and then have the skill to make conscious use of this understanding to help the persons concerned develop within the group and the group to realize its own objectives. In helping the group to determine its own objectives the worker permits the group to be as self-directing as possible and gives the members as much responsibility as they are able to carry at a given stage of their development. This does not mean that the worker's role is passive. It is an active role. Aronowitz and Weinberg make the point that group workers "attempt to influence and manipulate the group process and the collective minds of the members." In their discussion of the utilization of reinforcement theory in social group work they draw upon their experience with children's treatment groups in one center of a settlement complex. They say, "Social workers must recognize that they do manipulate group process and that they sanction or reinforce various kinds of behavior to achieve certain goals." [22]

The worker always endeavors to begin his work with the group where its members are in their own development and expects them to move only at the pace they are able to go. He must recognize the importance of a sense of timing and understand that it may be better at one time than another to attempt to stimulate interest in a specific project. As the worker helps to set the stage, he provides environmental stimuli and thus guides by indirection because he wants to help the group reach its own objectives without imposing his wishes upon the group.

The effective worker realizes that it is necessary for groups to express their negative as well as their positive feelings, and he is able to accept hostility without interpreting it as a personal attack on him as a worker. The worker gives genuine acceptance to the persons in the groups with which he works and helps the members to accept natural differences in one another. In so doing, the worker individualizes the members of the group and attempts to help them meet their special needs as group members within the framework of the group.

It is easy to write about how the group worker should function but it takes time to develop skill. In their studies of student performance Vinter and Sarri list ten areas where students experienced difficulty in developing competency: "1) skill in handling own feelings and needs; 2) skill in appraising own performance; 3) knowledge of influences on personality development, present attitudes and behavior; 4) skill in establishing goals for individuals; 5) skill in helping individuals to assume group roles; 6) knowledge of structures and processes of groups; 7) skill in establishing goals for groups; 8) skill in participating effectively in group interaction; 9) skill in effecting change in group structure and process; 10) skill in effecting change in inter-group relations; 11) skill in discerning group movement and change." [23]

The Group Worker and Group Objectives

The group worker has a special responsibility to be clear about what he is trying to accomplish with his group in terms of objectives. It has long been recognized that an effective agency must have clearly defined written statements of its objectives, or purposes. These objectives must be thoughtfully developed out of the continuous study of community needs. Furthermore, these objectives must be thoroughly understood by everyone who works for the agency and participates in the agency program. The over-all statement of purpose must be used as a basis for formulating the specific goals of divisions, departments, groups, and individuals in the agency. In addition, the statement of purpose is essential if the agency is to make periodic evaluations of its program.

As he thinks about purposes for his group the worker must first be clear about the meaning of the word. When we use the word "objectives," we refer to what we are trying to accomplish. Here our objectives are statements or formulations of what we are trying to do in group work. When our objectives are clear, we are able to select appropriate methods and appropriate program experiences as a means to the attainment of these objectives. The fact of the matter is that our aims and our methods are always interrelated. As John Dewey said:

An aim implies an orderly and ordered activity, one in which the order consists in the progressive completing of a process. . . . The aim as a foreseen end, gives direction to the activity; . . . it involves careful observation of the given conditions, to see what are the means available for reaching the end, and to discover the hindrances in the way. It suggests the proper order or sequence in the use of means. It facilitates an economical selection and arrangement. It makes choice of alternatives possible. . . . To have an aim is to act with meaning, not like an automatic machine; it is to mean to do something and to perceive the meaning of things in the light of that intent.[24]

Immediate objectives and long-term objectives are intimately related. Objectives serve the same purpose as a compass; that is, they guide the agency and the worker to a determined destination. Objectives are also useful in helping workers put forth the energy required to do the work of the agency. Donald K. David puts it:

Objectives are not merely goals; they are motivating forces for action, and we move toward them or retreat by concerted action. As a practical matter objectives which have been developed and defined by one group lose some and at times all of their motivating force for action when they are passed on to another group. The success of objectives in stimulating action is proportionate to the spirit of participation in determining the objectives. . . . Among people who are to take action the process of thinking about objectives is more important than the final words in which they are put on paper. The words of others may be mere platitudes; those you forge yourself have life. . . . Objectives in order to motivate a group to concerted action must be far enough away and general enough to motivate people with different characteristics to work toward the same goal, perhaps by different means. Action-stimulating objectives, therefore, must be close enough to excite individuals to action, far enough away to allow diverse people to work together, and not so far away as to induce despair.[25]

It is extremely important that everyone concerned with group work should devote a substantial amount of time to the working out of carefully formulated objectives. What are some of the values that result from this process?

1. When our objectives are clear, we are helped in the determination of the kind of service or program that the agency should provide, and our conception of purpose will control the specific emphasis of the program. Naturally, statements of purpose do not constitute a program, nor do they bring program into reality; but they do help us to know what type of program is most important to us.

2. Our objectives should be utilized at the point of deciding upon constituency or clientele with whom we work. It is practically impossible to make wise judgments regarding constituency, except in terms of agency objectives. It is equally difficult to develop satisfactory relationships between the agency and the constituency unless there is clarity as to the purposes to which all parties subscribe.

3. Our statement of objectives provides us with essential guideposts to the kind of leadership we need. This is important from the point of view of both paid personnel and unpaid volunteer workers. It will help the agency to outline the kinds of skills needed by all the people who work with agency groups.

4. Our statement of purpose can be utilized continuously in the process of financing the agency, providing plant and equipment, and dealing with all physical matters of operation. It is distinctly necessary to use the

agency purpose as a point of reference in budget making because what the agency is trying to accomplish should be the chief motivating factor in the way it allocates its funds.

5. Our objectives are put to work at the point of evaluation; in fact, a major aspect of the evaluation process revolves around the matter of purpose. When the agency faces the question of evaluation, it is compelled to use its stated purpose as the basis upon which it checks out its work. Thus, when purposes are clear, individual and group energy can be effectively mobilized and focused; priorities can be determined logically and soundly; programs can be measured; and public support will be sustained.

When we examine the statements of objectives from many different agencies we may draw certain conclusions. Though there may be differences in points of emphasis, practically every one of the agencies seems to be enunciating a basic philosophy about people and their needs. To this writer the objectives of social group work seem to be based upon the philosophy and conviction of group workers everywhere. Group workers believe that the person is more important than the activity. Group workers believe in the dignity and worth of every human personality. Group workers believe in the infinite capacity of people to grow and change. They recognize that growth comes from within and that growth opportunities must be provided so that these capacities for growth can be realized. Group workers believe, furthermore, that the people have the capacity to make wise judgments and when people are given an opportunity to accept responsibility they tend to behave in a responsible manner.

Group workers believe that personalities grow and develop in groups that accept them and are accepted by them. Therefore, the group worker, in addition to understanding the individual, must seek to understand the group in which the individual lives and has his being. Furthermore, group workers think of individuals as *whole* beings in their total environmental situation. The group worker no longer considers it good practice to work with segments of personality, for he now recognizes that what he does affects every area of the person's life. Group workers believe, too, that they must accept and work with persons as they are. If superimposed controls are overemphasized, spontaneous self-discipline will be defeated; if we are really concerned about people, we will cherish their freedom and individuality just as much as we cherish cooperative action and we will endeavor to free them for larger participation. Group workers believe that their leadership efforts must be democratic and a democratic leadership involves guidance, instruction, and a knowledge of persons and programs. Fundamentally the purpose of social group work is to bring about the highest possible development of human personality, dedicated and devoted to the democratic ideal.

When the group worker surveys the variety of groups for which he is responsible, he is confronted with the fact that there will be different objectives for different groups and different objectives for different individuals in his groups. It is neither possible nor desirable to suggest that there is any one way of determining objectives. Nevertheless, it is possible to point out certain things that every group worker must know and understand if he is to do a skillful job of determining purposes. Let us look at these things as a background for the determination of objectives.

The group worker must know and understand his agency and community setting. He must be familiar with the objectives, function, and policies of the agency. He must know the groups with which the agency works and the reasons for working with them. He must be familiar with the program of the agency and understand it in relation to group and community needs, and he must have a growing awareness of the agency in relation to other agencies and services. He must understand the nature of the community in which the agency and its groups operate, which means that he must have a growing fund of cultural, economic, and sociological background material. He must know about the availability of community resources and he must understand the larger socioeconomic picture and its meaning to groups.

Of course, it is important to emphasize the fact that the group worker must have an ever-increasing body of knowledge and an understanding of the groups with which he works. The worker should be aware of the significant factors in the history of each of his groups and of the similarities and differences among various types of groups. He should understand what groups need and want, and how his agency can be of service in meeting those needs and wants. He must work with the group to develop a statement of purpose in relation to agency function. He must have an understanding of program as a tool in the development of group members.

Naturally, the group worker must have an understanding of his own role in relation to his specific group. All of this means that he must become skillful in the acceptance of his group with its strengths and its limitations and must have skill in gaining acceptance by the group's members and in relating himself to the group on a professional basis. He needs to know how to study and analyze his groups to understand where they are in their development, and he will have to use skill in determining and assuming his role as a worker with individuals and with the group as a whole. He will try to exercise care to see that he does not superimpose his ideas and his conception of objectives, because objectives have little meaning to the group unless the members have had a part in determining them.

In connection with developing objectives for individual members, the group worker must understand why the individual comes to the group and what he wants to get out of it. The worker will need to have a constantly growing knowledge of all the individuals in his group—their cultural background, their home life, their schools, their occupations, their church, and their community interests. All this will help the worker to see the individual as a part of the group and the community. He cannot do a good job of determining individual objectives unless he is thoroughly familiar with the individual as a person. Once he has this information, he applies it in the group situation. The worker is called upon to accept individuals as different personalities with different needs. Then he must help individuals relate to the group through participation and help them gain acceptance and status. At times he will need to use his considerable skill in helping officers and group leaders perform their jobs without taking responsibility away from them. He will need to learn how to accept hostility and aggression, because many individuals need help with this very problem, and he will need to work skillfully with individuals in conflict without taking sides.

Thus, it is necessary that the group worker maintain a variety of complex relations simultaneously. As his skill in discovering individual needs develops, he will be able to use the group work process to help individuals meet these needs. He will become more skillful in pinpointing the specific objectives for specific individuals.

Throughout all this, the group worker must have a growing understanding of himself and his part in the group work process. He must accept and utilize supervision and must understand the mutual relationships that are called for in the modern social agency setting. He must develop his own awareness. He must develop insight and skill in handling his own feelings in the group situation. He should develop an increased understanding of his own attitudes and reactions. This development should be accompanied by a definite effort to modify his behavior when such behavior tends to get in the way of group growth and development. The more insight into his own motivations and feelings the worker has, the better able is he **to** create clear and specific objectives for his group.

In group work one of the greatest needs is for the thoughtful interpretation of its objectives.

This immediately raises a number of questions which must be answered: What should we endeavor to interpret? Should we interpret the objectives of group work? Should we interpret the functions of the agency? Should we interpret the group work process? Or should we try to interpret the role of the group worker? Then we need to ask ourselves to whom should we interpret group work? Who should do the interpretation? When should we interpret? What main concepts of group work do we wish to explain? What are the elements of comprehensive interpretation program? How do we interpret our work? How do we interpret our evaluation efforts?

It seems to me that we must be clear on what it is we are trying to interpret. If we are interpreting our purposes generally, then we must differentiate between what we do and what similar and allied professions do. If we are interpreting our agency function, we must determine whether we want to do so in broad terms or whether we want to refine it more precisely. If we are interpreting the group work process, then it seems to me that we have an entirely different problem. Technical and professional processes are always difficult to interpret. Usually the only way to interpret the group work processes is to describe in detail exactly what the worker does and why he does it. This would enable us to think through some of our basic concepts and would no doubt help us to arrive at a much better general understanding.

In addition, it seems important for us to be clear on the question: To whom are we interpreting our work? Some persons have much more understanding than others. Many times we fail to distinguish between the group that has had a great deal of experience with our agency and with our group work methods and a group that is new to us and new to what we are trying to do. We must, however, have a differentiated interpretation that is related definitely to the degree of understanding already possessed by our audience.

It seems important to suggest that one of the best ways in which to interpret group work is to use case examples, and actual excerpts from experience. This is one of the most effective ways in which to help people to understand what we are doing. Unfortunately, many group workers have not yet realized that it is possible to use the case example approach without violating confidence and hurting the individuals and groups involved. Material can be edited and modified slightly so as to describe the group activity and its meaning to individuals without sacrificing any of the confidential relationship.

Considerable thought must be given to the maintenance of a continuous, year-round, comprehensive program of interpretation. The matter of our objectives and purposes should be worked on in all of our leadership training courses and all of our supervisory work. We should pitch our program of interpretation on a positive level and should concentrate on clear specific illustrations of precisely what we are doing in our work.

The Working Agreement or Contract

It is essential that the group worker work closely and continuously with the group in the early stages of their relationship so that there will be agreement as to what they are trying to accomplish. The concept of the "working agreement" or "contract" has been discussed by a number of authors. For example, Frey and Meyer present their material this way:

In general the worker's exploration activities consist of making observations of the behavior of the members as individuals and as a potential group and giving members a chance to observe him from a safe distance. He offers activities which maintain the distance but which also provide bridges to closeness when the members are ready to use them. Activities open opportunities for further exploration of social capacities, frustration tolerance, controls, interest, skills. He verbalizes the obvious and ambivalent feelings about the group and gives permission for this study period to take place by not requiring commitment or a degree of involvement beyond each member's readiness. The testing so often referred to in our literature is accepted by the worker as the members' right to guard themselves in a new situation. His permissive, but limiting, protective, but enabling stance presents to the members an identifiable stable person about whom a decision can be made. The decision, of course, is whether to invest oneself in the group, in the worker and the agency. The decision to become affiliated with the other people in the group is not just a matter of liking or disliking them. In a social work group the struggle with accepting the stated purpose is tied in with the decision about future close association with people. As the purpose grows clearer, the working agreement becomes firmer. The worker's behavior as he helps members through the initial stages of the group sets the framework of the working agreement. The worker articulates the specific terms of the agency service as applied in this group and elicits members' reactions and feelings, both behaviorally and verbally. The verbal adult group can be helped to verbalize, the non-verbal group may need worker's clarification of evident feelings and responses. The working agreement is established as group and worker recognize why they are together and what is expected of each in this relationship. The working agreement becomes a reference point throughout the group life and is a dynamic force in accomplishing its objectives. This clear understanding of purpose is an important foundation for the development and maintenance of trust. Members should not be tricked into involvement under false pretenses if a helping relationship is to be established. The group which is not clear about its purposes and the working agreement can use this obscurity of purpose as a means of resisting deeper evaluation, greater self-awareness, and fuller responsibility. Handling such resistance is much more difficult for the worker who may not be sure of himself or what his and the agency's goals are. With those members in whom mistrust is a significant personality dynamic, the working agreement can be a source of reassurance and a damper on illusional ideas. To the "normal" person the working agreement expresses respect for him and helps him to engage in a responsible way in the group experience.[26]

Klein goes into the matter of contract in this fashion:

Contract is the agreement, usually verbal and non-verbal, between the worker and the group members and among themselves about the purpose of the group endeavor. The hypothesis is that if members do not know for what they are there, it is unlikely that they will be able to work to achieve the purpose, or be able to work together, or appropriately. The contract mobilizes and focuses the group energies. It is the premise that the group process is the change or growth-producing medium. For the group to move toward desired outcomes the group members must be aware of what they are working on and toward. . . . Contract also is an agreement about expectations of the reciprocal roles of the worker, the members, and the sanctioning agency. Clarity about reciprocal role expectations is important because it forestalls disappointments, frustrations, uncertainties, and also it gives some direction to what participants can work at and how. Like all contracts, it is negotiated by the participants and provides the framework, opportunities, and limits of the human encounters to follow. The contract is not immutable; it can be changed by the participants by negotiations when appropriate and as the need or desire arises. The setting of a contract insures the democratic rights of the members, emphasizing the egalitarian quality of the enterprise and, hopefully, minimizes control and manipulation. It is also an essential in the establishment of morale since morale presupposes acceptance of group goals.[27]

Schwartz discusses the concept of the working agreement in this fashion:

The agency, the worker, the group, and its members are related to each other by certain rules and requirements imposed upon them by the terms of their agreement. These requirements emerge first in the condition under which the group is established, its function identified, and its procedures initiated. Later, the rules are modified, amplified, and reinterpreted as their concrete implications become clearer in the events of group life. These expectations are not limited to those imposed upon the members by the agency, or by the worker; they are reciprocal in that each actor imposes certain restrictions and is bound by others. Thus, while the group and its members are held to certain policies and procedures, the agency and the worker are also limited by standards such as equal treatment, consistency in approach, the members' concept of fair play, and so forth. To the extent that the terms of the agreement are specific and unambiguous, the participants are free to pursue their tasks within the system in their own characteristic ways. Where the rules are, or become obscure and vaguely defined, the major energies of both worker and members become diverted to exploring the boundaries and testing the limits of the group situation. This leads us to the final task of the helping agent, in which he calls upon the participants of the learning group to face the necessities inherent in the conditions of their association. This definition of the requirements begins with the worker's first attempt to identify the specific responsibilities that have been undertaken by the agency, the group, and the worker himself; it continues as he monitors these realities and calls for clarification at those points where they become obscure.[28]

Goroff presents the best summary of the concept of the working agreement when he writes:

The process of establishing a working agreement is a crucial aspect of social work with groups. There are three basic components to the working agreement. The agency which offers the group service has reasons why they are providing this service. The individuals who join the group have their own purposes for coming and the social worker has his professional convictions about the service and also some concept of the roles he expects to perform in the group. The process of establishing a working agreement requires that the individuals jointly come to some agreement, which takes into account the expectations of the agency and the presence of the professional as well as their purpose for coming together. It is crucial that we stress the fact that this is a process—a series of events over a period of time. The working agreement will take time to establish. . . . The working agreement . . . helps all the members and the social worker to focus on the work to be done. Since it is a decision that the members of the group participated in making, it enables the worker to have some criteria to assess whether the group is addressing itself to the tasks or are they avoiding them? Also, it helps the worker and group members to recognize when unconscious or unavowed factors are brought into the group transaction. It is important to note that there are three levels of concern that each member brings to the group. The first level is the consciously avowed interests. These interests are those that people can and want to talk about. The second level is the consciously unavowed interests. These interests constitute the variety of conscious or near conscious concerns that people have but do not want to talk about, although they will often act on them. The working agreement provides a framework for the assessment of when unavowed concerns become a part of the transaction. The third level is the variety of unconscious needs that people have. These needs may from time to time find expression in the group. In addition, the process of establishing the working agreement involves the operationalization of the principle of self-determination. The members of the group jointly determine what they want to work on in conjunction with the social worker. The concept of "agreement" allows for mutually agreed upon changes or modification as the initial tasks seem to have been completed and the members of the group want to take on new tasks. The concept of agreement implies flexibility. Thus, one of the most important properties of a group is inherent in the process of the individuals working out the agreement which requires each individual to go beyond his own immediate concern in order to become a part of the group. If one of the problems an individual has is "exercising self-control," we may help him come to grips with this aspect of his personality more effectively through the group method than an interview encounter. To a degree, his individual self-centeredness is unwittingly supported in the interview encounter where he is the center of his own and the social worker's concern.[29]

NOTES

1. Helen Northen, *Social Work with Groups* (New York: Columbia University Press, 1969), p. 11.
2. William Fawcett Hill, *Learning Through Discussion* (Beverly Hills, California: Sage Publications, 1969), p. 16.
3. Philip E. Slater, "Role Differentiation in Small Groups" in A. Paul Hare, Edgar F. Borgatta, Robert F. Bales (editors), *Small Groups: Studies in Social Interaction* (New York: Alfred A. Knopf, 1966), p. 610.
4. Howard Baumgartel, "The Concept of Role" in Warren G. Bennis, Kenneth D. Benne, Robert Chin (editors), *The Planning of Change* (New York: Holt, Rinehart and Winston, 1961), pp. 373–374.
5. Henry Maas, "Concepts and Methods in Social Work Research" in Cora Kasius (editor), *New Directions in Social Work* (New York: Harper and Brothers, 1954), pp. 229–230.
6. Sebastian Tine, "Process and Criteria for Grouping" in *Social Group Work with Older People* (New York: National Association of Social Workers, 1963), pp. 99–100.
7. Alvin Zander, Arthur R. Cohen, Ezra Stotland, *Role Relations in the Mental Health Professions* (Research Center for Group Dynamics—Institue for Social Research, University of Michigan, Ann Arbor, 1957), p. 15.
8. *Group Treatment in Family Service Agencies* (New York Family Service Association of America, 1964), p. 17.
9. Northen, *op. cit.*, pp. 52–53.
10. Norman Goroff, "Social Group Work—an Intersystemic Frame of Reference," *Journal of Jewish Communal Service*, March 1971, p. 233.
11. Margaret E. Hartford, "Use of Social Group Work in Helping Members Accept Differences" in *Social Work Practice, 1964* (Published for the National Conference on Social Welfare by Columbia University Press, New York 1964), p. 233.

12. Virginia P. Robinson, "The Meaning of Skill" in *Training for Skill in Social Casework* (Philadelphia: University of Pennsylvania Press, 1942), pp. 11–12. Quoted in "What Is Social Group Work Skill?" by Helen U. Philips, *The Group*, Vol. 16, June 1954.
13. Hartford, *op. cit.*, p. 233.
14. Ruby B. Pernell, "Identifying and Teaching the Skill Components of Social Work" in *Educational Developments in Social Group Work* (New York: Council on Social Work Education, 1962), p. 23.
15. Northen, *op. cit.*, p. 19.
16. Margaret Hartford, *Working Papers Toward a Frame of Reference for Social Group Work* (New York: National Association of Social Workers, 1964), p. 5.
17. Hans S. Falck, "Social Group Work and Planned Change" in *Social Work Practice, 1964* (Published for the National Conference on Social Welfare by Columbia University Press, New York, 1964), p. 213.
18. Henry W. Maier, "The Social Group Work Method in Residential Treatment" in *Group Work as Part of Residential Treatment*, edited by Henry W. Maier (New York: National Association of Social Workers, 1965), p. 41.
19. Estelle A. Alston, "The Leader's Use of Self" in *Readings in Group Work* (New York: Association Press, 1952).
20. Nelson N. Foote and Leonard S. Cottrell, Jr., *Identity and Interpersonal Competence* (Chicago: University of Chicago Press, 1955), p. 57.
21. Pernell, *op. cit.*, pp. 20–21.
22. Eugene Aronowitz and Denise Weinberg, "The Utilization of Reinforcement Theory in Social Group Work Practice," *Social Service Review*, December 1966, pp. 390, 396.
23. Robert D. Vinter and Rosemary C. Sarri, "Learning Objectives, Teaching Methods and Performance Patterns in Group Work Education" in *Educational Developments in Social Group Work* (New York: Council on Social Work Education, 1962), p. 11.
24. John Dewey, *Democracy and Education* (New York: Macmillan, 1916), pp. 119–121.
25. Donald K. David, "The Objectives of Professional Education" in *Education for Professional Responsibility*. A Report of the Proceedings of the Inter-Professions Conference on Education for Professional Responsibility, held at Buck Hill Falls, Pennsylvania, April 12, 13, 14, 1948 (Pittsburgh: The Carnegie Institute of Technology, 1948).
26. Louise A. Frey and Marguerite Meyer, "Exploration and Working Agreement in Two Social Work Methods" in Saul Bernstein (editor), *Explorations in Group Work* (Boston: Boston University School of Social Work, 1965), pp. 10–11.
27. Alan F. Klein, *Social Work Through Group Process* (School of Social Welfare, State University of New York at Albany, 1970), pp. 50–51.
28. William Schwartz, "The Social Worker in the Group" in *The Social Welfare Forum, 1961* (Published for the National Conference on Social Welfare, by Columbia University Press, New York, 1961) p. 169.
29. Norman N. Goroff, "Unique Properties of Groups: Resources to Help People." Paper presented at the Child Welfare League Northeast Regional Conference, Hartford, Connecticut, April 30 and May 1, 1970. Mimeographed.

5

The Program Development Process

It is the point of view of this book that to be of maximum value program in group work should be person-centered and meet specific needs, should develop out of the interests and needs of the group members, should involve the members themselves in planning to the maximum amount of their ability, and should utilize the worker as a helping person rather than as a dispenser of entertainment.

The group worker is not there to "put on a program" or to "put over a program" but rather to help the group members *develop* their own program. There may be many situations in which "putting on" or "putting over" program is entirely legitimate, but such situations should not be considered as social group work. Goroff reminds us:

> Social group work in essence must always consider three basic components: 1) the relationship which exists among individuals, their subgroups and the group as a whole, 2) the dynamics pertaining to the group itself and 3) the relationship between the individuals in the group and their environing social and cultural systems. Unless there is this simultaneous concern over the links between individual and group, interaction within the group and the links between the group and significant others we would be hard pressed to recognize the efforts as social group work. Social group work as defined herein is applicable in any setting with any population whether it is perceived as being primarily concerned with corrective services for social dysfunctions or with normal growth and development—socialization. It is neither the target population nor the purpose for which the social group worker is engaged that is the significant determinant of whether social group work is being practiced. The significant determinant is whether the three basic concerns are present in the consciousness of the worker and if he has explicated these concerns with the members of the group in developing the working agreement with them.[1]

A fourth basic component of social group work is the program development process or the way that program activities are planned and carried out. Because of our belief that *persons* are much more important than programs, and because of our further belief that the *process* of program development is of the utmost importance, we have chosen to stress the basic understanding of the agency, the group, the individual, and the worker as prerequisites to the consideration of program. In this chapter we shall endeavor to put this material together at the point where the worker, the group, and the agency work together in fulfilling program needs.

The Nature and Purpose of Program in Social Group Work

A number of authorities have defined program in social group work. For example, Konopka says, "By *program* is meant any activity which the group does in the presence of the group worker during the course of group meetings. These activities must not be planned according to the particular needs or interests of the group worker himself, but only with reference to the group members. This principle includes diagnosis of individual and group needs and their assessment in relation to group and agency purpose as well as to professional values and ethics of human relationships." [2]

Falck declares, "Program activities are the mediating processes which carry the true meanings of member interaction. Through program they become anywhere from overtly apparent to dimly felt. Playing as well as talking; mimicry; symbolization; physical, instrumental behaviors; as well as pre- and unconscious anxieties, fears, guilt, and worry constitute the program or content of human interaction whether in intimate two-member or larger groups. Program comes from two sources: from each person and projected to others; and from others and absorbed by each member. Program is part of group interaction. Its variety is large. The message that program carries among members is potentially limitless." [3]

Middleman says, "This writer's point of view of just what comprises the program content of a group experience is a broad one. It is the accumulated totality of all the group does—both verbal and non-verbal—inclusive also of horseplay, cleanup, setting up a projector and such. It consists of both the constructive and the distracting activities that comprise the group's experience and the individual's tangential or related experience within the over-all group session. It may be initiated by the worker or by the group members themselves, arising spontaneously or as the outcome of deliberate planning. In time duration, program may range from a brief episode to an experience of several hours or to a continuing recurrent or developmental part of several meetings—perhaps ritualized into every meeting. Program is *what* is being done and *how* it is done, and, viewing it from the worker's point of view as he helps set it in motion, it includes the *why* of what is done. The program content, the worker's use of his relationship with the group members, and his effect upon their interactional process combine to become the social group work process itself—that precious entity through which the aims of the individual members, the group, the worker, and the sponsoring agency come to life. To put it another way, program is the vehicle through which relationships are made and the needs and interests of the group and its individual members are fulfilled. The goals for the useful program should be identical with the goals motivating the worker who is employing it. . . . A social group worker would use program then to help the individuals grow in self-value and to help the group become able to act on increasingly responsible social goals." [4]

Simply stated, program in social group work has come to mean anything and everything that the group does to satisfy its interests. At one time there was a tendency to think of *program* as being synonymous with *activities* or *events*. The group just had to be doing something of a highly active and visible nature all the time or it didn't have a program. Now we see that program is a concept which, when broadly conceived, includes the entire range of activities, relationships, interactions and experiences—individual and group—which have been deliberately planned and carried out with the help of the worker to meet the needs of the individuals and the group. Program is thus a process rather than the periodic culmination of a process. The festival that the group members have been working on for many weeks is *a part* of program, but everything that they have done in getting ready for it should be considered as the program of that group for that period of time.

As illustrated in Figure 5, any discussion of program in social group work must take into account such items as content and area, media of expression, and methods of conducting it. Program area or program content refers to a segment of life experience that has general meaning for the individuals at their specific point of development. For example, a great deal of program content in social group work centers around the area of recreation and wise use of leisure time. This is an important area for everyone because the way in which we use our leisure is of great social significance today. The area of citizen-participation in community or public affairs is also prominent in group work. Several agencies place a great deal of emphasis on the important area of home and family life, with the many problems of economics and social relationships involved herein. Health considerations loom large in the programs of many groups, as do matters of vocation, life philosophy, and interpersonal relations.

Media of expression in program refer to the specific means used by group members to plan and experience program in the area chosen. Parties, social events, dances, are means of providing leisure-time experiences which are recreational. Informal but planned group discussion is a prominent means of helping groups to think through both social and economic problems. The arts and crafts have tremendous significance in this modern era of machine technology. The drama may be not only a means of having a creative experience but also a way of deepening our knowledge of a community health problem. Music, too, becomes an excellent means of helping a group to experience harmonious relationships with other groups when all the members join in choral or orchestral unison. Group workers have long

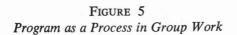

FIGURE 5
Program as a Process in Group Work

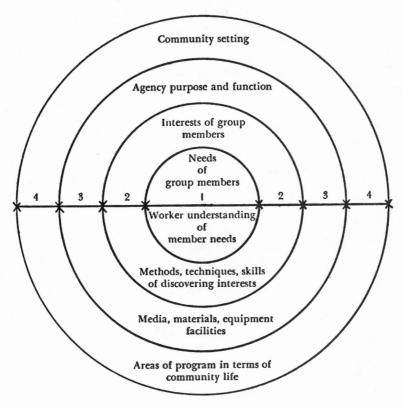

realized the great value of "seeing" and have used outings, trips, or excursions to help place their groups in firsthand contact with a new and different situation. These are but a few examples of media interchangeably useful in numerous areas of content.

The methodology of group work program is in itself a complex series of moves on the part of the worker with the group. The worker helps the group to select the areas of content and the media of expression. Even prior to this he may help the group to develop a functional organization of their members so that they can make responsible decisions. The discovery of interests and needs is, of course, an early step. Helping the group to modify interests by enlarging them or by deepening the interest is also involved. Much of program planning is discussional; therefore, the worker frequently has to help the group learn how to talk over the many aspects of a single idea. Groups must be helped to discover and use their own resources and those of the agency and the community. There is a great deal involved in stimulating people to action and in timing the work so that it unfolds at a suitable pace. It is no doubt far easier to "put on" a program for a group than it is to help that group develop its own program. The group worker who consciously relates the "what" of program (content) and the "how" of program (media) with the "why" of program (purpose) is obviously involved in a highly skilled job. He must have a keen appreciation of the backgrounds, points of view and aspirations of the group members and must avoid all tendency to superimpose his ideas and patterns of program. The program development process should be a blossoming of the group's own potentialities.

The Place of the Agency in Program

To the agency, program means the activities and services established as ways of achieving its purposes. In a recent agency self-appraisal [5] the following criteria relative to agency responsibility in the program area were suggested:

1. The agency has a comprehensive, written program policy statement indicating what kind of program it will make available to the community.
2. The agency has an active program committee charged with over-all program planning.
3. Departments or divisions within the agency have active program committees.
4. Agency program is consciously related to agency objectives.
5. Agency program is determined in the light of community situations and needs.
6. Hours and days of operation are related to community needs.
7. Program units are defined in relation to budget and personnel needs so that the agency has information on the costs of specific programs.
8. The agency has a defined policy it follows in establishing program groups.
9. The agency carries on a substantial portion of its program through small groups.
10. The agency is adequately staffed to implement its program.
11. The agency program includes a variety of activities.
12. The agency program is flexible and creative to meet emerging needs and changing current situations.
13. The agency program includes activities related to human needs in the community such as housing, education, civil rights, etc.
14. Group members participate in the formulation of program policies that involve their groups.
15. The agency has a plan for obtaining member opinion in determining program changes.
16. The agency keeps full narrative records of program groups.
17. The agency uses group records in program evaluation.
18. The agency has criteria which it uses in regular, periodic evaluation of program.
19. The agency is studying certain programs to see if they are no longer needed.

20. The agency program is coordinated with those of other agencies, public and voluntary.

21. The agency participates in joint program planning cooperatively with other agencies.

Certainly the agency is a very important factor in program development. If it ranks high in terms of the above criteria, it can be assumed that specific group programs are likewise well conceived.

Understanding Interests and Needs as a Basis for Program

Arbitrary division of the following material into discovery of interests and needs, group organization, and guidance of interaction does not imply that the program process is itself segmental. In actual work all these are interrelated and almost indistinguishable. The group worker does not say, "Now I am discovering interests; now I am translating these interests into needs; now I am going to organize; now I am working in the realm of group discussion." Rather, he recognizes that all these are subparts of the whole and are inherent in the group work process. We look at them separately at this point simply because by slowing down the process—even stopping it momentarily—we can see more deeply into the inner workings of the group. Northen says:

People come together in a group through some common need or interest. A complicated interplay of social relations among the members and the relations of each member to the group come into play. Members communicate their acceptance or rejection of each other, and they engage in certain activities. As they do so, a configuration of relationships develops, values and norms become established or modified, conflict occurs and is resolved, and a degree of cohesiveness develops sufficient at least for the survival of the group.[6]

There is a great deal of difference between *interests* of group members and *needs* of group members. An interest is a tendency to concentrate attention on an object, an idea, and whether it will help the group members to tell the worker what they want. During the informal reception process, new members with whom the workers talk can be encouraged to tell about what they have done and what they would like to do. In the early meetings with the group, alert observations and attentive listening by the worker will reveal various facets of interest. Oftentimes, the worker will use a kind of exposure device of showing groups what is going on in the agency and sometimes he may tell them what other groups have done or are doing. The use of publicity material and attractively arranged bulletin boards and exhibits can be a major help. Some workers use paper-and-pencil check sheets or conduct informal "group opinion" polls to find what might be interesting to the group.

When program interests begin to emerge from within the group, the worker needs to ask himself certain questions before deciding whether or not he has made a substantial discovery. Does this interest seem to represent in so far as possible the common interests of the group members? Does it seem to be a good starting point when considered against the background of this group? Is it in keeping with the resources and function of this agency? Does it have some possibility of both individual participation and cooperative group activity? Can the group take some responsibility of both individual participation and cooperative group activity? Can the group take some responsibility for implementing it?

Quite often in working with new groups the worker finds it difficult to locate a good starting point. It is never true that groups "just aren't interested in anything," but it is true that some groups are rather slow to express themselves. Many reasons may lie back of this lack of response. Perhaps unfamiliarity with what they might do is a reason. Therefore, the worker often suggests activity programs to groups and points out interesting possibilities. In so doing he is trying to free the group to respond and "open up," to let him know what they want and can do. When the worker decides that it is necessary to offer direct suggestions, he should be careful to present a number of possibilities so that group choice and group decision, even on simple matters, may have a chance to operate. Initial program suggestions should be relatively concise, simple and of limited-time duration. Long-term commitments tend to block rather than free the group to think of and offer their own ideas. Workers must of course be ready to help the group move away from worker-furnished suggestions when the group is ready to present its own ideas.

Another way in which interests may be discovered in early meetings with the group is the liberal use of questions. Through friendly inquiry the worker is often able to locate beginning points for program. Questions may be of an "exploratory" nature, such as "What are some of the fun things that groups like ours do around here?" Or questions may be of the "challenge or stimulation" type, such as "How about all of us trying to think of this as an idea?" Workers also ask "data" questions, such as, "How many of you have ever played this game?" "Choice or decision" questions on the order of "Now let's see if we can choose among all these possibilities?" should be used after the group has had time for careful discussion.

The job of interest discovery and the relating of interests to needs does not cease with the worker's early contacts with the group. In a sense, program development is continuous, and finding the beginning level is only one part of it. The worker has a function at the point of helping the group to enjoy a progressive series of program experiences which tend to parallel the group's development. The expansion of interests and the deepening of individual awareness is largely a matter of continuous interpretation and evaluation of programs as they are carried on. When the group discusses such questions as these—Is this what we really want to do? What did we get out of doing it? In what ways might we do it better? How should we change it if we were to do it again?—then the group is moving toward self-initiated change. Workers may be greatly concerned because, as they put it, "The group does the same thing all the time." It should be pointed out that many groups change very slowly and that all groups like to retain some of the old and established things along with the new. There is quite a difference between the expansion of an original interest, the broadening of general interests, and major shifts in interest. Groups that are "interested in everything," and as a result want variety, often are helped when the worker enables them to narrow their concerns and get a measure of focus.

In all this the group worker is an active participant who accepts his responsibility to help the group toward self-discovery. His role shifts as the group changes, and his duties depend upon the kind of response he is able to foster among the members of the group. A maximum of flexibility and a keen alertness to the moment at which the group is ready to act play a prominent part in the successful discovery of interests and their translation into needs.

Sometimes in his eagerness to get underway with a program the group worker makes the error of pushing too hard for the program that *he* wants the group to undertake. This is always unfortunate, for as Berelson and Steiner declare, "If the small group's activities are imposed from outside, the norms set by the group are likely to be limited in character; if they are determined from within, they are more likely to take on the character of ideal goals, to be constantly enlarged and striven for." [7]

Group Organization as a Part of Program Development

Every group that aspires to independence and self-determination must arrange its constituent members in such a way that they can be said to be "organized." The form of organization is in itself of minor importance. The function of organization is, however, of major importance. If a group is to develop and carry out its own program, it must have ways of making and accepting decisions, ways of assigning or delegating responsibility, ways of getting the whole group to participate in the planning, carrying out, and evaluation of the activities that make up the program, and ways of handling routine relationships with the agency and other groups. It is a part of the group worker's job to help groups create the type of functional organization that will make possible the sort of program the group wishes to conduct. The important thing about organization is its meaning and vitality rather than its form. The group worker does not "organize" the group, as may have been the case with some workers in the past. Rather, he works with the group at the point of creating a form or organization that will best serve its purposes.

Groups need help in answering such questions as these: How many and what kinds of officers do we need? But they can answer such a question wisely only if they have first located the jobs that need to be done. What rules of procedure should we adopt? is another common question. It cannot be answered clearly until the group agrees on what it wants to do and sees that, in order to accomplish its aims, a regular procedure is needed. Should we have a committee to do this for the group? is a natural question sure to arise. It, too, calls for thoughtful consideration before a yes or no decision can be made.

In general, the details of functional organization of the group should take shape as a natural process, as needs arise, rather than be superimposed by workers or agencies. It is very easy to overorganize a group on the theory that "everybody should have a job to do." Unfortunately it is very unfair and even harmful to pretend that people have a job to do when in reality no such job exists. Often workers and groups get satisfaction out of creating complex organizational superstructures, only to find that all their time goes into "keeping up the organization" and that there is no time or energy left for the real purpose of the group. A basic dictum would seem to be: Keep the form of the organization as simple as possible.

The worker has a great deal to do in pointing up what is involved in program decisions. When he asks, Who is going to do the work? or What jobs are involved here? he is helping the group to accept the fact that programs do not "just happen" but always require people who will take responsibility. In this connection there should be a clear understanding of duties and responsibilities and discussion of the time when the job is to be done. It is better to devote time and energy to careful planning than to endless checking up later because of initial misunderstanding. Furthermore, there is a great deal of skill required from the worker in helping officers, committee chairmen and others learn how to do their jobs and to do them in concert with others. The group worker must learn how to point out things without taking over and must know how to coordinate the separate efforts of a great number of different people, all of whom bear some of the load for the group as a whole. It is true that it might be a great deal easier for the worker to do it himself, but in so doing he defeats the purpose of group work, which is to get people opportunities to do for themselves and their group.

Guided Interaction—the Heart of the Program Process

In helping groups to develop and carry out programs we are working with areas of content, materials, organizational details, and other more or less visible items. While this is going on, we know that at a deeper level there are human needs which actually create the surface activities of program. Thus, in the program development process there are those things which meet the eye and ear, i.e., committees, meetings, trips, events and the like; but, more important, there is always a stream of emotion and feeling about the program that must be understood. See Figure 6.

FIGURE 6

The Streams of Program

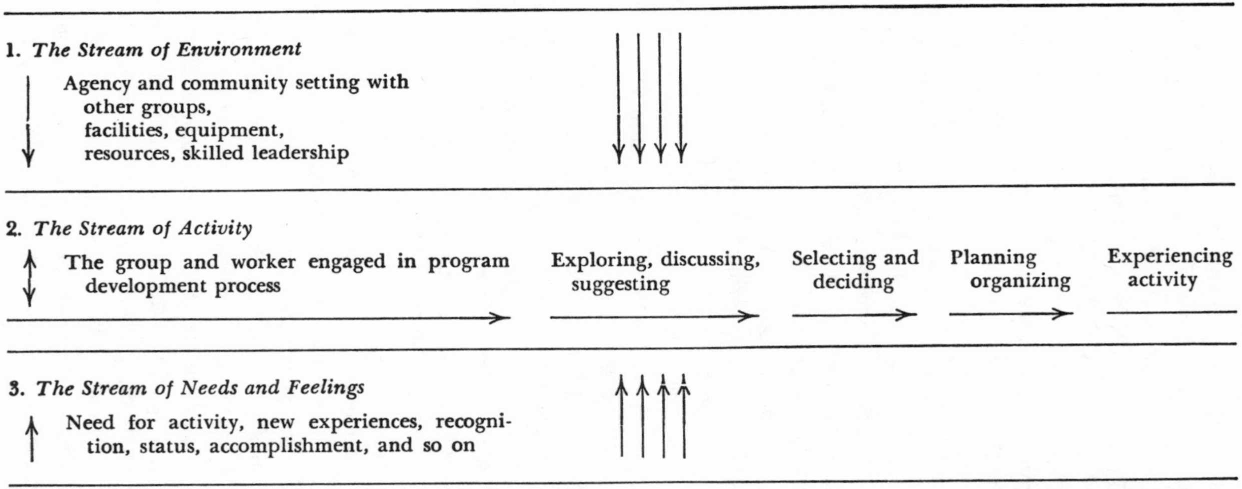

1. *The Stream of Environment*

   Agency and community setting with
   other groups,
   facilities, equipment,
   resources, skilled leadership

2. *The Stream of Activity*

   The group and worker engaged in program
   development process

   Exploring, discussing,   Selecting and   Planning   Experiencing
   suggesting   deciding   organizing   activity

3. *The Stream of Needs and Feelings*

   Need for activity, new experiences, recognition, status, accomplishment, and so on

In the center stream 2 we see the group and the worker together developing and experiencing program. They reach out to the top stream 1 and use the resources of the agency and the community. However, the bottom stream 3, which represents the needs and feelings of group members, furnishes the desire and motivation for program choice and implementation. As group and worker move along the stream of activity, changes occur in the other two streams.

Many illustrations of this phenomenon come to mind. Consider the group that always wants programs to be supercolossal, beyond its means, but—most important—"better than what another group did." When this group finds itself beyond its depth, it is too late for the worker to discover and take steps to improve an intense rivalry situation. Competition between groups frequently gets out of hand and creates many problems. Consider the group that is very protective of itself and quite unable to participate in program events with others who differ markedly from it. Perhaps the insecurity of the group makes it unable to broaden its outlook until a later time. Consider, too, groups that approach program in a highly tentative manner. They cannot make long-range plans or move beyond the simple, directly consummated event. Does this tell us something about the way the group regards itself and possibly something about its immediate past? During recent years many people have been on the move. They have a tentativeness about their lives and cannot settle down to involved programs. Consider, also, the influence of tradition on the program process. Many groups "did it that way last year" and the year before, for that matter. Traditions have meaning and value. They should be respected by the worker. Consider the wish of younger groups to copy programs from older groups and, in so doing, to receive the satisfaction that comes from doing what older people do. These and other examples reveal the dualistic nature of the program developmental process. Activity and interaction that begets the activity must be understood as a whole.

The social group worker's primary job in program development is to guide the processes of interaction among group members. Social group work utilizes the interaction of members around program in an agency setting with worker guidance. It is believed that this group work process results in the movement of individuals and groups toward objectives that are mutually compatible with the function of the agency. Interaction is illustrated in Figure 7.

Interaction refers to participating behavior of a reciprocal kind. It is the give-and-take of individuals who act and react. This "giving to and taking from" is really a single process which takes place within the group. The worker is responsible both for stimulating the "to and from" and for helping participation become channeled or focused on the goal to be attained. *Interaction itself is not an end but rather a means to the goal of the group.* It tends to take two forms: acts of initiation and responses to such initiatory acts. When group members present ideas or information, when they seek knowledge, when they show others how to do something, when they volunteer to take responsibility, they are interacting with their group members. Consequently, workers should be alert to the origin of ideas and then make certain that the group has a chance to respond fully. Responses may be positive, negative, or neutral. The response of one member to the idea of another member may be to accept it with slight modifications; this act then results in a new cycle of consideration. It has been well stated that

FIGURE 7

Guidance of Interaction—the Focus of the Program Process

Group work

The group
itself is
a major
tool of
personality
development

utilizes the interaction of members

Interaction is participating behavior of a reciprocal kind, give-and-take of
personalities that act and
react

Expression of interaction
Verbal communication
Body movements

Takes form of
Initiated acts
Responses to acts

Has dimensions of
Distribution—who?
Frequency—how often?
Duration—how long?
Order—sequence?
Direction—toward?
Content—what?
Meaning—why?

Resulting in dynamics
Acceptance
Status
Integration of group
Independence
And so on

around program in an agency and community setting

Program is a process
consisting of

Determining purpose
Deciding on activities
Assigning responsi-
bilities
Working together
Carrying out activities
Evaluating:
By group
By group with other
groups in agency
By group with
other groups
in community

with worker guidance

The worker plays
an active role in-
fluencing interac-
tion by

Helping group to
form
Helping group
develop
organization
Helping individu-
als to participate
Helping group
make decision
Interpreting
the agency
Enriching group
environment

resulting in movement to-ward objectives

objectives are

Individual	Group
Relationships	Feeling
Acceptance	Cooperation
Status	Achievement
Responsibility	Growth
Identification with group	and so on

interaction is not a matter of arithmetic or addition of responses but rather an interweaving or interpenetration of responses.

Interaction is a matter of degree rather than of type. In some situations, especially in cases in which the group is secure and morale is high, group members work together with surprising speed and thoroughness. Almost everyone participates and has a chance to express himself, and the product of the interaction is substantially a group product. With other groups the reverse is true, and the worker has to back up and begin almost at the beginning again. Clearly, the kinds of relationships that exist among the members and between the members and the worker determine the degree of interaction that will obtain. Until the individuals actually become a group and can communicate with each other, the degree and duration of purposeful interaction will be less than at a later time. Beginning-level program with newly formed groups should concentrate on things that will help such groups to develop a consciousness of one another, a consciousness of being a group.

Understanding the Dimensions of Interaction

After working with groups for a period of time, the group worker becomes aware that the process of interaction has many dimensions. He begins to watch for certain things to happen, and in so doing he understands more fully the meaning of the behavior being displayed. Some of the important dimensions of interaction that the worker should have in mind are:

1. *Distribution*—who is participating—should be studied. After a few meetings the worker can recall who is participating and who is not and will become aware of the demanding member and of the member who does not participate at all.

2. *Frequency*—how often and how many times the member participates —can be observed. Some members seem to be involved in everything that is going on, and others participate less frequently.

3. *Duration*—how long participation lasts—is considered. Here the worker will note that some members seem to be actively involved throughout most of the meeting while others enter in only now and then and briefly.

4. *Order* of participation is important to understand. Some members always speak first and others wait awhile. Member A may not participate until member B has had his say. Member C may always enter in after the worker has made a comment. Member D may watch for opportunities to insert his specific feelings.

5. *Direction* of the interaction should be noted. Usually there are two broad categories of direction: toward persons and toward objects. Sometimes the worker will observe that a member always responds to another member but will not respond to the worker. Sometimes the interaction is

directed toward the task at hand, and other times it is off the track and seemingly out of focus.

6. *Content* of interaction is usually both program- and personality-centered. Group members may be talking about a forthcoming program event and simultaneously reveal their preferences for certain persons to be in charge of certain parts of it.

7. *Meaning* of the interaction is evaluated by the worker, who endeavors to assess the positive and the negative aspects of member responses. He asks himself: What does this comment by this member mean in terms of how he is getting along in the group? Does this specific response mean that the member is becoming a part of the group, is gaining acceptance, is developing his identification with the group? Is the individual's failure to respond due to lack of familiarity with the subject at hand or is he fearful of revealing his attitude?

In connection with his preparation of the record of the meeting, the worker will endeavor to re-create in his mind the various dimensions of interaction outlined above.

Five factors, taken together, influence the interactional capacity of the group: the relationships between group members, the relationship between the worker and the group, the conscious bond of need and interest which holds the group together, the goals for which they work, and the social situation in which they find themselves. As he gives guidance to group interaction in relation to the program development process, the group worker is demonstrating the group work process. The group work process is in operation when the group worker consciously guides and utilizes the interaction among group members for individual and group development. It is important to emphasize the fact that in the group work process the worker participates actively in directing the interaction of members so that the experience will meet their needs as individuals and at the same time assist the group to move toward some satisfying group achievement which is mutually determined.

Program Planning With Large Groups

More and more the group worker is called upon to help large groups develop and plan program. Frequently reference is made to "mass activities," but it is difficult to define exactly what these words mean. Presumably reference is being made to large social recreation programs, such as dances, or to open forum discussions, large classes, athletic tournaments, or canteen and lounge activities, game rooms, and the like. It seems that when group workers use the phrase "mass activities," they are thinking of large groups, say thirty to one hundred or more persons, who have come together for some specific program event. Such a large group may be composed of a number of smaller groups, or it may start out as a large group. Some groups that start as small groups may grow to such a size that they no longer enjoy the characteristics of the small group. To this writer it seems preferable to think of groups as small or large rather than to refer to the large group as a "mass."

It can by no means be said that large groups are in themselves undesirable or unproductive. Large groups generally have a different purpose than have small groups. They may meet different needs of individuals, and they are obviously set up to function in different areas of program. Since group work is a method useful in helping persons develop as individuals, the question seems to be: To what extent is social group work useful as a method in developing program with large groups? In the judgment of the writer social group work has much to contribute in the large group situation. The application of group work methodology should not be strictly limited to the small cohesive friendship group.

Many agencies are now working with substantial numbers of large groups. There are some very good reasons for the trend toward selective large-group participation. There has been a tremendous increase in population during the past twenty years, and this has put a great deal of pressure on agencies to provide service. Because there are not nearly enough agencies and because agency budgets are inadequate, it has been necessary to provide service to large groups if any kind of program is to be offered.

If it can be assumed that large groups in themselves are neither good nor bad and that the success of any group program depends largely upon the kind of professional leadership it has, then it should be possible to locate many ways in which group work method can be helpful with the large group. Essentially it seems that the problem of the group worker in the development of program with large groups is one of finding ways to individualize the experience and ways to increase individual participation that will lead to the acceptance of responsibility on the part of the individual. The worker can, however, increase the degree of individualization and the amount of individual participation by concentrating his attention on helping to create a setting, or atmosphere or climate, in which there will be a maximum degree of intimacy and individualization. He can see to it that members are thought of, regarded, liked, and treated as individuals even though there may be a large number of them.

The worker can also help the large group divide its members into a number of subgroups of either short-term or long-term duration. The process of planning group program can be participated in by a large number of members on different occasions. The use of a steering committee or planning or executive committee will enable certain members of the group to take responsibility for the whole group. If there is sufficient rotation of responsibility in jobs of this kind over a period of time, a large number of persons can have experience in doing something for the group.

The planned subdivision of a large group engaged in program activity can amount to the creation of a number of small groups and can help individuals become a part of the small group during the specific event or session. In addition, the group worker has an opportunity to refer individuals from large groups to small groups, and often the large group provides a way for an individual to get started in an agency program. Alertness on the part of the group worker will frequently result in his locating of individuals who need special help. This may require a specialized interest and a specialized focus, so that the individual can be helped to relate to another resource. In thinking about the use of social group work with large groups it seems more and more evident that much of the problem resides in the failure of the group worker to realize that within the large group there are always many possibilities for individual assignments and many possibilities for helping the individual increase the amount of his responsible participation.

Let us bear in mind that group workers should endeavor to use as much of their group work knowledge and skill as possible in all group situations, small or large. Program development is a continuous process that calls for the involvement of as many group members as possible.

Criteria of Effective Process and Program

The group work process is operating at its best when the agency, the worker, and the group provide an environmental setting in which the full interplay of personalities upon one another is not only permitted but definitely encouraged; help individuals to participate in the discussion of goals, the formulation of plans, and the carrying out of program activities; emphasize cooperative, joint activity, in which working together serves to integrate individual, group, and agency in a mutually satisfying effort; work for a system of group organization and social control that makes it possible for the individual to function as an individual but at the same time allows him to choose to act collectively with others in socially valid ways. Group workers who believe in the group work process know that program is important but that the *way* in which that program is planned and conducted is of greater importance.

In summary, the program development process involves several definite steps which can be listed as follows: the continuous discovery of interests and needs, the selection of a starting point or beginning level of program, the analysis of what is needed in the way of work responsibilities to carry out the program, the allocation of duties to various members, the coordination of individual efforts and the creation of a group unity, the experiencing of the program choice, and evaluation before moving on to the next program.

Our programs in social group work must meet the following criteria of effectiveness:

1. Program should grow out of the needs and interests of the individuals who compose the group.

2. Program should take into account such factors as age of group members, cultural background, and economic differences.

3. Program should provide individuals with experiences and opportunities which they voluntarily choose to pursue because of their inherent values.

4. Program should be flexible and varied to satisfy a variety of needs and interests and to afford a maximum number of opportunities for participation.

5. Programs should evolve from the simple to the more complex, with movement coming as a result of group growth in ability and readiness. Movement from initially "personal" to "social" or "community" concerns should be an ultimate objective if our programs are to have greater social signficance.

NOTES

1. Norman Goroff, "Social Group Work—an Intersystemic Frame of Reference," *Journal of Jewish Communal Service,* March 1971, pp. 229–230.
2. Gisela Konopka, *Social Group Work: A Helping Process* (Englewood Cliffs, New Jersey: Prentice-Hall, Inc., 1963), p. 170.
3. Hans S. Falck, "Social Group Work and Planned Change" in *Social Work Practice, 1964* (Published for the National Conference on Social Welfare by Columbia University Press, New York, 1964), p. 218.
4. Ruth R. Middleman, *The Non-Verbal Method in Working with Groups* (New York: Association Press, 1968), pp. 66–67.
5. Harleigh B. Trecker, *Guide for Agency Self-Appraisal* (New York: Federation of Protestant Welfare Agencies, Inc., Revised Edition, 1965), pp. 14–15.
6. Helen Northen, *Social Work with Groups* (New York: Columbia University Press, 1969), p. 18.
7. Bernard Berelson and Gary A. Steiner, *Human Behavior: An Inventory of Scientific Findings* (New York: Harcourt, Brace and World, Inc., 1964), p. 336.

6

Individuals–Working
With Them in the Group

The group worker works with groups, individuals, and especially with individuals *in* the group. Although his basic approach is directed to the group, his aim is to help individuals use their association with others in the group so that they will grow and develop. As Falck puts it:

> The role of the social worker with the growth-oriented group is to help the members use the group experience to grow and develop, either within the context of their normal developmental needs or in relation to their social and emotional problems. The primary purpose of the . . . group is to provide each member with a means of maintaining or improving his social functioning. To achieve this purpose each member must put something of himself into the group and contribute to its health. This . . . clearly implies that the group is a means to an end and not an end in itself.[1]

For the most part the group worker works with individuals while they are actually with the group. Here the worker's focus is upon the individual *and* the group simultaneously. The group worker also works with the individual outside the group. Prior to, after, or in between group meetings, group workers have frequent meetings with individuals and equally frequent opportunities to be of help to them. In these instances the worker is giving help to the individual *as a member of the group*. He is not assuming a casework relationship. The group worker may help the individual to obtain casework service or other kinds of specialized aid outside the group, and in so doing he is utilizing his skill in making a referral. Under such conditions he may work along with the caseworker, cooperating in a general treatment program but carefully confining his efforts to work with the group aspects of the situation.

Some of the general questions that the worker may ask with reference to the individuals in the group are: How can I tell when the individual is ready for group experience? What kind of group is better for a certain kind of individual personality? What should I try to understand about the individual prior to group placement? How do individuals become a real part of the group? How do they gain acceptance and status? How can I help new members in their efforts to become accepted? What can I do to help the individual who is having difficulty in getting along with others?

Why Individuals Form or Join Groups

The individual wants to be a part of a group because some need of his can be met better as a member of a group than in any other way. Though individuals may not understand exactly what it is they are after when they voluntarily join groups, there is always a reason, or a combination of reasons, for doing so. Sometimes the reasons are expressed verbally and are at variance with the real reason, which they either do not know or cannot verbalize. Because of the purposeful nature of human behavior, the group worker knows that each member of the group has a need for something which he proposes to get from his participation with the group. The group worker tries to find out what the individual wants and tries to help him satisfy his wants by means of the group. Tropp says:

To be in a group means to have the resources available to satisfy some of the most fundamental human needs. It means, first of all, belonging, which itself says a great deal, because all human beings have a deep need to belong, to others and with others. Belonging implies acceptance by others, and that acceptance is a basic kind of affection from one's fellow human beings. To be in a group also means having opportunities for self-expression under circumstances in which others can appreciate it, so that it becomes achievement and brings recognition—and these are great supporters and strengtheners of that precious feeling of self-worth so necessary for mental health. Finally, to be in a group means having the opportunity to experience that important communal balance of freedom and limitation, which is at the root of social responsibility, one of the hallmarks of social maturity.

The group is not only an alliance through which normal needs can be met; it can also be a natural healer of hurts, a supporter of strengths, and a clarifier of problems. A group may serve as a source of strength and support for those whose inner strengths have been weakened. It may serve as a sounding board for expressions of anxiety, hostility, or guilt. It often turns out that group members learn that others in the group have similar feelings weighing them down in their aloneness, that they are not so different or so alone—and learning this in live confrontation with one's peers is a most powerful change-inducing experience. In fact, one of the key virtues of the group method is that the people are indeed readier to take help from one another than from a worker.

Further, in a group, one may discover that one does have differences from others and that one must contend with these differences in the process of group conflict and group criticism. As this is discovered, one may either affirm one's differences or see a necessity for changing. Thus, the give-and-take of group life can deeply affect one's attitude toward oneself and toward others. It leads to an increased capacity for objective judgment, increased self-control, clearer perspective on one's own needs, greater acceptance and understanding of the situation in which one finds himself, more effective use of the services being offered, and, finally, increased social responsibility and preparation for effective living in the larger society.[2]

When we discuss the question "What do individuals want from group experiences?" we discover that, first and foremost, they want to *belong* in a psychological sense. They want and must get more than symbolic membership identification if they are to remain in the group very long. To belong, they must be accepted by the group and must accept the others. They become a real part of the group by identifying themselves with it and by playing a role within it. Groups grant or withhold status to individual members on the basis of the role that the individual assumes and plays. Differences in individual status are a result of the value that the group attaches to a certain role at a certain time. Being a member of a group and achieving a real feeling of belonging are of great importance to the individual.

When thought is given to the terms used in group work and when their meaning is examined, important aspects of the problem come to light. Webster's Dictionary tells us that a *member* is "one of the persons composing a society, community, or party; an individual who belongs to an association." It says also that *to belong* is "to be attached or bound to or connected with by some relation." It would seem that the word "relation" is the key to the problem. When persons join a group they do not join a building or a program. They join with *other persons* who are working toward an ideal or a purpose. Hence, belonging refers to a quality of human relations among persons. Joining or taking out a membership may be a nominal or even an intellectual experience, but *belonging is essentially an emotional experience.* Persons who really belong to a group develop an inner feeling of warmth, pride, sharing, devotion, affection, and respect with reference to the others and to the purpose of the group. Belonging means to be a part of something—a real part of it, and this feeling comes as a result of definite experiences with people.

Thus, when group workers talk about membership and its meaning they are not referring to membership campaigns, or drives. They are not talking about the act of handing over a sum of money and receiving a card to carry in wallet or purse. They are not talking about the buying of services or privileges, worthy and legitimate as these may be. They are talking about a psychological process of growth in human relationships through which members become belongers. Belonging is related to *people and purpose* rather than *place and program.* Belonging is a voluntary response freely given. It calls for something on the part of the person who wishes to belong and on the part of the group too. Real belonging is a living companionship or fellowship between people.

It is true that not all persons want to belong to a group, and not all who do belong reach the same depth or intensity in their relationship. Thus there may be various degrees of belonging and ever-present change in the quality of the connectedness. Some persons may become members of a group without a very clear notion of what they are joining or why they wish to join. With them there may be a period of time wherein they do not *belong* in a psychological sense and must be helped into this relationship by the skill and understanding of the agency worker and the group members. As they experience the feeling of belonging, they acquire the language of the group, and a shift from "my" and "mine" to "we" and "ours" in their conversation is observable.

In the movement from the first joining of an association or becoming a member of a group to becoming one who can be said to belong, a number of things happen. In the realms of thinking, feeling, and acting changes are noted. The person who belongs accepts the *purpose* of the group, interprets it, works for it. There is a commitment to the ideals and aspirations of the group. True, the member may seek modification in the purpose of the group as circumstances change and new needs arise. Such changes, however, grow out of the work of the group, and each individual has a voice in the refocusing of purpose. The person who belongs accepts and carries responsibility in behalf of the group according to his abilities and strengths. He makes an investment in energy. He becomes a part of the propelling force and does not go along "just for the ride." In addition, belonging requires the member to accept the ways of work of the group, the "ground rules" so to speak. Here, again, he may strive for modification in the methodology of the group but does so openly and in concert with others.

As an individual becomes more and more a part of the group, he tends to help others to experience a similar relationship; he wants to help others to belong because of what belonging means to him. Later he may adopt a critically evaluative attitude toward his group and what it does. This change makes for alertness and helps keep the group growing in effectiveness. Thus the person who belongs has a *function* to perform, and this function grows as he grows in understanding and insight toward those in the group and the purpose for which they strive.

Often this process is slow. Usually individuals go through steps or stages in their identification with their group and their agency. It is necessary for the group worker constantly to apply what is known about the ways in which individuals may be helped to achieve this relationship of genuine belonging.

The group worker must ask at least two basic questions at this point. They are: Under what conditions will this feeling of belonging grow? How can I help to bring about this relationship between persons?

Fortunately, there are some things that are known. First of all, from study and research we learn about the dynamics of attitude change. If we expect a member to become one who *belongs,* we must have the right conditions for this to happen. For example, we know that the social and group atmosphere, or climate, is an important factor. When there is warmth, friendliness, intimacy, and *time,* then the seeds of belonging can be sown.

Then, too, we know that when purposes are stated with clarity and directness, when they "make sense," many persons will be helped to determine whether or not they *want* to belong. Purpose grows into conviction only when the individual is able to express the purpose simply, forcefully, and in language that is alive and meaningful. We also know that when time is given to a new member relatively early in his experience, a sense of belonging will develop more rapidly. The intake, or reception, process is crucial in helping the person to understand what he is joining, who his fellow members are, and the way in which they work together to attain their goals.

And, finally, we know that persons differ in their use of groups and associations because membership in a group is a very individual matter. Therefore, the membership process must be individualized, and a conscious plan formulated for each individual which takes into account background, interest, needs, and other factors. Because of this need for indvidualization the small group setting seems to more quickly and more frequently foster the feeling of belonging.

At the beginning of the relationship between the group and the individual in a social group work setting, the individual makes his way into the group situation by feeling himself completely accepted by the worker. Workers who have been accepted by the group thus become a bridge or avenue over which the new person can pass to gain acceptance from the members.

Northen writes about the power of acceptance in these words:

A feeling that one is accepted in a group and that he, in turn, accepts other members is a powerful dynamic in the process of change. All people need to feel accepted. Acceptance denotes the quality of being regarded favorably by the group to the extent that continual interaction with others is possible without undue threat. As a person feels accepted, his self-esteem rises. He becomes more open to new ways of feeling and thinking. He feels comfortable enough to reveal some of his feelings, aspirations, and concerns to others. He can dare to look at the unacceptability of some of his behavior, utilizing the knowledge for growth and change. As he feels accepted, a member tends to enhance his identification with the group which, in turn, enhances the group's impact on his attitude and behavior.[3]

As the individual begins to get a warm response from the worker and others in the group his self-confidence increases. He may then proceed to simple tests of his own abilities by offering to assume a minor and temporary responsibility for some phase of the group's activity. The group subjects the individual to a period of testing and the individual in turn discovers what he must do to gain acceptance and status. The accompanying

Figure 8 illustrates the various kinds of behavior likely to elicit acceptance or rejection from the group. The process of social adjustment is two-way and continuous. The way the individual feels about the group and the way the group feels about the individual are basic material for the sensitive group worker, who must realize that, in the individual's struggle to become a part of the group, there is a never-ending flow of emotion.

FIGURE 8

Individual Behavior and Group Acceptance

The Individual Who Behaves

This Way	This Way
Is likely to get acceptance and status from the group:	Is likely to be rejected and denied status by the group:
Accepts the goals of the group	Disparages goals of the group
Responds positively to ideas of group members	Responds negatively to group ideas and programs
Takes responsibility; works for the group	Does not accept responsibility
Contributes skill and treatment	Talks too much, dominates, tries to take over group
Shares with group members	Violates or flouts group rules
Accepts rules and limits of the group	Constantly complains
Defends the group	Is selfish; does not share

Becoming a part of a group is thus a gradual process for the individual. It is a relative matter, too, for some persons want to penetrate into the group only so far and others have needs which can be met only by means of very strong attachments. The intensity factor is also important, since some persons relate much more rapidly than do others. There will be noticeable fluctuations in group acceptance, for the course of individual adjustment is seldom straight ahead but is more likely to be forward, then backward, then forward, and so on.

As the individual becomes a part of the group, we can observe certain characteristics in his behavior. He may start to speak the same language as do the members. He accepts all or part of the goals of the group and tends to make those goals his own. He learns about and agrees to the limitations that group life always imposes on individuals. He seeks acceptance from certain individual members and may become a part of a subgroup. He shows his confidence in the group and the ideas expressed by its members. He may come to the defense of the group when he feels it is threatened. As he assumes responsibility in behalf of the group and is allowed to put talent and skill to work, he begins to feel that his contribution means something. The individual wants the group to care about him, to like him and to appreciate his efforts no matter how small they are.

In this process the individual learns that to become a part of a group he must give up some of his individuality. His prejudices, biases, blind spots, and unfounded fancies must be sacrificed. He must control himself more than before and must deliberately handle himself with firmness, especially when the group is putting him through certain tests of affiliation. Learning to share materials or ideas with other persons is partly a matter of modifying established habits and points of view. The greater the difference between the individual and the group, the greater the adjustment problem. Since becoming a member of a group is a matter of role playing and interaction between the individual and the group, the group's feeling about the new member is important.

Some of the inner and seldom expressed questions that groups have about individuals who seek admission: Will he fit in? What will he contribute to us? Will he take his share of responsibility? What are his skills? Is he too superior and thus a threat to us? Or, is he so inferior that he will retard our progress? Whom does he know and what do they think of him? Will his reputation enhance or weaken our position in the agency or community? Answers to such questions are sought indirectly, and the new individual undergoes a series of introductory experiences that tend to present him with the customs, traditions, and codes of the group. The way in which he is helped to understand what is going on will determine, at least in part, the speed with which he becomes a part of the group. In all of this the group worker has a very real function. The essence of this function is the way he works with the group, for, as Klein reminds us, "Social work through group process relies upon group forces as the primary medium for growth and change. The function of the worker is to permit the group to become a supportive medium and to allow group processes to nurture and succor each member. The focus of the work is upon the group and the group processes." [4]

The great meaning of the group to the individual is stressed by Tropp who observes:

When one gets down to the central core of what really happens that makes the group experience so meaningful and so useful, one discovers the simple truth that people with similar interests, similar concerns, or similar problems can help each other in ways that are significantly different from the ways in which a worker can help them in a one-to-one relationship. This is not to say the group method is better—simply that it is different; and because it is different, it may be more effective for certain purposes. The key difference is that the members of the group take help from one another. And this is the way it has always happened in life; people have, from time immemorial, helped each other, sans benefit of therapy. Just as people do not have to be taught to breathe, so they move to help each other.[5]

Situations in Which the Group Worker Works With the Individual in the Group

When we analyze recorded experience with a view to highlighting situations in which the group worker works with the individual in the group, we discover that many of these situations are repeated. Some examples based on an analysis of several groups are:

1. The group worker is working with the individual when he tells him about various groups to which he might belong and helps him to make a choice from among several group possibilities.

2. The group worker is working with the individual when he helps him to become a part of a group by accepting him and by introducing him to others in the group. As Falck says:

> The most valuable part of the worker's activity is to help group members relate to one another. He helps the clients develop into a group in which each person may have a given place, a role, and a more or less characteristic way of acting. With the worker's guidance, the members may become aware of the efficiency, or lack of efficiency, of their behaviors, as reflected by the reactions of other members. Thus members can be helped to learn what kind of behavior "works," what kind brings satisfaction, and what kind brings punishment. Frequently, the worker can involve group members in a discussion of their behaviors in relation to one another, their feelings about one another, the experiences they find pleasant, and the experiences they find painful. The worker can guide the group process by intervening to ask a question or make a comment or an interpretation or by engaging in such nonverbal behavior as silence or reflection. The worker helps the group develop a reality of its own, which is reflected in the kinds of evaluation members make of one another's behaviors, perceived motivations, guesses, and judgments. In other words, a considerable amount of the worker's skill lies in knowing when and how to intervene in the ongoing group process. Effective use of his many tools, combined with his disciplined emotional investment in his clients, produces the artful practitioner.[6]

3. Individual work is being done when the group worker works with persons who have assumed leadership responsibilities within the group. The worker aids in planning, defining responsibility, setting standards of performance, and in helping individuals to evaluate the way in which they have done their work.

4. The group worker works with individuals who have difficulty in carrying through on responsibilities they have assumed. By helping the person to gain insight at the point of understanding why he has not been able to perform his tasks and by helping the group to understand all that is involved, the group worker is frequently able to convert otherwise negative experiences into positive gains for the individual and the group. Sometimes individual loads must be lightened and responsibilities reallocated.

5. The group worker is called upon to help individuals who have great difficulty in adjusting either because of highly aggressive behavior or because of excessive withdrawal. Frequently, such persons have strong feelings of hostility toward the authority of the agency or to other adults. They must work out their feelings in the setting of the group, but they need help in doing so.

6. The group worker helps individuals who are in danger of being made scapegoats by the other group members. As Feldman declares, "Scapegoating, social rejection, and intense personal dislike constitute focal practice concerns for social group work. For the most part, practitioner interest in such processes devolves from the frequency of their occurrences in social work client groups, from legitimate worker concerns regarding their potentially maladaptive consequences for individual group members, and from worker recognition that the small group milieu affords multiple focuses for effective intervention." [7]

7. The group worker individualizes by encouraging members of great capacity to develop their leadership skills and to take on successively more advanced responsibilities.

8. The group worker may help individuals to withdraw from groups that are not suited to their needs, from which they cannot depart because of strong guilt feelings associated with "quitting" or "failing to make good."

9. Work with individuals is being done when the group worker works with the group's elected representatives who serve on agency or community intergroup councils.

10. When the worker makes a referral of a member to some other specialized resource agency or worker, he is naturally concentrating attention on individual needs.

These examples of individualization are but a few of the possible ways in which the group worker actually works with individuals in the group.

Kindelsperger and Ryland offer the following specific suggestions for helping individuals within the group:

Ahead of Time Preparation. Gain as much knowledge of each individual as possible, his assets and liabilities, his interests and capabilities; help in choice of the group best for him; have awareness of the developmental level of the group as a whole and the stage of development in relation to a given individual.

Acceptance by the Worker. This adds support and security. Give direct expression of interest in the member, such as calling him by name; give reassurance of this interest, for once is not enough; discuss his special interests; stay near a timid member, a new one, or when special support is needed, but be careful not to alienate the group; give encouragement for achievement, praise where praise is due—whether it be for skill in activities, control of feelings, contribution to the group; perhaps participate in activity in a one-to-one basis, later drawing in other members.

Help Member Become Accepted by Other Members. Take direct steps to help him relate to others—introduce him, for example; help him find some common bond or interest with others; use his special skills to augment the group's program, build esteem, and promote relationships; use such mechanical means as rearrangement of seating or subgroups for special jobs; enlist the help of other members who feel secure in the group to help a new or low status member become accepted (the worker may at times interpret needs); make skillful use of program to change subgroups, give leadership roles, develop special projects or programs needing a variety of skills which individual members have.

Protection of Member. Direct hostility to self to relieve member. Identify with individual or subgroup, supporting their stand to some extent: "They have a point, let's listen"; redirect activity or discussions to a less sensitive area, at least for the time being; support officers or leaders, helping them to lead and assume proper role; reinterpret for the member to the group, rewording, or explaining words or actions to make it possible for him to do so.

Let Matters Take Their Course. This kind of inactivity must be carefully gauged and good judgment used. It may be too traumatic and ego deflating for the member and the limits imposed by the group may be destructive for other group members. However, it may result in subsequent change of behavior because of a desire to stay in the group. Guilt of other members may result in later overappeasing behavior.

Positive Use of Limitations and Authority. Set structure within which members are able to function safely; help group set limits (group values), sometimes through helping officers to function better; help group improve decision-making methods so that elimination and subjugation are not used as ways of authority; expose member to group pressure; help him limit his own behavior; help him face reality, sometimes through accepting his own limitations, physical or otherwise; set direct limits on the basis of need; protect the group from the individual who would destroy it through limiting individual expression; use agency policies to limit, reassure, and interpret.

Skilled Use of Program. Behavior may change if the individual is helped to acquire skill and resulting feeling of worth and identity. Use program to help acquire status and acceptance, face reality, experience limitations through those set by activity, develop leadership skill, experiment with ego adaptation.

Verbalization. Bring out into the open at the proper time for discussion and evaluate the feelings around the situation. "You can feel without knowing, but you can't know without feeling." [8]

Working With Individuals to Develop Their Leadership Capacity

Every group worker realizes that group members differ in their talents and abilities and that some are more capable in the realm of leadership than are others. It is necessary for the group worker to be especially interested in locating those individuals who show signs of being able to assume leadership responsibilities. If the group is to carry on its own program, it must have leadership from its own members; otherwise, the worker finds himself carrying far more responsibility than is wise or desirable. Consequently, the worker finds it necessary to work with those individuals who are carrying leadership duties, and, in addition, he needs to help every member gain an opportunity to try out his specific strengths. It is the hope of group work that persons will be able to carry over their leadership skills into other group situations as they move beyond the agency setting.

The worker usually has a role to play with the individual who is an elected or appointed leader within the group. Officers and committee chairmen need help in understanding their duties and in planning their work.

They need suggestions as to how they may approach their jobs and how they may influence others in the group. Through such devices as executive committees and planning conferences the group worker has an opportunity to help these key individuals see their role in relation to the others who hold similar posts. Frequent individual conferences with the worker are often required by newly chosen leaders so that they may become secure in their new jobs. There is usually a very real need to help the individual who has selected or been given a leadership responsibility to develop a style of leadership that will be acceptable to the other members of the group. Problems around the use of authority are common, and more likely than not the inevitable discouragements of slow group response will need talking through with newly chosen member-leaders. The tendency on their part to want to go too fast will bear watching by the group worker.

It is easy for the group worker to fall into the comfortable habit of encouraging hard-working, able group-member leaders to continue in a given responsibility when it would be better for them to move on and let someone else have a chance. Consequently, member-leaders have to be helped to give up leadership roles in the group and to take responsibility in some larger unit in the agency or the community. This is one means of opening the way for others to have leadership opportunities; also, it is a means of finding individuals to take responsibility for intergroup and interagency activities which transcend a single group.

The way in which the group worker works with the group through group member-leaders is in a large measure the key to the wider realization of social group work with larger groups.

Working With the Individual Who Has Difficulty in Adjusting

For most individuals who have been properly placed in groups the process of adjustment is generally smooth. Adjustment is often a matter of maturation, and as Klein points out, "Group experience plays an essential part in the process of maturation. The group seems to meet certain psychological needs, such as the development of independence, the identification of social roles, the identification of social skills and attitudes that are acceptable to one's peers and to the larger society, and the development of values that mark growth from egocentricity to socialization. The process is one in which the individual learns to meet his personal needs in such a way as to, at the same time, gain favorable acceptance from others." [9] But for some group members there are problems of adjustment which require special attention from the worker. When an individual is having difficulty in becoming an accepted part of the group, the group worker studies not only the individual but the group as well. In addition, the worker studies how he feels about this individual and what the individual's behavior is doing to the group. This is highly significant because it tends to diminish the worker's natural wish to place the burden of the adjustment on the individual when in reality the group situation may be an unwise one for a certain person.

The group worker studies the composition of the group. Is it too large or too widespread in age or background for this individual? He studies the formal organization of the group. Perhaps there is too much or too little. Standards may be too high or too low. The group may exert too much pressure for this member now. The program of the group may be too difficult or too easy. Perhaps lack of skills on the part of certain individuals causes them to rebel against a given type of program. The emotional tone of the group is examined. Perhaps the underlying hostility and competitive feelings of the group did not emerge until this particular individual came into the group. The group may become very punitive to the individual who cannot adjust and thus will make it advisable for the worker to protect the individual by suggesting that he withdraw from the group.

Actually, the group worker should take three steps when the individual has failed to make a satisfactory group adjustment. First, the worker should try to understand the reasons for the individual's behavior toward the group. Second, he should try to understand his own response as a worker to this individual. Third, he should seek to understand what the individual's behavior is doing to the group and how the group is responding to him. It is impossible to study individual maladjustment in the group as if it were an isolated phenomenon. There are always multiple causes and effects of individual difficulties in the group.

What is the meaning of the individual's behavior? What lies behind it? What does it represent? What does it do to the group? What does it do to the worker? What can the worker do about it? Answers to these questions will enable the worker to proceed on a sound basis.

The individual behavior responses that require considerable understanding and help from the worker are many and varied. One group of workers analyzed their experience with groups and developed the following list of individual adjustment situations with which they were called upon to work during a brief period with so-called "normal groups."

1. Individuals with almost insatiable drives for dominance had to be helped to restrain their tendencies to "take over" the group.

2. Extremely passive individuals, who were shy and withdrawn, needed help in asserting themselves and in taking some share of responsibility for the group.

3. Markedly dependent individuals, dependent on the worker or other members, indecisive and unable to move, had to have patient help first in making small decisions and then in moving on to larger ones.

4. Individuals who assumed responsibility and then did not carry through often incurred the wrath of the group and needed help in understanding the meaning of their duties and obligations to other group members.

5. Individuals whose response pattern was highly negativistic frequently got in the way of group progress and needed help in shifting to a positive response pattern.

6. Some individuals unable to accept limits or in conflict with authority behaved so as to "get the group in trouble" when they violated agency, community, or group rules. These ranged from minor incidents to major cases of outright conflict. In his research on authority relations and disruptive behavior in small discussion groups Burke[10] points out that the type of leadership found in the group is of great importance.

7. Individuals sometimes had a false notion of their status in the group, and in their anxiety over wanting status they "spoke for the group" or "committed the group" to something different from that which the group actually wished to do.

8. Individuals who made excessive use of the group to air their own troubles, grievances, or complaints about the world were in need of help in controlling their feelings.

9. Individuals rigid in attitude and conduct and lacking in the resiliency required by rapidly changing group situations created problems requiring special attention.

10. Persons whose performance never measured up to their talk, whose fantasies got in the way of real achievement, represented another category of individual need encountered by the group worker.

Why do individuals behave in this manner? They *say* they want to belong to the group, but they *do* many things that annoy the group and hinder their chances of getting acceptance. We need to consider the person's need to be both dependent and independent and the resultant feelings of ambivalence which arise as persons work through their conflicts. Every individual has conflicting emotions or drives which need resolution. From infancy through the late years the individual needs the love and affection of others. As a baby he is utterly dependent upon the adults in his world to provide physical and psychological care. As a child he needs change, and he wishes to become independent from adult care, yet he realizes that it is comfortable to be dependent and precarious to assume too much independence. Consequently, he wavers back and forth, not fully understanding the dual nature of his feelings. He may struggle to impress upon people the fact that he is independent, yet he feels inwardly that he is not and really wants to be a part of a well-knit group. Eventually, he must work out a style of living or adjustment that allows him to be sufficiently like others to belong, yet sufficiently different to be a person in his own right. Social group work in a sense provides a "proving ground" or "laboratory" in which the individual can try out various means of solving his conflicts without danger to himself or others.

Of first importance in social group work is the fact that the individual's ability to adjust in a group work situation always depends in part upon his present and previous group experiences. Scheidlinger states:

Each member can be assumed to bring with him to the situation a complex patterning of conscious and unconscious attitudes toward himself, toward other people, and toward group experiences in general, i.e. toward groups as a gestaldt. Attitudes toward concurrent or antecedent group experiences are likely to be revived; in addition, under the tensions inherent in group participation, deeper and forgotten attitudes and levels of perceiving are reactivated as well.[11]

The success with which he has utilized family, school, work, and other groups will determine the ease with which he can come into a happy relationship in his agency group. Lack of affection at home may create in the child or youth an intense need to be affectionately received by the play group, and he may try too hard to get this kind of response. Insecurity in a job or vocational group may carry over and prevent the individual from plunging himself very deeply into affairs of the group. Repeated frustrations in other settings may make the individual feel forced to rid himself of aggression in the group. It is of tremendous importance that the group worker understand what the individual's behavior does to him as a *worker*. Dominant, passive, dependent, irresponsible, negative people are disturbing to inexperienced and unprepared workers. They not only "bother" or "upset" the worker but may threaten the worker so much that he wishes those persons were no longer in the group. The group worker may become upset because he thinks such behavior will undermine the group. Perhaps he thinks the agency, through its executive board, may become upset. Hence, the glare of agency opinion may blind the worker. What others think of the worker may dictate his reaction toward a group member who is having trouble in adjusting. Inability to adjust may be interpreted by the worker as a stern reflection on his work. The worker's response to needy individuals is thus of vital significance. He must have a clear picture of his own reaction.

The worker next examines the group. How does the group respond to the "difficult" individual who has a need for special help in adjusting? How does the group feel about this individual? How are feelings shown or expressed? A group may accept the aggressive dominance of an individual because it is so insecure as a group that it cannot do otherwise. It may resist, even retaliate, by excluding or putting out such individuals. It may ignore the person and slowly apply pressure so that the "nonco-op" is forced out if he does not learn to conform. In this area it is especially evident that groups respond very differently to what may seem to be identical situations. *Groups respond to the needy individual on the basis of what they have been and now are as a group.* If groups are themselves secure, they can endure much more from individuals in the way of deviant behavior.

Workers who are insecure themselves may tend to seize upon the notion that they must "protect the group" against the threats of the needy individual, especially when expression of that individual's need takes the form of aggressive behavior. Many times we have heard workers exclaim, "She will break up the group!" "He is spoiling all the fun for the others." Groups often make the same accusations. To be sure, such behavior is annoying and irritating, and it is a nuisance to the group and to the worker. However, there is a difference between behavior that merely annoys a group and behavior that really hurts the group and the members in it. If every worker and every group moved to exclude each of the individuals who at some time or another annoyed a group, there would not be any groups. If group morale is so fragile as to be destroyed by a single upset person, then it is questionable whether it is a sound group in the first place. We must remember that the individual's adjustment to society can take place only if he has groups to adjust to. Quick exclusion from a group that the individual is trying to cultivate cuts down the time in which he can adjust. Therefore, it seems logical to suggest that the group worker encourage the group, in so far as possible, to grant the individual a continuing opportunity to adjust and work with the group.

The above discussion does not preclude the fact that some people are not ready for groups and must be removed or temporarily excluded. Frequently, this is a matter of faulty admission procedures or poor group placement. In such instances, prompt individual help is needed. Thus, when we study the total situation of the individual who is having difficulty in adjusting we see that it has three parts—*individual, group,* and *worker*—all related and interlocking. Whatever the worker does with the individual will affect the group and vice versa. The worker himself is involved and he must consciously understand his own feelings so that they do not block his efforts to help the individual. The above discussion is illustrated by the accompanying Figure 9.

Several avenues of procedure are open to the worker as he speculates about how to help the individual. He may decide to try giving help to this individual by means of working with the group. In so doing, he assumes that the group is strong enough to "take" the difficult individual and that the individual wants the group enough and has sufficient potentialities for change to subject himself to group controls. Along with this, the worker may decide to work directly with the individual while he is a member of the group and in the actual presence of the group. Thus he may limit the individual's participation, curb his aggression, or redirect his energy. Sometimes the group worker will decide to try to help this individual outside and away from the group but in terms of the individual's problem as it affects his group adjustment. A fourth thing he may decide to do is to work for a referral of this person to specialized help such as social caseworkers can give. Before discussing group work and casework relationships we shall do well to examine the extent to which help can be given through the medium of the group.

The worker must make a decision as to the nature of the individual's difficulty, the depth of his need and the duration of the maladjustment. If there is evidence that the individual has one or two friends in the group it may be that the three of them can be assigned to some special task, and the individual can gain status in this way. If the individual has some special

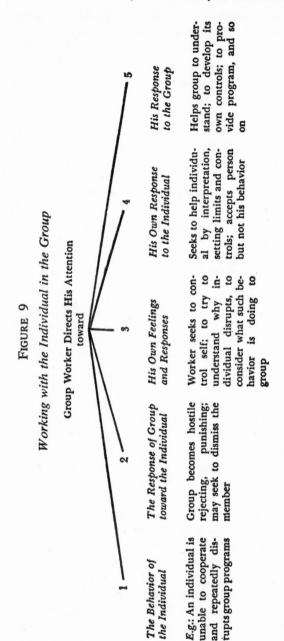

FIGURE 9

Working with the Individual in the Group

Group Worker Directs His Attention toward

1	2	3	4	5
The Behavior of the Individual	*The Response of Group toward the Individual*	*His Own Feelings and Responses*	*His Own Response to the Individual*	*His Response to the Group*
E.g.: An individual is unable to cooperate and repeatedly disrupts group programs	Group becomes hostile rejecting, punishing; may seek to dismiss the member	Worker seeks to control self; to try to understand why individual disrupts, to consider what such behavior is doing to group	Seeks to help individual by interpretation, setting limits and controls; accepts person but not his behavior	Helps group to understand; to develop its own controls; to provide program, and so on

ability which can be displayed for the benefit of the entire group it may be an entering wedge for a better adjustment. Rules and conduct regulations made by the group and enforced by them can be a positive means of correcting individual tendencies to violate group behavior norms.

Sometimes the worker interprets the behavior of the individual to the group by asking the members if they have ever felt or behaved in a similar manner and what they think the reasons were. The worker realizes that in so far as possible the difficult group member should be given protection from the group if too severe controls imposed by the group would have a tendency to create more aggression. The worker must let the group know that he is aware of the bother and discomfort such persons cause the others in the group. He neither condones or condemns the individual's behavior or the group's attitude. He does not deny unpleasantness but admits that it is present and seeks to find ways of correcting the situation.

The poise and equilibrium displayed by the worker has an effect on the individual and on the group. When the individual discovers that the worker likes him, accepts him, and is responsive to him, even though a previous episode may have been extremely negative, he may have less need to be negative. Frey observes:

It is the worker's supportive, warm, good parent relationship that helps relieve the anxiety and tension of an individual faced with the multiple demands of his own style of response to life's "normal" problems or "nuclear conflicts," and to the peculiar demands upon him as a member of a specific network of psychological interactions. The worker's acceptance, understanding, advice, and tangible aid can help the individual meet these demands and handle the anxiety, pressures, and tensions that exist in most groups. Of course, this support is provided during the group meeting and outside it according to individual need and group circumstances.[12]

Workers can be of help to individuals by working with the group on the basis of step-by-step or situation-by-situation analysis of individual problems. Individual adjustment is always a slow process. If a person can do one thing well and receive credit for it, he may have laid a foundation stone for future progress. If groups will understand and deal with specific situations one at a time and by means of concrete, observable experiences, they may be better able to help the individual who is confused and in conflict. Frequently, the setting of time limits will encourage a group to work along with an individual during an agreed-upon period during which he may be able to make the necessary adjustment.

By working with the group and helping it to understand what may be behind the individual's behavior, the group worker may make it possible for him to remain in the group and simultaneously get outside help that will facilitate the adjustment. Or if the individual has to withdraw temporarily from the group, the way may be left open for him to return at a later time. By casework help the individual may be able to develop self-insight and modify his behavior sufficiently, so that he will find it easier to get along in the group.

In helping an individual member to become able and ready to receive casework service, the group worker concentrates upon interpretation. He interprets what the caseworker is there to do. He should be careful to include both the individual and the group in his interpretation. He should emphasize the fact that the individual's behavior can change when there is willingness to respond to expert help.

Relationship Between Social Group Work and Social Case Work

Social group work and social casework services are integral parts of a broad community services program. Both are needed because individuals receiving casework service frequently need group experiences, and individuals in group work programs often need casework help. In addition, discoveries and advances are being made in both casework and group work, and so workers in either one have the possibility of learning from the other. Coyle puts it:

> The group worker needs also certain knowledge and skills which are common to all social workers. He must know how to establish contact with individuals in his group who need more help than the group can provide. This requires the ability to recognize symptomatic behavior, and to establish a relation with the individual. In most instances . . . the group worker cannot himself undertake an individual relationship of the casework variety. This is not because he may not be equipped or able to do so but because to do so would confuse his role with the group and often make it impossible for him to fulfill it. In this, the group worker, like the teacher, has other functions which will be hampered if he embarks on intensive individual relationships. He should, however, be able to recognize need for personal help, to know available resources in casework or other services and to be able to make the necessary referrals. He should also be able, of course, to receive referrals and to place individuals in helpful group situations. In this he uses largely the diagnosis of others but applies to treatment his special tools available through program and relationships in groups.[13]

Coordination should not prove to be too difficult when we consider the fact that both group work and casework hold to basic concepts and principles which are, if not identical, highly similar. Consider the fact that casework and group work both work for the betterment of the individual. The purpose of both casework and group work is to be of help to the individual in some phase of that individual's relationships. The focus of the method is the person primarily and the problem or program secondarily. Group work and casework are based upon a dynamic understanding of the individual's needs *in* his social situation. There is mutual acceptance of the principle of starting where the individual or group may be at the moment and going no faster than he or it can go. The right of the individual and group to self-determination is central in the philosophy of both group work and casework. Each calls for a worker able to understand and accept persons as they are and able to create a positive working relationship between himself and the individual or group. Glasser and Burns say:

Basic to the two direct-practice methods is the worker-client relationship. A distinctive difference between the two methods, however, is that in group work this relationship often takes place in the context of the group, and, further, the practitioner must direct his understanding and interventions not only to individuals but also to the group as a whole and to the interactions among group members. This difference leads to variations in practice. . . .

There are, nonetheless, certain common aspects of this relationship which can be viewed as part of the total process. In both group work and casework the interactional situation between the client and the worker is essentially quasi-contractual. That is, the worker and the client must arrive at some agreed-upon reciprocal expectations concerning the ends and means of the treatment process. In addition, practitioner behavior is guided by professionally determined expectations. For the worker in each method there is an expectation of impartiality, of service ideals, of commitment to the values and ethics of the profession, and of objectivity and professional discipline based upon self-awareness.[14]

In both casework and group work the process is developmental, and programs grow out of the process of interaction between the worker and the individual or group. The ultimate test of either casework or group work is what happens to the individual person.

Coordination between casework and group work services must be motivated by and founded upon a desire on the part of workers to provide the best possible service to individuals, groups and communities. There must be a willingness, on the part of caseworkers, to understand what group workers do and can offer and a willingness, on the part of group workers, to learn about casework programs and the conditions that underlie the use of these programs. A number of different plans of coordination have been in effect. In some agencies caseworkers and group workers are employed as staff personnel. They work with the same general clientele and provide both services when needed. In some situations agencies specializing in casework service work with agencies specializing in group work service and have agreements regarding referrals and staff cooperation. In some communities group work agencies have pooled their resources and have obtained casework consultants on a cooperative basis, sharing the time of a caseworker with several other agencies. Here the caseworker may be a consultant to the group work staff and may do some work with individuals on a casework basis.

In situations in which cooperative programs have been tried, caseworkers have discovered that group workers can provide certain definite things for individuals whose group association needs are not being met. Recreational or leisure-time opportunities can lead to informal education and to satisfying group relations for the client of the caseworker. On the other hand, individuals referred to caseworkers by group workers can get help with their problems which cannot be solved in the group. They can get specialized help from other community services when aided by the caseworker, who has the knowledge, skill, and time to work on an individual basis. Frequently, caseworkers can work with the families of group members who are in need of help at this point. By working closely with the caseworker it is possible for the group worker to make the individual's group experience more meaningful.

The fundamental questions that arise when this subject is investigated are as follows: How can caseworkers and group workers become more conscious of the services each stand ready to render? How can group workers and caseworkers become more sensitive to the individual's need for additional help? How can workers judge the individual's capacity to relate himself successfully to a group or to accept help from casework? When is the individual ready? What points should be kept in mind in preparing the individual for referral? How much interpretation should be done? What kind of continuing cooperative relationships should be established between workers after referrals?

Referral of Individuals to Other Resource Agencies and Workers

The group worker is frequently asked by members of the group: "Where can I get help on my school program?" . . . "What kind of job should I try to get?" . . . "Should I change jobs?" . . . "Where can I get my eyes examined?" . . . "Do you know why there is so much conflict between my mother and me?" Queries of this kind are symptomatic of unmet needs which neither the worker nor the group can do much about in the setting of the group. They call for the referral of the individual to other resources.

Similarly, the group worker often locates persons who seem to have a need for specialized help but who are unaware of it or unable to ask for help. These instances are difficult to handle. No blanket approach will do, because persons are different and their status in the group and with the worker differs. In some cases the group worker may initiate a direct conversation with the individual, saying he has observed what seems to be a need and saying further that there are workers who may be able to help. The extent to which a group worker takes initiative in calling the attention of the individual to his needs and resources depends upon the kind of relationship the worker has with the individual and the timing and circumstances.

No matter whether needs are voluntarily expressed or pointed out by the worker, the process of referral to other resource agencies and workers is a very important one. Referral in social group work is the process of helping an individual in the group become related to another resource. This resource may be a worker within the agency or in another agency. The referral is made for the purpose of providing specific additional service. Designation of referral as a process implies that it has a beginning and an ending. It begins when the group worker and the individual recognize the need for supplementary help from another worker. Following this, there is a joint exploration of available resources and preliminary selection of the specific agency or program. It may be necessary to arrange for a conference with the worker in the receiving agency before the details of the actual referral can be worked out.

A great deal is involved in preparing the individual prior to the definite appointment with the other worker. After the individual and the receiving agency have come together it will be necessary to arrange for a follow-up conference between the group worker and the worker in the receiving agency. Decisions must be made as to which worker will assume primary responsibility and in what manner the workers will cooperate so that their separate approaches are mutually understood.

The details of the referral process will vary in terms of the specific case and specific agencies involved. Certain general principles can, however, be stated as guides to the development of skill in this important area of service.

First, the referral must always be individualized. Each referral is different. Group workers must study the individual and his needs and so interpret the availability of service that it will be voluntarily sought.

Second, the purpose, or aim, of the referral should be clearly understood by the worker, by the individual who is being referred, and by the receiving agency worker. The group worker must be allowed sufficient time for work with the individual and with the receiving agency to define the reason for the referral and to anticipate results. Referral is always a means to an end and that end should be conceived as better service for the person.

Third, to be most effective, referrals should be personalized. When the group worker knows the purpose, function, procedures, and personnel of the agency to which the individual is being referred, he can interpret all of this to the person and make the referral easier and less threatening. Referrals should be made to the worker in the receiving agency by name, at a stated time, and with a written note of introduction if the individual is not known to the new worker.

Fourth, preparation of the individual for referral and preparation of the agency to receive the individual are very important. The group worker should give a general description of the receiving agency and what the individual will find it to be like when he goes. Naturally, workers must avoid committing the receiving agency to any specific service, because they will not know what they can do until they have made a study of the situation. Workers who make referrals should avoid asking the receiving agency for any special privilege or deviation from established policies, procedures and routines they consider necessary for the satisfactory carrying on of their work.

Fifth, the worker should interpret the individual being referred to the receiving agency and should share verbally or by correspondence pertinent information requested by the receiving agency. Churchill observes from the point of vantage of the child guidance agency:

Disturbed peer relationships are among the most frequent symptoms for which children are referred. Diagnosis of the problems of the child should include adequate data about peer difficulties. The traditional model often fails to provide these. Our reporters, parents, teachers and children themselves rarely give a clear picture. Often they give conflicting reports. The individual evaluations clarify why such problems arise in terms of intrapsychic distress but frequently fail to clarify how they are manifested socially and how they create secondary social problems. The group worker can provide additional information. For example, the group report may show that a child behaves in a grossly different manner with children or with children and an adult, than he did when he was seen individually.[15]

Sixth, the group worker should be prepared to work with the group at the point of interpretation, especially when referral means the temporary removal of the individual from the group. Though it is neither necessary nor wise to magnify or place undue emphasis on referrals which have been made, it is far better to discuss the matter with the group in a matter-of-fact way than to permit lack of knowledge to create group anxiety.

And *seventh,* immediately after the referral has been made, the follow-up process should begin. The group worker should take the initiative in determining with the receiving agency worker what kind of continuing cooperation between workers is needed. They should determine mutual and independent responsibility, the kinds of informational reports to exchange, and the frequency of conferences if the case is to continue over a period of time.

When group workers accept the fact of their own limitations and begin to use referral sources to the full, they actually build group work practice beyond the level of *specialization* to the higher level of *integration* that is so essential if the individual is to receive the greatest possible benefit from community services.

NOTES

1. Hans S. Falck, "The Use of Groups in the Practice of Social Work," *Social Casework,* February 1963, p. 65.
2. Emanual Tropp, *A Humanistic Foundation for Group Work Practice* (New York: Selected Academic Readings—a Division of Associated Educational Services Corporation, 1969), p. 4D.
3. Helen Northen, *Social Work with Groups* (New York: Columbia University Press, 1969), p. 25.
4. Alan Klein, *Social Work Through Group Process* (School of Social Welfare, State University of New York at Albany, 1970), p. 53.
5. Tropp, *op. cit.,* p. 4D.
6. Falck, *op. cit.,* p. 66.
7. Ronald A. Feldman, "Group Integration, Intense Personal Dislike and Social Group Work Intervention," *Social Work,* July 1969, p. 30.
8. Walter L. Kindelsperger and Gladys M. Ryland, "The Meaning to the Individual of Participation in Group Life" in *Use of Group Methods in Social Welfare Settings* (New Orleans: Tulane University School of Social Work, 1957), pp. 3–4.

9. Alan F. Klein, "Individual Change Through Group Experience" in *Social Welfare Forum, 1959* (Published for the National Conference on Social Welfare by Columbia University Press, New York, 1959), p. 136.

10. Peter J. Burke, "Authority Relations and Disruptive Behavior in Small Discussion Groups," *Sociometry*, September 1966, pp. 237 ff.

11. Saul Scheidlinger, "Identification, the Sense of Belonging and of Identity in Small Groups," *The International Journal of Group Psychotherapy*, July 1964, pp. 293–294.

12. Louise A. Frey, "Support and the Group: A Generic Treatment Form," *Social Work*, October 1962, p. 38.

13. Grace L. Coyle, "Some Basic Assumptions about Social Group Work" in Marjorie Murphy (editor), *The Social Group Work Method in Social Work Education*, Vol. XI, *Curriculum Study* (Council on Social Work Education, New York, 1959), p. 102.

14. Mary E. Burns and Paul H. Glasser, "Similarities and Differences in Casework and Group Work Practice," *Social Service Review*, December 1963, p. 419.

15. Sallie R. Churchill, "Social Group Work: A Diagnostic Tool in Child Guidance," *American Journal of Orthopsychiatry*, April 1965, pp. 581–582.

7

Group Work With Special Groups

There has been a dramatic increase in the use of social group work with special groups and in special settings. A rich body of experience has been recorded in the literature especially during recent years. Schwartz and Zalba [1] in their comprehensive book describe group practice in such settings as public schools, slum hotels, hospitals, public welfare, trade unions, residential treatment centers for children and prisons. Earlier Konopka [2] wrote an outstanding book on group work in the institution and has recently revised it. Hundreds of articles in the professional journals testify to the fact that social group work has made a major contribution to meeting the special needs of people in a range of settings much wider than the traditional settings where group work practice began.

It should not be surprising that group work has been so valuable to people with special needs. Somers points out:

A small group which is meaningful to its members affords an ideal means and context within and through which individuals can be helped to work on dependence-independence conflicts, to deal with problems of loneliness and loss, to work on problems of identification and self-regard, to master social skills which are crucial to carrying out life tasks in various stages of development, and to develop and practice within a more protected social environment, some of the changes in feeling and action which characterize more adequate and satisfying behavior for the individual and for his society. We know that if the present begins to hold more satisfactions for the individual in relationships which are meaningful to him, he can utilize his strength and energy to give and to live beyond himself. The future for him and for his society becomes not only more tolerable but more inviting.[3]

Thus, all people regardless of their situation or their problems need group experience. And the group can be of help to many people who are in special situations. Furthermore, the group worker can often reach people and provide services that other workers are less able to offer. In addition, the

142

group worker can often team up with other workers to provide more comprehensive services. In some cases the group worker and the caseworker constitute an interrelated prime helping team.

In this chapter we want to present some examples of group work with special groups and in special settings. We want to summarize some of the learnings from these experiences and offer suggestions for many group workers who will work with some of these special groups as they pursue their professional practice.

As one searches the rich accumulation of literature presented over the past decade or so it is evident that the small group is now an accepted medium for helping people in a great variety of situations. One is also struck with the different names given to such work. Many, of course, call it social group work and then attach the setting such as the hospital or the chronological age group such as older persons. Others refer to group therapy and, to a limited extent now, psychiatric group work. Group treatment is often used and so is group counseling. Group education, a long-standing term, is used now and then.

It is sometimes difficult to figure out the differences between these terms. Frequently the difference arises out of the background of the writer. Oftentimes the difference resides in the goal to be accomplished by the project. No matter what name is used in all of the examples, *the group* is primary and through the group with the help of the worker an attempt is made to bring about change in the individual through guided group interaction.

The examples that have been selected for inclusion at this point represent the wide range of opportunities that are now open to group workers. By going directly to the practice reports of these writers it is hoped that learning by the reader will be enhanced and that the experiences reported will be of value to workers who may find themselves in similar situations or with similar problems.

Group Work in a Juvenile Detention Center

Goldberg [4] gives a detailed and analytical account of group work practice in a juvenile detention center. Even though detention centers are short-term care facilities for the children, Goldberg points out that "it is hoped that the detention will be a therapeutic experience designed to begin or continue society's efforts to rehabilitate the offender and prevent recidivism." He outlines the following purposes for the group work program:

1. *It sought to facilitate adjustment to detention.* One goal was to maximize the positive potentials and to minimize the stresses and strains. It goes without saying that the more energy invested by the youngster in fighting detention, the less he has available for utilizing the experience productively. The more that he tends to view the institution and its personnel as punitive and antiyouth, the more difficult it will be for him to utilize the helping resources available. We had no aspirations that we could make the child happy to be detained

but we did hope to assist him to accept as fully as possible the fact of, and the reasons for his detention.

2. *It sought to further diagnostic understanding.* The group workers helped to collect data which might be useful to the court in planning toward the child's future. Not uncommonly, this is a basic purpose of the temporary detention facility. It was hoped that the opportunities for intimate observation of, and participation in, the group living situation would provide an understanding of the child which would not be readily accessible elsewhere. Such diagnostic impressions would complement those collected by other staff and departments.

3. *It sought to contribute to the beginning treatment process.* It was hoped that through the therapeutic handling of individuals in the group-living situation, the children would develop greater insight into the meaning of their peer and adult relationships and further, that they would clarify their value systems as they conflict with the world about them and increase their concern and desire to do something about the factors which have produced delinquent behavior. An integral part of this purpose was the desire to facilitate more active participation by the child in planning that will affect his future. It was thought that as a result of our relationships with the children, they could be helped to see the advantages in more open sharing and active participation with the probation officer and others who were making decisions which would influence their future lives.

4. *It sought to meet normal growth needs.* There was recognition that regardless of the degree of delinquency, these youngsters were in the midst of a crucial developmental phase and that confinement frequently frustrates normal growth needs. The provision of opportunities for choice in some areas of their daily lives, for self-expression and the development of leadership qualities, and for participation in activities that offer a sense of achievement is illustrative of the needs our services tried to meet.

5. *It sought to influence the institutional milieu.* Ways were sought to assist in the development of a climate which facilitated the achievement of over-all objectives. It was obvious that our limited service would have little positive effect unless what we were doing both supplemented and was supplemented by the efforts of the institution as a whole. We sought to participate with others in such a way that the maximum amount of cooperation could be secured.

It is probably clear that this listing of objectives is a mixture of ends and means. The goals of understanding individuals and creating the right agency climate are indispensable means to the end of individual growth and change. We have presented them in this fashion because they seem to flow so naturally from the setting in which they developed. In actual practice, our efforts to understand the children were as much on our mind as helping them to adjust to detention.[5]

Goldberg then goes on to describe several kinds of group services that were developed at the center:

1. *The group as a whole.* The group of primary concern to the staff was the living unit, housing from fifteen to more than thirty members. This group, analogous to a ward or cottage in other institutions, is the one in which the members spend much of their time. It is the child's "family" during his detention, and within it he eats, sleeps, and plays. If his problems and needs are dealt with satisfactorily in this group situation, it is likely that he will make good use of the total institutional experience. In so far as his problems and needs are not met, the reverse may be expected. All the group workers were assigned at least some responsibility for direct work with one living unit. The frequency of contacts varied between two and three sessions weekly.

At the outset, the problem was to establish a professional helping relationship with the youngsters. The group workers described themselves as social workers but differentiated their functions and method from those of the probation officer and the caseworkers within the institution. Frequently, the development of this beginning relationship seemed most achievable through activity-centered program, and, as a result, the students planned activities in which the majority of the children participated. In addition to group discussions, these sessions included active games in the gym, crafts, and a combination of quiet and active games in the living unit. The response to the group workers in these units was almost universally positive. It seemed to make no difference how apprehensive the workers were initially, the youngsters were eager to see them. This points up one of the well-known effects of detention upon adolescents: confinement with little opportunity for free choice produces tension and boredom. Thus the initial response to the workers can be explained by the youngsters' desire for outlets to satisfy normal growth needs.

Within a relatively short time other helping potential began to develop through providing services to the living units directly. Youngsters who were most frightened by detention and most apprehensive about the future began to utilize the [workers] in clarifying these issues for themselves: "Why am I here?" "Why hasn't the probation officer visited?" "Why does he think I shouldn't go home?" "Why can't my parents visit more frequently?" "Why does it take so long?" The more pressing these questions were, and particularly in cases where individuals had not found other staff members with whom they could discuss them, the more use of the workers was made.

As the relationships within the group stabilized, there were additional opportunities for the group worker to participate in the interacting process of the group living situation to achieve certain purposes. There was often much conflict and tension within these groups. In the process of daily life in close proximity, emotions were expressed and displaced in these interpersonal relationships. The group workers handled as much of this as was possible. At points, the best they could do was to set limits on how the conflict could be expressed. At other times, it was possible to explore the conflicts sufficiently so that the individuals involved could completely resolve them.

A major requirement for achieving almost any objective for individuals in groups is the development of a sufficient level of cohesiveness within the group. This opens up potentials which would not otherwise be present. The achievement of an adequate level of cohesiveness within the unit living was an elusive goal of the group work service in this setting. Because of the high rate of turnover and the heterogeneity of several of the living units, it was difficult to find ways to produce the desired group bond. We knew that such "we" feeling might emerge out of the mutual recognition that the group had the potential for meeting members' needs. The group workers struggled to identify the need-meeting potentials of the groups and to make these as explicit as possible to the youngsters. The achievement of this group condition was often influenced significantly by the arrival and departure of youngsters, a factor which the group workers could not control. It was apparent, however, that through the appropriate use of activities, at first largely worker-introduced and then increasingly involving the members of the group in discussion and choices, there began to develop a level of group feeling which might be used to enhance the positive potentials of the group living experience. As the group meant more to the members, it was more likely that isolated youngsters would receive support. Moreover, domineering and manipulative members would be more apt to confront obstacles, in the form of group solidarity, to their efforts narcissistically to use the group. In this connection, it should be noted that the group was the same whether the social group [worker] happened to be the leader or whether it was led by other institutional staff members. As cohesiveness within the group began to develop, it often produced better communication between the group and the staff.

Since the unit group experience represented such a crucial piece of the institutional environment, the group workers attempted to help it serve over-all goals. Their efforts were somehow to relate to this rapidly changing collection of individuals in such a way that they would become a *group*—a significant setting within which the individual's problems might be worked on and his needs met. The workers tried to help the groups to agree that they wanted something (even if it was only a gym period where everyone had a fair chance to participate without fighting) and then to organize themselves to get it. While the specifics varied from unit to unit and worker to worker, this was the essence of the process in working with the unit groups.

2. *Subgroups.* On occasions when the living unit housed more than thirty members, it became extremely difficult to work with the entire group, a factor which was further complicated by heterogeneity along other dimensions. For instance, one of the boys' units included youngsters from eight through fourteen years of age. Wherever it seemed appropriate, an effort was made to work with significant subgroups of units that had already been assigned to one of the group workers. In this boys' unit, during the first semester, one worker met with the entire unit two sessions per week. In the second semester, as the size of the unit increased, it was divided by age, and the worker met with the younger children once a week, the older children once a week, and the entire unit once a week. This made it possible to individualize the members of the group to a much higher degree than had formerly been the case. While to some extent this did impede the development of a group bond, nonetheless it stimulated the development of closer relationships among subgroup members which was especially useful for the younger children and also contributed to their accessibility to other staff.

Another use of subgroups occurred in the older girls' living unit when several girls were awaiting transfer to a state correctional institution. The interim was longer than usual, and eight or nine older adolescent girls were awaiting transfer for several weeks. This created distinctive subgroups and produced a great deal of conflict, with the "uncommitted" children being very much threatened by the "committed" children. The social group worker therefore met with each subgroup separately as well as with the group as a whole. Results similar to those which had occurred with the boys were noted. Communication between the worker, other staff, and the subgroups was markedly facilitated. A much fuller understanding of their responses to this situation was procured. As a result of the expression of their feelings and reactions and the acceptance of them by the institution and its staff, there was some reduction in tension and conflict.

A somewhat different approach was used at one point. It was decided to form a small group of younger boys for whom, it was hypothesized, the detention experience created the greatest stress. The group worker met twice weekly with this group throughout a semester. While the problem of helping the group develop a significant bond was accentuated by the fact that this subgroup was together as a group only when the worker met with them, it was thought that for many of these individuals the experience had made an important contribution. In the first place, it provided an opportunity for them to be separated from the larger group living situation in which adjustment was more complicated. This produced a better opportunity for self-expression and participation in activities which were designed primarily in terms of their developmental stage. Among the products of this group experience was the drainage of tension which developed out of the daily life stresses. A good deal of griping and complaining occurred during the group sessions. As the worker began to understand and handle them it became apparent that these problems often had not been expressed directly to other staff members outside the group. It might be mentioned that this illustrates how a person's location in group and organizational social structures often influences how accessible and responsive he may be to efforts to help him. In this case, the youngsters were apparently so threatened by their group living situation, and so powerless in the larger unit group's social structure, that they had been unable to discuss some problems until this group was formed. To some extent, conflict between the younger and older members was brought into the open and handled by both of the subgroups, the social group worker, and child care personnel. While the "normal" antagonisms between younger and older subgroups living in close proximity were not eliminated, they did seem to be reduced, and the precipitating factors seemed to be better understood by all parties. Some of these youngsters were very much supported by their close relationship with the worker.[6]

Goldberg then offers material on work with individuals and participation in the administrative process. He concludes that the contribution of group work has been highly significant.

Group Work in the Youth Correctional Field

Saleebey [7] in his writing about youth correctional centers places emphasis on work with groups:

The Center's treatment program will consist primarily of problem-solving by each of the living units [groups]. Problems that each person faces—within the Center or outside in the community—are subjected to group analysis and group decision. Every facet of life is examined in searching detail. Attitudes and impressions are challenged as soon as they are expressed. No one can exist in this kind of a situation without deep introspection and the development of a rationale for his attitudes and behavior. . . . In the group-based treatment model, each group is "closed" in the sense that once the group is formed at the very beginning of the program, it maintains its identity as a problem-solving group until its members are discharged from probation or otherwise removed from the program. This "closed" plan allows for continuity in the personal relationships developed during the group's experiences as residents of the Center.[8]

Sidman and Sidman [9] present a detailed and comprehensive report on the use of community volunteers as discussion group leaders for juvenile probationers. They enumerate some of the rationale behind the use of groups and volunteer discussion leaders as follows:

1. No one has all the solutions to adolescents' problems in living; therefore, the burden remains on the individual youngster to search into himself for answers to his problems. But this is a difficult task to accomplish alone. With a good guide or friend to help, most persons, including adolescents, can go far towards resolving day-to-day problems by probing into the whys and where-fores of their own behavior as well as the behavior of significant others.

2. Just learning to verbalize issues gives one skills that can be generalized to other situations, e.g., getting jobs, school problems, and so on.

3. Several opinions on problems discussed provide a coverage of issues not usually found in one-to-one counseling relationships; also, group togetherness and social pressure on one's behavior (both positive and negative) play an important role in groups as they do in the society at large.

4. The chances of missing some of the various subtleties of human behavior and emotions are lessened in a group situation by virtue of the fact that several people are listening and responding to every statement.

5. Adolescents gathered in a discussion group that is led by an accepted adult, are encouraged to explore the ways they are behaving in the group and to develop alternative ways of handling interactions with others in the group and outside of it.

6. Learning how to talk about emotions, such as anger, rather than acting out these emotions, is a skill that can be derived from these groups and applied to everyday living.

7. Learning how to respond to and help others through exchanging advice and ideas can be very helpful in teaching the probationer skills about getting along with people.[10]

Grob and Van Doren [11] give an interesting account of what they call aggressive group work with teen-age delinquent boys at a private institution in the Midwest. They tell about a summer work program in which the boys worked voluntarily in small groups on campus beautification. Even though the work was physically demanding the boys did a tremendous job over the hot summer months because they were given the opportunity to plan their projects, formulate goals, and they could see the tangible results of *their* efforts. Remarkable behavior changes carried over into cottage life and other phases of their life at the institution.

Scarpitti and Stephenson [12] write about the use of small groups in the rehabilitation of delinquents. They call their work guided group interaction, which has been defined as "using free discussion in a friendly supportive atmosphere to re-educate the delinquent to accept the restrictions of society by finding greater personal satisfaction in conforming to social rules than following delinquent patterns." [13] "It is a form of group therapy in which the anticriminal attitudes of the group are internalized by the delinquent as a result of the group's influence upon him. In guided group interaction the major emphasis is on the group and its development as a rehabilitative agent. The role of the trained group leader is to support and guide this development rather than to psychoanalyze or counsel members of this group. This particular version of group therapy has been adopted as the basis of rehabilitative programs in large, custodial institutions as well as at small, residential group centers. However, in the program described [here] it has been extended outside of the residential institution with no apparent loss of effectiveness." [14] At the group residential center described in the article the boys return to their homes each night and remain home during the weekend. Scarpitti and Stephenson go on to say:

> The guided group interaction sessions (with ten boys in the group) are seen as a medium through which each boy becomes aware of and develops insights into his own problems and those of the group. Through face-to-face interaction with his peers, the boy is given an opportunity to understand the motivation for his behavior and the consequences of his deviation. Within this group discussion the boy learns new attitudes that provide him with the proper motive to change his behavior. However, while the guided group interaction sessions are an important part of the therapeutic program they are only one part of it. The total program is looked upon as an integrated whole in which therapy is continually taking place. In this light, the group is seen as a mechanism of change facilitated by the specific program elements, length of stay, and the social relationships which develop within the group.[15]

Group Work With Drug Addicts

Psychologists Kruschke and Stoller [16] make a contribution to group interaction theory in their account of an intensive group experience for drug addicts in a correctional setting. While they would not be apt to consider their work social group work and social group workers would doubtless agree that it is not, what they did is of general significance. They write:

The potential of groups for the possible rehabilitation of antisocial deviants, such as the drug addict, is being recognized increasingly. As a consequence, interaction groups are beginning to play a central role in a variety of programs which have attempted to deal with the addict population. . . . Accelerated interaction is a time-limited form of marathon therapy. Its major characteristic is its dependence upon continuous group interaction over several days. Instead of the conventional form of meeting for an hour or two periodically over an indefinite period, members of an accelerated group are removed from their customary environment and immersed in interaction for several days. Continuous interaction over a prolonged period has a number of consequences. It permits an intensive treatment situation within a relatively brief time. It constitutes an experience which has a profound impact on the individual who goes through it. The degree to which it stands out from the rest of his daily life experiences enhances the special excitement and potential meaning it might have for the participant. . . . Another of the outstanding consequences of such an arrangement is the development of intense involvement of the group members with each other, leading to considerable sharing and a high level of intimacy. For most participants such a group represents their first contact with the possibilities of opening themselves to others in a mutual manner. It represents an experience which affects them in manifold ways, in particular, through firsthand development of closeness and by aiding participants to sense the consequences of their own particular way of moving through the world.[17]

In reviewing the learnings from intensive group experiences with youthful addicts the authors summarize:

The following are some of the immediate consequences of employing the accelerated group as a part of the over-all group program in the therapeutic community atmosphere of the Rehabilitation Center.

1. *An accelerated and increased knowledge of the addicts by the group leaders.* The knowledge is gained through an experience that reduces somewhat the usual staff-inmate distance. This means that the staff is in a position to see the addict in a significantly different light than usual and can have a greater appreciation of the capacities and potentials, as well as limitation of those he is to treat. . . .

2. *A decrease in the staff-addict barrier.* Just as the staff usually learns about the addicts in a very narrow situation, so the addicts built myths about the staff to explain away the specialized role-playing in which they inevitably see them. When the two simultaneous "myth-cultures" become somewhat eroded through the sharing of a mutual experience of the group, barriers are invariably reduced.

3. *An accelerated and increased knowledge of the addicts by the other addicts.* Intimacy develops in the accelerated group situation differently than in the ordinary dormitory friendship in that it is accompanied by unpleasant feedback as well as disagreement over the consequences of actions. Thus, mutual knowledge and involvement breaks out of the usual format which often supports self-destructive behavior.

4. *An accelerated and increased awareness on the part of each addict of*

*what he is doing in the world, the consequences it has for him, the effect
it has on others, and possible avenues of change which are open to him.*

5. *The establishment of a meaningful model of group participation which
the participants are able to transfer into other group situations.* One of the
long-term effects of the accelerated group is that the participants see what is
possible in the accelerated setting and carry their expectations, based on this
experience, back into the regular group program of the institution in which
they participate. Furthermore, they function in an even more straightforward
manner and actively encourage others to do the same in these groups. This
has a definite impact on these groups, changing them significantly in the direction of more honest and immediate participation.

6. *A specific change of attitude by the participants and a more positive outlook in the dormitory setting which results in an increased appreciation and
utilization of the institutional program.*

7. *A significant shortening of the length of time individuals spend in the
institution.* [18]

Group Work in a Women's Prison

Peirce [19] describes a social group work service in a women's prison. He
spells out the underlying philosophy of the program in these words:

For the social group worker the primary client and the basic unit of service
is the group. The group as the unit of social service is used to enable the
individual to enhance his social functioning. . . . The social group worker is
concerned with social reality and its impact on his client. He attempts, through
group experience, to help his client identify and evaluate social reality so the
client can consciously choose to come to grips with reality in the manner most
fitting him. Implicit in this formulation is the group worker's goal of helping
both the group and the individual member function in a responsible manner
acceptable to society. The primary helping forces generated by the use of the
social group work method are: 1) The conscious disciplined use of the
relationship the worker has with group members. 2) The helping potential
available in the relationships the members have with each other. These . . . may
provide valuable individual support, help with measuring and defining social
reality, and other growth-producing stimuli. 3) The help that comes from the
"group as a whole." In particular, the elements of personal support, individual
status, and the help in testing and evaluating new ways of relating and adapting
are crucial. Furthermore, as the group member experiences satisfactory social
relationships within the group he is able to try out these patterns of social
functioning outside of the group while the group continues to provide the
social laboratory for further interpersonal experimentation. This focus on the
meaning of the group as a separate and distinct entity is probably the feature
that most distinguishes social group work from other helping processes used
with groups. The social group worker purposefully focuses on developing
group identity, group bond, group "esprit de corps" and group standards and
controls. As group members develop a sense of the group as something more
than a collection of individuals interacting they are able to use this identifica-

tion with the group as a force for modifying their own behavior and attitudes. Often one is able to risk change or growth because "the group is behind me." [20]

Peirce goes on to point out:

Any program of group services must be based on the solid foundation of a well structured program of individual services. With this in mind, the following functions of the group work program were postulated:

1. It would provide a specific helping service to some prisoners in need of help who were unable or unwilling to seek help individually. . . . The specific group social service offered was aimed at helping group members with their problems around their placement in a maximum security cottage.

2. It would provide help in identifying some of the prisoners in particular need of individual help.

3. It would help develop greater staff awareness of inmates in need of help.

4. It would, for some, provide the stimulus to seek individual treatment.[21]

After reviewing the experience with the group Peirce said:

One of the results, at least temporary, of participation in the group was reduction in tensions and acting-out behavior. It would be shortsighted, though, to see the goals of such a group as confined to the essentially limited one of adaptation and adjustment to the prison structure. Beyond these, members used the group sessions to experiment with and develop new modes of social behavior. They were able also to use them as means of projecting themselves beyond the self-defeating, vicious circle of griping and acting out. Members related not only satisfactory achievement but achievement beyond the minimal, such as exceeding work quotas, job promotion, and moving out of themselves to help others. In other words, there was evidence that experiences in the group were enhancing the social functioning of its members to the extent that clear signs of developing social responsibility were observed in the behavior of group members.[22]

Forthun and Nuehring [23] present a rich account of group work in a maximum security prison for men. They point out the values of the program and offer suggestions for the further development of this work.

Group Work With Wives of Police Officers

The Department of Police in a western city conducted a series of small group meetings with the wives of police officers "to expose the wives to the specific problems encountered by police officers in their roles as members of the criminal justice system, specifically, members of law enforcement agencies. . . . The [experimental] group was created in view of the high divorce rate presently among police officers. Feeling that the demands of the job places unusual stress on marital and family relationships, the architects of the course . . . saw a need to improve communication and understanding between officers and their wives regarding the nature of the officer's job. . . . To achieve the objectives of improved communication and understanding they . . . sought to create an atmosphere where the unique problems of the wives could be shared and accepted, thus helping the wife to adjust to the radical changes in home life which result in her husband's appointment." [24] Wives who participated agreed that they had received much by sharing their concerns with others in a similar situation.

Group Work With Relatives of Alcoholics

Bailey [25] reports on the group work being done with relatives and friends of alcoholics:

Al-Anon is a fellowship for relatives and friends of alcoholics, similar in philosophy, structure, and program to the related and better known fellowship of Alcoholics Anonymous. Most Al-Anon members are wives of male alcoholics, although many groups include a few men who are husbands of alcoholic women, as well as other relatives. The drinker may or may not still be drinking, and he may or may not be a member of A.A. According to their own statement of purpose, Al-Anon members "are banded together to solve their common problems of fear, insecurity, lack of understanding of the alcoholic, and of warped family relationships associated with alcoholism. [26]

After studying the program it was found:

The probability of the husband's affiliating with A.A. and beginning to recover from his alcoholism was increased when the wife participated in Al-Anon. Her attitudes appeared to be less condemning and she had gained greater freedom in discussing her husband's illness. The emphasis on alcoholism as a combined mental and physical illness, which characterized the Al-Anon women, is not only in accord with current medical knowledge, but also reflects a reduction in moralistic interpretations and the sense of shame that have contributed to past feelings of despair. Mental illness is still heavily stigmatized in our culture. Inclusion of a physical component makes alcoholism more concrete and treatable, and the outcome more hopeful. [27]

Group Work With the Alienated Child

Kolodny [28] has written a comprehensive article based on his rich experience as director of group work for a children's service association. He tells about the impact of peer group activity on the alienated child. His use of the phrase alienated child "is intended to convey the notion that the child is usually not simply forced into isolation by others, but contributes to his rejection by them and may indeed seek such rejection." [29] He goes on to say:

We are aware that alienated youngsters are found in a number of different clinical categories. Our contribution to their total treatment—and many of these youngsters are receiving individual help from caseworkers or psychiatrists —is rather single-minded and, in one sense, unvaried. It consists of providing them with a social club experience with their peers under a social work-trained leader. Through facing the demands of peer group interaction, such as self-confrontation, sharing, and the rewards it offers, freedom of self-expression, group support during anxiety-provoking experiences and the like, the social club experience is intended to help alienated youngsters to discover that their characteristic defense of flight is not necessary, and that emotional closeness to their fellows need not be feared. My own feeling is that given professional leadership, or leadership under professional supervision, a children's activity group, whether it be for disturbed, mildly disturbed children, or those who are functioning relatively well, can offer certain helpful emotional experiences which are important to all children. These include: gratification of emotional needs for status; the opportunity to establish close relationships with peers and to correct distortions in perceptions of peers; the opportunity for the release of some feelings that otherwise have to be controlled, with nonpunitive consequences; the experience of receiving ego support, through acceptance and limitations reasonably applied from a relatively objective adult; the opportunity for social testing and for the discovery of social strengths from emotional interchange, leading to an increase in social skills; the chance to increase the range of one's modes of expression through observation of peers who become models for identification and to find substitute modes of gratification through an enlarged repertoire of play skills; increased self-awareness and understanding of the possible implications of maladaptive behavior; the opportunity to master anxiety-producing situations by utilizing the support of the group; and the opportunity through the assimilation of groups' norms to modify one's system of controls, either by relaxing overly severe controls or by developing controls which were previously lacking.[30]

Kolodny points out that group work has a different aim than group psychotherapy:

It is concerned with fostering cohesive tendencies in groups. We help members organize and structure the group experience. Considerable attention is devoted to the cooperative planning of the activities, the decision-making process, and the mastery of social and/or physical skills. As a result, the social group worker may assume a variety of roles, such as teacher of skills, program adviser, or mediator. In general, he is more active than the group psychotherapist in initiating activities, guiding group interaction, and limiting the amount of acting out. In our agency we are more concerned with individualization and less with group goals than in, let us say, the usual group work agency, settlement house, or community center which may serve relatively normal youngsters. We share with the group psychotherapist an intense concern with the psychodynamics of each member's behavior. However, unlike the group therapist, who, by design, does not actively involve himself in programming, we try—by no means always successfully—to use whatever understanding of psychodynamics we possess in helping the group to plan its activities.[31]

Kolodny details the goals for one group in the following discussion.

What are our workers in these activity groups trying to do with the disturbed youngsters we serve? Consider our experience with a group made up entirely of alienated youngsters who were responding poorly to the conduct, academic, or socializing requirements of a school system in a nearby suburb. Below is a statement of goals developed by the worker and his description of his role during the three-year service effort:

"My operational objectives [he wrote] were as follows: with those whose sense of helplessness was at once concealed by and reflected in their tendency to attack, project, and deny, I wanted to help them to discover and experience their own abilities to make a friendly or hostile world for themselves; for this reason it was essential to try to help them to own their own actions and feelings. Since all of the boys had weak or absent fathers and overpowering mothers who were hostile to their growing up and toward any displays of appropriate masculine assertiveness that might accompany it, I wished to provide them with a different perspective on aggression and some motivation to risk themselves in competition. I sought to create those conditions—the company of peers on a regular basis, the availability of gratifying activities and attention from an inquiring, challenging, yet supportive adult—under which each member could achieve some mastery over physical tasks and social events in the presence of what has been called "a validating audience." I wanted also to actively reinforce any willingness on the part of a member to hazard an investment in the making and keeping of friends.

"The role which I as a group leader took in attempting to implement these objectives was an active one, designed to retard rather than elicit a great deal of regression, and directed at members' capacities to judge and to learn from current experiences rather than toward their reliving and working through in direct fashion, feelings connected with earlier trauma." [32]

Group Work With Street-Corner Girls

Ackley and Fliegel [33] described their work with adolescent girls of a special youth program in a large eastern city. This was an experimental method of street-corner social work to reach girls as well as boys. They said, "Teen-agers use the street corner as an extension of their living room. They gather outside rather than in an overcrowded home where parents or siblings may listen or bother them. On the corner there is room for everyone; there they can be independent of their parents, and there they can learn the skills of social interaction." [34] In establishing their identity as a social worker they said, "Essentially it involved 'hanging' on the corner with the teen-agers—listening, occasionally joining the conversations, and sitting in the local candy store, drinking Cokes and listening to the jukebox." [35] They also found that "in the area of programming, the worker had to be much more active in presenting new ideas to the girls than was necessary with the boys. The girls' lack of immediate interest in a girls' club or a ball team made it more difficult to offer them concrete services or interest them in new program ideas. At first the worker was primarily a passive observer within the 'hanging' [around] activity. Sitting, eating, watching the girls dance—often with each other—gossiping, listening to records or [viewing] TV, and being on hand while watching the boys, were all considered program and were most common at first in our work. After three or four months, the worker with the group of thirteen- and fourteen-year-old girls was able to interest them in forming a club and engaging in such activities as using the tape recorder, cooking, eating, paperbag dramatics, sociodrama, finger painting, movies, clay, aggressive games with a minimum of organization, bowling and trips." [36] They discovered that "with extremely hostile and suspicious girls, establishing a relationship with them through the group seemed most successful. They need the security of the group, its support in testing the worker, and group approval before beginning to trust the worker and use her more effectively on an individual basis. The worker needs to be flexible, moving from group to individual and back again as the need arises. The older girls especially need and want individual help, and this should be the goal. There needs to be more than weekly contacts with these girls. The worker needs to be more verbal, active and available in the neighborhood, where they are most comfortable. She needs to be able to respond in an appropriate manner to what they feel to be crisis situations." [37]

Group Work With Adolescents at a Psychological Services Center

Braverman,[38] writing from her perspective as a social worker at a center for psychological services, describes the importance of the informal peer group as an adjunct to treatment of the adolescent. Because many adolescents with serious behavior problems had difficulty in entering into a casework relationship at the guidance center they set up a loosely structured lounge program where boys and girls who had individual interviews scheduled could drop in before or after their interview sessions. She says:

We decided to structure the group program loosely rather than make it a club because we wanted to avoid any element of coercion or exclusiveness. We felt that participation in the group must be completely voluntary and strictly fun. This was important because the youngsters had no choice about coming to the center for their individual sessions since their parents had insisted on it. To give the youngsters a sense of freedom the lounge room door was left open and the program was unplanned and spontaneous. . . . The role of the group worker was simply to make the young adolescent clients feel comfortable in the group, to help them mingle, and to protect the weaker members from any viciousness on the part of the stronger. There were games lying about and blackboards on the walls. Occasionally someone brought a guitar, but most of the youngsters' time in the lounge was spent in chatting. We succeeded in creating the casual, light atmosphere we wanted, in making the youngsters feel they could just sit around and talk if they wanted to, play a game of bingo or hangman if they wanted to, or go out for a snack together if they wanted to. . . . Feelings of anxiety, guilt, and fear were particularly strong among the young adolescents. Added to their age-specific feelings of this kind were anxiety at having to face the fact that serious problems had made it necessary to come to the clinic, embarrassment at being singled out from among their peers at school, and fear of the adult worker. These youngsters' associations with their peers in the group program helped alleviate these anxieties and fears at the outset of treatment. Meanwhile, the workers maintained casual relationships with them, discussing only subjects that were not emotionally tinged and often playing games with them. We relied on the sense of identification and the support provided by the group experience to keep the young adolescents from bolting from treatment at the start. After a time, they came to trust their individual workers, and casework treatment could begin. During the second phase of treatment there was a greater focus in the individual sessions on daily incidents that made the clients "feel bad." Though little attempt was made at developing insight in the youngsters, lest their anxiety be increased, the workers' focus on their problems was, of course, threatening. The group again provided them with the support they needed to be able to tolerate the shift in treatment: though their relationships with one another were not close enough at this stage to provide a basis for verbal support, the mere fact that they liked each other dispelled the threatening feeling that they were "kooks." The next stage in the clients' use of group came when the quality of their relationships with their workers changed. As they began to feel closer to the workers, they became more able to talk about painful things and were gradually helped to develop some insight into their behavior. Frightened by this experience, our adolescent clients at different times and in different ways (in actions or in words) used the group to give vent to feelings of anger at their individual workers. They also gained support by talking with other members of the group about their experiences in handling their everyday problems; for example, homework, parental controls, relationships with the opposite sex, spending money, and so forth. Thus they were able to allay some of the anxiety about themselves that was aroused in the individual sessions. When threatening subjects came up again in their individual sessions, they were readier to work them through. . . . In addition to the therapeutic experiences the adolescents had with their individual workers, the experience of being in a group had value for them in itself. It gave them an opportunity to develop social skills in a protected setting. The group worker helped the isolate to mingle more easily, did not allow the more aggressive members of the group to intimidate the more timid, and encouraged any signs of leadership. . . . The goal of the lounge program had been achieved; not one of the young adolescents in our caseload left treatment.[39]

Group Work With Mentally Retarded

Gershenson and Schreiber [40] report on their pioneer efforts in social group work with mentally retarded teen-agers in a large city. They review eleven years of decentralized community-based program for these youngsters. They point out:

Children learn to live with others only through group experience. However, the retarded child is often caught in a vicious spiral that is negative and limiting to his social development. The lack of social experiences leads to social retardation and ineptness in chronologically appropriate social skills, accompanied by emotional difficulties arising from feelings of rejection and deprivation; and the lack of social skills further limits the opportunities the retardate has of participating in social experiences. Mentally retarded children must be taught many things which normal children learn spontaneously or incidentally. Often they must be taught to play and to be helped in developing creative qualities that give them fun and pleasure. When this has been achieved the retardate can gain the same satisfactions from participating in social activities as other people. These satisfactions derive from: a) being recognized and accepted in the group situation; b) a sense of accomplishment in activities in which he is successfully interacting with his peers; c) the experience of self-expression, especially when making positive contributions to the group's activities; d) the enhancement of self-esteem; e) and the feeling of belonging.[41]

Gershenson and Schreiber then spell out five purposes for the group work program:

1. A medium of enjoyment for mentally retarded children and youth.
2. A setting which will aid them in social adjustment—one which provides a small, intimate, face-to-face experience with others of the same age, including members of the opposite sex.
3. Experiences to help them develop simple, useful skills that they can carry over to the home, to the community, and perhaps to employment.
4. Experiences to help them accept themselves and the limitations imposed by their retardation, as well as to utilize their capacities to increase their feelings of self-worth.
5. A means of freeing parents for a few hours weekly of the supervision of the retardate and of helping them to carry over into the home and community attitudes that will promote increased independence in their children.[42]

From their experience they draw general observations on group work with the retarded as follows:

1. Retardates, like other individuals, can be expected to react differently to group experiences. . . .
2. The individual's needs take precedence over the group's needs. . . .
3. Program is planned to provide individuals with opportunities to experience success. . . .
4. Expectations of the level of an individual's performance must vary in relation to the intellectual, social, and emotional aspects of behavior. . . .
5. Group activities must be carefully selected to suit the functioning level of the group.[43]

Mandelbaum [44] writes about the group process in helping parents of retarded children.

Using the group process to help parents is an increasing clinical practice in service to the mentally retarded. The worker who attempts the process must be skilled in dealing with persons in one-to-one interviews, preferably before he attempts to deal with them in groups. If he chooses the group method because he is discontented with the one-to-one method he should know that in trying to help individual parents through group process he takes on a task of greater complexity, one requiring an understanding of the dynamics not only of individual behavior, both normal and abnormal, but also of the behavior of groups.[45]

Beck [46] has prepared a brilliant guide for working with the closed, short-term group as a treatment adjunct for parents of mentally retarded children. Her very complete treatment of the subject is a substantial contribution to the literature.

Schreiber and Feeley [47] describe group work with the brothers and sisters of the mentally retarded in a richly detailed article. They show how experience in such groups helps these siblings to understand better the situation in which the retarded youngster finds himself.

Group Work in the Field of Rehabilitation

Citing an extensive body of literature from the field of rehabilitation, Gust [48] concludes:

Group work or group counseling can be employed in almost any situation and with any type of disability group or client problem. In addition, the practice of group counseling as with individual counseling, appears to have shifted from emphasis upon treatment applied to the individual to client self-help and personal responsibility. This sense of personal responsibility can be fostered through various group procedures. . . . Groups provide the opportunity for members to learn from each other through sharing ideas, common concerns, and possible solutions to problems. Being able to share fears and apprehensions with others is helpful because of the cathartic effect—getting it off one's chest—and because of assuring group members that they are not alone, that others have similar or worse problems than they do. Because of positive peer pressure, individual group members often develop better personal appearance and habits and begin helping one another by listening empathetically and giving realistic suggestions.[49]

Gust then stresses the importance of the professional worker:

The first step in developing a positive emotional climate is taken by the counselor. As he relates with the individual and the group, he must help them become aware of their feelings toward each other and about themselves. As each person is helped by the leader to express his feelings about himself, it provides a real contribution or commitment to the group and enables the members to learn more about each other. This process of sharing real feelings with each other provides the basis for further movement within the group.

To the extent that individual members are honest with and accept each other they will achieve a level of functioning allowing them to begin working effectively. Once the relationship has been formed, the group can begin to work together toward the consideration or solution of the common problem. For example, in a group focusing on getting along on the job, the members can share positive and negative experiences, fears, apprehensions, as well as ideas and plans, without fear of retaliation or hostile criticism from group members. In addition to being accepting of one another, members will be more receptive of materials and information made available by the group leader. When problems arise within the group they can be worked through if members follow the initial process of openness toward each other combined with warmth and acceptance. These general steps illustrate the cycle involving relationship development, problem solving, relationship maintenance, and eventual group dissolution when tasks have been completed. . . . The process of group interaction and movement provides members with an example and an experience of working together in a group. This experience for many members is their first in a positively functioning group and gives them a model for future action in their own social, work, and home groups. Learning these positive relationships in the group counseling setting can often facilitate changes in the member more quickly than individual counseling, since reality testing with associates is constantly available. Between meetings the individual may be willing to try out new techniques learned in the group. This speeds up the change process. The individual counseling experience can also be enhanced by allowing the individual to try some of his ideas in a protective yet "lifelike" group setting.[50]

Group Work in Residential Treatment

In his discussion of social group work in residential treatment Maier says:

The group, as an arena for trying out and living out *new experience,* becomes especially relevant in residential treatment. Residential treatment serves individuals who cannot benefit from ordinary reflective and relationship therapy, otherwise they could have been helped through some form of out-patient treatment. For these clients the essence of therapy becomes located in the series of experiences they find within the residential treatment program. For them treatment is anchored in the experiences of discovering the consequences of behavior and actual effective coping with the tasks before them. Social group work efforts become especially relevant, because in group work the worker is preoccupied with the activities of the group and with the opportunities for each group member to demonstrate to himself and in the presence of others his actual competence and his questions about areas of incompetence. Group experiences can become the most vital resource for ego development.

Different role of the group worker. Social group workers function in different roles in institutional settings. The multiplicity of their professional functions suggest that they need to continue to examine and define their special task for themselves and their colleagues. If a social group worker is called on to function as a supervisor of group living staff, training specialist, or administrator, he will undoubtedly bring to bear this specialized knowledge. His professional alignment remains with social work; his professional functions, however, are those of a supervisor, teacher, or administrator, whichever is demanded of the particular situation. Most important, he does not practice social group work within any of these tasks just outlined. . . .

In social group work practice, as in all social work intervention in general and in residential treatment specifically, the social group worker utilizes the social group work method in order to engage his clients and himself in a purposeful group experience. His objective is to enhance the social functioning of each client preventively and rehabilitatively. The social work group provides the worker with his arena of practice. By means of the group sessions the worker introduces conditions in and through the group that serve as intervening, that is, associate, experiences to each client's ongoing life experience and his family, peer, school, work, and/or other community life. The content and focuses of the group worker's intervening activities in any setting are based on three major considerations:

1. The nature of the clientele who, with the worker, make up the group.
2. The context in which the group experience proceeds.
3. The formation and acceptance of treatment objectives by the worker and his clients.

In brief, social group work intervention is based on each client's personal circumstances, the circumstances of the social group work experience, and the continuous understanding about the intervening group experience as a means in context for effecting change within each client's personal life situations.[51]

Out of her experience and research in group work in residential treatment centers Konopka says:

The group worker's present functions in treatment centers seem to be:
1. Participation as a responsible member of the clinical team in observation of the child and helping with diagnosis, using his particular skill of observation of individuals in group interaction.
2. Giving direct services to the children through work with therapy (activity and discussion) groups and with representative groups of children, such as house councils.
3. Supervision and coordination of the group living situation by working closely with house parents or group counselors.
4. Work with parent groups when possible.[52]

Kirby summed up eight ways in which the group worker could be of service in the institutional setting:

Some of the major areas of professional service which a professional group worker is prepared to offer in the institution are briefly:
1. The direct practice of social group work with small groups of clients or patients.
2. Working with other staff members toward helping them understand the group process.
3. Sharing with other staff members the group worker's observations and recommendations with reference to individual and group behavior.

4. Sharing with other staff members the group worker's observations and recommendations with regard to social climate and group living factors in the institution.

5. Analyzing the need for and recommending the formation of various kinds of groups to meet the needs of the individual clients of the agency.

6. Assuming the responsibility as a professional group worker for helping to maintain the limits and standards of the agency.

7. Accepting responsibility for co-ordinating and enriching the recreational program along with supervising and training recreational staff and volunteers.

8. Interpreting the agency program to the community through contacts with volunteer groups, community agencies, service clubs and similar organizations.[53]

Group Work With Foster Parents and Children

There are many reports on the use of group methods with foster parents and children.

Watson and Boverman [54] offer a thoughtful analysis of experiences with preadolescent foster children in group discussions. They started the groups to "learn more about foster children and their problems." The eight- to twelve-year-olds revealed their feelings about being foster children and it became easier for the agency staff to help them adjust to their situation as foster children.

Mills, Sandle and Sher [55] describe the process of developing a discussion group with a selected number of foster mothers of latency-age children. In establishing the foster mothers' training group the following goals were stated:

1. Develop a sense of camaraderie among the mothers through increased communication and exchange of opinions, resulting in improved morale.

2. Instill a sense of loyalty to the agency through participation in what might be viewed as staff functions; increase realization of foster mothers that they are functioning as extended staff of the agency.

3. Give emotional support and recognition for the child-rearing services offered by these mothers.

4. Enhance child care skills through group discussion and contact with group leaders; encourage a problem-solving attitude in child rearing, and the habit of seeking advice when needed.

5. Give more efficient surveillance of mothering practices by foster families than would be provided by home visits with caseworkers; such direct "feedback" from foster mothers would then aid in adjusting agency policies in the interests of the mothers and their children.

6. Teach group methods to the children's Home staff to broaden their professional skills and encourage use of group techniques.[56]

Mills, Sandle and Sher then go on to say:

Twelve mothers with latency-age children in their care were selected initially. It was felt those selected were the ones who might benefit most from a group experience. The age of the foster children was chosen as the main basis for organization, since this might furnish a common focus of concern for the group.[57]

The writers tell about the many items that came up in the discussions:

The variety and complexity of child care issues generated for discussion within the group was somewhat surprising and quite stimulating to the group leaders. The spontaneous discussion of so many issues certainly reflected the concern and dedication of these foster mothers and their charges and seemed to justify the initiation of the mothers' group to help resolve child-rearing problems.

The quick response of the mothers to the discussion group appeared to reflect their desire for recognition as a resource of the agency, and, in fact, many of our foster mothers were "senior staff" in both age and child-rearing experience. . . . Information on a foster child's background was supplied by the [agency] at the time of placement. The mothers felt they were in the dark about child-rearing strategy under such circumstances, and requested more information about the natural parents, previous foster placements, and the intellectual and emotional prognosis of children placed in their care. The motivation behind such questions seemed to be the mothers' concern about the degree of responsibility they should be prepared to assume for the progress of their charges. There was recurrent discussion of the effects of heredity on a child, and the relative effects of early trauma on children. In all such discussions could be seen the deep desire of the mothers to have a realistic yardstick for measuring their success or lack of it, and to understand the limitations that early trauma or heredity might produce in their children.[58]

In summing up their experience, Mills, Sandle and Sher say:

Formation of a foster mothers' group to discuss child-rearing issues was initiated as a supplement to existing caseworker home visits in a private children's agency. Twelve planned sessions were conducted by a casework supervisor and psychologist, assisted by a recorder-summarizer who recapitulated the content of each session at the close of each 1½-hour meeting. Objects of the discussion were to create a climate of loyalty and involvement of the mother with the agency, increase morale through better communication among the mothers, share experiences in child rearing to provide a higher level of mothering skill, provide improved supervision of foster care by staff, and provide the [agency] staff with a demonstration of group process methods to broaden their professional skills.

Experience with the first foster mothers' training group has provided significant feedback on foster care policies of the agency, increased communication between foster mothers and agency, heightened morale and indentification, and provided an important sounding board for the mothers to test out and check their child-rearing practices. Continuation of these groups is planned with increased staff participation.[59]

Doll wrote up the experience a large eastern city public child welfare agency had with a series of group meetings of foster parents. Among the learnings she reported were:

1. Foster parents who felt threatened by their neighbors' negative attitude toward foster care have gained a feeling of support from identifying with each other as members of a group.

2. Foster parents who have been hostile and difficult to work with in a one-to-one relationship have been willing to discuss their problems of child management with other foster parents.

3. In general, the participating foster parents have gained perspective on their foster-care problems through learning about the problems of other foster parents.

4. The foster parents have often worked out ways together of handling the typical behavior problems of childhood and adolescence.

5. Some of the participating foster parents have formed friendships with each other that have led to friendships between their foster children.[60]

Hanwell sees many values for foster parent groups. He writes:

For foster parents, participation in [group] education groups contributes to several areas of their development. The group experience helps them gain a sense of identity as foster parents. They learn from each other and feel less isolated when problems arise. They begin to discover that some difficulties which they encounter with foster children are typical rather than a reflection of their own inadequacy.

Knowledge of child development and of the special needs of foster children helps the foster parents to understand the children placed with them, and contributes to development of skill in coping with children's feelings and behavior when they first come to the foster parents' home. They gain some understanding of natural parents and the problems leading to placement of children.

Foster parents become more aware of their own roles as they learn about the over-all welfare program and the place of child welfare in it, as well as policies pertaining to public and private agencies. As they understand the agency and its complexities as well as the reasons for its policies, they begin to identify with the agency and their criticism of the agency becomes more constructive. Foster parents' identification with the agency seems to result in less turnover of foster parents and a reduction in replacement of children.[61]

Stanley evaluates the first meeting of a group of prospective foster parents as follows:

In our evaluation of this meeting, we felt that the following had been accomplished:

1. The responsibility of the agency had been established.
2. A positive identification with the agency's goals and staff was begun.
3. An understanding of the importance of the foster parents' job with the agency was started.

4. A beginning movement toward seeing the needs of children above the immediate request for children was stimulated.

5. Some factual aspects of foster care had been made clear.

6. Some indirect teaching of how to be foster parents was accomplished.

7. The importance and expectation of foster father were stressed.

8. Expectations of self-involvement had been set up.

9. Some people would reject foster parenthood.

At the end of this meeting there were some who stood together, talking. A few questions were asked of staff members. The tone was exciting, friendly, and an air of anticipation pervaded.[62]

Stanley goes on to say:

In the use of this method, we feel there must be trust and respect among the staff. Each must fulfill his own role comfortably. The leader should be willing to find his way with a group. We do not feel that he or she must have group work experience, but he must have knowledge about foster care and conviction about people's ability to involve themselves in a discussion about it. We further feel that the applicants should enjoy the meetings. We have purposefully used the change-of-pace technique. We have used lightness, even to emphasize a serious point. We have especially used a light touch to desensitize a point. This lightness does not in any way reflect the main theme, which is quite serious, and which the applicants recognize fully. We have trained the Supervisor of the Foster Care Unit in this district to use this method. We have flown in a supervisor from another district to observe a series of meetings and plan to help her use the method in her district.

We believe that the quality of these homes surpasses the quality of other foster homes in this district. We have continued to use this method of study in this district exclusively, and our subsequent observations are similar. Five series of meetings have been held. However, we are certain we have lost some good applicants because they would not or could not come to the meetings. We may have lost them in any event. We will never know. We do know we have gained excellent homes. Whether these foster parents could perform their duties as well if we had used the more traditional method of study, we also will never know. We earnestly believe it is a method which could profitably be explored further, for we are of the opinion that some life energies have been freed. This energy is being expended creatively with the children. To us, this is the true test.[63]

Carter [64] tells how the division of foster home care in a large city department of social services added group services for adolescent foster children.

From the outset, the division saw the program as a way to help adolescent children in foster care solve their problems through the group method. Its objectives were to help them overcome the difficulties they were having with their foster parents, teachers and other school authorities, and community authorities. . . . The division hoped that as the adolescent foster children solved some of their problems they would develop better relationships with their foster parents and other adults and that improvement in this direction would carry over to a better use of their caseworkers' services.[65]

They organized six groups, one of fourteen- to fifteen-year-old girls, one of sixteen- to seventeen-year-old girls, three of fourteen- to fifteen-year-old boys, and one of sixteen- to seventeen-year-old boys. The groups met biweekly September through June after school at the agency or in other community resources. Groups averaged eight to twelve members in size. Carter warns that "group work with adolescent foster children offers no short cut to an agency. On the contrary, group work creates the need for more services. As the group [workers] listen to and learn from the adolescent foster children, they gain new insight. This new knowledge has been invaluable to the division in its attempts to match its services to the needs of adolescents." [66] Carter saw real value in the groups. "The climate of the group, which lends itself to the development of self-confidence in the adolescent and trust in the leader, has definite carry-over into life. Through the group, many adolescent foster children are now able to handle some of their unresolved feelings concerning their natural parents and as a result, have better relations with their foster parents." [67]

Goldstein [68] reports on seven years of experience with group programs for foster parents in a voluntary agency. These groups were designed to improve the competence of foster parents and enhance their status within the agency. A study of the experience "identified ten major points that would have to be kept in focus in developing and operating an expanded group program:

1. Staff members have to be available to the foster parent groups on a sustained basis.

2. The staff members have to be flexible enough about their working time to participate in evening meetings or Sunday events.

3. Agency suggestions about programming cannot be imposed on the foster parents but can only be introduced as the foster parents are ready for them.

4. Out of respect for their "quasi-professional" status, the foster parents must be encouraged to assume responsibility for planning and handling their meetings.

5. To function adequately as "quasi-professional" persons, the foster parents need to have a complete picture of the agency's operations and some knowledge of the other child welfare programs in the community.

6. Because foster-parenting is a speciality for which formal training has not been developed, one goal of a group program must be to teach the participants how to fulfill better their role as foster parents.

7. Participation in a group program can help foster parents who have few opportunities for socialization compensate for this deficiency by giving them a closer identification with the agency and the broader community of child welfare services than they had when they became foster parents.

8. Through participating in programs with other couples who are caring for foster children, foster parents—who often feel isolated in their work with

children—can come to see the problems of foster children and their natural parents in broader perspective.

9. All foster parents cannot be expected to participate in the group activities, but in order not to cause confusion for those who do, communication needs to be kept open between the caseworkers in charge of the group activities and the caseworkers who work individually with foster parents.

10. The principle of confidentiality of information must be respected in regard to children and foster parents, although in group activities the foster parents will inevitably come to know a good deal about each other.[69]

Group Work With Unwed Mothers

Barclay [70] describes a group approach to young unwed mothers in which a public assistance agency, a settlement house, and a family service agency demonstrated effective collaboration in a family life education program. In the eastern city she wrote about, "There was a particular need for reaching out to the great number of unmarried women living in the area alone and away from home . . . many young unmarried pregnant women and mothers in the area were without family ties but also acutely unfamiliar with the community and almost completely socially isolated." [71] In writing about the group that was established she said, "As the meetings continued and I began to uncover the concerns and needs of the young women in the group it became my goal to offer them an experience that would bring them and their children into the community from which they felt so much apart. A great deal of time has been devoted to helping them become aware of resources within the community and enabling them to make effective use of them. Much has been effected through group discussion, as the mothers have exchanged ideas and experiences and supported and encoraged one another." [72]

Barclay went on to declare:

Various elements in the group process and experience . . . contributed to the gradual development of feelings of self-worth on the part of these young women. To begin with, they were listened to and their worries and feelings were carefully elicited. As common concerns to all were identified and focused on, there developed a phenomenon that is universally observed in such discussion groups; one young woman would speak of a problem that seemed to her unique; another group member would expand on the same problem or one just as worrisome; and finally, someone would remark in surprise and with some relief that she no longer felt so alone and different from other people. The discovery by group members of the universality of human problems and the concurrent feelings of helplessness, anger, guilt, remorse, or despair is one of the principal phenomena in group experience that serves to mitigate disabling feelings of personal inadequacy and to create a common bond among group members. Even so, as the young mothers began to share experiences, it became clear that not everyone was at precisely the same point in ability to respond appropriately to problems and to deal with them. The mothers began to learn from one another as I continued to elicit ideas and to expand on them out of my knowledge and experience. As I identified and pointed out the underlying concerns that often were expressed in veiled terms, they became more available for consideration. After a while a feeling of group solidarity or cohesiveness became something almost palpable, expressing itself in a variety of ways. The group members began to discover strengths they had not known they had. Through a process of identification with me and with one another they began to try their wings, giving one another both challenge and support. The experience of speaking up in a group and being listened to with interest and respect and of having suggestions or ideas referred to in a subsequent session as having been helpful or at least thought-provoking clearly enhanced their self-confidence.[73]

Group Work in Adoption

Group work has been used successfully in the child welfare field of adoption. Chappelear and Fried [74] write about helping adopting couples come to grips with their new parental roles. They describe an agency's experience in holding group discussion with couples who had already had children placed in their homes. Biskind [75] describes the group method in services to adoptive parents. Sacks analyzes the group method in services to foster parents and preadoptive children.[76] Dillow remarks that "the two adoption agencies with which I have worked in the last several years are both using the group method as part of the home study and have found it generally more effective in helping couples prepare for adoption than the individual home study alone." [77] In his paper on using groups for the study of prospective adoptive couples Celli [78] makes a convincing case.

In talking about the goals for setting up these groups to evaluate the suitability of prospective adoptive homes Celli says:

We agreed that we would put more emphasis on the educational aspects of preparing for adoptive parenthood than on the evaluative aspects. While not denying our job of assessing suitability for adoption, we wished to get across to couples that one of the primary purposes of the group home study was to help them achieve a high degree of readiness for adoptive parenthood. It was felt that this would free couples from concern over the prospect of being evaluated and allow them to direct more energy into constructive use of the group as a means of grappling with issues pertinent to adoptive parenthood. We were aiming at getting a truer picture of couples' initial feelings about adoption so as to help them grow in readiness to adopt.

We also wished to provide an atmosphere in which to see that others shared many common concerns. The fact that all others in the group were initiating a request for a child would in itself enable couples to experience a supportive feeling. We theorized that this would provide a common purpose and bond among couples so that the group would have an almost built-in measure of cohesion at the outset.

We also felt that a group atmosphere would minimize couples' feelings of dependency in relationship to the agency. We wanted the group to provide more room and freedom for people to initiate and work into roles as adoptive parents that would be most meaningful for them. People are different and they prepare for adoption in different ways. There are different approaches to handling issues of adoption, many of which are appropriate. With many diverse opinions that would emerge in a group, couples would have a chance to test their own ideas against the opinions of their peers, rather than imagining they have to match wits with any agency representative. Such an exchange of opinions would allow couples to draw more upon their own ideas in dealing with issues of adoption.

We finally anticipated that the group program would allow us to benefit from more feedback from people than is usually the case in individual contacts. We had observed that people had seemed to draw support from the group to the extent that they were freer in their interchange of opinions with the agency. This type of feedback could only help us in further refining our practice, knowledge, and skill.[79]

Celli describes the development of the group program as follows:

After some experimentation we have developed a format for the group program that seems to be most useful for us and for the couples involved. The group meets once a week, consecutively, for three weeks; couples are seen during the fourth week in their homes and at the last meeting in the agency in the fifth week. We have found that the group seems to develop more easily if the meetings are held weekly rather than spaced out further. The fourth meeting in the homes gives an opportunity to discuss with couples their reaction to the group, and to explore any areas we feel are important based on their participation, and it encourages couples to bring up anything of concern to them.

Two social workers are present at all of the sessions. One worker functions as leader of the group, while the other assumes the role of co-leader. The function of the co-leader is to amplify and support the leader in his direction of the group. He may add to the leader's comments or further explore areas which emerge in group discussion. Either the leader or co-leader visits a couple in their home during the fourth week. We have found many practical advantages to having two social workers participate in the group meetings. Couples derive more assurance that a final decision as to their readiness to adopt will be made by more than one person and that their request for adoption will be given a fair hearing. They also seem to gain a greater degree of security and identification with the agency through having contact with two of its representatives. The social workers also derive benefit from each other's support in dealing with areas of discussion in their group. Each worker assumes responsibility for visiting half of the couples in the group in their homes and dictating a completed record.

Each group consists of seven or eight couples. If groups are much larger, it is difficult to individualize the couples within them.[80]

Celli writes about the role of the worker and the contract that is established with the group:

The idea of setting a contract has been most helpful in creating an atmosphere in which leadership of groups is most effective. It involves conveying the purpose of the group home study early to the couples who participate in it. It can be viewed as a set of role expectations and obligations. We outline what we as an agency expect of couples during the group meetings and what they can expect of us. Considerable time is spent during the first meeting being fairly specific with couples in the group with enough structure and security to share their own ideas with us. The contract involves covering several points. We indicate to couples that there are two purposes to the meetings: to help us evaluate a couple's potential readiness for adoption and to help couples prepare for adoptive parenthood.

We indicate that we will be discussing:

1. The type of child they wish to adopt—boy, girl, nationality, etc.

2. Their attitudes toward natural parents—what type of information do they wish, why do these release children for adoption, etc.

3. Telling a child of adoption—when to tell, how to tell, what to expect as a child grows.

4. Their fertility problem—what information do they have, how did they react to it?

5. What type of people are they—what have been their family experiences, how will they anticipate they will deal with parenthood?

It can readily be seen that these are general areas which allow for a wide latitude of discussion and interaction. We feel these are content areas, to be explored with couples, that are important to us as an agency to know in order to make a wise decision in placing a child with them. From our experience having such a guide helps couples begin to grapple with issues of adoption.

We do not, however, follow a rigid format or feel that we have to discuss specific areas at specific meetings. It is to be expected that each group will be unique and should be encouraged to deal with specific areas of importance to that particular group as they develop. In practice, every effort is attempted by the group leader to make this a relatively fluid situation. The group is allowed to start in any direction that seems most important to it. As the discussion and interaction expands, use can be made of the content material provided by the group.[81]

In evaluating the program Celli says:

We have found that the response of couples to our program has been in general a very positive one. Couples are usually reluctant to terminate the program at the last meeting and often ask that they be able to attend meetings in the future after they have received their child. From our observations the program appears to enable couples to maximize and build on their existing strengths as they approach adoptive parenthood. As a result they tend to have a positive identification with the agency and a greater willingness to share their experiences with us. The tendency has been observed by others during postplacement group meetings and seems to hold true for our group home study program as well. It has been especially interesting to see the effect on people as they become free to share doubts and fears as well as positives. When others in the group indicate they have similar doubts this in itself is usually enough to alleviate them.

At this point we have tended to put in groups couples who are most ready to adopt. As a result we find that in most groups there is a minimum need for intervention on the part of the worker. The groups gather a momentum of their own as the meetings continue, with greater interaction among the participants. Participants look less to the group leader for direction or answers and more to other group members. As issues are discussed and resolved in the group, they gain greater reliance on their own ability to deal with them. We feel this provides people with a greater confidence in their ability to assume the role of an adoptive parent.[82]

Group Work in Family and Children's Agencies

There is a growing body of experience on the use of groups in family and childrens' agencies. The Family Service Association of America has reported:

The family agencies that embarked on the first group treatment programs did so because of their conviction that the method had a potential for increasing the effectiveness of their helping services. They recognized that the group process added a new dimension to the traditional one-to-one helping relationship and believed that this new form of treatment would add depth and breadth to the clients' therapeutic experience. Over the years, considerable attention has been given to the dynamics of the process and to determining which kinds of clients can make constructive use of it. It has been used both as the only form of treatment and as a supplement to casework treatment.

The response from Member Agencies to a questionnaire indicates many types of groups have been organized. It seems likely that other types may be organized in the future as caseworkers acquire knowledge and experience in the method and deepen their skills.

The composition of groups may be planned by sex, age, marital status, or presenting problem, in various combinations. A group may be composed of adults who are married, it may be limited to men or women, or open to both; and the members selected may have similar or different presenting problems. Groups may also be formed of adults who are single, divorced, or widowed to help them deal with the problems characteristic of their marital status; these groups may be mixed or limited to one sex. Elderly men and woman may be included in one group or be separated by sex; the focus may be on a particular problem or on the general adjustment problems of this stage in the life cycle. Groups may be composed of adolescents or of latency-age children, usually of the same sex; special attention is given to their maturational problems.

In general, the groups in family agencies are composed of clients who have considerable motivation for seeking help and are willing to involve themselves emotionally in the experience. Group treatment has also been found effective with socially insecure and deprived persons who tend to resist and evade individual interviews.[83]

The same report indicates:

In group treatment, as in individual treatment, the medium through which change is effected is the interpersonal relationship. In the group situation the primary relationship of each member is with the therapist, but the network of peer relationships also serves therapeutic ends. The interaction between the various members, and between each member and the therapist, provides the channel for the communication of ideas and feelings. The discussions of the members' problems serve the same purpose as similar discussions in individual interviews. A unique feature of group treatment is the opportunity it provides for clients to discover that others have encountered similar problems, which itself is a relieving experience. The acceptance and encouragement that the members receive from the therapist and from one another help reduce anxiety and guilt. As their sense of worth increases, they have less need to defend themselves with denial projection and rationalization.

Through the group interaction the members manifest, in both their verbal and their nonverbal communications, their basic personality patterns and characteristic defenses. In the discussions, their modes of thinking and behaving come under the scrutiny of the group. Each person may be challenged by some members and supported by others. The members thereby become more aware of their impact on people and more sensitive to the needs and feelings of others. Through identifications with other participants and the therapist, they absorb new ego-ideals, standards, and modes of behavior. The group interaction also provides a means of working through negative and hostile feelings toward key persons in the present and in the past. These and other facets of the group process must be understood and handled by the therapist if he is to help each member gain maximum benefit from this form of treatment.[84]

In a landmark book on the fundamentals of group treatment Levine says:

Purpose is the core of group function and the ideal method for selecting a purpose for a social work treatment group is to begin with the identification and common needs among individuals in an agency or worker caseload. This idea is simply the basic social work approach of beginning with the detection of need. In the case of a potential group service, the need should be common to all the prospective members.

When the agency develops its purpose for establishing a group on the basis of detected common needs among individuals in a caseload, there is some assurance that the purposes of individual members for joining the group will be similar and in harmony with that agency purpose. A confluence of the purposes of the agency and individual members later develops into a dynamic group purpose through the group treatment process. The result is a healthy alignment of the three major kinds of purposes—the agency's, individual group member's, and group's. This alignment of purposes is the foundation of sound group treatment in accordance with social work objectives. Group purpose becomes the source for both the energy and the focus of the group effort. The worker can then help the group to use its energies to focus on solving problems. A confluence can be facilitated through groups formed by the agency in the manner just described. However, in natural groups, the worker may not be able to begin with an easily detected and common need. Natural groups are usually already formed when a worker is first contacted. Typical of these groups are the family, the adolescent gang, or even a long-standing friendship group in a psychiatric ward.[85]

Dillon [86] describes the experience of a casework agency in using group interviews for intake purposes. The agency found the group interview especially helpful with mothers of disturbed children. Response was good; mothers examined their own attitudes and behavior in regard to their children; and they showed a willingness to help one another. She sums up the experience as follows:

Group intake does not preclude an individual, personal approach to each client. Rapport has been easily established not only between the counselor and each client but also among the clients themselves, and it lays the groundwork for the establishment of a relationship in therapy. No client has objected that she did not have enough time to present her problem. No one has expressed concern about the violation of confidentiality. And clients have not been antagonistic toward one another.

Our experience, though limited, indicates that the self-awareness that is essential for the success of therapy can be achieved through the group members' interaction. We also believe that group intake has had a salutary effect on communication within the clients' families. Some mothers have reported that after the group session they have been able for the first time to discuss with their husbands and children not only the problem that was troubling them but also their own feelings and attitudes.

The intake session has proved to be an educational introduction to counseling for the undecided client who does not know whether he needs counseling help and for the client who is afraid of counseling because he does not understand it. In the intake session the client sees counseling in action; he learns what will be expected of him in the counseling process because he has a direct experience of what counseling entails.

We are convinced of the administrative and therapeutic benefits of group intake.

For the first twelve sessions scheduled, one hundred and fourteen invitations were extended; ninety-three mothers attended, and twenty-one mothers canceled their appointments. Seventy-nine mothers requested further help, and fourteen mothers expressed their belief that they had received enough help in the intake session to manage on their own. We were able to screen more applicants than we could have handled in individual sessions.

One of the outcomes of group intake is the formation of ongoing therapy groups. One group of five mothers is still in progress; a second group of five mothers, which met weekly for three months, has terminated. These mothers, feeling increased personal security through their development of understanding of themselves and of their child and his needs, reported improvement in the child's adjustment. Because adequate and effective communication had been established between the parents, and between the parents and the child, there was no need for direct treatment of the child to be undertaken.

We have also concluded that group intake is therapeutically helpful to each client who participates. Many of the therapeutic techniques used in individual counseling are also effective in group counseling. Moreover, the techniques of group psychotherapy are applicable in groups formed for the purposes of screening applicants, and some of the same therapeutic gains are made.[87]

Mabley [88] reports on the use of group application interviews in a family service agency. After considerable experience with this new approach she concludes:

The information gained in group application seems to more than balance the data not obtained. We do not learn as much of the history of the problems or of the applicants' early life experiences as we would learn in an individual interview; however, we frequently learn some of the early history as applicants refer back to the reasons for their feelings or behavior. The relationship to the application worker is, of course, diluted in a group situation. It may be true, however, that the group application meeting is beneficial in guarding against too much revelation in a first interview. Moreover, applicants do not have as much of a problem in separating from the group application worker as they do from a worker with whom they have had an individual session, and they are less likely to have an illusion that they have solved their problems in one interview. The presenting problems are less comprehensively reviewed in a group session than in an individual interview, but we find we can secure all the information we need at the time as well as receive signed permission to obtain additional pertinent information while the applicant awaits service.

The number of applicants who follow through with their request for agency service is impressive. Out of 58 people representing 42 families seen in 13 group meetings during the first three months of our experiment, one family was referred to the court, several were given emergency service, and 24 families were offered ongoing casework service. When appointments were offered, 23 of the 24 accepted; the couple who did not wish further appointments had made application for help twice in past years and had never continued. In contrasting the responses of applicants held on a priority waiting list at the central office with the response of our district waiting list, we found that 72 per cent and 96 per cent, respectively, continued. The result of group application interviews as manifested in a desire for continued service is encouraging.[89]

Cyrus [90] describes a treatment group composed of ten disadvantaged mothers served by a family casework agency in a large midwestern city:

The decision to offer treatment to a group of dependent, deprived women was based on several factors: concern for, and interest in, this particular clientele; knowledge of the need of these women for feminine identification with a warm supportive caseworker; understanding that they shared common problems and had similar personality structures and family backgrounds.[91]

She further reports:

The group process added depth and breath to the therapeutic experience of these women. Most important perhaps was that [they had] a positive family experience within which they learned to give to one another, to share the mother figure and to acquire through an educative experience a few of the tools they needed to achieve healthier family life. These women are better able to deal with current problems and reach out for further help when they cannot effectively cope with their difficulties. It is my conviction that the value of introducing group treatment into our program was successfully demonstrated.[92]

Group Work in Health Settings

In a survey made by the National Association of Social Workers Committee on the Utilization of Group Methods in the Health Field it was found that "there is social work with groups in health settings. . . . Pediatric, geriatric, medical, and surgical services in hospitals, rehabilitation centers, and outpatient clinics were among the settings where social work with groups was reported. Among people served in these groups were cardiac, neurological, cancer, tubercular, arthritic, and cirrhotic patients. Handicapped, isolated children, handicapped housewives, persons with metabolic diseases, and handicapped elderly persons were also involved in groups meeting in the community. The description of this practice disclosed that there were many kinds of groups with many purposes and a wide range of objectives, including education, treatment, orientation, and socialization. A few programs, chiefly those found in rehabilitation centers or pediatric services of hospitals, were designed to counteract potentially destructive emotional reactions to illness and institutionalization such as dependency, isolation, depression, and anxiety. For the most part, the material examined by the committee described work with reality-oriented groups, focused on personal and social problems encountered by patients in relation to their illnesses and disabilities. Intervention was directed toward those issues and difficulties which were, or might become, obstacles to recovery and effective social functioning." [93]

Frey gives a helpful "checklist of things to do in starting formed treatment groups:

1. Study the needs or problems of the total patient population.
2. Decide which of these can best be met by using the group approach.
3. Select individually those patients who seem to need assistance in resolving these problems.
4. Interview these patients and observe them in their natural groups.
5. Formulate a beginning psychosocial diagnosis and treatment plan for each.
6. Compare this plan with the plans for other potential group members.
7. Compare these to the originally conceived purposes for the group.
8. Determine if there is a central harmony or compatibility among these various objectives.

9. If in harmony, form a group by again interviewing the patients about their possible participation in the group and begin to set the working agreement with each.

10. If the results of the study process point to a different but more vital need or problem than originally designated, reformulate an appropriate plan.

11. If the results show quite differing needs and treatment plans among the group members, regroup accordingly.[94]

In discussing the approach to patients in hospitals Frey and Meyer say:

Another population to which the group worker reaches out is patients in a hospital. It is common practice in hospitals to search out individually those patients with special needs in order to assign them to groups. Less usual is the approach to a ward group in which the aim is to intervene in the ongoing daily group processes in order to guide them toward therapeutic ends or at least to prevent them from being anti-therapeutic. In these instances the population may not feel a pressing need for help with problems of group living and may not want it after it is offered. In the mental hospital, the patients may not be permitted a choice about participation or they may be so disoriented that they seem unable to make a choice. Despite these obstacles exploration proceeds apace and the working agreement with its verbal and non-verbal elements is eventually achieved.[95]

In his writing on group programs in a general hospital Hirsch [96] describes the development of a comprehensive range of social services and sees group work an inherent part of the total. He points out the many opportunities present in the general hospital setting to "nurture the development of group treatment by social workers." [97] He says the "hospital consists of one great complex group entity . . . multiples of small group societies namely wards." [98] He tells about working with "subgroups of patients [that] collect in all corners of the wards." He says, "We need to reach out to them in their natural groupings and by joining them we can intervene constructively in affecting attitudes and reactions that might otherwise prove detrimental to maximum use of hospital care. Also, by involving ourselves in the little clique on the ward, we have opportunities to make use of informal contacts to guide us in determining needs and goals for the more structured types of groups." [99] He points out, "Social workers in a hospital setting deal with clients who are facing critical health crises that in turn result in serious and far-reaching psychosocial crises in their and their families' current life situations. Relatives usually are particularly concerned about patients' care and are ready to participate in any program that the hospital advises. By and large, patients and relatives are particularly eager to join with others facing the same crises when offered the opportunity to do so. Time and place do not constitute great obstacles in a hospital. Patients are physically accessible. The urgency and concern of relatives make them more available than one would expect." [100]

Hagberg [101] offers a warm report on social casework *and* social group work methods in a children's hosptital. She concentrates on teen-age groups in her article and tells about how caseworkers and group workers cooperated in providing services to these youngsters, many of whom faced long-term hospitalization. She says:

The group worker used three techniques in developing the teen program: working informally with the teen-age boys on a one-to-one basis and in small groups, working with organized groups, and working as a member of the total hospital team. He defined the purposes of group work . . . as follows: 1) to help the teen-agers cope with the normal stresses of adolescence as well as with the stresses of hospitalization; 2) to develop tools to help them cope with the problems of chronic disease; 3) to enhance their social functioning; 4) to develop and work within an emotional climate, or "norm," of the teen unit; 5) to help the youngsters understand that they are not completely controlled by the environment, but could constructively change parts of it. As the program developed, the group worker organized a teen council elected by the patients, on which the head nurse and the group worker also served. . . . The group worker was given responsibility for directing group work with all adolescent boys, taking social histories on their admission to the hospital and carrying through with individual casework services for these boys and their parents.[102]

Hagberg then tells how some of the caseworkers began to use the group work method with teen-age girls' groups. She says:

The major purpose in combining methods was to enable social workers to give needed intensive casework to more children. Initial goals were similar to those described by the group worker, although the caseworkers placed greater emphasis on the use of the group to help individual children. Gradually the caseworkers noted other benefits from group work and evolved the following goals: 1) to alleviate the children's anxiety and pent-up anger over illness and hospitalization; 2) to provide an opportunity for patients to master the trauma of illness; 3) to give hospitalized children a constructive experience in socialization as well as to protect them from feelings of separation and isolation; 4) to help prevent psychological or emotional damage; and 5) to facilitate the caseworker's efforts to help children individually with their problems. In all [the hospital] has had six activity groups for patients: teen-age boys, teen-age girls, two groups of younger girls, and two groups of younger boys. All activity groups have therapeutic overtones. Each group met weekly but members were not required to attend. Membership was open to all patients in the specified age range, changed frequently with admissions and discharges.[103]

In evaluating the work Hagberg says:

The many kinds of nonverbal communication in group interaction speed the social worker's understanding of each child. The social worker has an opportunity to test a child's concepts of reality, and to observe the way a child socializes with other children. By comparing his own observations with the parents' reports, the social worker often reaches greater understanding of the quality of the parent-child relationship. Meeting with a group of children, most of whom have problems, makes heavy demands on the social worker. . . . The social worker must relate to and show his empathy for several children at the same time. Often such a public demonstration of understanding and respect for the individual child means more to him then the understanding shown the child when he is alone with the social worker. . . . In a group session, the social worker observes the patterns of interaction that he once only heard about secondhand. Often after a meeting when feelings are still high, the social worker can find out just what is bothering a child. Sometimes the child reveals a problem while the group action is going on. The children themselves are expert in confronting each other and the social worker has to be alert to scapegoating. With sensitive intervention, however, he can guide the children into finding ways to cope with each other. The clown learns to relax and yield the spotlight; the coward, to stand up for his rights; the bully to develop empathy for his victims; the troublemaker, to discuss his problems openly instead of provoking others to act out his aggressions. . . . No child ever really has a social worker all to himself. The combination of group and individual treatment gives the social worker a chance to help a child learn to realize that life in a hospital—as elsewhere—demands a certain amount of sharing.[104]

Hagberg closes by observing:

The most important benefits to the hospital from the use of the combination of social work methods are improved collaboration with other professional staff members and a greater emphasis and interest among the staff in creating a healthy emotional climate.[105]

Rostov [106] has made a critical review of the literature on group work in the psychiatric hospital. In her examination of 48 bibliographical references about adult inpatients she considered six major areas: background information, goals and values of group work services, functions, relationship to other services, relationship to social service, and implications for practice. She says, "Social group work is practiced in a variety of settings. The psychiatric or mental hospital is one area that has recently incorporated this approach into its program. It is as one of the methods used in the total treatment process of the therapeutic milieu that group work in the psychiatric hospital functions." [107] She summarized the contributions of group work in these words:

The goals and values of group work in the psychiatric hospital [are] to socialize, including the use of groups, forming satisfying social relations, establishing an awareness of others, promoting sharing, learning and relearning social skills; to offer ego supports and develop ego strengths as well as broadening interest and scope of activities, building self-confidence, self-esteem, self-worth, achieving tangible things, developing acceptance and recognition, channeling intellectual capacities into constructive uses, and increasing self-expression; to test reality and see cause-and-effect relationships; to increase responsibility, develop good judgments and self-controls, and handle group living problems; to influence one another in a positive way, develop better morale, and challenge group hostility; to feel and exert some control over one's future; to adjust to a new mode of living and interrupt the deterioration process and counteract the regression of institutional living; to prepare and test for discharge and return to community life; to promote insights, develop the proper perspective on problems and feelings, and release and drain off tensions; to accept and understand one's illness and prepare for and use the individual and other therapies more positively; to increase the opportunities for observation and diagnosis by the staff.[108]

Somers lists some learnings from social group work practice in clinical settings. She says:

We have learned that the small group can provide a laboratory for insight and for change for the individual, and a kind of laboratory or anchorage in the reality of social expectations. The social inappropriateness of the immediate behavior is often quite clear, as are the present realistic consequences. Individuals can learn to face and handle realistically the problem in social relationships growing out of the group itself and can try out alternative and new ways. The professional worker is often able to see the acting out of the provocative behavior—the individual in action, reacting, and interaction in a way which may aid in diagnostic clarification and in sharpening of the worker's social treatment focus and goals. . . . The small treatment group can become and must be maintained as the bridge to the individual's capacity to utilize in other groups what he has learned in the treatment group.[109]

With reference to social group work in the health field Klein summarizes several guiding principles:

1. The purpose of the group should always be clear to the worker.
2. The needs and problems of the individual, his motivation and capacities, opportunities available for help—all these factors must go into diagnostic consideration of the worker in determining the choice of treatment method for the individual.
3. Group purpose and individual diagnosis serve as a guide to determine the composition of the group.
4. In determining composition of the group, the worker must attempt to predict transactions between the worker and group members, and among the group members.
5. The worker in the group has a professional responsibility to know and, when necessary, to control what is happening in the group. He must see diagnosis and evaluation as a constant and fluid process in his ongoing work with the group. He should focus this diagnosis and evaluation on the individual's use of the group and on the movement of the group as a whole. He should know when the individual is hurting the group. The worker must be able to judge when it is necessary to remove an individual from the group. It, at times, may become necessary despite careful selection of group members.[110]

Group Work With Older Persons

Maxwell sees it as follows:

The special dimension of need by older people for group participation stems from the intensification of specific needs as one gets older because of the "roleless role," and the deficits which can and do occur. Groups present unique opportunities for meeting these needs:

1. Changes in physical and psychological capacities require understanding and acceptance of these changes, necessitate substitutions and reorganization of patterns of behavior. Groups of peers who have lived or are living through these changes can provide a support and an understanding most helpful to individuals when the atmosphere, values, and leadership of the group provide a constructive milieu.

2. Groups can provide the opportunity to renew old friendships and develop new ones to replace the loss from death of old friends, family and marriage partners.

3. Community groups and organization memberships increase in importance as a means of providing identity for older people. A person's identity is closely allied to his group affiliations. When "Who is he?" is asked, the question is directed to family, occupation or profession, company or organization worked for, or organization represented. Mobility has decreased the value of family name as indentity. With retirement, identity through the employing agent, occupation or profession decreases or is lost. Loss of identification decreases the sense of self-worth and worth in the eyes of others. There are few doors open to "Joe Smith, Retired."

4. Groups are the means by which an older person belongs to something larger than himself or his family. They serve as a means through which an individual can act in unison with others to express a point of view, to accomplish tasks, to make his voice heard in the community and the world, to feel useful.

5. Status and recognition are achieved for an individual within a group in the broader community. Self-esteem is so closely related to the job one does and the money one earns from it that retirement can easily mean a loss in self-esteem. To be valued by a group for what one contributes rebuilds one's esteem.

6. Every group requires its members to meet some set of expectations. They may cover ways of behaving, kinds of grooming and dress, manners, beliefs, types and quality of activities. Older people in the "roleless role" have no expectations of what they shall make of their retired or older years. Group membership can undergird and broaden, focus and define ways of giving meaning and purpose to these added older years. It should be clear that group participation represents far more than filling time or having fun. Certain basic and essential human needs of older people can be fulfilled only through group participation.[111]

In his writing on group work with older adults, Goroff makes the point that workers must define the older adult population conceptually before it is possible to develop satisfactory programs. If one sees the older adult as being only in the terminal stages of life without developmental needs, then it is useless to see group work as making much of a contribution. However, if one views him as a growing, developing individual with never-ending needs, then group work can meet some of these needs. Group work can contribute much in helping the older adult to adopt to his situation and learn how to fulfill new social roles such as "being a good friend, caring for other people, and enjoying mutually satisfying activities." [112] Goroff says, "Do not do for the group that which they can do for themselves. Do not solve their problems, help them solve them themselves. Do not become their spokesman, help them select their own spokesman. . . . We are working with people who have spent a lifetime coping with problems and resolving them, making decisions and assuming responsibility for them. They have not lost this capacity." [113]

Lowy [114] presents a rich discussion of meeting the needs of older people on a differential basis. Rose [115] writes on social and cultural factors that must be understood if one is to comprehend the place of older people in American society. Busse [116] describes psychological and physical factors in aging. Rank [117] writes about group experience in a day center for older adults. Shore [118] outlines group experience in a home for the aged. Harlow [119] details group experience with older persons in a psychiatric hospital.

Silverstein [120] reports on a new venture in group work with the aged. She tells how elderly persons responded to group work service and used their experience and sensitivity to help their neighbors and to participate in community affairs. Her work was carried on with aged tenants of a big city housing project. Some of the elderly were incapacitated because of illness and at times they were in need of emergency care. Floor captains were chosen to help their fellow older persons who could not care for themselves completely. The floor captains were organized into a group to help them learn their new roles and responsibilities. She concluded:

> In this experimental use of the group work method with elderly persons who had a particular function as floor captains in a public housing project it was again demonstrated that older people, given the opportunity to use their knowledge, experience, and sensitivity, can continue to be constructive participants in the affairs of their community. Too often in our contact with them we forget that they have much to offer both as individuals and as members of the community.[121]

Group Work in Schools

A relatively recent development has been the use of social group work in the schools. Traditionally, school social work has centered its service around the social casework method. As Johnson points out, the specific function of the school social worker is ". . . to add his professional competence to that of other specialists in the school in order to help children who are not learning or are not achieving expected educational goals to make maximum use of the opportunity to learn and to develop into social beings in society. In carrying out his functions, the school social worker is engaged in two kinds of activities: those which focus on a particular child and those which focus on the welfare of school children generally." [122] Clearly the statement allows for the use of social group work as one way of helping certain children with certain needs.

As Crowthers points out:

Peer group associations, whether natural groups or structured into agency and/or school programs, have always been an integral part of the basic social structure of schools, both in the classroom and outside the classroom. We could cite a myriad of examples: the chumship groups of small boys cohesively cooperating with heretofore flaunted school rules so they can get out at the first possible moment to play ball; the dynamic interaction of the power structure and subgroups in an elementary schoolroom with the rolling up the aisle of apples, oranges, and bananas as the means of peer group communication resulted in that never-to-be-forgotten height of *esprit de corps*—the surprise fruit shower for the teacher.

We have a long history of structured group activities both within the school itself as the extensive extra- or co-curricular approaches have developed, and as various agency programs have been offered at times within the school or related to the school.[123]

Crowthers then develops the group approach to helping children in the school setting by stating:

The frame of reference for this particular approach to our topic therefore includes several propositions.

Proposition 1. Every social worker in every setting has need to understand the dynamics of group behavior. Various methods of teaching this approach have been developing in social work education. The only agreement among educators is that there is no one pattern, method, or system and all are in a constant stage of revision.

The potential of this proposition as a diagnostic and treatment tool can only be suggested here. What is the nature of the child's social hunger? How is he accepted by his peers? Is he chosen on teams? Is he always the last to be chosen? If he has begun to feel better about himself through work with him and his family, what about the group into which he must fit? Have the teacher and the classroom group changed their ideas of him? Can they be helped as a group to recognize and accept the change? . . .

Proposition 2. Every social worker in every setting has need for skill in facilitating the helping process in and through the group. A helping process can and does frequently occur among the members within a group whether or not the group is designed for this purpose or whether or not there is professional intervention to facilitate the helping process. Facilitation of this helping process can be a legitimate target of professional intervention at a number of levels, not only at the treatment group level, as a worker carries his total professional responsibility. A social worker, as a professional worker, makes a contract with society to behave in a responsible way, and to make use of his knowledge about the psychosocial needs of individuals, in any situation in which he may find himself in connection with his duties.[124]

Wittes and Radin in writing about group work with parents in a compensatory preschool program in a midwestern city make a significant contribution. Their early education program included a parent-group work program designed to help lower-class mothers of preschool children to change their child-rearing attitudes and practices. The leaders of the experimental program reported that "at the end of the year there was a significant difference in child-rearing attitudes between the experimental and the control mothers, as indicated by the amount of change in their responses to items on questionnaires." [125]

Wyers [126] writes about adaptations of the social group work method in the school setting. In a most interesting article he describes what he calls "cluster groups," "classroom groups," "splinter groups," "telescopal groups" and "socioeducational groups." It is useful to look in detail at how group work was carried on in these groups:

Cluster groups. Children who were the classroom scapegoats and isolates were frequently referred, but it was not possible to follow the traditional practice of grouping them together: only one or two such children were referred at a time by each school, and the schools were too far apart to permit interschool groupings on the basis of core difficulty. Innovation was required, and it was decided to group children who were functioning adequately around a child whose behavior was dysfunctional, the central client.

Prerequisite to such an approach, of course, is the permission of the child for the worker to discuss his problems with the other children in the group, whom he has been asked to select and to ask for assistance in resolving his difficulty. Also prerequisite is preparatory work with the child and a willingness and ability on his part to accept the confrontation of his peers in the cluster group. Preparatory work is done with the helpers, or auxiliary group members, as well. The nature of the child's difficulty is candidly discussed with the helpers, and an appeal is made for their participation.

Generally cluster groups meet from four to six times. Throughout, the content of the meetings centers on the presenting difficulty—a frank discussion of it, the primary client's point of view, the perceptions of the auxiliary group members, and the transactional nature of the problem. Discussion is guided toward linking the client with his peers in extra-group situations, both in the classroom and elsewhere. As group cohesion develops, the auxiliary members become more supportive of the primary client and are themselves able to explain their roles, both in the group and outside it. The primary client, responding to their support and encouragement, can become less defensive; scapegoats can become less needful of assuming the role of attacker and attacked, which is so often characteristic of them.

Final meetings of cluster groups can be profitably focused on fun. Participants frequently bring food or drink, wanting to give to the group. Generally ample but real praise can be given to the primary client for his social growth.

And praise can also be given to all the members for their participation and success in the group experience. The dissolution of the scapegoat situation can be examined, and suggestions for future interactions can be made.[127]

Classroom groups. Certain formal referrals indicated the presence of diffuse personal and group malperformance. Informally, too, it was brought to the group worker's attention that certain entire classrooms were upset, for reasons that were either vaguely defined or unknown. Discussion and observation were utilized to make evaluations of these classroom groups, and various sources of difficulty were identified: uneasiness with selected teachers, anxiety on the part of certain teachers, guilt over scapegoating, overidentification with allegedly persecuted class members, tensions between subgroups within the classroom, and suppressed anger resulting from a discrepancy between the teacher's and students' expectations about classroom behavior. Obviously the unstable situations caused by such emotional problems were not conducive to social growth and educational achievement. And so, as teachers were able to permit it, large group or classroom group work was used to alleviate distress.

In this adaptation of social group work the class is the social group experiencing dysfunction. This approach departs from the traditional model in that membership is not selective, and there is no individual diagnosis, although certain members may be precipitating or forcing the imbalance.

The group worker confronts the classroom group with the major problem. He may indicate that it has been suggested to him either by the teacher or by a student. He must obtain a consensus that the identification is an accurate one. He must also obtain the group's agreement that it can operate more efficiently if a solution can be found.

Generalized, but focused group discussion can be used, and also role playing. A release of group feeling is sought, and alternative solutions of the problem are suggested. Role playing is particularly valuable when group members are not cognizant of their feelings or are unable to articulate them. With such an approach three group sessions are usually enough to bring about relief from the symptom, and it may be alleviated in just one meeting.

Though the treatment of the group is psychosocial, it must be specifically related to the over-all purpose for which the group generally convenes. If the problem of the group is not significantly alleviated after several sessions, subgrouping is indicated.[128]

Splinter groups. It became apparent that certain scapegoats and other socially alienated children were not helped by approaches requiring them to leave their classroom groups. In fact, leaving the classroom further complicated their social relationships. These children needed social engineering that would help them establish better relationships with their peers and elevate their social status; it was within the group that the solution lay. Thus, for such children social work groups were formed within the classroom group.

Splinter groups are set up in much the same way that cluster groups are, though the treatment approach has a somewhat different basis. A primary client is identified, his permission to reveal his difficulties is obtained, and the auxiliary members of the group are chosen by him. The classroom group is then prepared in the presence of the primary client; explanations are made of why the subgrouping is occurring, how its members are selected, and what its activities will be. Whenever possible, the activities of the splinter group are designed to parallel those of the larger group.

Work with such splinter groups is traditional group work with one major variation, the arena in which the group experience is occurring. The classroom group is cognizant of the small group's activities and is, at least symbolically, integrated with it, for the members of the larger group intermingle with the members of the splinter group except during the actual time of its meeting. They have no undue curiosity about what happens to the primary client and picture themselves as a part of his social development. Frequently the subgroup becomes so attractive that extra-group members wish to participate in its meetings. This attractiveness elevates the status of the subgroup, thereby elevating the status of the primary client. And usually only four to six meetings of the subgroup are necessary to ease the primary client's problem.

The splinter group approach lends itself well to all kinds of group discussion. Confidentiality does not become an issue, for there is small likelihood of a breach of confidence in such a visible endeavor.[129]

Telescoped groups. Frequently time will not permit lengthy group development. This necessitates group work that can be completed in a short period of time.

A telescoped or short-term group usually meets from four to six times. The members are aware at the outset of the abbreviated nature of the group experience. They are selected on the basis of current difficulty and are grouped around core dysfunction. Group development, however, is accelerated. The members know the purpose of the group and why they were selected. The group program is usually planned during the first or second meeting, and it is frequently necessary for the worker to be more active in the planning efforts than he would be with a longer-term group. The activities must be highly gratifying, ego-supportive, and directly related to the treatment goals. Time limits can be used to force interaction between group members when it might otherwise take longer.

The telescoped group has received much attention in recent years. It is not a replacement for longer-term treatment, but it can provide support and problem alleviation for selected individuals. For the telescoped groups in this project, the group members were selected on the basis of their amenability to short-term intervention, and the treatment emphasis was on highly structured, ego-supportive programming.[130]

Socioeducational groups. The need for parental involvement in a school program designed to help children with behavioral or educational problems became obvious. And it was found that large numbers of parents—as many as thirty—could be formed into short-term groups, educationally focused but problem oriented and programmed to meet only six or seven times.

Prospective members of such parent groups must be screened in advance. They are informed that a group is being formed to offer guidance to them because they are experiencing difficulty in their role performance as parents. They are also informed that the duration of the meetings and the programming will be tailored to help them correct their faulty role performance.

Group sessions are planned in conjunction with the group members. Films, discussions, guest speakers, role playing, and formal presentations can all be used to meet the mutually agreed-upon goals. The worker uses his repertory of group work techniques to question, stimulate discussion, provide educational leadership, and offer continuity to the ongoing life of the group. Such a group differs from a family life education group in that it is person oriented rather than subject oriented. At the same time it differs from group counseling in that the members do not focus exclusively on their own very individual problems.

The socioeducational group convenes because of an observable dysfunction on the part of its members. Programming is based on the meeting of their needs, socially, emotionally, and educationally. The large size of the group does not permit discussion of the intimate problems of the members, and yet the content of the meetings is based on those problems, even though they are not always consciously identified.[131]

Group Work in Public Welfare

One of the rapidly growing applications of group work is in the field of public welfare. This has been especially true during the 1960's and early 1970's. With millions of persons in need of and receiving public welfare services, state and local governmental units in the public welfare field have found group methods to be of considerable value.

When the situation in which needy families and adults find themselves is reviewed it seems certain that group work can be of real help. These persons are often lonely and in great need for companionship and the warmth of human association. Their environment of home and community is too frequently barren and their financial resources are of course sharply restricted. To find joy, recreation, and relaxation is difficult and often impossible. Families which are broken or otherwise incomplete fail to provide for the needs of the remaining members and substitutes are needed. Confined and restricted by educational inadequacies, work opportunities are hard to find, thus further hampering the social experience of these people. When illness, disabilities, and other handicapping conditions are present additional problems are posed. If spirits are low and morale shattered by the blows of recurring crises, the understanding of others can do much to restore hope and rebuild the faltering ego. When the agency providing service is large and complex the small group can be used as a helpful framework for explaining how the agency operates and the mutual responsibilities involved.

The literature dealing with group work in public welfare has grown remarkably in recent years. Fenton and Wiltse [132] made a landmark contribution in their book on group methods in the public welfare program. They describe 25 group service experiences in 13 county welfare departments in California. The Federal Government has published three helpful monographs.[133] One entire issue of the distinguished *Public Welfare* journal was devoted to the subject of group work services in public welfare settings with Schwartz [134] providing a thoughtfully researched comprehensive article. In addition, the journal gives state-by-state summaries of exciting work that is going on.[135] Feldman provides another article reviewing experiences and offering perspective on the future.[136] Some of the states have prepared helpful training brochures.[137]

In his survey of group service programs in public welfare in a large western state, Feldman notes:

Group programs at the direct service level were found to serve one or more of the following nonmutually exclusive purposes: 1) to *inform* clients about agency standards, rules, and procedures, 2) to *educate* clients and to develop specific client skills, 3) to *counsel* clients about problems related either directly or indirectly to their public welfare status, and 4) to *rehabilitate* clients with certain social, psychological, or physical problems. Two global criteria were found to comprise the major bases for composition of direct service groups: first, all or most of the clients in a given group were recipients of a similar category of public welfare service, such as old age assistance; or second, the clients manifested similar types of social, psychological, or physical problems, such as groups of alcoholic welfare recipients. The following selection of client groups served by the six agencies from 1963 through 1966 aptly illustrates the broad range of services provided: intake groups; boarding home license applicants; boarding home operators; foster care applicants; foster care parents; preadoptive applicants; adoptive parents; blind public welfare recipients; recipients of old age assistance; socially isolated AFDC mothers; foreign-speaking AFDC mothers; mothers of preschool children; mothers of school dropouts; mothers preparing to enter the labor market; unwed mothers; parents of retarded day care children; mentally retarded adults; emotionally disturbed adults; preadolescent children; adolescent school dropouts; mentally retarded children; emotionally disturbed children; "unemployable" clients; alcoholic clients; and, family counseling groups.[138]

Foster says that the people whom the public assistance program is set up to serve are not just financially needy people:

They are people in double jeopardy, so to speak. Bound up in their financial need is another problem too. They are needy and old. They are needy and disabled. They are needy and blind. They are needy and a parent is gone. From this viewpoint, we see the applicant for public assistance as one whose problem of financial need is complicated by another specific problem which affects and is affected by his financial need. . . .

For the older person, diminished physical energy and increased social isolation are very often accompanying factors to financial need. In many instances, the worker is the only individual on whose attentions the older person has any claim. We are concerned with what help we can give the person in handling the physical aspects of his day-to-day living and in identifying potential sources of family or neighborhood help before crises arise. What help can we give the older person to remain in his own home and, when this is no longer possible, what help can we give in securing alternative living arrangements related to his need? [139]

. . . .

If one is old and no longer has money, the range of opportunity to make one's own decision becomes very narrow. The question changes from what kind of a roof would I like over my head to will there be any roof. It is more difficult to participate in social and community life. Not only because of lack of money but because of loss of family and friends and of decreasing physical energy. Just living from day to day can present a problem. Likewise, the child whose father is gone or the person who has a serious disability will find there are often unsurmountable obstacles in the way of achieving, without help, the values and satisfactions which in our country are regarded as the cultural heritage of all of us. Viewed in this likeness, the focus of our helping is not just concerned with the obstacle itself but with how it may be removed or its effect ameliorated in order that the person can live a more constructive life and be a more constructive member of society.[140]

In discussing some predictable effects of financial need Foster goes on to say that financial need places "limitations on social participation and impairs social relationships." [141] There may be a withdrawal from interest groups because of negative feelings of difference. Sometimes a person assumes that his associates will think less of him because he is no longer self-supporting and sometimes the person simply does not have suitable clothing to wear to church or special events. Quite frequently there is withdrawal from social groups because of inability to do one's share through lack of money to pay dues, contribute to the organization, frequently go to group meetings or to visit friends. Often there is no time to participate, especially if the mother is working full-time and trying to care for her children and her home.

Foster says that with older persons there is an increasing social isolation brought about through the death of family or friends, physical limitations or communication because of failing eyesight, impaired hearing and the like. Retirement from daily contact with employees is another contributing factor to isolation. When the children grow up and move away this also makes for loneliness.

Shoemaker, a pioneer in the use of group work in public welfare, observes:

While we wish to avoid stereotyping public assistance clients, many have in common definable problems which by their very nature present a challenge to the social worker, whether caseworker or group worker. However, the nature of some of the problems does mean that group work may be helpful where casework has not always been. Social isolation, family relationship, and social adequacy are some of the areas in which group work can offer distinctive help. In addition to these relationships, which are clearly social work's province, other areas of social functioning, such as parent and family life education, can be dealt with effectively through the group process and, depending upon a group's purpose and auspices and the worker's function, can validly be claimed for social group work.[142]

Shoemaker points out the importance of having the group work service thoroughly understood and lists some basic considerations:

For the trained group worker in public assistance all the issues mentioned— use of the group as the major service in the setting, use of programming, balance of the group function—must be viewed in the context of the complexities of the public assistance program. There is need for much independent judgment on the part of the professional in terms of how to intitiate and integrate group work into the program. Clients present so many needs that almost any effort will show some positive results. Thus, the primary question of where the use of group work will have the greatest impact includes many other questions relating to staffing, inservice training, and so on. While it is not strictly a practice problem, the fact remains that the administrative problems are so great that the group worker needs to be a functioning part of the public assistance agency if he is even in the capacity of consultant. In a number of instances, group workers have been hired by public assistance agencies with rather disastrous results as the agency was not ready for the introduction of group work and the workers were not sufficiently knowledgeable and skillful to help the agency become ready for their use.

The results of the demonstration in the Baltimore department make me hopeful of the possibility that group work will come into its own in the public assistance program. While this use of group work is an issue in itself, already we are seeing both some of the problems and positive results. The continuity of the services of one worker, the socialization process of the group experience, the readiness to share in a group, are all evident. One of the major problems is that of timing, of establishing a rhythm for group and individual contacts. While his work load is no heavier than that of the caseworker, the social worker who uses both group and individual approaches experiences the stimulation-exhaustion cycle more frequently, with the impact of both upon himself. Whether this is a training phase cycle is not yet clear. Also, the use of both stirs up the clients to use resources within and outside the agency. While this is a hoped-for result with any method, the insistent demands of the group call for immediate action.[143]

Bell and Kaplan described the work being done with a group of mothers who were receiving Aid to Families with Dependent Children. A voluntary community agency worked with the public welfare agency in getting the group started. The aim was "to help these women become more socialized, to restore their self-confidence, and to give them an opportunity for constructive activity. . . . Depression, isloation and low self-esteem were seen to be the characteristics of the mother who is supported by the AFDC program and who lives alone with her minor children and must therefore care for them unassisted by their father." [144] The authors reported that "the group has engaged in a wide range of activities, which can be categorized under three general headings: 1) sessions aimed at ventilation of feelings and concerns; 2) educational meetings; 3) recreational and social activities. These overlap however, and two or more take place in a single meeting. . . .

After considerable thought, the members reached agreement that the purpose was fourfold: 1) to help themselves, 2) to help their children, 3) to serve the community, and 4) to serve the center (the sponsoring agency)." [145] Bell and Kaplan went on to say, "As the group structure evolved, so did the relationships among the mothers. Their mutual support was evidenced by their informal contacts with one another outside the group meetings." [146]

Youngman has written a comprehensive article on social group work in the Aid to Families with Dependent Children program. After outlining some of the problems these families face she describes the social group work services offered to them:

Social group work services offered to AFDC clients at the Department of Public Welfare are short-term discussion groups. During the past winter, I have served six groups of between six and ten members. These groups met for one hour per week for six weeks. Caseworkers selected and interviewed the clients whom they felt could use a group experience in accordance with the purpose of the specific group. Participation was voluntary. One group was formed for mothers who had made a satisfactory plan for their children, wanted to find a job, but had not been successful. Their common problem was employment. Another group were mothers who had children committed as delinquents to a Maryland training school. Their common problem was to understand better the child's behavior and their own responsibilities in preparing for his return home. Another group were mothers who had severe difficulty in providing a satisfactory home for their children on the assistance grant. Their common problems were that the agency questioned their ability to give their children adequate care and to use the available help.

Another group was made up of parents who were both in the home. The husband was incapacitated, but physically able to attend agency group meetings with his wife. Their common problems were those that arise during whole family adjustment to the illness of the breadwinner and those economic adjustments to the AFDC grant. Two groups of mothers were new recipients; they had been receiving AFDC for only a month. Their common problem was recent financial dependence, facing their present social situation, and planning their future.

Group relations, characteristically unique to social group work, have several specific qualities that enhance the social functioning of group members. There is an opportunity for professional relationship with the social group worker as well as the relationship with peers. An opportunity exists for members of the group to give help as well as to take help. Motivation for change is stimulated as the member tries to live up to the expectation of the group. Making social contact and universalizing the problem helps the member feel less alone, a part of a whole.[147]

An excellent summary of the use of the group method as a resource for welfare clients has been prepared by the U.S. Department of Health, Education, and Welfare:

The group method, long known as an effective problem-solving process, is relatively new to the public welfare field. A welfare agency in Richmond, Virginia, is demonstrating how this method can be used to help public assistance clients identify their problems and view them more realistically. By sharing ideas and experiences, both insight and mutual support develop from the knowledge that others have similar problems, and this in turn generates new energy to cope with them.

The goal is not primarily to find employment for those involved but rather to show that recipients with common concerns can help each other when brought together in an effort to recognize and understand their human needs. This can lead to somewhat better lives within their present situations, and in some cases to a desire for education or training as a means toward greater independence. The project is divorced from the eligibility process. Its main purpose is to teach an approach to problem solving rather than to resolve specific problems.

Findings and Their Implications for Action

Involvement of Total Agency Staff. Cooperation of the total agency staff is vital to the success of this approach. The referral system, paticipant preparation, and integration of the group experience into the ongoing program require good communication and cooperation between the work group and other casework staff, since both seek to meet the needs of clients.

Group Formation. Clients demonstrating a need for help and a desire to participate in group activity are referred to the project by their caseworkers. These clients have problems typical of the Public Assistance Group: financial worries, difficulties in family relationships (especially parent-child), poor home management, little or no vocational or educational skills or training, feelings of loneliness and suspicion, chronic illness or physical disability, and an apathetic attitude with lack of motivation for change. They are grouped to bring together those with common concerns, such as AFDC mothers, unwed mothers, older citizens, married couples, graduating high school students, teen-agers, alcoholics, mothers living in a public housing project, and unemployed but employable men. Sixty-five per cent of the persons being served in this project are AFDC mothers. The group meets once a week for 2 hours for a total of 12 sessions. Baby-sitting and transportation are provided to all clients needing such services.

Training Sessions. Four of the regular casework staff were selected to test the hypothesis that it is possible through intensive training for staff without previous group experience to become skilled group leaders. In the initial training sessions, special attention was given to planning agenda and methods of approach, defining group goals, and discussing specific problems likely to occur in the group sessions, such as poor attendance, lack of group cohesion, and extreme hostility or verbosity.

Once the staff trainees had gained confidence and skill in the group approach, the discussions moved to content areas: the difficulties of rearing a child with one parent, the resentment faced by a welfare child, the unwed mother's wish for male companionship, and the place of unemployed men in the poverty culture. Discussion, role playing, and special task assignments were some of the methods used in the training sessions. In addition to the weekly training sessions with the project consultant, each worker met individually with the project supervisor to discuss specific needs. Without this intensive training, it would probably have taken many months of trial and error to achieve the same quality of group leadership.

Group Leader. Much of the success of the group sessions depends on the skill of the group leader in creating a relaxed atmosphere of mutual trust where the clients will discuss their feelings and problems, for without this there can be no deeper understanding of themselves and their situations. The leader must also have confidence that the group can fined its own solutions with minimum guidance.

Planning for each session is vital if there is to be meaningful exchange. Although the group leader should be flexible and sensitive to the client's needs, she must also remain alert to the direction the group is taking and the issues coming up for discussion, and be prepared to facilitate a full exploration. For each session, the leader prepares an objective based on the needs of those in the group, their areas of interest, and the agency goals. In the early sessions, group purposes and goals are interpreted in order to alleviate the participants' suspicions and convince them they can function more independently and effectively.

The attitude of the leader is just as important as the techniques employed. If she is to bring the clients to a more realistic appraisal of what they can do for themselves, the leader must understand and be sensitive to their deep and recurring problems, their unhappiness with life, and their apparent apathy and its causes. This depth of understanding can be acquired only by listening and being open to influence and change. The group leader must be able to *demonstrate* her belief in the dignity of all people and must serve as an example and source of encouragement. In other words, she "leads a vision" which is neither moralistic nor neutral but is instead a belief in the ability of all to understand themselves better and use this insight to improve their lives.

Group Progress

Ventilation. The first session of the group often opened with ventilation of hostility toward the welfare agency. Suspicion, fear, anger, and mistrust presented the main obstacles which had to be overcome before the group process could take on meaning and begin to deal in a therapeutic way with the complex problems of these welfare clients.

Group Identity. In the next few sessions most groups moved from expressions of hostility, guilt, and anxiety to a strong group identification where they could share experiences. The group bond was usually formed when a specific incident took place, as when one member presented a provocative, commonly felt problem. As one worker put it, "We hit the nerve of the group purpose and every individual felt it as her own." As the group senses this purpose, meaningful discussion begins and those involved in it become more receptive to hearing what the problems are and what the solutions might be. Tuned in to the needs of the recipients, the leader helps them translate their feelings into words, and in many cases into action.

Progress of Participants. As the group gained momentum and strength, the individuals did also. In addition to providing mutual support and exchanging practical information, such as how to stretch the budget, the clients, by sharing feelings about common concerns, often generated in each other the realization that there *were* positive steps they could take to begin coping with what had once seemed to be insurmountable problems.

Group workers found that it was not always necessary for the group to solve specific problems, but merely through discussion to suggest clues for problem solving that would excite the clients to new strength. The initial and most visible evidences of a change in self-concept were improved appearance and more fluent speech. By their comments participants began to show progress in the areas of personal and family conditions and relations with the agency. One remarked that she was no longer "smart" with her caseworker because "we understand each other better now."

The group experience was for many clients the first time they had been accepted and understood as individuals with human needs. Greater dignity and feelings of self-esteem could be seen in a variety of subtle and obvious ways. The content of their lives and their own happiness seemed to improve. With the help of the leader and other members of the group, many began to feel they could change their lives. Having acquired these feelings of greater self-worth, some began to desire financial independence, and this frequently led them to seek education or employment. Although not an immediate goal of the project, this was a bonus often achieved.

Caseworker Growth. The project has benefited the group leaders as well as group members. By mutual interaction, staff members involved have acquired new perspective and insight into the clients' needs and motivations. They have gained a fuller appreciation of the maturity, strength, and ability which the participants can muster to cope with their frustrating situations. Such a change in attitude can be a valid and useful tool in providing for the many unmet needs of welfare recipients.[148]

Coleman describes her work with a group of unemployed blind adults who had become homebound and were unable to travel about the community by themselves and had very few social contacts except through occasional visits from relatives. In her group several members lived in convalescent homes. Others were residing with relatives or friends. She says:

We had to exercise a high degree of sensitivity and understanding in order to encourage group members to participate in activities.

It was important to recognize that, in order for these adults to begin to participate in activities which sighted adults enjoy, certain attitudes and skills would have to be developed. During the first stages of participating in a new activity some discomfort and hard effort would be necessary until they gained the confidence and basic skill to enjoy the program as a form of leisure-time activity. We observed this during the initial stages of participation in new activities, over and over again as the full realization of the disability was brought home to them emotionally. They became aware of what things they could not do or had difficulty in attempting. They were conscious that there were sighted adults watching them as they made sometimes awkward, sometimes successful attempts. We stressed the importance of companionship in activities—a companionship of blind adults—as well as the companionship of sighted adults who could use encouragement and a guiding hand to help them learn a new skill.

The use of group discussion proved to be an effective tool in helping the individual in the area of social adjustment. One incident occurred with a newly blind man who joined the group through a referral about a year after the group had started. Although it had been explained to this man by the referral worker that he would be entering a group of visually handicapped adults, it was obvious that, because of his intense emotional concentration on himself as newly blind, he was unable to absorb the fact that others might have become blind like himself. Upon entering the group he talked of nothing but his inability to see, and how discomforting it was to him. I restrained the urge to explain to him that there were other blind adults in the group, wondering what their reaction to his comments would be. The other blind group members, interestingly enough, sympathized with him and did not at first indicate to him that they were also blind. Rather they began to start a conversation about all the active things they had done that week. One adult had shoveled snow from the driveway in front of her house, one had walked along a busy highway several miles, one had taken the bus and transferred four times to get to his destination. As the new member of the club began to lament that he could not do any of these things because he was blind, one of the members gently told him, "Oh, but you must try; you see we have succeeded and we are all totally blind also."

It was essential for the worker to keep in mind the importance of directing group discussion so that it was kept at a positive, constructive level. To encourage a discussion about blindness per se tended to produce nothing but a gloomy group atmosphere which isolated members in their depression. On the other hand a discussion about some of the feelings expressed about common incidents which occurred to members, accompanied by constructive suggestions on how to cope with these situations, produced a positive, optimistic group feeling tone.

We began to understand the meaning of dependency in the relationships of a blind adult through observing his reaction with staff and volunteers. One could often sense the frustration engendered in the blind adult because of the conflict of wanting to be totally independent but having to be dependent upon another adult for some necessities. We encouraged staff and volunteers to emphasize independence as much as possible and to underplay, in the presence of others, dependency needs. Most volunteers learned that the most helpful relationship with the blind adult was an individualized one in which they participated on the same level with him in activities and social conversation, structured situations for maximum independence and were available when special assistance was required.

A visual handicap does not automatically imply disability. It is important that social workers encourage communities to re-evaluate existing services to the blind adult, and to begin to take a fresh look at providing and expanding services not to a dependent group of people but to a group of individuals with varying needs. With guidance and encouragment visually handicapped adults do have the potential to become responsible and contributing citizens within the community.[149]

Saul, Eisman, and Saul [150] discuss the use of the small group in the helping process with the blind. Their account gives firm support to the fact that group work is a valuable diagnostic, evaluative and therapeutic tool in the process of rehabilitation for persons with visual handicaps.

Summary

There can be little doubt that social group work has been found to be helpful to many people with special needs and in special settings. In addition it seems clear that the use of this method will continue to grow and increase as more trained workers become available. While predictions are always hazardous, it is possible that group work will become one of the most rapidly expanding specializations in social work. Certainly it is safe to suggest that more and more social workers will be working with groups for at least a part of their professional practice. Furthermore, many other agencies can be expected to explore and experiment with group work as a viable part of their service offerings.

There are, of course, similarities and differences in the many examples referred to in the preceding pages. As for similarities, each example calls attention to people in a small group. In each example some kind of change in the situation or the behavior of the individual is sought. All of the groups have a worker or a leader. None of them are leaderless. The vast majority of the group are voluntary although most of them are in a sense formed. There are time limits on most of the groups and some are strictly confined to setting. For the most part group work tends to be one part of a wider and more encompassing range of services. In some cases group work is the primary method of service and in others it is secondary. In some cases efforts are made to create a strong group bond or cohesiveness; in others this is less so. In most cases there is a central focus on the individual and a reasonable expectation that by being a part of a group and by group interaction the individual will be helped in some manner. A minimal amount of group organization is characteristic of many of the examples. The results of the experience seem on the whole to be positive.

Any organization or institution that wishes to use social group work or an adaptation of it with their clients must consider certain questions before embarking on the program. First, thought must be given to *purposes,* or specifically what they hope to accomplish by planned and guided group experience for these particular persons. A realistic determination of purposes to be achieved is of course a prerequisite to determining whether or not the program is successful. Second, the *needs* to be met by the group experience must be carefully determined insofar as this is possible. Inasmuch as persons vary markedly in their situations it is clear that some more than others will need what group work can provide. Third, the *selection* of the clientele to be served by the program requires a careful and thoughtful procedure. Since not everyone can participate in or benefit from groups, critical decisions as to need and readiness must be made. Categorically, the emphasis should be placed on *voluntary* participation and free choice insofar as this is possible because it is known that persons get so much more when they decide to be a part of something. Fourth, the *formulation* of the group requires much advance planning and consideration because only if care is given at this step can there be a reasonable chance for group survival. While rules are hard to specify it does seem evident that the starting point is better when the group is kept quite small. Fifth, the kind of *worker* required and the role ascribed to that worker need to be thought through. Of course, the worker requirements stem from the conception of objectives or purposes held for the group. Sharply detailed professional service goals obviously demand a highly trained professional worker. On the other hand, less behaviorally oriented goals such as information giving or sharing may be achieved by a worker with a different background. Clearly the worker, professional or nonprofessional, full-time or part-time, paid or volunteer, must have a deep understanding of the group process, the area of need in which the members find themselves, and the formation of the agency in its special setting.

NOTES

1. William Schwartz and Serapio R. Zalba, *The Practice of Group Work* (New York: Columbia University Press, 1971).
2. Gisela Konopka, *Group Work in the Institution*, Revised Edition (New York: Association Press, 1970).
3. Mary Louise Somers, "Potentials for Use of the Social Group Work Method in the School Setting," Institute Paper, mimeographed (University of Connecticut School of Social Work, 1964), pp. 9–10.
4. Theodore Goldberg, "Group Work Practice in a Juvenile Detention Center," in *Social Work Practice, 1965* (Published for the National Conference on Social Welfare by Columbia University Press, New York, 1965), pp. 119–138.
5. *Ibid.*, pp. 120–121.
6. *Ibid.*, pp. 123–128.
7. George Saleebey, "Youth Correctional Centers: A New Approach to Treating Youthful Offenders," *Federal Probation*, March 1970.
8. *Ibid.*, p. 52.
9. Jack Sidman and Leona Kay Sidman, "Community Volunteers as Discussion Group Leaders for Juvenile Probationers" in *Volunteer Programs in Courts* (Washington, D.C.: U.S. Department of Health, Education, and Welfare, Social and Rehabilitation Service, Office of Juvenile Delinquency and Youth Development, 1969) pp. 229–261.
10. *Ibid.*, pp. 230–231.
11. Harry E. Grob, Jr., and Eric F. Van Doren, "Aggressive Group Work with Teenage Delinquent Boys," *Children*, May–June 1969, pp. 103 ff.
12. Frank R. Scarpitti and Richard M. Stephenson, "The Use of the Small Group in the Rehabilitation of Delinquents," *Federal Probation*, September 1966, pp. 45 ff.
13. Lloyd W. McCorkle, "Group Therapy in the Treatment of Offenders," *Federal Probation*, December 1952, p. 23.
14. Scarpitti and Stephenson, *op. cit.*, p. 45.
15. *Ibid.*, p. 46.

16. Douglas Kruschke and Frederick H. Stoller, "Face to Face with the Drug Addict: An Account of an Intensive Group Experience," *Federal Probation,* June 1967, pp. 47–52.
17. *Ibid.,* pp. 47–48.
18. *Ibid.,* pp. 51–52.
19. F. J. Peirce, "Social Group Work in a Women's Prison," *Federal Probation,* December 1963, pp. 37–43.
20. *Ibid.,* pp. 37–38.
21. *Ibid.,* p. 38.
22. *Ibid.,* p. 42.
23. Gerald J. Forthun and Ronald E. Nuehring, "The Prison-Group Work in a Maximum Security Prison" in William Schwartz and Serapio R. Zalba, *The Practice of Group Work* (New York: Columbia University Press, 1971), pp. 199–220.
24. *Seminar for New Officers' Wives,* Criminal Justice Education and Training Center, Providence Heights, Issaquah, Washington, April 8, 1971. Community Relations Division, Department of Police, Seattle, Washington.
25. Margaret B. Bailey, "Al-Anon Family Groups as an Aid to Wives of Alcoholics," *Social Work,* January 1965, pp. 68 ff.
26. *Ibid.,* p. 68.
27. *Ibid.,* p. 74.
28. Ralph L. Kolodny, "The Impact of Peer Group Activity on the Alienated Child: Experiences of a Specialized Group Work Department," *Smith College Studies in Social Work,* February 1967, pp. 142 ff.
29. *Ibid.,* pp. 142–143.
30. *Ibid.,* pp. 143–144.
31. *Ibid.,* p. 146.
32. *Ibid.,* pp. 146–147.
33. Ethel G. Ackley and Beverly R. Fliegel, "A Social Work Approach to Street-Corner Girls," *Social Work,* October 1960, pp. 27 ff.
34. *Ibid.,* p. 27.
35. *Ibid.,* p. 28.
36. *Ibid.,* p. 30.
37. *Ibid.,* p. 30.
38. Shirley Braverman, "The Informal Peer Group as an Adjunct to Treatment of the Adolescent," *Social Casework,* March 1966, pp. 152 ff.
39. *Ibid.,* pp. 153–154.
40. Sidney Gershenson and Meyer Schreiber, "Mentally Retarded Teen Agers in a Social Group," *Children,* May–June 1963, pp. 104 ff.
41. *Ibid.,* p. 104.
42. *Ibid.,* p. 104.
43. *Ibid.,* pp. 106–108.
44. Arthur Mandelbaum, "The Group Process in Helping Parents of Retarded Children," *Children,* November–December 1967, pp. 231 ff.
45. *Ibid.,* p. 231.
46. Helen L. Beck, "The Closed, Short-Term Group—a Treatment Adjunct for Parents of Mentally Retarded Children" (Washington, D.C.: U.S. Department of Health, Education, and Welfare, Welfare Administration, Children's Bureau, 1965). Reprinted 1967. Pamphlet.
47. Mayer Schreiber and Mary Feeley, "Siblings of the Retarded—a Guided Group Experience," *Children,* November–December 1965, pp. 221 ff.
48. Tim Gust, "Group Counseling with Rehabilitation Clients," *Rehabilitation Record,* January–February 1970, pp. 18 ff.
49. *Ibid.,* pp. 19–22.
50. *Ibid.,* pp. 23–24.
51. Henry W. Maier, "The Social Group Work Method and Residential Treatment" in *Group Work as Part of Residential Treatment,* edited by Henry W. Maier (New York: National Association of Social Workers, 1965), pp. 28–29.

52. Gisela Konopka, "Group Work in Residential Treatment: An Historical Review" in *Group Work as Part of Residential Treatment,* edited by Henry W. Maier (New York: National Association of Social Workers, 1965), p. 25.
53. Dorothy F. Kirby, "A Group Work Program in a Children's Institution: An Administrative View" in *Social Work with Groups, 1958,* Selected Papers from the National Conference on Social Welfare (New York: National Association Workers, 1958), p. 14.
54. Kenneth W. Watson and Harold Boverman, "Preadolescent Foster Children in Group Discussions," *Children,* March–April 1968, pp. 65–70.
55. Robert B. Mills, Rose R. Sandle, and Monroe A. Sher, "Introducing Foster Mother Training Groups in a Voluntary Child Welfare Agency," *Child Welfare,* December 1967, pp. 575–580.
56. *Ibid.,* pp. 575–576.
57. *Ibid.,* p. 576.
58. *Ibid.,* p. 577.
59. *Ibid.,* p. 580.
60. Adolin G. Doll, "Group Learning for Foster Parents in a Public Agency," *Children,* September–October 1967, p. 187.
61. Albert F. Hanwell, *et al., A Guide for Foster Parent Group Education* (Boston College Graduate School of Social Work, 1970), p. 3.
62. Ruth Light Stanley, "The Group Method in Foster Home Studies" in *Social Work Practice, 1963* (Published for the National Conference on Social Welfare by Columbia University Press, New York, 1963), p. 226.
63. *Ibid.,* p. 234.
64. Woodrow W. Carter, "Group Counselling for Adolescent Foster Children," *Children,* January–February 1968.
65. *Ibid.,* p. 23.
66. *Ibid.,* p. 26.
67. *Ibid.,* p. 27.
68. Harriet Goldstein, "Group Learning for Foster Parents in a Voluntary Agency," *Children,* September–October 1967.
69. *Ibid.,* pp. 180–181.
70. Lillian E. Barclay, "A Group Approach to Young Unwed Mothers," *Social Casework,* July 1969, pp. 379–384.
71. *Ibid.,* p. 379.
72. *Ibid.,* p. 381.
73. *Ibid.,* p. 383.
74. Edith M. Chappelear and Joyce E. Fried, "Helping Adopting Couples Come to Grips with Their New Parental Roles," *Children,* November–December 1967.
75. Sylvia E. Biskind, "The Group Method in Services to Adoptive Parents," *Child Welfare,* December 1966, pp. 561–564.
76. Gerda G. Sacks, "The Group Method in Services to Foster Parents and Preadoptive Children," *Child Welfare,* December 1966, pp. 568–571.
77. Louise B. Dillow, "The Group Process in Adoptive Homefinding," *Children,* July–August 1968, p. 153.
78. Vincent F. Celli, "Using Groups for Study of Prospective Adoptive Couples," *Public Welfare,* July 1969, pp. 272–278.
79. *Ibid.,* pp. 274–275.
80. *Ibid.,* p. 276.
81. *Ibid.,* pp. 276–277.
82. *Ibid.,* pp. 277–278.
83. *Group Treatment in Family Service Agencies* (New York: Family Service Association of America, 1964), p. 12.
84. *Ibid.,* pp. 24–25.
85. Baruch Levine, *Fundamentals of Group Treatment* (Chicago: Whitehead Company, 1967), pp. 4–5.
86. Vera Dillon, "Group Intake in a Casework Agency," *Social Casework,* January 1965, pp. 26–30.
87. *Ibid.,* p. 29.

88. Albertina Mabley, "Group Applications Interviews in a Family Agency," *Social Casework*, March 1966.
89. *Ibid.*, pp. 88–89.
90. Ada S. Cyrus, "Group Treatment of Ten Disadvantaged Mothers," *Social Casework*, February 1967, pp. 80–84.
91. *Ibid.*, p. 80.
92. *Ibid.*, p. 84.
93. Louise A. Frey (editor), *Use of Groups in the Health Field* (New York: National Association of Social Workers, 1966), pp. 10–11.
94. *Ibid.*, p. 30.
95. Louise A. Frey and Marguerite Meyer, "Exploration and Working Agreement in Two Social Work Methods" in Saul Bernstein (editor), *Explorations in Group Work* (Boston: Boston University School of Social Work, 1965), p. 7.
96. Sidney Hirsch, "Group Program in a General Hospital: A Consideration of Differential Factors," *Journal of Jewish Communal Service*, Spring 1969, pp. 248–253.
97. *Ibid.*, p. 248.
98. *Ibid.*, p. 248.
99. *Ibid.*, p. 249.
100. *Ibid.*, p. 249.
101. Katherine L. Hagberg, "Social Casework and Group Work Methods in a Children's Hospital," *Children*, September–October 1969, pp. 192–197.
102. *Ibid.*, p. 193.
103. *Ibid.*, pp. 193–194.
104. *Ibid.*, p. 196.
105. *Ibid.*, p. 197.
106. Barbara W. Rostov, "Group Work in the Psychiatric Hospital: A Critical Review of the Literature," *Social Work*, January 1965.
107. *Ibid.*, p. 23.
108. *Ibid.*, pp. 24–25.
109. Mary Louise Somers, "Potentials for Use of the Social Group Work Method in the School Setting," Institute Paper, mimeographed (University of Connecticut School of Social Work, 1964), pp. 12–13.
110. Alan F. Klein, "Theoretical Framework" in *Social Work with Groups*, edited by Claire R. Lustman (Veterans Administration Hospital, Pittsburgh, Pa., March 1963, mimeographed, 147 pages), p. 23.
111. Jean M. Maxwell, "Helping Older People Through Social Group Work" in *Potential for Service Through Group Work in Public Welfare* (Chicago: American Public Welfare Association, 1962), pp. 8–9.
112. Sebastian Tine, "Process and Criteria for Grouping" in *Social Group Work with Older People* (New York: National Association of Social Workers, 1963), pp. 94–95.
113. Norman N. Goroff, "The Use of Social Group Work with Older Adults—Promise and Problems, Principles and Practices," Paper, mimeographed (University of Connecticut School of Social Work), pp. 4–5. Presented at the Consultation Workshop on Services to the Aging Sponsored by the Connecticut State Department of Aging, Litchfield, Conn., March 19, 1970.
114. Louis Lowy, "Meeting the Needs of Older People on a Differential Basis" in *Social Group Work with Older People* (New York: National Association of Social Workers, 1963), pp. 43 ff.
115. Arnold M. Rose, "Social and Cultural Factors" in *Social Group Work with Older People* (New York: National Association of Social Workers, 1963), pp. 9 ff.
116. Ewald W. Busse, M.D., "Psychological and Physical Factors" in *Social Group with Older People* (New York: National Association of Social Workers, 1963), pp. 21 ff.
117. Betty Jane Rank, "Content of Group Experience in a Day Center" in *Social Group Work with Older People* (New York: National Association of Social Workers, 1963), pp. 101 ff.

118. Herbert Shore, "Content of Group Experience in a Home for the Aged" in *Social Group with Older People* (New York: National Association of Social Workers, 1963), pp. 108 ff.

119. Minnie Harlow, "Content of Group Experience in a Psychiatric Hospital" in *Social Group Work with Older People* (New York: National Association of Social Workers, 1963), pp. 124 ff.

120. Sandra Silverstein, "A New Venture in Group Work with the Aged," *Social Casework*, December 1969, pp. 573 ff.

121. *Ibid.*, p. 580.

122. Arlien Johnson, *School Social Work* (New York: National Association of Social Workers, 1962), pp. 87–88.

123. Virginia L. Crowthers, "The School as a Group Setting" in *Social Work Practice, 1963* (Published for the National Conference on Social Welfare by Columbia University Press, New York, 1963), p. 70.

124. *Ibid.*, pp. 72–73.

125. Glorianne Wittes and Normal Radin, "Two Approaches to Group Work with Parents in a Compensatory Program," *Social Work*, January 1971, p. 43.

126. Norman L. Wyers, "Adaptations of the Social Group Work Method," *Social Casework*, November 1969, pp. 513–518.

127. *Ibid.*, p. 514.

128. *Ibid.*, p. 515.

129. *Ibid.*, p. 516.

130. *Ibid.*, p. 517.

131. *Ibid.*, pp. 517–518.

132. Norman Fenton and Kermit T. Wiltse, *Group Methods in the Public Welfare Program* (Palto Alto, California: Pacific Books, Publishers, 1963).

133. See Harleigh B. Trecker, *Group Services in Public Welfare* (Washington, D.C.: Department of Health, Education, and Welfare, Welfare Administration, Bureau of Family Services, 1964), *Helping People in Groups*, Six Background Papers from the Workshop on Group Services, April 19–23, 1965 (Washington, D.C.: U.S. Department of Health, Education, and Welfare, Welfare Administration, Bureau of Family Services, 1965); Marjorie Montelius, *Working with Groups: A Guide for Administration of Group Services in Public Welfare* (Washington, D.C.: U.S. Department of Health, Education, and Welfare, Welfare Administration, Bureau of Family Service, 1966).

134. William Schwartz, "Group Work in Public Welfare," *Public Welfare*, October 1968.

135. "Group Work Services in Public Welfare Settings," *Public Welfare*, October 1968.

136. Ronald A. Feldman, "Group Service Programs in Public Welfare: Pattern and Perspectives," *Public Welfare*, July 1969.

137. See Kermit T. Wiltse and Justine Fixel, *Use of Groups in Public Welfare* (California State Department of Social Welfare, September 1962); also *Guide for Use of Group Methods in County Welfare Departments* (California State Department of Social Welfare, September 1962).

138. Feldman, *op. cit.*, p. 267.

139. Helen B. Foster, *Services in Public Assistance: The Role of the Caseworker.* Public Assistance Report No. 30 (Washington, D.C.: U.S. Department of Health, Education, and Welfare, Social Security Administration, Bureau of Public Assistance, Division of Program Standards and Development, Undated), pp. 4–5.

140. *Ibid.*, p. 19.

141. *Ibid.*, p. 27.

142. Louise P. Shoemaker, "Group Work in Public Welfare" in *Social Work Practice, 1967* (Published for the National Conference on Social Welfare by Columbia University Press, New York, 1967), p. 127.

143. *Ibid.*, pp. 135–136.

144. Courtenay W. Bell and Harvey L. Kaplan, "Public-Voluntary Sponsorship of a Mother's Group," *Social Casework*, January 1964, p. 21.

145. *Ibid.*, p. 22.

146. *Ibid.,* p. 23.
147. Louise C. Youngman, "Social Group Work in the AFDC Program," *Public Welfare,* January 1965, pp. 28–29.
148. "The Group Method: A Resource for Welfare Clients," *Research and Demonstrations Brief,* April 1, 1970. Prepared by the Research Utilization Branch, Division of Research and Demonstration Grants, Office of Research, Demonstration, and Training, Social and Rehabilitation Service, Department of Health, Education, and Welfare, Washington, D.C.
149. Nancy Coleman, "Social Group Work with Visually Handicapped Adults." Paper presented at the Alumni Conference, School of Social Work, University of Connecticut, April 7, 1962. Mimeographed.
150. Sidney R. Saul, Nadine Eisman, Shura Saul, "The Use of the Small Group in the Helping Process," *The New Outlook for the Blind,* April 1964, pp. 122–125.

8

Evaluation of Social Group Work

Evaluation is that part of social group work in which the worker attempts to measure the quality of a group's experience in relation to the objectives and function of the agency. Evaluation may be centered upon individual growth, program content, or worker performance because all these aspects tend to influence the general achievement of the group. When individuals, groups, and workers are studied in an attempt to ascertain their growth and development, subsequent experiences can be better provided to meet newly recognized needs.

Evaluation calls for the gathering of comprehensive evidence of individual member growth. It is necessary to interpret and integrate this evidence into an individual-member summary related to the level of development he had achieved at the time of entry into the group. The same process applies with reference to the group and the worker. Actually, to be most valuable, evaluation should be thought of as *continuous* rather than periodic. It is an integral part of good group work. In the accompanying Figure 10 the on-going nature of the evaluation process is pictured.

Evaluation begins with the formulation of specific objectives for individuals and groups. It is then necessary to clarify the objectives by identifying individual and group behavior which can be properly interpreted as representing growth for the persons involved. The next step is the provision of program experiences designed to offer opportunities for adjustment and growth. These experiences may be of long or short duration, depending upon the nature of the immediate and long-term objectives which underlie them. The worker then must keep full records of the behavior of the individuals and study their response to the group program, worker, and one another. In making such evaluative studies, the worker applies criteria of growth and development and makes judgments as to what the behavior response means to specific individuals and groups in their situation.

Usually the evaluation process results in the modification of objectives for both individuals and groups. If interpretation of the evidence shows

FIGURE 10

Evaluation of Group Work

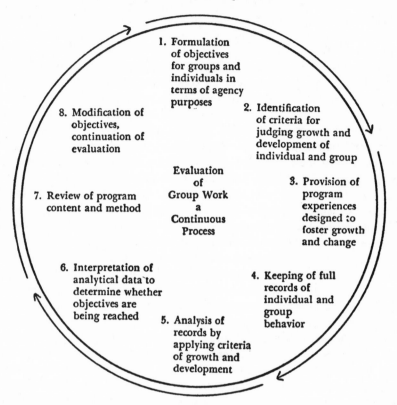

that the prevailing program is meeting needs, it may be continued. If it appears that the group situation should be altered to improve the quality of experience provided, changes can be made. Evaluation is of paramount importance because through it, and it alone, is it possible for workers to know the extent to which they are accomplishing their objectives. Without continuous evaluation objectives become outmoded, programs become static and groups fail to meet needs. It is a fundamental obligation of every worker and every agency to rethink and reorganize its practice in the light of thoughtful evaluation.

Evaluation of the Agency

The agency in which social group work services are carried on must be evaluated from time to time. Certainly this is a task to be led by agency administration but it is also important that group workers have a role in the evaluation process. It would seem clear that the better the agency the better the chances that group work services will reach the goals that have been set for them.

To evaluate the agency it is necessary to develop criteria of good practice. The suggested criteria for use in evaluating organizations providing social welfare services which follow should be of help in this regard.

1. *The Criterion of Purpose.* An effective agency has clearly defined statements of its objectives or purposes which have been thoughtfully developed out of the conscious study of community aspirations and conditions and which are thoroughly understood by those who work and participate in the agency porgram. The agency purpose is appropriate for community support, although new objectives usually require organizational effort to attain new community support. Furthermore, the agency is peculiarly able to work toward the social goals explicit within its purpose with some reasonable expectation that the goals are achievable.

2. *The Criterion of Community Setting.* An effective agency has defined, or its auspices define, the geographic or political territory within which it will operate program. It endeavors to understand basic physical, social, and cultural facts about its area and to use such information in planning its work. On the basis of ongoing fact-finding and research, it defines and redefines requirements and aspirations of the population it intends to serve. It conducts research studies into specific problems and conditions, using emerging useful concepts. It has an understanding of what the focus is during the next five to ten years within the community and institutional systems of which it is a living part.

3. *The Criterion of Constituency.* An effective agency has made decisions regarding the constituency with which it will endeavor to work. It seeks to understand the people with whom it works and it endeavors to help these people become related to the agency as a whole. The relationship of the constituency to the adult voting membership or delegate body, if any, is clear. An agency committed to social welfare has an unequivocally open policy of accepting into constituency and service status *all persons and groups* with the social condition or problem to which the agency directs its program. This means *no* barriers to user, board or staff status based on race, ethnicity, national origin, creed, prior criminal record, age or sex except in such organizations which may be organized within tested Constitutional protections to serve exclusively particular constituencies within these categories.

4. *The Criterion of Program.* An effective agency has activities and services established to achieve agency purposes based on participant requirements and social conditions. The program has sufficient depth, diversity and design to meet the needs of individuals, groups, neighborhoods, and communities. Program complies or is moving steadily toward compliance with high standards of each specific service and should reflect a high level of performance. Normally an agency's minimum standards are the national or federal ones within its field of service or service system.

5. *Criterion of the Board.* An effective voluntary or private agency has an elected board of directors charged with the responsibility for directing the affairs of the agency in harmony with its stated purposes and within the framework of democratic administration. An effective public agency has a board appointed by competent authority. A public agency board is charged by law or regulation with the responsibility of either directing the affairs of the agency through policy determination or advising the political decision makers and chief executive of the organization. A quasi-public agency board has particularistic patterns of authority and responsibility. Whether voluntary, public or quasi-public, a board is broadly representative of the community and the constituency served by the agency. There are specific terms for board membership, and preferably provisions for board rotation. The board is organized in a committee structure which provides for study activity and decisions of less than fundamental policy between board meetings. The majority of the board members are active participants and attend meetings without absence except for prior requested absence for good reason. It is evident also that the executive and the board are working together to solve the common problems of the agency.

6. *The Criterion of Administrative Personnel.* An effective agency has administrative personnel and management practices which are designed to facilitate the work of the total organization and the attainment of its goals. In the management process the chief executive officer of the agency is, of course, the central figure. It is to be expected that he will be educated for his duties and will carry these duties on in concert with the other members of his professional, clerical, and maintenance staff who share management tasks at various levels and over various spans and kinds of program. The chief executive officer is competent to manage internal and external activities and resources, the formal and the informal systems, and the long-range and the day-to-day interests. A critical test of any chief executive officer is his active facilitation of the effectiveness and efficiency of his staff, and his capacity to attract and develop competent personnel.

7. *The Criterion of Professional Personnel.* An effective agency is staffed by a sufficient number of qualified professional personnel to provide services focused upon the attainment of the agency's goals. Qualified professional personnel implies attitude, insight and skill equal to the task, qualities usually the result of personal maturity, undergraduate education, special training, and, to the greatest extent possible, graduate education pertaining to the assigned responsibility. The agency has a comprehensive program of supervision or consultation aimed at the continuous improvement of worker performance. It has written job descriptions and personnel policies. There is a clear pattern of staff responsibility and authority. Employed staff receive adequate salaries and there is reasonable provision for expenses in line of duty, participation in educational courses and conferences, health programs, retirement plans, and other employee benefits typical to the community. Agency policy encourages participation of its staff

in professional associations and allows participation in labor organizations.

8. *The Criterion of Volunteer Personnel.* An effective agency has a systematic plan for the recruitment, selection, training, and supervision of volunteers who assist in program leadership. These volunteers are chosen on the basis of explicit qualifications. They are persons of various social statuses, age, and some come desirably from the users of the service.

9. *The Criterion of Facilities.* An effective agency has the use of adequate facilities where it conducts its work. These facilities, including equipment, are designed to implement the program objectives of the agency. They are maintained in attractive, clean, safe, and workable condition. There is a property maintenance plan for the immediate care and for long-range capital improvements. The location and distribution of facilities is based on accessibility and sound principles of urban planning for community facilities.

10. *The Criterion of Financial Resources and Practices.* An effective agency has financial resources and fiscal practices adequate for the objectives the agency seeks to obtain. Its operating income and expenditures are kept in balance, or knowingly out of balance. Its capital funds are carefully invested and supervised. There is an annual audit by an impartial firm. Full and adequate records are maintained of all funds entrusted to the agency. There is adequate insurance coverage, including workman's compensation, insurance for fire and water damage, public liability on motor vehicles, and, when appropriate, provision of a plan for health and accident insurance for service users such as campers, twenty-four-hour-care residents, and others away from their homes in agency programs. Agency financial practice recognizes the financial participation of persons served, either through taxation, contribution, fees and dues, or a combination thereof. Fees and dues schedules are to be developed with their possible impact on program objectives in mind quite as much as increasing agency income.

11. *The Criterion of Relationship with National Organizations.* The agency is a local affiliate of an appropriate national organization, or working to make itself eligible for membership in such a body. An effective agency establishes and maintains cooperative working relationships with its regional and national or federal organization. It participates in organized activities and conducts its work in accordance with the national or federal organization's stated principles and practices, if these principles and practices are consistent with the ethics and principles of the relevant professions.

12. *The Criterion of Community and Public Relations.* An effective agency maintains cooperative working relationships with other community agencies. It develops interagency collaboration on behalf of specific clients, patients or members. It collaborates with other agencies in community planning. It is an active participant in its fund-raising campaign for financing social welfare whether or not it is a receiving agency. It endeavors to create community understanding of its work and the community problems

or goals it focuses upon. It interprets supportively the purpose and program of all standard-meeting social welfare organizations. It is a social critic whenever social conditions which hurt people go unchanged and whenever standards are clearly violated.

13. *The Criterion of Reporting and Appraisal.* The effective agency maintains a systematic and clear set of records and reports of individual and group constituency and their activities, progress toward specific objectives, role of staff with service users, and financial receipts and expenditures. On the basis of these records and reports, and other information, the agency board, committees and staff periodically appraise the agency's past efforts, present status and future direction. Objective self-appraisal, and appraisal in conjunction with other community agencies or over-all community study, is an important requirement if the agency is to remain effective and efficient in view of changing community conditions, evolving community policies, and new professional developments. A responsible agency promptly shares essential and appropriate reports with its local planning body and the agency's national or federal organization because it knows that its own accumulated experience is important in helping to shape local and national policies and plans. From time to time an organization encourages evaluation by outside qualified social science and professional persons.

14. *The Criterion of Relationship with the Central Planning Bodies.* An effective agency works cooperatively with one or more central planning bodies. It thus contributes its experience and expertness to plans for all people and ensures an opportunity for the plans of other agencies to affect planning within the agency. It takes its plans for review amid a more comprehensive planning process and receives consultation before instituting major changes in its service area or program.

15. *The Criterion of Long-Range Planning.* An effective agency makes long-range plans for the strengthening of its work. The agency has a committee on agency development and future planning. It makes careful analyses of trends in the volume of its service. It is to be expected in times of rapid population increase that agencies will seek to enlarge their program and to serve more people. However, evaluation for long-range priority direction within social welfare suggests organizational focus upon *particularly damaged population groupings* and to modifying the program and the organization itself even drastically, when necessary, in order to improve its effectiveness. Unless an organization is effective in the long range, is the sanction of society merited? [1]

Problems in Evaluation of Small Groups

Determining what happens to people in small groups has always been a difficult task and will continue to be so. Davis highlights this when he writes:

The investigation of group behavior poses problems not generally encountered in the study of individuals. The problems arise from the fact that a group is composed of several subjective processes. Each person reacts to a social situation in a rather different way, and there is no single conscious experience to call the group's own. In attempting to understand group phenomena, the early student of social behavior drew heavily upon his own experience in groups and upon his observations about the collective actions of others near and around him. Whereas the early experimental psychologist could supplement his own observations of behavior by requesting verbal reports from a subject responding to a stimulus selected by the experimenter, the early social psychologist found it impractical, for obvious reasons, to request a group to report directly on what "it" was doing. More recently psychologists have turned to direct and systematic observations of groups, but even this poses very difficult measurement problems. If we were to consider at length the problems associated with the direct observation of active groups, we would discover that accurate observations and the acquisition of an orderly empirical record of interpersonal activities constitute troublesome difficulties that are still imperfectly resolved, even in the study of simple laboratory groups.[2]

Phillips and Erickson in their writing on interpersonal dynamics in the small group observe:

Small group activity can be measured by graphs, charts, attitude scales, evaluation questionnaires, or quality of input. Members can be asked to express their personal satisfaction or lack of it. Reports can be subjected to content analysis. But, whichever of these ways is selected, part of what we are looking for is omitted. Somewhere in the interaction, and in what it does inside the individual, lies the real essence of human interaction, and we cannot yet get at this with any known instrument. Thus, each participant in and student of the small group must rely to some extent on his personal experience and feeling as he attempts to explain behavior or to plan it.[3]

In spite of the problems in creating a system of evaluation for social group work a number of people, over the years, have made creative contributions. Some of these will be examined in the section which follows.

Approaches to the Evaluation of Group Work

In a pioneer effort to evaluate social group work Bernstein [4] presented his "Charting Group Progress" approach. He developed charts on group evaluation, individual evaluation, and the member's group contribution. Under the heading of group evaluation he listed and explained such criteria as attendance, group organization, group standards, wider horizons, social responsibility, enriched interests, handling conflicts, leadership and participation, cooperative planning, group thinking, group loyalty and morale, and decreasing need for the leader. Criteria used in connection with the individual evaluation chart included attendance, new skills and interests, wider loyalties, degree and range of participation, leadership, breakdown of prejudices, status in the group, symptoms of maladjustment, health, vocational development, and educational developments. Under the heading of the member's group contribution both constructive and destructive behaviors were cited. In spite of the fact that the Bernstein "charting" approach was developed some years back there is much to be said for it today and certainly it still offers a way of getting into evaluation that is indeed helpful.

In her writings on group work services in public welfare Montelius lists "ten realistic measurements of results" in terms of what may happen with public welfare clients who have taken part in experimental group programs. They are:

1. Has there been a change in the appearance of the client?
2. Is the client more articulate? More expressive?
3. Is the client interested in learning about child care, budgeting, the schools?
4. Does the client seem to have more knowledge of the Welfare Department, its rules, limitations, function?
5. How does the client view his relationship with the social worker? Is there any change in this relationship?
6. Has the client indicated any interest in outside activities such as adult education, YWCA activities, church groups?
7. Has the client indicated more interest in learning a skill, going to work, or seeking a job?
8. Is the client more inclined to use community resources, such as the county hospital, camps for the children, local playgrounds, nursery schools?
9. Does the client express concern for other group members when they are ill or in some kind of trouble?
10. Has the client taken responsibility for any group activity or helped in planning an activity? These would be immediate indications of the effectiveness of the group experience for agency recipients. Later the agency could determine whether any gains made were sustained and whether the agency itself had moved toward making needed services more readily available by participating in the development of community resources needed by clients, providing additional agency services, and so on.[5]

In her classic paper on evaluating movement of individuals in social group work Northen and her committee reviewed, compared, and evaluated many statements of group work objectives to answer the question, "What do we hope will happen to a particular group member because of this experience?" After much discussion and many revisions the following statement of objectives of group work was developed:

The general goal of all social group work is to effect changes or adaptations in an individual's attitudes, relationships, and behavior to the end that he may develop greater personal adequacy and improved social adjustment.

Next was the determination of criteria. Three major areas were selected:

Changes in attitudes. A crucial test of the effectiveness of social group work is the extent to which a person has changed in his attitudes toward himself. In other words, have his feelings about himself changed? For example, does he depreciate or value himself? To what extent does he accept his own family and cultural background? How does he feel about his limitations? How much insight does he have into his feelings and behavior? Changes in a person's attitudes toward other people are also important. What value does he place on other people? How does he feel toward people who differ from him in ability, cultural background, or social class? Attitudes toward ideas is the third component of this criterion. Does the person belittle or respect the ideas of others? How able is he to look at two sides of a question? How insistent is he that others accept his ideas?

Changes in relationships. Closely related to attitudes is the way in which a person relates to other people—to the group worker, other members of the group, his family, peers of the same and opposite sex and persons in positions of authority. In each of these relationships, what role does he have? How consistent or conflicting are these roles? How affectional or hostile does he feel toward others and how does he express these feelings? How easy is it for him to make new friends, share his feelings, ideas, and possessions with others? To what extent does he trust others and they him? What is the range of his friendships and how stable are they? Does he see other persons as they really are or are his perceptions distorted? Does he withdraw from others or move out toward others? How does he handle competition?

Changes in other behavior. As a result of social group work practice, it is expected that there will be changes in a person's behavior at home, school or work, and in the community. Does the person, for example, dress differently? Is he more or less destructive of property? To what extent is his behavior within the socially acceptable norms for his age group? To what extent is he able to live within the law and the regulations of the groups to which he belongs? To what extent have behavioral symptoms changed, such as swearing, physical complaints, stealing, and fighting? How well does he handle responsibility? The committee working on the project read, judged, and analyzed fourteen summaries of individuals to determine the extent to which these individuals had changed as a result of group experience. They conclude: "The study has suggested that there are general objectives of social group work that hold true regardless of the setting in which social group work is practiced and that the same general criteria can be applied to the study of individuals receiving group work service. It was suggested that individuals are helped, through social group work, to change their attitude toward themselves and other people, to improve their relationships with others, and to behave in a way that brings them satisfaction and that is within the expectations of society. The study has suggested that social group workers can agree on the amount and direction of movement made by individuals in relation to the criteria. It has indicated that records can be prepared which are suitable for use in a study of movement but that most workers need considerable help in learning to write such records.[6]

The meaningful involvement of youth in group work programs has long been cited as a basic goal. The Sherifs say:

Any activity, any program should be in the nature of a challenge to youth, requiring concerted planning and action. Involvement in the planning and execution affords, at the same time, the occasion for the individual to test his acceptance or rejection by others, an occasion for him to prove himself to others, and an occasion personally to excel in the process. When policy is formulated, action programs outlined, and facilities provided in harmony with this principle, a self-image will emerge in the youth that he feels as his own free creation and, hence, something to be cherished and lived up to in its practical implications. The alternative in which programs are worked out only by adults for the benefit of youth with the intent of doing something to them is bound to share the fate of all such ill-conceived policies. When we are made to take part in programs which are not of our own free initiation or free choosing, we simply go through the moves. The benefits are only transitory at best. We may drag our feet or evade them when we can with immunity, as has been the case with regimented programs and activities in which the individual himself is not ego-involved as a personally committed and aspiring active participant in concert with others important in his eyes.[7]

In an outstanding discussion of youth involvement Weber and Custer [8] refer to a pronouncement of the Federal Government some years ago:

That if children and young people are to become the self-reliant, self-disciplined, and thinking adults so essential to the success of a democratic society, these children and young people must be recognized as increasingly capable of managing their own affairs and of sharing responsibility for the affairs of the community. That opportunity must be provided for a genuine partnership between young people and adults in community planning for the welfare and growth of these young people. These two principles must be applied to all phases of community life. In the family, the church, the school, and the community the child must be treated as a responsible person and accorded the dignity that is his right as an individual.[9]

This philosophy was extended, sharpened, and put in operational terms by Shmelzer in her definition of youth involvement:

Generically, youth involvement refers to varying sets of procedures that can be employed to enable youth to participate directly in the activities, programs, services, etc., that are designed to affect them. In the youth involvement type of project, youth are not only recipients of services, not exclusively the objects of action, but key figures in developing and/or dispensing services—therefore also subjects of action.[10]

Using the criterion of youth involvement and the above definition of it, Weber and Custer present both historical and contemporary examples of how youth have been encouraged to develop programs for themselves with appropriate agency and institutional support.

In an important study which dealt with the evaluation of change through the use of the group work method with delinquent girls Konopka and

Czaky listed eleven categories "selected as essential to gauging movement through group work process." These categories were:

1. *Insight into Responsibility for Self.* Movement should be toward acceptance of personal responsibility and accountability vs. total projection of responsibility onto outside forces.

2. *Prejudice.* An adversely biased opinion: In this context especially biased opinions in regard to individuals of different races, color, creed, national origin or socioeconomic groupings. Movement should be toward less bias and more acceptance of differences.

3. *Self-Concept/Self-Image.* A negative self-image seems typical of many delinquent girls. Movement should be in the direction of a realistic self-assessment with acknowledgment of strengths and weaknesses.

4. *Capacity for Trust.* Pervasive distrust of people seems to be characteristic of the delinquent adolescent. Movement should be in the direction of a capacity to trust adults and contemporaries but not in an indiscriminate way.

5. *Ability to Make Own Decision.* In a complex society an unusually high amount of decision-making is demanded. Capacity to make rational decisions and to weigh different circumstances and consequences needs conscious development. Movement should be in the direction of making rational decisions without unduly being swayed by emotion or the influence of peers.

6. *Interpersonal Skills.* The interdependence of human beings demands development of one's own personality at the same time as consideration of others. Movement should lie in the capacity to put into practice this dual demand.

7. *Social Relationships.* It is considered in our society that one of the major tasks of adolescence is to come to terms with heterosexual relationships. A healthy attitude is considered one which allows for feelings of romantic love as well as the capacity to develop general friendships with boys and girls. Movement should be in the direction of this dual capacity.

8. *Role and Role Conflict.* This concept is related to the problem of the changing role of women in today's society. Movement should be in the direction of each individual's accepting her own most appropriate role.

9. *Preparation for Work.* In our society today, it is considered appropriate for an adolescent girl to prepare for gainful employment. Movement should lie in the direction of acceptance of preparation for it.

10. *Capacity to See Reality.* Delinquent adolescent girls seem especially prone to distort reality situations by either remanticizing them or seeing them in an exaggeratedly negative light. Movement should be toward a capacity to assess situations in a more rational way. This applied in this context relates especially to relationships with boys.

11. *Degree of Acceptance of Prevailing Societal Mores.* Specific societal mores in which movement had to be judged were: 1) acceptance of preparation for work; 2) acceptance of delayed gratification; 3) ability to profit from past experience; 4) respect for personal and property rights; 5) abstention from overt physical aggression; 6) avoidance of promiscuity.[11]

These eleven categories were developed into a three-page rating schedule and then two groups were selected for evaluation. Written records of group sessions were analyzed. The basic approach yielded positive findings and was judged worthy of further development and refinement.

Some Criteria of Good Group Work

Evaluative criteria for group work should take into account the several phases of the group work whole. Inasmuch as social group work involves individuals, groups, workers and agencies, it is necessary to see what good group work practice calls for in the way of specific behavior of each.

Effective group work depends largely upon what happens in the *group itself*. Good group work results—

(1) when the members of the group propose, plan, carry out, and evaluate their own program experiences with the assistance of the group worker;

(2) when the members of the group enjoy status and a relationship of mutual acceptance which makes for social adjustment. Evidence of this status and acceptance appears in the interactions and relationships among the members of the group;

(3) when a group works together cooperatively and democratically with a wide range of participation—if possible, every member participating to the extent of his ability;

(4) when the behavior of the group is such that it accepts help, guidance and counsel from the group worker and other resource persons in the agency and community;

(5) when a group develops not only consciousness of its own self but also wholesome relationships with other groups in the agency and the community;

(6) when the group shows evidence of a developing social consciousness which enables it to take responsibility for leadership in vital affairs of the community.

Additional criteria of good group work can be formulated in terms of *worker behavior*. Actually, the way in which the worker carries out his responsibilities influences the extent to which the group can be a positive resource for individual development. Good group work demands the following behavior of the worker:

1. The worker must formulate objectives, know what he is trying to do, and know what he wants to have happen as a result of planned group experience. These objectives must be thought of as integrated with those of the agency.

2. The worker must develop an effective working relationship with the members of the group. This relationship is a prerequisite to satisfactory work because through his relationship the worker stimulates, guides, and influences the group but does not dominate it.

3. The worker has conscious understanding and skills which he uses to help the group members do things for themselves in relation to their readi-

ness and ability rather than in terms of a prescribed program. Some of the understandings and skills include the recognition of what it is that holds the group together, the use of group controls, the ability to help members of the group into participating relationships, and the ability to motivate the group into action.

4. The worker recognizes that every individual is different and has specific needs which may be met through group experience. The worker's understanding of the individual is developmental rather than final, and it is his responsibility to continue to search for a deeper and more complete understanding of the individuals with whom he works.

5. The good group worker accepts his responsibility to keep adequate group records and uses his records in the continuous evaluation of his work.

The *behavior of the agency* as represented by its administrative and supervisory staff, as well as its direct workers with groups, is an important aspect of good group work. Effective group work cannot be done unless the agency wants to do it and guarantees the conditions under which it can be done:

1. Good group work requires that the agency have a clearly stated and clearly understood purpose based upon community, group and individual needs.

2. Agencies must have a policy of grouping which deliberately encourages the use of basic groups—that is, groups known to be influential in the lives of group members. Well-formed groups consciously integrated with the total agency are essential.

3. The agency must have a democratic basis of organization and administration, so that groups will have an opportunity to share in the important affairs of the agency insofar as they are able.

4. Group work is possible and probably better when the agency recognizes the importance of personnel standards, is thoughtful in the supervision of workers and gives thorough educational supervision to their efforts.

5. Inasmuch as group work is a developmental experience which depends in large measure on the worker's understanding of individuals in their life situation, the agency must have a system of intake and recording which secures information about individuals and makes it available for workers to use in their work.

6. Whenever the historic and continuing purposes of the agency are expressed in member and leadership commitment which they seek to manifest in program directed to community, group, and individual needs, there is evidence of good group work.

When groups, workers, and agencies apply these criteria to their own behavior, it then leads to a consideration of effective group work in terms of individual growth and development. Though personality changes very slowly and many so-called intangibles are involved, it is possible to locate at least a few criteria which have general application to the *individual*. It is good group work—

(1) when the individual has received sufficient acceptance from the group members that it can be said "He belongs" or "He is a part of the group";

(2) when the individual has a role to play in the life of the group, a role which gives him status and a position of value and importance in the group;

(3) when the individual is helped to an acceptance of the need to co-operate and share in the purposes, plans and activities of the group. It is in this way that he becomes able to utilize group offerings positively for his own growth;

(4) when the individual with special needs is helped to recognize these needs and helped to obtain specialized services from community resource agencies if his needs cannot be met in the group;

(5) when individuals become able to accept people who differ from them and become able to take social responsibility for the wider affairs of the agency and the community.

Though the twenty-two criteria used in the four sections above are not mutually exclusive and must be considered as interrelated, they constitute a general base from which agencies and workers may proceed to formulate more specific items for their own use.

Group Records—the Basis for Evaluation

If workers are to do a sound job of evaluating their work with groups they must keep group records. The major value of the narrative process record from the standpoint of the worker is that such records help the worker to do a more effective job with his groups. Every other purpose is in a sense a subpurpose of this major one: *to improve the quality of experience provided for the group.* By writing a complete process record of everything he does while working with the group, the worker is helped to think, to analyze and to evaluate. The record is thus a tool in the process of understanding the group and learning how to help it. When the worker puts in writing what happened in each group meeting, what he did, what problems he faced, and what questions arose in his mind, he is thinking into the group situation.

Process records are written by the group worker *primarily for himself and for his own use* continuously throughout his relationship with the group. These records help the worker to become more aware of the members of the group as individuals. He can see emerging and changing interests of individuals; he can see evolving needs and how these needs are being met. He can see the development of skills and social attitudes; he becomes sensitive to special problems which may interfere with the individual's full use of the group. Process records show the worker the variety of interpersonal relationships which take shape within the group. The emergence of a group consciousness can be seen as can subgroupings. The acceptance of the individual by the group is reflected by his change in status which can be discovered from reading accumulated records. The development of the worker's relationship and role can be ascertained from careful recording of what he does while helping the group. Attention becomes focused upon the status of the group in the agency and in the community as intergroup relations are recorded. Changes in the goals of the group become more evident, and member interests outside the group are seen from a review of the record.

As the worker writes his records after each meeting, he develops a picture of the group that can be passed on to his superior. Together, worker and supervisor can focus their attention on the group situation as experienced by the worker. The record is thus a stimulus to interaction between the supervisor and the worker. Records enable group work supervisors to keep in touch with many groups for purposes of coordinating the total program of the agency. Records are useful as a basis for evaluating the group experience of the members and for helping the worker in individual and group supervisory conferences. When new workers are assigned to groups, past records become useful at the point of orientation and help new workers to understand the kind of experience the group has enjoyed prior to the coming of the new worker. Records are valuable to other departments of the agency if it is large; and they are important in the planning of referrals of individuals to community resource agencies.

The underlying function of recording is to improve the quality of service to the individual. Hence, recording enables agency administration to judge the quality of its service, the need for its service, and the needs of its constituency or potential constituency. Records are useful to administration in determining whether its services meet the needs of the community, whether the quality of service is in line with processes and objectives of the agency, and whether there is a need to change policies and practices. Furthermore, well-kept records are useful in interpreting group work as a method in social work. Agency boards and community groups can be helped to appreciate the need for added facilities, equipment, and staff. When a review of the records of several groups reveals common problems, it is possible to utilize such factual information as a basis for the selection of staff members and for staff training. Staff assignments to groups can be made with greater intelligence when there is a record of the development of the group.

Meaning of the Record in the Group Work Process

What are we attempting to record when we record the group work process? This is the most important question to answer and understand. Partial answers may be found in this list of items:

First, when we set out to record the group work process, we write about individuals and their responses to one another in a given group situation. In other words, we write about the behavior of the individuals in the group.

Second, we write about the type and extent of participation of individuals who are working, playing, thinking, or otherwise acting together in the group. We concentrate upon what individuals do as they associate with one another.

Third, we note and record the origin and the development of ideas, including their acceptance or rejection by the individuals involved. We look for the interplay of minds and the stimulation of individuals by other individuals.

Fourth, we put down exactly what the group worker does as he carries out his helping role with the group. In addition, we record what the worker thinks and feels about the group situation and what he hopes to accomplish as he works with it.

Fifth, we put down movement, growth, and change as we see it in individuals and in the group as a whole.

Sixth, we write about the relationship between the group and the agency and include community relationships when these are signficant in understanding the group.

Recording the group work process thus implies that we shall concentrate upon *individuals* working together in group situations, *relationships* among individuals as reflected by their participation, *interaction* within the group and between groups, ourselves as *workers* present to exercise a helping role. This may be restated as: *who?*—the members of the group; *what?*—the things they do together; *how?*—the way in which they do things together; *why?*—the reasons why we think certain things occur or fail to occur.

In the beginning, workers who are learning how to record the group work process discover that their job consists of alert observation and sensitivity to what is happening in the group; selection of what to include; organization of material selected; the actual write-up; analysis of the material written; interpretation and utilization of the material in next steps with the group.

The Content of the Narrative Record

The writing of the narrative record is but one part of the worker's job in group work. For some workers, especially for those new in the field, it seems to be a difficult part, and they frequently ask, "What do you want me to include in my records? Do you have an outline that I may follow?" An outline or list of what to include in the record is but a reflection of the work philosophy of the person or persons drawing up the outline. When workers have good insight as to the basic principles of social group work, the items included in content lists tend to emphasize or illustrate these principles. Because groups are different, any list or outline of what to include in the record must be something to select from and to be guided by only in a general way. It is doubtful that any group meeting could possibly include all the items that might be listed in a comprehensive outline. At the outset, workers should be encouraged to include everything that they see as important in understanding the group. As the worker develops security and skill with a given group, changes will come about in the recording. The worker will see more than he saw at first. He will recognize the importance of his own role within the group and will comment upon it more fully. He may discover perplexing and conflicting situations which need further study, and so he will include more interpretation and evaluation in the records. Various items which might appear in the records of a group which has been meeting for some time include the following:

1. The record should include basic identifying information about the group, its name, the date, time, and place of its meeting; the names of individuals present and absent should be listed and new members properly noted. The physical setting within the agency or away from the agency should be mentioned at the beginning of the record as well as any important observations on weather or other conditions which might affect the attendance.

2. The record should include mention of individuals by name; what they do, what they say, and how they get along in the group should be recorded along with the sequence of their participation. Specific contributions of individuals should be mentioned as they interact with other members of the group. The emotional quality of participation, as reflected by behavior toward other individuals or the worker, is important and should be included.

3. As the worker works along with the group he will become aware of the group as a whole. But by putting down what the group does in its activity program, by noting positive and negative response to experiences, and by recording what the members says about their group in relation to the agency, the worker becomes conscious of the group as it moves through various phases of its development.

4. The relationship and role of the group worker should be included. When the worker provides materials, makes arrangements, introduces new members, offers suggestions, leads discussion, participates in activities, interprets the agency, or in any other way enters into the affairs of the group, it should be recorded.

5. At the close of each meeting's record the worker should include a section of evaluative comments regarding what happened during the meeting. This section can consist of questions, explanations as to why things occurred or failed to occur, and tentative plans for the future. Such comments or meeting-by-meeting evaluations are exceedingly important and frequently are longer than the actual meeting record.

6. The worker should include both planned and informal meetings with individuals before, after, and between group meetings. If the worker works with committees that are a part of the group, these meetings should also be described. Individual conferences between the worker and officers of the group, and meetings that the worker established for the purpose of locating

program resources should be included. The goal should be to make the record as complete as possible.

The Principles of Recording

The best discussion of the principles of recording is found in Lindsay's book.[12] She lists and describes five basic principles. These are: the *principle of flexibility,* and by this she means that the record must be adapted to the agency's purpose because group work practice and agency purpose are inseparably interwoven; the *principle of selection,* which implies that the worker does not include everything in his record but selects significant material in the light of individual and group development; the *principle of readability,* which is based on the thought that form and style are important and that clarity of expression is essential for all written material; the *principle of confidentiality,* which says in substance that the record is a professional document and that as such its contents are guarded by a sense of professional ethics; the *principle of worker acceptance,* which underlines the fact that the worker must accept his responsibility to write records because of his conviction that records have value in rendering high-quality professional service.

These principles become self-evident when we consider the various ways in which workers use their records to improve upon their work with their groups.

Using Process Records—What We Learn from Analyzing Them

The worker's use of records begins when he starts to write, because the primary value of records is in helping the worker think through his work with the group. The record should be reviewed before each meeting with the group, since in so doing the worker will be helped to recall salient features of the group's development. After a period of work with the group the accumulated body of information in the record should be studied with a view to ascertaining trends and movements. Record usage thus centers around both immediate and long-term goals.

Good records enable the worker to see and understand the kind of relationship he has established with the group. They show his sensitivity and the way in which he picks up group leads or fails to respond to requests for help. Records make it possible for the worker to learn how his role has changed as the group has developed and reveal the kind of problems the group has encountered in carrying out program and in meeting specific situations.

Records help the worker to deepen his understanding of individual and group behavior and indicate the point at which the individual and the group have arrived in their development. Individuals who need special attention emerge, and the extent to which their needs are being met in the group can be seen. Individuals with leadership abilities can be helped to greater responsibility for the affairs of the group when they have been located by means of the record.

In general, records are most useful at the point of evaluation of the group work process. In fact, it is doubtful whether evaluations of program, individual growth, or worker performance can be satisfactorily made without records. Although partial judgments can be made on the basis of memory, thorough evaluation is possible only if adequate records have been kept.

NOTES

1. Jack Stumpf and Harleigh B. Trecker, *Some Suggested Criteria for Use in E aluating Organizations Providing Social Welfare Services.* Mimeographed. Rev.sed 1971.
2. James H. Davis, *Group Performance* (Reading, Mass.: Addison-Wesley Publishing Company, 1969), p. 1. Reprinted by special permission from Davis, *Group Performance,* 1969, Addison-Wesley, Reading, Mass.
3. Gerald M. Phillips and Eugene C. Erickson, *Interpersonal Dynamics in the Small Group* (New York: Random House, 1970), p. 225.
4. Saul Bernstein, *Charting Group Progress* (New York: Association Press, 1949) in Dorothea F. Sullivan (editor), *Readings in Group Work* (New York: Association Press, 1952), pp. 46 ff.
5. Marjorie Montelius, *Working with Groups* (Washington, D.C.: U.S. Department of Health, Education, and Welfare, Welfare Administration, Bureau of Family Services, 1966), p. 49.
6. Helen Northen, "Evaluating Movement of Individuals in Social Group Work" in *Group Work Papers, 1957,* National Conference on Social Welfare (New York: National Association of Social Workers, 1958), pp. 29–30.
7. Muzafer Sherif and Carolyn Sherif, *Reference Groups* (New York: Harper and Row, 1964), p. 315.
8. J. Robert Weber and Carson Custer, *Youth Involvement* (Washington, D.C.: U.S. Department of Health, Education, and Welfare, Social and Rehabilitative Service, Youth Development and Delinquency Prevention Administration, 1970).
9. *Recommendations for Action.* Prepared for the U.S. Department of Justice by the panels of the National Conference on Prevention and Control of Juvenile Delinquency (Washington, D.C.: U.S. Government Printing Office, 1947), p. 81.
10. June Schmelzer, "Youth Involvement: A Position Paper" (Washington, D.C.: Office of Delinquency and Youth Development, 1966), p. 27.
11. Gisela Konopka and Vernie-Mae L. Czaky, *An Approach to the Evaluation of Change Through the Use of the Group Work Method* (Minneapolis: School of Social Work, University of Minnesota, October 1965, mimeographed), pp. 10–13.
12. Anne W. Lindsay, *Group Work Recording—Principles and Practices* (New York: Whiteside, 1952), pp. 95–106.

9

Basic Principles of Social Group Work

The group worker must understand the basic principles of social group work and must be guided by them in his professional practice.

Principles are guiding assertions, or statements, that have come from experience or research. They are generalizations based upon what has been observed in good practice with groups in different situations. Basic principles on working with people in groups to help them grow and change have been formulated by a number of writers.[1] The suggestions given here seem to this writer to be of most help to the worker. And the worker must have more than an awareness of principles as words. He must have knowledge of the thinking and assumptions that underlie the principles. He must realize what acceptance of the principles means in terms of his behavior as a professional worker.

Principle of Social Work Values

In social group work as in all of social work the values of the profession are the foundation upon which services are developed and made available to persons who need them. The group worker must understand and accept these values and be guided by them.

Central to this principle is the social worker's belief in the dignity and worth of all people and in their right to participate in making decisions about matters which affect them. Group workers who accept social work values and are guided by them believe deeply in freedom of expression and respect the rights of individuals in this regard. The human personality is considered to be capable of growth and change when the environment is favorable to this and when appropriate assistance is made available. The individual and his needs is always the primary focus of the group worker. An essential attribute of social group work is the constant realization by each individual of his full potential toward self-realization.[2]

Principle of Human Needs

In social group work as in all of social work human needs are the basis for the provision of services and programs. The group worker must accept the fact that the meeting of human needs is his primary obligation.

The principle of human needs implies that the worker will seek always to understand the conditions out of which needs arise and that he will work to eliminate unfavorable conditions insofar as is possible. The worker will study the community to discover points of stress and he will anticipate emerging needs to be better prepared to meet them. He will seek to help his group become related to all of the forces making for the enrichment of community life and the strengthening of community services.

Principle of Cultural Setting

In social group work the culture of the community must be understood inasmuch as it influences the way needs are expressed, services are created and utilized by the people who need them. The group worker must have an ever-increasing knowledge of the community.

Every community service agency exists in a cultural setting which in itself is always changing. The beliefs, views, values, prejudices, experiences, and feelings of the people in a given situation constitute the basis for their behavior. The group worker who recognizes this fact seeks to sharpen his awareness of the nuances of cultural determinants and tries to work in ways that will utilize the cultural strengths in his setting. Programs and services should recognize prevailing cultural forms and should be carried forward in ways which support the growth of positive cultural change.[3]

Principle of Planned Group Formation

In social group work, the group is the basic unit through which service is provided to the individual; consequently, the agency and workers responsible for the formation of groups or the acceptance into the agency of already-formed groups must be aware of the factors inherent in the group situation that make the given group a positive potential for individual growth and for meeting recognizable needs.

Behind this principle is the fact that groups, like individuals, are different. Groups are likewise evolving, developmental, ever changing. Central to group work is the fact that groups are tremendously influential upon the behavior of individuals. The influence of the group on the person is not necessarily social or positive. It may be the opposite. Consequently, the group in social group work must possess elements of conscious design and plan. It must contain a social growth potential for the members in it. The fact that it is a group in a social agency setting with a worker makes it distinctly different from nonagency groups. Agency, group, and worker in unison agree that certain positive values are in reach of this group if they will strive to attain them together.

The group worker who accepts this principle and its implications will study groups already formed and give help to groups on the threshold of group formation. However, he will not seek to require all groups to be alike nor expect them to meet identical needs. His skill will be evident in the way he consciously gives aid at the point of group formation. If groups are already formed, he will help them to create a satisfactory association with the agency when it is evident that such association will be mutually desirable. He will help individuals without group contacts to become a part of appropriate organized units.

Principle of Specific Objectives

In social group work, specific objectives of individual and group development must be consciously formulated by the worker in harmony with group wishes and capacities and in keeping with agency function.

Here we accept the fact that the individual in the group in the agency with a worker constitutes an inseparable whole. Individuals want and get different things from groups. Agencies and their workers must be aware of what people want from group experiences and help them to get it. Different people in different groups at different times get different results from their experiences. What they are likely to get and what it is potentially possible for them to get become concerns of the group worker. Objectives thus become a controlling force in the present life of the group.[4]

The group worker who recognizes the need for consciously formulated specific objectives for individuals and groups becomes a purposeful, rather than an unfocused, worker. Group work becomes planned rather than haphazard. It, of course, remains informal, but "informal" does not mean that it is without deliberate plan and purpose. When the worker focuses on individual and group objectives, he reduces the likelihood of permitting his own needs to get in the way of the group. When he works with a group to help the members see their strengths and limitations and set their objectives accordingly, he is helping to convert random human energy into powerful personality resources. When he presents the agency's consciously formulated purposes, which say what it believes in and what it is there to do, he is exercising his skill in agency interpretation and objective formulation. When the individual can feel and say, "That is what I want," and when the group can also feel and say, "This is what we want," and when the worker can feel and say, "This is what you and I and our agency are agreed is within the realm of desirability and possibility; let's work together on it," the group work objectives become the truly democratically conceived goals that they should be.

Principle of Purposeful Worker-Group Relationship

In social group work, a consciously purposeful relationship must be established between the worker and the group members based on the worker's acceptance of the group members as they are and upon the group's willingness to accept help from the worker because of the confidence the members have in him and in the agency.

This principle assumes that it is both possible and necessary to create an effective working relationship with a group before the worker can be of help to the group. It supposes that the character of such a relationship can be defined and understood. Effective relationships grow out of the mutual acceptance of each other by worker and group. The worker's relationship with the group is in itself a major tool. The quality and strength of the worker-group relationship determine the extent to which the group can be helped to the fullest realization of its potentialities.

When group workers adopt the procedures suggested by this principle, they begin their work motivated by an initial desire to understand the group as a basis for helping it. In the past, some workers may have been initially preoccupied with group mechanics, structure, and organizational aspects. They "organized groups" according to preconceived patterns. Now, workers are much more interested in the human or individual aspects of the group. By encouraging the group to "be itself" and by accepting it as it is, the worker becomes accepted and helpful to the group.

Principle of Continuous Individualization

In social group work, it is recognized that groups are different and that the individuals utilize group experiences in a variety of ways to meet their differing needs; consequently, a continuous individualization must be practiced by the worker. Groups and the individuals in the groups must be understood as developing and changing.

The fact that communities, groups, and individuals change is always a strong element in professional social work practice. Perhaps to the social worker the "law of change" is primary. The worker's belief in the capacity of most people to change, when given adequate opportunities for, and help in, changing, underlies and reinforces much of his methodology. To work with groups in awareness of their differences as well as of their similarities is a relatively new and basic principle in social group work.

When the group worker individualizes a group, he accepts the naturalness of difference. When he sees groups as ever changing and developing at different rates of speeds, he eliminates arbitrary expectations as to response and accepts the importance of flexibility in his work with the group. He asks: Where is this group now? How have its members changed? What is likely to emerge in the future? What is this group trying to become?

What does this imply for me as a helping person? Planning *for* the group is replaced by a process of planning *with* the group.

The worker will constantly endeavor to help the group assess its own development. He will want it to develop insight into its needs, capacities, potentialities, and limitations. He will point out progress and will indicate directions for the group to take in the light of its developmental status and its readiness to assume responsibility.

Inasmuch as it is rare, if at all possible, that individuals will make identical adjustments to the same group situation or use the same group experience to meet identical needs, the worker is consciously aware of how individual group members are behaving. The worker thus expects a variety of individual responses rather than a uniformity of response. He accepts the unevenness of individual ability and growth. He endeavors to help individuals understand themselves and works with the group to help it modify its behavior toward individuals who have special needs.

Individualization is continuous on the part of the group worker who accepts the certainty of change. The next step with the group grows out of the worker's conscious attempt to understand what has happened in all past experiences with it.

Principle of Guided Group Interaction

In social group work, the primary source of energy which propels the group and influences the individual to change is the interaction, or reciprocal responses, of the members. The group worker influences this interaction by the type and quality of his participation.

When people are together in groups, the possibility of interaction or interstimulation is always present. Though reciprocal responses may be released by different mechanisms and may have a lower or higher degree of intensity and continuity, the fact remains that this influence of person on person is a major dynamic in social group work. The social group work process implies a harnessing, direction, and conscious utilization of the natural social processes of interaction. The presence of a worker, whose role is to influence actively the type and degree of interaction, converts the social process into the social group work process.

The worker thus operates on the principle that he is there with the group to release and increase the interaction rather than to minimize it or keep it from emerging. He is aware of the basic importance of interaction among members of the group and consciously limits the amount of interaction between himself and the group. He does not presume to tell the group what to do nor does he decide things for the group. He enhances the interactional potential by helping members to assume participating roles, though this may mean that it is necessary to limit temporarily the participation of others or to point out new roles for them to play so that opportunities may be broadly distributed.

The worker who defines his responsibility in relation to the degree of interaction, present and potential, utilizes methods that stimulate the group to the fullest possible analysis and understanding of their own situation. He tries to give depth to group discussion by helping the group ask and answer: What must we endeavor to understand about this situation? Is this course of action superior to any other we might take? What are the alternatives? What are the consequences of our proposed action?

The worker is willing to share his own beliefs with the group when the group wishes to know them, but he is careful so to present his material that the group does not acquiesce to his position but continues to think matters through and ultimately reach a judgment of its own. Though there is always a measure of identification between the worker and the group, the primary identification should be between the members of the group themselves.

Principle of Democratic Group Self-Determination

In social group work, the group must be helped to make its own decisions and determine its own activities, taking the maximum amount of responsibility in line with its capacity and ability. The primary source of control over the group is the group itself.

The principle of self-determination in group work assumes that groups accepted into a relationship with the agency have the right to make choices and the potential capacity to make satisfactory decisions. It further assumes that individuals and groups can develop in social responsibility only when they are given opportunities to behave responsibly. Since duties accompany rights, conscious judgments must be made on how much responsibility a group should be asked to assume at any point in its development.

When the group worker sincerely wishes to implement the democratic ideal of self-determination, he begins with the premise that groups have the right to accept or reject agency services. Acceptance of the agency and the worker comes about after the worker has interpreted the function of the agency and his own role. Agency limits that might seem to restrict the group actually become a positive support for the group to use in furthering its own immediate aims.

There is a very real difference between "knowing what is best" for a group and *knowing the group* so as to help it determine what is better for it. The worker thus gives up any need to have "power over the group" and, instead, works with the group on the basis of his ability to share his wider experience, competence, and expertness. At times the worker may have to assume a temporarily authoritarian role with certain individuals to permit the group to become self-determining. In many instances the worker must first help the group to develop a conscious group self before it can become responsibly self-determining. The emphasis of the worker will shift as the group changes. His aim, however, is to encourage an ever-increasing capacity on the part of the group to take responsibilty for its actions. When the group worker gives vitality to the principle of self-determination, it is interesting to note that he is less likely to feel "personally" responsible for success or failure of the group; rather, he recognizes that social group work is a matter of agency, group, and worker accepting proportionate amounts of responsibility and working together.

Principle of Flexible Functional Organization

In social group work, the process through which the worker guides the group in setting up formal organization is just as important as the actual structural details of that organization. Formal organization should be flexible and should be encouraged only as it meets a felt need, is understood by the members and can function accordingly. The formal organization of the group should be adaptive and should change as the group changes.

Every group possesses an informal organization or arrangement of its constituent members. Such arrangements enable the group to function, to get its work done. In social group work the group is deliberately purposeful; consequently it needs a degree of formal organization to aid it in furthering its purposes. Formal organization enables the energies of group members to become properly channeled. An orderly identification and arrangement of the jobs to be done gives individuals a chance to assume duties and gives the group the chance to select its own leaders. Carefully developed procedures and policies of operation lend stability and certainty to group life. Group efforts, hitherto random and without design, become focused when suitable organization is made available.

However, since groups are different, they need a type and plan of organization to meet their peculiar characteristics. They need less or more organization as circumstances arise. The process through which the group discovers its need to organize its efforts is an excellent vehicle for growth. The experiences the members have in solving organization problems are just as valuable as are other kinds of program experience.

There is a great difference between "organizing a group" and helping a group to organize itself. The group worker must consciously control his own wish for organization of the group until needs are explored, objectives tentatively set, and specific functions determined. Officers, committees, chairmen, rules of procedure, and the like are important, but the group must be helped to make its own decisions about them as needs arise. Though it sometimes seems that groups may want the worker to superimpose a form of organization, it is almost certain that such requests actually reflect ambivalence and lack of sufficient opportunity to clarify needs.

The worker has a specific responsibility in helping the group to determine the qualifications required for all major leadership assignments so that persons who assume those jobs may know what is expected of them. He will work with the persons who hold office or otherwise serve the group and help them to fulfill their respective roles. He will guard against the temptation to "take over" when persons momentarily falter in their efforts. He will help the group to judge the effectiveness of its leaders.

In general, the form of organization should be kept simple and direct. Groups that are allowed to become "overorganized" often find their excess structure a distinct handicap, and frequently its presence retards, rather than enhances, the flow of interaction. Though formal group organization must possess a degree of stability, crystallization and rigidity can set in to the detriment of the group. It is sound for groups to modify their form of organization and to change assignments as the group changes and as other people become able to take over specific responsibilities.

Principle of Progressive Program Experiences

In social group work, the program experiences in which the groups engage should begin at the level of member interest, need, experience, and competence and should progress in relation to the developing capacity of the group.

The principle of progressive program experiences implies that there is a starting point for group work program and that definition of that starting point is important. The differences between groups with respect to interests, needs, and abilities are especially pertinent in the program development process. Programs which might seem incidental, even superficial, to an outsider are often quite real and meaningful to the group. Though it is possible to impose program patterns on groups, it is clearly unwise if the objectives of group work are stated in terms of individual and group growth in democratic skills.

The provision of exposure and experience supplant coercision and dominance in democratic group work. The group worker may make suggestions as to possible programs, but he is careful to extend a variety of choices and he endeavors to relate those possible choices to the level of the group. He is satisfied with small beginnings and fosters initial programs of short duration. He is anxious to utilize the suggestions of the group and prefers to withdraw his suggestions when the group is ready to put forth its own.

The group worker gives help to the group in planning and carrying out its program wishes. By means of evaluation it is possible for worker and group together to move in a direction of more complex program experiences. As success in relatively simple activities makes for security, groups are enabled to undertake more involved sequences of program. To a great extent, progress in program experiences is dependent upon the group's willingness and ability to accept the worker's help in continuously evaluating the contribution of activities as they take place.

Principle of Resource Utilization

In social group work, the total environment of agency and community possesses resources which should be utilized to enrich the content of the group experience for individuals and for the group as a whole.

We assume that the group is always a part of a setting. This setting consists of the agency and the community. Thus, the group must be understood as it is influenced by its setting. There is always a relationship of mutual stimulation between the group and the setting. The worker will wish to see the group in this larger setting and will endeavor to help the group utilize all available resources.

The worker has a role outside the group as well as with the group. He builds up his fund of knowledge about the community and frequently makes his knowledge available to the group. In a sense he is an interpreter of the community and may serve as liaison between the group and the community. The skill with which the worker is able to relate the group to the agency and community is made apparent by the status the group enjoys and by the facility with which it draws upon its adjacent environment.

Principle of Evaluation

In social group work, continuous evaluation of process and programs in terms of outcomes is essential. Worker, group and agency share in this procedure as a means of guaranteeing the greatest possible self-fulfillment for all.

We assume that evaluation in social group work is not only possible and desirable but necessary. The process of evaluation is itself neutral and non-threatening. If there is sufficient clarity regarding the objectives sought, close scrutiny that reveals where we have succeeded and where we have failed is rewarding to all concerned.

The central importance of carefully written group records becomes clear when we accept the principle of continuous evaluation. These records represent the accumulated evidence we must have to make adequate judgments regarding the extent to which objectives have been attained.

Principles Will Change as Group Work Develops

The principles of social group work are dynamic. These principles, which study and experience have indicated as being essential to effective group work practice, will change. With further experience and study our understanding of these principles will deepen. Workers will develop new insight into the skills needed for the successful application of principles. With further study of social group work as a method we can expect new statements of principle to emerge. Considerable work is yet to be done toward fashioning a theory and practice of social group work that will produce in participants outcomes more closely approaching the maximum of possibilities.

NOTES

1. For discussions of principles see: Ruth E. Smalley, *Theory for Social Work Practice* (New York: Columbia University Press, 1967), pp. 175 ff.; Gisela Konopka, *Social Group Work: A Helping Process* (Englewood Cliffs, N.J.: Prentice-Hall, Inc., 1963), Chapter 8, "Principles of Social Group Work Practice," pp. 155 ff.; Emanuel Tropp, "Social Group Work: The Developmental Approach" in *Encyclopedia of Social Work, Sixteenth Issue* (New York: National Association of Social Workers, 1971), Vol. 2, pp. 1247, 1248; Charles D. Garvin and Paul H. Glasser, "Social Group Work: The Preventive and Rehabilitative Approach" in *Encyclopedia of Social Work*, Sixteenth Issue (New York: National Association of Social Workers, 1971), Vol. 2, pp. 1265–1266.
2. For a rich discussion of values see Saul Bernstein, "Values and Group Work" in *Further Explorations in Group Work* (Boston University School of Social Work, 1970), pp. 119 ff.
3. For a penetrating discussion of the culture concept see Albert S. Alissi, "Delinquent Subcultures in Neighborhood Settings: A Social System Perspective," *Journal of Research in Crime and Delinquency*, January 1970, pp. 46 ff.
4. For a brilliant discussion of objectives see Louis Lowy, "Goal Formation in Social Work with Groups" in *Further Explorations in Group Work* (Boston: University School of Social Work, 1970), pp. 94 ff.

PART II

SOCIAL GROUP WORK PRACTICE—
SELECTED RECORDS, DOCUMENTS,
AND TEACHING AIDS

1. Defining Social Group Work

The following material sketches various efforts made over a thirty-year period to define social group work. Dr. Grace L. Coyle in her 1935 piece offered a succinct and sharply drawn statement seemingly limited but nonetheless basic to later formulations. Then in 1949 Dr. Coyle, serving as Chairman of the Committee on the Function of the Professional Group Worker for the American Association of Group Workers, presented the classic "Definition of the Function of the Group Worker." This far-reaching declaration has stood the test of time. In the early 1960's Dr. Margaret E. Hartford summarized a brilliant "Frame of Reference for Social Group Work" for the Group Work Section of the National Association of Social Workers. This comprehensive statement served to move group work ahead. Finally, Dr. Robert Vinter seems to have narrowed the definition of group work in his article for the distinguished *Encyclopedia of Social Work 1965*. Students are urged to read these pieces from the standpoint of common elements and developmental trends.

Group Work . . . is an educational procedure aiming at the development and social adjustment of individuals through voluntary group association usually carried on in leisure time. It needs to be distinguished on the one hand from the case approach which deals with individuals in a one-to-one relationship between client and worker, and from the mass approach which handles hundreds in mass recreation or education with little or no individualizing possible. Group work relies for its effect upon the interaction of a face-to-face group of people bound together by a common interest. These groups vary in size according to the type of person and interest involved, but in order to make group work possible they need to be sufficiently small and stable to allow

233

for mutual acquaintance among the members and some knowledge of individuals on the part of the leader.*

In May of 1949 Dr. Grace L. Coyle, Chairman of the Committee on the Function of the Professional Group Worker for the American Association of Group Worker presented the following "Definition of the Function of the Group Worker":

The Group Worker enables various types of groups to function in such a way that both group interaction and program activities contribute to the growth of the individual, and the achievement of desirable social goals. The objectives of the group worker include provision for personal growth according to individual capacity and need, the adjustment of the individual to other persons, to groups and to society, and the motivation of the individual toward the improvement of society; the recognition by the individual of his own rights, limitations and abilities as well as his acceptance of the rights, abilities, and differences of others. Through his participation the group worker aims to affect the group process so that decisions come about as a result of knowledge and a sharing and integration of ideas, experiences and knowledge rather than as a result of domination from within or without the group. Through experience he aims to produce these relations with other groups and the wider community which contribute to responsible citizenship, mutual usderstanding between cultural, religious, economic or social groupings in the community and a participation in the constant improvement of our society toward democratic goals. The guiding purpose behind such leadership rests upon the common assumption of a democratic society; namely, the opportunity for each individual to fulfill his capacities in freedom, to respect and appreciate others and to assume his social responsibility in maintaining and constantly improving our democratic society.

Underlying the practice of group work is a knowledge of individual and group behavior and of social conditions and community relations which is based on the modern social sciences. On the basis of this knowledge the group worker contributes to the group with which he works a skill in leadership which enables the members to use their capacities to the full and to create socially constructive group activities. He is aware of both program activities and of the interplay of personalities within the group and between the group and its surrounding community. According to the interests and needs of each, he assists them to get from the group experience the satisfactions provided by the program activities, the enjoyment and personal growth available through the social relations and the opportunity to participate as a responsible citizen. The group worker makes conscious use of his relation to the group, his knowledge of program as a tool, and his understanding of the individual and of the group process and recognizes his responsibility to individuals and groups with whom he works and to the larger social values he represents.†

* Grace L. Coyle, "What Is This Social Group Work?" *The Survey*, May 1935, p. 138.
† *The Group*, May 1949, pp. 11–12.

Group work is a way of serving individuals within and through small face-to-face groups in order to bring about desired changes among the client participants. This method of practice recognizes the potency of social forces that are generated within small groups and seeks to marshal them in the interest of client change. The composition, development, and processes of the group are deliberately guided by the practitioner toward achieving his service goals for the clients. Intervention in the experience of the group is the primary means of effecting change, although practitioners engage in many other activities with or on behalf of their clients in addition to conducting group sessions. The group is viewed as a small social system whose influences can be managed to develop client abilities, to modify self-images and perspectives, to resolve conflicts, and to inculcate new patterns of behavior. Achieving such changes among group members has significance only if the changes can be stabilized beyond the duration of the group experience. Persons selected for service through group work are manifesting difficulties, or are believed likely to do so, in important phases of their social functioning; problems of school performance and adjustment, marital conflicts, violation of legal norms, pervasive disturbances in social relations, and so on. Service is directed at ameliorating these difficulties or at developing individual abilities so that clients may function with greater effectiveness and satisfaction. The results of group work service are to be assessed, then, in terms of improved performance in these social role areas, not merely in terms of changed behavior within the treatment group.*

Frame of Reference for Social Group Work †

Social group work is that method of social work in which the group experience is utilized by the worker as the primary medium of practice, for the purpose of effecting the social functioning, growth or change of the group members. The social group worker's practice includes a number of different activities depending on agency setting and job definition. The group worker's functions may include services to groups and individuals, administration, supervision, organization, program planning, and coordination, intake and group placement, record keeping or community and public relations. All of these activities and others are considered aspects of social work practice. The social group work *method* may be distinguished as those specific activities of the worker with or in behalf of the group in which the group experience is used for the benefit of the members.

Within the context of professional social work, social group work incorporates values, purposes, knowledge and sanctions common to all of social work. The difference between social group work and other methods of social work lies:

* "Social Group Work" by Robert Vinter in *Encyclopedia of Social Work*, (New York: National Association of Social Workers, 1965) pp. 715–716. Used with permission.

† From Margaret E. Hartford (ed.), *Working Papers Toward a Frame of Reference for Social Group*. Prepared as a project of the Committee on Practice of the National Group Work Section of the National Association of Social Workers, 1959–1963. Bernard Schiffman, Chairman (New York: National Association of Social Workers, 1964), pp. 4–6). Used with permission.

1) In its methodology.
   The social group worker functions primarily with the group as his major method of helping. His use of individual methods or intergroup methods, although vital to his practice, are secondary.
2) Differential use of common bodies of knowledge.
   The social group worker draws heavily upon individual personality theory, sociocultural theory of society and personality, interactional theory, and he may draw upon social psychology and group dynamics more than the other methods of social work.
3) Different emphasis of some of the purposes toward which social group work is directed.
   He uses his method toward the restoration of personal and social dysfunctioning and the prevention of social and personal breakdown, but also toward the promotion of normal social growth especially in stress periods, and to provide opportunity for personal enhancement and to develop citizen participation. In these three latter purposes social group work may differ in some degree from other methods of social work practice.

Settings. The social group work method is employed in a variety of settings or types of agencies and organizations. These include neighborhood and community services, group services, youth services, hospitals and clinics, correctional institutions, schools, residential treatment centers, institutions for aged, ill or people with special problems, churches, family and child welfare services, public assistance and camps. Though the purpose, focus, goals and the sanctions of the services are conditioned by the setting and the clientele, the group work method is practiced in essentially the same form regardless of setting.

Focus. The social group worker, in providing service, gives simultaneous attention to the group processes, and to the functioning of the individual members. He draws upon knowledge and skill in understanding and affecting group processes as well as knowledge and skill in working with individuals within the group. This dual focus is a particular characteristic of social group work practice. The social group worker may organize the group or may intervene in an already existent group in such a way that the group experience will provide a helping milieu for the individual members in accordance with their social needs. In group work practice the group development is sometimes seen as an end in itself.

Purposes

The social group work method is used to maintain or improve the personal and social functioning of group members within a range of purposes. Groups may be served for corrective purposes when the problem is in the person of group members or in the social situation or both, for prevention where group members are in danger of dysfunction, for normal growth purposes particularly at critical growth periods, for enhancement of the person and for the purpose of education and citizen participation. Any group may be served for any one or all of these purposes simultaneously, and the purposes of the service may change through time, but are related to the social functioning needs of the particular group members within their social context and within agency focus and goal.

1. *Corrective Purpose.* In instances where there is or has been social or personal dysfunctioning or breakdown within individual members, or within their social situations, the group experience may be utilized to provide corrective experiences. In these instances something may have gone wrong or never developed within the person or within the social situation. A group of people may have similar problems or be affected adversely by their social situation. Examples of such problems include delinquents, emotionally retarded people who need social experiences guided by a strong adult, people suffering from physical or emotional breakdown or social isolation, or people who are demoralized by socially, economically and culturally deprived social situations. In these examples the group with the group worker may provide the necessary corrective experiences to provide growth or change.

2. *Preventive Purpose.* In instances where individual group members or the group as-a-whole may exist in circumstances where there is danger of deterioration in personal or social functioning, the group experience may be used to maintain current level of functioning to prevent personal and social breakdown. Under these circumstances the group with the social group worker may provide a constructive program of mental health, provide alternatives from the surrounding delinquency or other social problems, present alternative values, provide motivation for change from prevailing cultural trends, or provide an opportunity for early detection of potential emotional problems and offer alternative resolution to personal pressures, or provide supports for people thought to be under stress and in danger of deterioration.

3. *Normal Social Growth.* The group experience guided by the worker may help to facilitate the normal social growth process and the extension of effective social functioning, particularly for people in stress periods. The social group worker through his interventions helps the group to provide preparation for and adaptation to new situations such as occur in migration or immigration, approach to marriage or parenthood, growth into new age roles such as adolescence, youth, adulthood or old age. The guided group experience may provide social associations and peer relations necessary to facilitate the progression through the normal developmental periods, and to extend the range and quality of social relationships.

4. *Personal Enhancement.* Through collective experience and interpersonal exchange the individual develops skills, expresses latent talent, fulfills potential for growth and finds enrichment of life which could not be achieved as adequately through individual experience. Such groups would include some of the creative arts, interests, intellectual and philosophical discussions, or action groups in which the individual member grows and finds a fuller life experience through the group, not available to him through individual activities. The social group worker may facilitate the group processes so that such experiences may be found by the individual members.

5. *Citizenship Responsibility and Participation.* The social group worker guides the group toward experiences which provide for the members the incorporation of democratic values for themselves, for the group as a whole, and for the wider society. The emphasis in this purpose is on the value development and change within the members that incorporates belief in

rights and dignity of all human beings, not just practice in democratic procedures. By being helped to participate actively in group life, individuals may learn to lead and to follow, to take part in the decision-making process, to assume responsibility for themselves and others, to delegate, to think independently and collectively, to abide by decisions to which one has agreed in the group, and to assume some responsibility for society.

Knowledge

The social group worker draws upon, integrates and applies several bodies of knowledge including personality theory, group theory, sociocultural theory, knowledge of social welfare organization, and knowledge of program media, and theory of group work method.

1. *Personality Theory.* The social group worker uses dynamic theories of personality by which he can understand the meaning of individual behavior from an intrapsychic and interpersonal or social view. The social group worker uses generalized knowledge about expectations of personal and social behavior at various stages of development within the cultural context. Knowledge is also used of the effects of the sociocultural and group experiences on personality development. The social group worker employs this knowledge in his activity with the group in order to provide the opportunity for helping the individual members to grow, change, or correct their social functioning. This knowledge is drawn from biology, physiology, psychology, psychiatry, social psychology, anthropology, and education.

2. *Group Theory.* The social group worker uses theory and concepts about groups by which he can understand and also intervene effectively in the processes of groups. Some of the elements or processes he needs to understand are: the group formation, continuity, and dissolution processes, the elements of group composition, goals, structure and functioning, patterning of relationships, group influences and controls, deliberative process and decision making, the nature of group cohesion and morale, and the cultural properties of groups. The social group worker draws his group theory from social psychology, sociology, anthropology, psychiatry, and to some extent theory about groups that have developed within the practice of group work itself.

3. *Sociocultural Theory.* The social group worker draws upon knowledge of the nature, function and structure of society and culture, subcultures and substructures including reference groups, social, ethnic, social class, family, geographical, and occupational organization. He uses systems theory, social change theory, and organizational theory and some of the theoretical formulations of social dysfunction, such as anomie, disengagement, minority status, economic depression, etc. He draws this knowledge of social theory from sociology, anthropology, economics, social psychology, and political science.

4. *Knowledge of Social Welfare Systems.* The social group worker uses a body of knowledge about the organization of social welfare systems, public and private, the nature and function of resources and the interrelatedness of the social welfare services. The worker uses knowledge of the need systems and the various approaches to need meeting and problem solution at the community level. This knowledge stems from social work and social welfare organization,

social sciences, and some knowledge developed within community organization practice.

5. *Knowledge of Program Media.* The social group worker uses knowledge about the nature and functions of various program media for personality development, for facilitating social, intellectual and physical growth, for stimulating motivation for change and for facilitating group development or change. Program media used in social group work may be verbal and non-verbal and includes arts and crafts, dramatics, music, sports and games, discussion, camping and camp crafts, dancing and trips (among others). The sources of this knowledge beyond social group work itself are education, physical education, recreation, adult education, and the arts. The social group worker needs enough knowledge about the uses of the various media to be able to be selective in the program which he introduces or facilitates from the suggestions of members, appropriate for the particular members in the specific group.

6. *Practice Theory.* Specific practice theory relative to the use of social group work remains to be fully developed and tested. However, practicing group workers and educators do use theoretical formulations based on the accumulation of wisdom, knowledge and clinical experience, and the integration and application of knowledge from the basic sciences and other professions.

Some of the elements of practice theory follow: The Group is the means for providing social group work service. The worker gives attention to the growth of members in the development of themselves and their group through their interactions and activities with each other and with the worker. As part of the service the worker may find it necessary or deem it important to engage in individual conferences with members or in behalf of members, but this is related to the use of the group as the major medium of service.

Service is provided to groups and individuals by the social group worker on the basis of diagnostic thinking about and feeling for the particular people in the specific group in their circumstances and within the defined service area or agency framework. Decisions about service are made at the administrative, programming and staffing level as well as with individuals and in the group, based on an assessment of need in light of focus, goal, and resources. Diagnostic thinking includes an awareness of the differential social functioning needs and strengths of the particular individuals which may be amenable to growth or change within the group experience. Diagnostic thinking also includes an assessment of the group as an entity in light of a theoretical formulation of the nature of groups.

The social group worker's interventions take the form of interaction or relationship with members and group, the facilitation of interpersonal relationships among members and promotion of group action through various group activities or program media toward the end of growth or change of the group and the individual members in accordance with members' and worker's goals determined in the diagnostic process.

The social group worker's constant evaluation of the process of growth and change taking place within the group and with the individual affect his intervention and methods of procedure.

Technical Skills

The technical skills of the social group worker exist in practice, and are developed from clinical experience, and the application of existent theory. The social group worker uses his knowledge, makes an assessment of the needs and strengths of the members and of the group and intervenes with the group using a range of technical skills. Most of these technical skills remain to be described, elaborated and operationalized, while others need to be tested for further theoretical support. Some of the technical skills of the social group worker which have been identified are as follows:

1. Skill in relationship with members and in the facilitation of relationship between and among members.

2. Skill in diagnosis or assessment of the social functioning needs of individuals and of the group using an integration of the several bodies of knowledge.

3. Skill in systematic observation and assessment of individuals, groups, social situations, and problems to determine need for service.

4. Skill in forming, continuing and terminating groups.

5. Skill in intervention in group processes.

6. Skill in leadership in handling structure and authority, facilitating and guiding the group.

7. Skill in involvement of group members in planning and group activity.

8. Skill in analysis of program media and in use of program media with group.

9. Skill in recording.

10. Skill in use of agency resources.

11. Skill in facilitating the use of community resources.

12. Skill in use of professional judgment in choice of actions related to individuals and groups.

13. Skill in evaluation of professional activity and of individual and group movement.

14. Skill in communication of attitudes, feelings and opinions.

Values

Social group work practice as one of the methods of social work is influenced and bound by the philosophy, values and ethics of the profession. It rests upon a belief in the dignity of all men, and the social responsibility of men for their fellow men. The social group worker, therefore, accepts the specific responsibility to perform professional practice for the benefit of the group members and the welfare of society, and works toward the extension of the democratic ideal.

2. References on the History of Social Group Work

For those who wish to acquaint themselves with the history of social group work the following references should be helpful:

1. Grace L. Coyle, "Social Group Work" in *Social Work Yearbook 1937* (New York: Russell Sage Foundation, 1937), pp. 461–464.
2. Margaret E. Hartford (editor), *Working Papers Toward a Frame of Reference for Social Group Work* (New York: National Association of Social Workers, 1964), pp. 62–79, Chapter 5, "The Search for a Definition—Historical Review" by Margaret E. Hartford.
3. Ernest V. Hollis and Alice L. Taylor, *Social Work Education in the United States* (New York: Columbia University Press, 1951), pp. 39–41.
4. Gisela Konopka, *Social Group Work: A Helping Process* (Englewood Cliffs, N.J.: Prentice-Hall, Inc., 1963), Chapter 1, "History of Social Group Work."
5. Ruth R. Middleman, *The Non-Verbal Method in Working with Groups* (New York: Association Press, 1968), Chapter 1, "The Evolution of Social Group Work," pp. 25–63.
6. The periodical *The Group,* Volume 1, Number 1, February 1939, through Volume 17, Number 5, June 1955. *The Group* was published by the American Association for the Study of Group Work from the beginning in 1939 to 1946 when the American Association of Group Workers was established. After 1955 when the A.A.G.W. joined with other professional organizations to found the National Association of Social Workers, group work articles appear in *Social Work,* the quarterly journal of N.A.S.W.

3. A Guide for the Study of the Group

The following outline is offered as a guide for the student who wishes to understand his group either at the beginning of his relationship with it or after he has spent some time working with it.

A Guide For the Study of the Group

A. *History of the Group*
 1. When did the group begin?
 2. How, by whom, and for what reason was the group started?
 3. What agencies have worked with this group in the past?
 4. What type of group is this: interest group, class, club or other?

B. *Group Characteristics*
 1. What is the age range of the group members?
 2. What is the sex of the group members?
 3. What cultural backgrounds or national origins are represented?
 4. In what ways do group members spend most of their time? In school? At work? In other ways?
 5. What form of organization obtains at the present time?
 6. What is the quality of relationship among members?

7. Does the group seem to have any prominent subgroups?
8. Is there evidence of social control patterns operating within the group?
9. What seems to be the status of the group in the agency and the community?
10. What has been the past experience of the group, and how do the members tend to evaluate it?
11. Does there seem to be a balance of active participation among the members of the group?
12. Is the group growing or diminishing?
13. How does the group admit new members?
14. How does the group carry on its affairs of business and program?

C. *Individuals in the Group*
1. What is the age, sex, race, occupation, educational background of each individual?
2. What is the individual's status in the group? In the agency? In the community?
3. How does the individual relate to other individuals? Who are his friends? With whom does he participate easily?
4. What are the individual's interests and abilities?
5. What has been the individual's previous experience in groups?
6. From what kind of home and community environment does the individual come? ·
7. To what extent does the member participate in the activities of the group?
8. How much initiative and responsibility does the individual take in the affairs of the group?
9. Does the individual now hold an office, chairmanship, or other leadership responsibility?
10. With what other groups is the individual active in the agency or community?

D. *The Worker-Group Relationship*
1. Who were the former workers with the group? What was their relationship? What do group members say about them?
2. What is the present worker's relationship with the group? What does the group expect from the worker?
3. What is the present worker's relationship with individual members?
4. How does the present worker define his role with the group?
5. What use will the group make of other workers as resource people or special program aides?

E. *Program*
1. What has the group done in the way of program and what are its present interests?

2. How has program been planned and carried out in the past, and what is the present method of program implementation?
3. To what extent does the program seem to meet the needs of the group?
4. To what extent has program progressed from simple to more complex activities?
5. Are the facilities and resources adequate to meet the needs and interests of the group?
6. Is the program in harmony with the purposes of the sponsoring agency?

F. *Individual and Group Objectives*
1. What are the needs of individuals and to what extent can the group meet these needs?
2. What are the immediate and long-term objectives for this group?
3. Which individuals need special help from the worker and group?
4. To what extent has the group had successful experiences in the past?

G. *Level of Group Development*
1. Where is the group now in terms of its development as a group?

4. Stages of Group Development

The material on stages of group development presented below is offered as a means of acquainting the student with a variety of approaches to this important matter. It is suggested that these approaches be compared and that an effort be made to relate specific groups to the models given here.

Stages of Development in Social Group Work *

The five stages through which members and groups as a whole will pass in the course of their development are: (1) pre-affiliation, (2) power and control, (3) intimacy, (4) differentiation, and (5) separation.

Stage 1: Pre-affiliation—Approach and Avoidance

The initial period of group association is one in which the members are becoming familiar with one another and the situation, and have not yet formed close ties. Relationships are usually non-intimate and a good deal of use may be made of rather stereotypic activity as a means of getting acquainted and at the same time retaining some distance and protection. The group and the

* James A. Garland, Hubert E. Jones, Ralph L. Kolodny, "A Model for Stages of Development in Social Work Groups" in Saul Bernstein (ed.), *Explorations in Group Work* (Boston: Boston University School of Social Work, 1965), pp. 21–41. Used with permission.

worker tend to be seen as reflections of other groups and leaders with which the individual has had contact in his social experience (as distinguished from families). Members' ambivalence toward involvement is reflected in their vacillating response to program activities and events. An on-again-off-again attitude toward such things as parallel versus interactive play, accepting versus not accepting, and responsibility versus avoidance in cleanup and planning are quite common. The basic struggles in this ambivalent, pre-affiliative phase when viewed in the light of the closeness dimension is one of approach and avoidance. Whether the group members elect officers and plan a month in advance at the first meeting or lurk outside the clubroom furtively peeking in the door, they are probably experiencing some kind of anxiety about becoming involved and are attempting to find ways within their framework of social experience to accomplish this process of exploration and affiliation. . . .

Stage 2: Power and Control

Once the basic problem has been solved as to whether the group experience is potentially safe and rewarding, and worth a preliminary emotional investment, members begin to lock horns with the power and control issues of group life. The problems of status, ranking, communication, choice making and "influence" come to the fore. There is a testing of the group worker and other members, and an attempt to define and formalize relationships and to create a status hierarchy. Physical strength, aggressiveness, mental agility and skill in whatever endeavors the group considers to be of high value must be discovered. Cliques form and alliances are made, at times, for the purposes of mutual protection. These may vary in size from two against the group to the total group against one. This latter situation sometimes arises out of the need of the group to protect itself from the very powerful and aggressive member, or from the pyschic danger posed by a deviant or handicapped member. It is at this time that scapegoating first appears and, with it, an attempt to exclude individuals from membership.

The relationship which appears to be most significant in connection with the power-control issue and which has the greatest effect on the nature and intensity of intragroup control dynamic is that between the worker and the group. The worker has the ability to give or withhold in material or emotional terms and this may include food, handicraft materials, the use of sporting equipment, a meeting room or an automobile, extra time for meetings, or personal attention for individuals. His role as a therapist, teacher, parent, agency, community or social class representative, however the group perceives him, gives him a potential for influencing the affairs of the members that is at the same time comforting or overwhelming. A rather striking example of the impact of this potential is the amount of energy an antisocial gang will sometimes invest in keeping the group worker from being admitted to their system and from "taking over."

Stage 3: Intimacy

The third stage of development is characterized by an intensive case of personal involvement, more willingness to bring into the open feelings regarding club members and worker and striving for satisfaction of dependency needs. Sibling-like rivalry tends to appear as well as overt comparisons of the group to family life. There is a growing ability to plan and carry out group projects, although this proficiency declines as interpersonal conflicts arise. There is a growing awareness and mutual recognition of the significance of the group experience in terms of personality, growth and change.

Stage 4: Differentiation

The stage of differentiation is one in which members begin to accept one another as distinct individuals, to see the social worker as a unique person and to see this group experience as a unique experience from which each can find an acceptable intrapsychic equilibrium. As clarification of and coming to terms with intimacy and mutual acceptance of personal needs brings the freedom and ability to differentiate, and to evaluate relationships and advance the group on a reality basis.

Stage 5: Separation

The fifth stage is that of separation. The group experience has been completed and members may begin to move apart and find new resources for meeting social, recreational and vocational needs. The process of termination in this stage may involve some regression and recapitulation, both spoken and acted out, of former group experiences and relationship patterns. In addition to permitting of anxiety over separation and loss, the recapitulation serves an evaluating function, helping the group to rethink and assess the meaning and value of the total experience. If the group experience has made a significant impact on the group members, the assumption is that it now becomes the frame of reference for approaching new social, group, and familial situations.

Phases of Group Development *

The phases and the events which characterize each are detailed below, in the order in which they are typically identified.

1. *Origin Phase.* This phase refers to the composition of the group and is distinguished primarily for analytic purposes, because events occurring are at least a precondition for later development.

2. *Formative Phase.* Initial activity of group members in seeking similarity and mutuality of interests is the outstanding characteristic of the formative phase. Initial commitments to group purpose, emergent interpersonal ties and a quasi-structure are also observable in this phase.

3. *Intermediate Phase I.* This phase is characterized by a moderate level of group cohesion (i.e., interpersonal bonds among members), clarification of purposes, and an observable involvement of members in goal-directed activities.

4. *Revision Phase.* In this phase, a challenge to the existing group structure

* Rosemary C. Saari and Maeda J. Galinsky, "A Conceptual Framework for Group Development" in Robert D. Vinter (ed.), *Readings in Group Work Practice* (Ann Arbor: Campus Publications, 1967), pp. 76–77. Used with permission.

can be expected, accompanied by modification of group purposes and operating procedures.

5. *Intermediate Phase II.* Following the revision phase, while many groups gradually progress toward maturation, the characteristics outlined in Phase 3 may again appear; however, the group generally manifests a higher level of integration and stability than that of the earlier intermediate phase.

6. *Maturation Phase.* This phase is characterized by stabilization of group structure, group purposes, operating and governing procedures, expansion of the culture of the group, and the existence of effective responses to internal and external stresses.

7. *Termination Phase.* The dissolution of the group may result from goal attainment, maladaptation, the lack of integration, or previous planning to terminate the group.

Stages in Group Development *

Groups come into being in such ways as: (1) functions of associations, institutions, and government; (2) deliberate developments for special purposes, such as working agencies, social welfare programs, military organizations; (3) spontaneous developments out of current needs, such as the gang developing for protection; (4) permanent aspects of the culture, the family; and (5) related to interest, such as the team in formal games. . . . These stages of development may be regarded as symptoms of group movement in the direction of group competence. They are a convenient, theoretical device for bringing together a large body of observation of group properties. No group ever fits exactly into these categories, and all groups do not go through all the stages.

Varying degrees of tension, spontaneity, conflict, comfort, and response are seen in these stages. Each stage may be described in terms of the operational concept (indicated by the tentative title), the behavior, and the direct experience.

First Stage: Approach or Orientation. The behavior of adults tends to be that of conventional approach, while children present a range from noncommittal, evasive behavior to the conventionalized approach. Behavior is tentative and wary, sometimes provocative, with most members being relatively passive as they assess possible social threat. Leadership may appear as some staff members offer committing suggestions. In terms of internal awareness we speculate that the individual may be anxious regarding the response he will receive and fear possible domination, aggression, isolation, rejection, hostility (his own and others toward him) but anticipates satisfying reassurance.

Second Stage: Relationship Negotiation or Conflict. Behavior varies. The more aggressive begin to bid for the responses they wish, the roles called for by their needs, which are not necessarily known to the individual. The passive members are still largely passive. There is some tentative commitment by a larger number of members and from experimental aggressiveness, hostility, and demands. In terms of individual awareness, tentative establishment of some

---

* Walter L. Kindelsperger and Gladys M. Ryland, "The Meaning to the Indivdual of Participation in Group Life" in *Use of Group Method in Social Welfare Settings.* (New Orleans: Tulane University School of Social Work, 1957), pp. 8–9. Used with permission.

reassuring relationships and freedom of self-expression and assessment of dangers is made with more reassurance. The shy person may still be fearful of commitment, but in general, anxiety is reduced on the part of most members.

Third Stage: Group Role Emergence. The behavior indicates that the majority of the members have found the response and roles which promise the needed satisfaction; on the other roles they compromise, substitute, cooperate, and accommodate their points of view. There is some repression on a subconscious level. Definite group structure acceptable to the majority appears as the dominating content of the helper. Speculating on personal awareness it is probable that responses and roles satisfying to the individual are brought into the structure or old roles are accepted; there is the beginning of confident commitment and trust. Considerable identification with group roles—the development of "we" feeling and "our" club—shows personal investment in the group.

Fourth Stage: Vacillating Group Role Dominant. The behavior here shows the emergence of well-developed group roles newly accepted by the majority but with considerable ambivalence and vacillation. Group structure seems well developed but this appearance is apt to be deceptive; leadership groupings are well established. The experience provides increasingly satisfying responses. There is greater "we" feeling and identification with group roles and structure on a conscious basis.

Fifth Stage: Group Role Dominance. The behavior shows strong group structure attachment and acceptance of roles is well established. Techniques of group adjustment are well accepted; leadership functions are partially established and behavior roles are dynamic. Individuals have probably realized and sustain self-satisfaction with strong personal needs satisfied in a dynamic manner and a strong identification with group roles on a less conscious basis with belonging and ease predictable.

Sixth Stage: Institutionalized Group Role. Behavior shows that only rigid group structure and rules limit behavior. Group roles become less and less dynamic. The direct experience indicates that specialized satisfaction is to be found only in rigid roles which are not dynamic in nature and these demand roles dominate the members.

5. Program Planning in Social Group Work*

 I. All program is based on interest and needs
   A. Interest is determined by:
    1. Stated desires—skills
    2. Developed skills—mastery
    3. Pleasant experiences—fun
    4. Has met recognized and unrecognized needs
    5. Normal interests of age—sex group
   B. Needs which may be met in program are:
    1. Physical growth and neuromuscular control
    2. Intellectual stimulation and growth
    3. Acceptable release for emotions

* An outline developed by (Mrs.) Louise P. Johnson, Assistant Professor, School of Social Work, University of Iowa. Used with permission.

4. Patterns and disciplines which limit and influence behavior and provide security
5. Development of socialization skills including:
    a) Gaining acceptance through skill in activity
    b) Increasing status
    c) Providing opportunity to make and carry out decisions
    d) Aiding individuals in relating to others
    e) Providing patterns for settling conflicts and establishing controls
    f) Opportunity to express friendliness, affection, indifference, and hostility
    g) Providing diagnostic material
    h) Modification of interest and development of new interests

II. Criteria for good program
    A. Grows out of interests and needs of members
    B. Takes in account factors of age, cultural background, setting
    C. Provides experience and opportunity to choose and develop new interests, deepen old interests, normal growing-up experiences, work with others
    D. Is flexible and varied, maximum opportunity for participation
    E. Evolves from simple to complex
    F. Adheres to agency policy

III. Program Process
    A. Discover interest and need
    B. Select beginning point or level of program by considering:
        1. Attention span
        2. Frustration tolerance
        3. Socialization level
        4. Physical level
            a) Coordination
            b) Skill
        5. Intellectual level
        6. Emotional level
            a) Handling of aggression
            b) Judgment
            c) Psychosexual development
        7. Specific skill level
    C. Decide on activity considering A and B
        1. Set goals
        2. Try out activity
        3. Adapt as necessary
    D. Analyze what is needed
        1. Staff
        2. Equipment
        3. Supplies
        4. Area
    E. Allocate responsibility for specific tasks
        1. Worker
        2. Members

F. Carry out activity (role of staff)
   1. Present activity to group
      a) Be positive in your attitude yet accept members' negative feelings
      b) Show rather than tell
      c) Proceed from simple to complex
      d) Set limits
   2. During activity
      a) Help individuals participate
      b) Help group form and develop
      c) Help group make decisions
      d) Maintain previously set limits
      e) Observe behavior and relationships
      f) Enrich group experience using own interests, experiences, and skills as appropriate
G. Evaluation
   1. Activity
      a) Was it appropriate to interest and need of group?
      b) Were goals met?
      c) Was preparation sufficient?
   2. Individual response
   3. Group response

6. The Hill Street Cadets: The Worker and a Teen-Age Group Take Stock

Agency and Community Setting

The Hill Street Neighborhood Center is a private agency, established to render community educational and recreational service to individuals on a group basis through participation in a variety of group activities. Groups range from formal types, like the Boy and Girl Scouts, to informal play groups with a variety of groups in between, serviced and supervised by group workers. The agency staff through the Intergroup Council often develop special large-scale programs such as festivals, celebrations, forums and the like.

Hill Street consists of several buildings, a gymnasium and auditorium combination, the main building housing the clubrooms and providing offices for staff members; a music, art, and library building and a clinic are also a part of the setup. There is an outdoor playground which has a director, an assistant director and four group workers with two full-time special activity persons and four part-time workers who help on special interest programs, including modern and classical dancing, dramatics and choral groups.

The function of the agency is stated as: a community agency where children, youth, and adults of both sexes are provided opportunities for personality development and social adjustment through recreation and informal education. The agency is situated in a neighborhood of varied cultural groups where, through clubs, classes and other groups, persons are helped to take social responsibility for community welfare. Members discover talents, broaden their interests, and learn to work together. No restrictions as to sex, race, religion, residence, or economic status. Membership not obligatory.

The agency is located in the heart of the Hill Street District adjacent to the central manufacturing area of the city. There are many nationality groups within this area, and they utilize the agency activities daily. It is open to all, from very young preschool children to the older adults. The community consists of moderate-income families predominantly, but some are in need of economic assistance. Close to the agency are the Greenview Playground and Henderson Recreation Field which are operated by city and county government. There is one high school within this vicinity. There are several grammar schools and junior highs.

The Worker's Background in Group Work

As my father was a Scout Commissioner, it was expected of me, I suppose, to join the Boy Scout "Cub" troop when I was ten. This I did. Scouting was fun when we planned and conducted our own program. Later, at the Y, twelve of us fellows who were better than average in aquatics formed the Swimming Club. From the time I was twelve years old until I left college, this club was to be an important group experience. One of the Y staff was our club adviser. Meetings were held once each week, but we members were together at least five times a week. The Swimming Club soon became more than just a swimming club. We studied lifesaving, officiating at aquatics, Indian lore, social dancing and handicrafts. We "talked" religion, politics and "girls." We hiked through the country, traveled to other cities and competed with other swim teams.

Summer boys' camp experiences provided other important elements of my group life. Under supervision of what must have been fairly well-trained counselors, I, among 300 other boys, received a full measure of understanding—the word is deliberately used—the responsibilities of cooperative living. Our games, food, sleeping quarters, trips, plays, and campfires were based on the intimate unit of ten boys and a counselor. The effect was so profound that I find myself leaning on those experiences in carrying out my work. There was a very happy balance of free time and planned program. I recall resenting only one aspect of camp life which was compulsory, and that had to do with religious functions. In the four summers I attended camp, only one program failure remains with me. Once only was a project tried which was initiated from "above" with little or no consultation of the campers who were to participate. We were asked to construct, in the sand, a huge bas-relief map of the camp. We were under the direction of one of the camp staff, and although we worked like Trojans and came up with a fairly presentable piece of work, we all hated doing it and would gladly have done KP or other distasteful jobs rather than participate in this "creative" effort.

My work as a volunteer helper in a "group work agency" began when I was sixteen. At that time, I assisted a professional worker in swimming instruction and lifeguarding. Later, I helped to teach crafts and lead discussions in classes and groups. This was not social group work, although it had some of the elements of it. The main element lacking was a focus on helping persons through the use of the group experience. Obviously, as a teen-ager I had limited insight and skill in that, although I could teach skills successfully.

Sometime during my eighteenth year I received my first pay for assisting in the athletic and craft program at the Y. After completing high school and entering college, I spent three summers as a counselor at camp.

My first real experience as a social group worker came while doing supervised field work in graduate school. Under faculty and agency supervisors I learned some basic skills and insight in helping individuals in groups in their development toward personal and social maturity. I had been on the staff of Hill Street for three months when I began working with the Cadets.

Individuals in the Group

The Cadets were organized five years ago. Of the fifteen original members, Freddy B., Frank J., Sam H., Kenneth E., Mike F., Wilfred L., Walt G., George A., Alex G., and Paul B. were still active in the group when present worker was assigned.

When first organized, these boys were ten, eleven, and twelve years old. They began as an athletic club, participating in seasonal sports the year around. Gradually, they took on other activities and adopted a club structure and constitution. Volunteers, sometimes a father of one of the members, had worked with the group. Some of the recent workers were dominating. The group was without a worker eight months before present worker came. The Cadets are fifteen to seventeen years of age as the record begins.

Individuals in Following Record

Freddy B., seventeen years of age, tall, slender, nervous, hyperactive, great need for attention and a leadership role. Tends to dominate and run things. An only boy, home troublesome, eventually moved across town to live with a married sister.

Alex G., fifteen, a husky fellow, active in football only. Was sergeant at arms. Usually quiet, becomes loud when trying to gain recognition.

Sam H., sixteen, tall, good-looking, athletic, quiet, reserved. Not too active in club—follows along.

Frank J., seventeen, an only child, nice-looking, athletic, ambitious as to status in club. Good leadership qualities, but needs better control of feelings. More practice and tolerance needed.

Harry S., fifteen, a nervous fellow, introvert, impatient, a perfectionist. Eventually resigned from club to join a new group which offered opportunities for an ideal situation as he saw it.

Don T., sixteen, a cynical, seemingly asocial fellow. A poor cooperator in the club and on the athletic field.

Gerald A., seventeen, a good-looking fellow, genial, a bit vulgar in his sense of humor and in things he thinks the club should do. An instigator on a more playful level.

Kenneth E., seventeen, only came to meetings a couple of times, not very interested in the Cadets.

Paul B., fifteen, plump, good-natured and well liked. Unable to compete too well athletically, but tries hard.

Wilfred L., sixteen, good-looking, athletic, good-natured and well liked. Like Sam, follows along, but does more pushing below surface.

Ned R., fifteen, a new member, smaller than most of the fellows, not athletic, but quite well liked. Rather quiet.

Mike F., seventeen, tall, athletic, quiet, likable, interested in club to the end.

Louis W., fifteen, a new member, attended infrequently because of music lessons which came at the same time as the group meeting.

Walt G., seventeen, well-built and, like Kenneth, losing interest in the group.

Dick R., sixteen, a sincere, level-headed fellow, not too well accepted, largely because his interests were not in keeping with those of the other members. Friendly with Frank.

George A., sixteen, a pleasant fellow, good thinker and well accepted. Lived on other side of town but occasionally attended meetings.

First Meeting

While waiting for the meeting to start, Mr. O., the supervisor, introduced Worker to Freddy, president of the Cadets, and he in turn introduced Worker to the boys present and to each of the members as they came in. Alex barged in, walked over to Worker, and said brusquely, "Are you the new adviser? I'm Alex G., glad to meet you."

Freddy called the meeting to order, sent Alex upstairs to get Harry, the secretary, and proceeded to ask for committee reports. The reports were brief and were given without enthusiasm. Harry hurried into the room and upon request of Freddy immediately began a reading of the minutes, which amounted to a rather emotional tirade that there were no minutes, there were hardly any fellows at the last meeting and if the club was going to keep on this way, there'd be no club. Too, "What this club needs is new fellas."

The president then proceeded with old business. This consisted of a brief discussion of a proposed party. However, Gerald, who was to have arranged for a house, had forgotten to do so. One of the other fellows thought that he might be able to get his house.

Next, the question of basketball was brought up. Freddy suggested that the club team might enter another tournament. Don thought that one tournament was enough. There were a few comments and the matter was dropped.

The president then brought up the question of T-shirts that the club was to buy for the members. There were a few comments on the weak condition of the treasury. It was decided that the purchase of T-shirts would be looked into. Freddy asked for a volunteer to investigate the price and where they could be bought. Paul offered to look into it and then added that he thought he would have time to do so.

In the way of new business, Freddy suggested the possibility of having a raffle, in order to raise money for the club. There was considerable discussion on this. Paul expressed the general consensus, saying, "We just ran a raffle three months ago and if we tried another one it wouldn't look good, as everyone would think that all our club is interested in is making money." The idea of a raffle was dropped.

Freddy then told the club of some books on sex that he thought the club should order by mail. He said, "We should get them and all of us should read them. We should know about such things. We'll need it later on. It's good stuff." Nothing further was said.

Don suggested that the club should do something over Thanksgiving. A number of ideas were advanced: a hayride, a trip to the mountains, going on one of the tours of the city, a hike. Some of the pros and cons of each were briefly discussed, the fellows jumping from one thing to the next. No agreement was reached. Don suggested that the club go ice skating. He said he thought it was fun and was sure the fellows would enjoy it. Mr. O., the supervisor, suggested that Worker had had experience with ice skating and could probably go with the club and help them out. Worker said that he would be glad to go skating with the club and help those fellows who might have difficulty. A discussion of what skating rink should be used and what night to go followed. Frank asked Worker what rink he thought best and what night. Worker suggested the Midtown Rink because it was close, as well as being one of the nicer rinks in town, and suggested a week night as being less crowded. (The fellows had expressed some concern about choosing a night when the rink wouldn't be too crowded.) Mr. O. offered a suggestion that the Wednesday night before Thanksgiving might be a good night, there being no school the next day. The club agreed that this would be the night. Freddy asked Frank to inquire about price, etc., and report back to the next meeting. Worker suggested that Frank go out and phone the Midtown. Mr. O. wrote Frank a note so that he might use the agency phone. He returned and informed the club that the admission was

50 cents and skate rental 25 cents, the evening skating session beginning at 8 o'clock. Freddy asked the fellows to meet at the agency at 6:30 P.M. and asked that everyone try to come. Also, he suggested that each of the members spread the word around and try to get others to join them.

Harry got up and told the fellows that the club should make up its mind to really work together, that the club should really start over and get going. Too, that if Worker would be willing to be adviser to the club, it would help a lot. There followed some discussion about having Worker advise the club for a trial period. Freddy offered the thought that, after all, Worker might have his own ideas about whether or not he wanted to work with the club. He then asked him to tell the club whether or not he would be their adviser, what he thought was wrong with the club, and what he thought the club should do. Worker told the boys that he would very much like to be with the club, that after a few meetings they could decide whether or not they wanted him to continue. As to what was wrong with the club, Worker suggested that he didn't feel he had known the club long enough to offer criticism. He said that he thought there were certainly enough members for a good club. Too, that the fellows had shown enough spirit and interest and that they were certainly alive and moving, and saw no reason why they couldn't correct their weaknesses as they went along and in time create a strong, active club.

Don asked Worker to tell the fellows something of his experiences, so that the club might know something about him. Worker told the fellows of his interest in athletics and gave a brief account of some of his athletic experiences. Too, he related some of his work experiences, in the shipyards, on the waterfront, etc. and suggested that he might tell the boys some of his other experiences should they be interested.

When the boys heard that Worker had gone to college, Freddy asked him if he would tell the fellows some of his experiences at college. Worker promised to do that at a later meeting. The fellows also commented upon the possibilities of a football team, with Worker coaching them. Worker's closing comment was that he thought they were a swell bunch of fellows and that he would like to "stick around." The general reaction seemed to indicate that Worker would be acceptable to the boys.

Freddy asked Worker how long he would be able to stay with the club, as he felt it wouldn't be too good if he only stayed a short time. He said that usually when an adviser left after only a few months with the club, a lot of the members would quit too. Worker said that he thought he would be able to stay for at least a year.

The two visitors (prospective members) were asked to leave the room while the fellows voted on them. Bob was discussed first. The general feeling expressed was that Bob had previously belonged to the club, hadn't stuck with it when the club was having a rough time, and was now interested in joining again because some of the girls he was interested in were sympathetic toward the Cadets. Too, the boys felt that Bob was of the opinion that he could join the club whenever he wished. It was decided that he should not be allowed into the club. Worker suggested that the boys should explain to Bob why he was being refused membership and that possibly he could apply again in a few months' time. At that time, if the boys felt he was ready for membership, they might vote him in. They agreed not to vote Bob in.

Bob was brought into the room. Freddy asked him to face the members, introduce himself, tell the boys something about himself, and explain why he wanted to join the club. Bob gave for his reason for seeking membership, "desire for social activities" and then added "athletic." Freddy proceeded to explain that his reasons weren't satisfactory and related his poor association with the club thus far. He then enumerated some of the qualifications desirable for membership and suggested that Bob apply again in a few months if still interested and that if the boys thought he was acceptable, he might be voted in at that time.

Ned was then called into the room. The president explained that the fellows felt he was really interested in the club and chummed around with most of the fellows, and for these reasons he had been voted in.

Freddy asked Frank, Harry, and Mike to stay for a short executive meeting, and also asked Alex and Wilfred to remain for a few minutes. The meeting was then adjourned.

Harry spoke to Worker after the meeting, saying, "So you think we have enough members to get the club really going? I hope you're right." Worker asked him if he had any ideas for someone to represent the club at an organization meeting of an Interclub Council. Since Harry seemed anxious that the club be well represented, Worker suggested that he go down and represent the club.

As Worker was leaving, Freddy related a brief account of the history of the club. They had started over five years ago when a group of the boys had organized a kids' football team. At that time they were called the Diamonds. They engaged in various athletic activities, were primarily a sports club. Later they changed their name to the Cadets and have belonged to the agency ever since. Freddy apologized to Worker for the behavior of the boys saying, "They are really not like they acted tonight, but are a swell bunch of guys. You'll see." He added that the club really needed an adviser as they hadn't had one for quite some time. Freddy's last remark was, "The boys like to hear about your hockey and football experiences— they envy you."

Worker's Comments

Since it was the first meeting, with Worker up for approval as adviser, Worker felt that most of the overtures should come from the boys. When they asked him for some of his background, Worker felt that athletic experience and working around the country would go over with fellows of this age.

In planning the skating party, Worker's suggestion that they phone for the necessary information immediately was for the purpose of the club's experiencing a feeling of actual accomplishment, of something definite being done. They had jumped from one thing to the next in most of the meeting, without any concrete results. Worker's suggestion in regard to refusing Bob's request for membership was also for the purpose of the club's experiencing the feeling of doing something complete in itself, and doing it satisfyingly. Worker's remark that he would like to "stick around" was on the basis of feeling that the club had reacted favorably to his account of his background, as was evidenced by some remarks of the boys. Worker felt that the boys would at this point accept such a positive expression of desire to advise the club.

The meeting seemed to be held together by little more than routine business. Jumping from one item of business to the next, without any definite results, seemed to indicate a need for coordinate leadership. Freddy, the president, seems to dominate the club, along with Frank, the treasurer, but this may be because of a lack of interest on the part of the other members.

Second Meeting

Worker spoke with Freddy before meeting and was told that the club was unable to go skating because of a hockey game at the Midtown. They were sorry about this outing's falling through. (Worker was ill and could not attend.)

Later, Worker saw Frank who said that they were quite disappointed about last Wednesday and that there had been some talk about the club breaking up. He felt that for one thing each fellow left it up to the other one to come to club meetings. Frank told Worker Freddy would be late, but that he would start the meeting. He went looking around the building for the rest of the members and a few minutes later came back to ask Worker what time he wanted to start the meeting. Worker told Frank to start the meeting whenever he felt that enough of the fellows were there. Worker asked Frank into the office and helped him to plan an agenda.

Frank called the meeting to order and asked for committee reports. There were no committee chairmen present, so Frank gave all committee reports. He announced the basketball game this Thursday night against the Cardinals and asked all the fellows to be out. The question of another skating party was brought up, and after some discussion it was decided to go a week from Friday night. Frank then reported on the coming basketball league at the gym and on the fact that the Cadets had been invited to enter a team.

Frank suggested to the fellows that, if they wanted to learn to dance,

Miss H., the dance instructor of the agency, would teach them privately. Worker asked Mr. O. to give the boys more of the details. Mr. O. explained that Miss H. would very likely meet with the club early in the evening for half an hour or an hour and suggested that Worker see her about this. The fellows indicated that they would take advantage of this opportunity and come at 7:00 next Tuesday night.

Freddy joined the meeting. Don, Alex, and Sam simultaneously commented on Frank's brief, hurried way of running the meeting. They suggested he slow it down so that the fellows could talk about some of these things. On a number of occasions Worker whispered to Frank to have some discussion on the item that he had brought up.

Louis W., a prospective member, was asked to leave the room while the fellows voted on him. The fellows felt that Louis was "OK" but some of the boys pointed out that as soon as Louis came into the club some of his friends, whom the club were opposed to, would try to get in. However, they finally agreed that if Louis was voted in they were under no obligation to accept any of his friends. Frank called him in and had him face the boys and then began to make an acceptance talk. He was at a loss for words. Paul, sitting beside him, tried to prompt him, but unsuccessfully. Freddy interrupted saying, scornfully, though good-naturedly, "Let me do it," and proceeded to accept Louis into the club.

Sam asked what had happened to the thirty dollars that Walt, former treasurer, had. As far as the fellows knew he still had the money. Some mention was made of visiting him, but the matter was dropped at that. Paul informed the club members that a local football team had challenged their club to a game. Worker interrupted this new item of business by asking the fellows what they planned to do about Walt and the thirty dollars. He went on to suggest that the club clear up one thing at a time, instead of jumping from one thing to the next. Worker suggested that they appoint a couple of fellows to see Walt immediately, make some definite arrangement, and report back at the next meeting. Alex and Sam were appointed for this work.

The discussion then returned to football. At this point, Walt came into the meeting and immediately turned the money over to Frank. As for football, the fellows tried to arrange for a practice Sunday morning saying that Worker could give them some plays; however, too few fellows thought they could make it Sunday morning, and the idea was dropped.

Worker's Comments

In planning the agenda with Frank, Worker tried to point out a few of the loose ends—"ignored business of the club"—that should be discussed at the meeting.

Worker again tried to influence the club in the direction of getting things done so that there might be some feeling of accomplishment. At this point

Worker does not feel that he should force himself on the club to too great an extent. A more permanent and satisfactory relationship will be established if Worker moves slowly and in such a way as not to become too much a part of the neagtive side of the adult authority conflict which Worker senses is notably present in the attitudes of the majority of the members and which, of course, is characteristic of this age group.

Criticism of the way Frank was handling the meeting is significant. The fellows do feel the need for participation—for active discussion. The committees seem to offer little, if any, opportunity for participation and expression. They seem poorly organized, hazily defined, lacking in work to do and they appear to have very little significance. The executive committee needs revitalizing.

Third Meeting

Freddy called the meeting to order. Paul was asked to take minutes. Freddy called for a collection of dues. Most of the fellows paid up, but in a way that showed little respect for this phase of club procedure. Kenneth in particular displayed a negative response and Worker heard him remark that he wasn't going to pay any more money to the club.

Freddy spoke of the tournament basketball game that the club had lost on a forfeit because the members failed to appear. There was very little comment on this. Freddy seemed at a loss for words, and Kenneth said what a dead meeting this was. He then indicated that the fellows had decided to drop the idea of entering the league at the gym. This, too, evoked little comment. Freddy then brought up the question of the proposed ice skating party this Friday night. He asked how many planned to go and no one raised his hand. The fellows were quite passive to the business of the meeting thus far. Wilfred suggested going to the hockey game this Saturday night, and for the first time the fellows showed some interest.

Worker asked if the boys were very well acquainted with the game. They responded in the negative, and Worker suggested that he might give them a "chalk talk" on the game. This suggestion was favorably received. Paul left the room for a few minutes and Freddy suggested waiting until he got back. When he returned, Worker gave the chalk talk using the blackboard to diagram hockey formations. The fellows were enthusiastic about the description of hockey and asked many questions and made a lot of comments.

At the completion of the chalk talk, the meeting was adjourned. The boys left the room "throwing" imaginary blocks and "stickhandling" their way down the hall. On the way upstairs Louis thanked Worker for the talk. Gerald added his thanks and the rest of the fellows echoed theirs.

Fourth Meeting

The boys came in a body and Frank called the meeting to order in Freddy's absence. After a bit of horseplay, the meeting finally got under way. Frank asked Harry to read the minutes of the last meeting.

Frank read a letter of resignation from Kenneth, who said he felt that it would be impossible for him to remain with the club. Frank called for some discussion and proceeded to call on each member, going in rotation around the room. Wilfred thought that Kenneth should be asked to come down to the meeting and explain in person why he was leaving the club. George took the same stand. Alex thought they should give him a bad time of it. Gerald exclaimed, "Let's kill him!" and then in a more sober voice indicated that Kenneth should be made to pay up all back dues and agreed with the others that he should appear before the club and explain his resignation. Harry arose, saying, "I know you guys aren't going to like this," and went on to explain that if a fellow wanted to quit the club, certainly that was his business and he had a right to do so. Worker commented that Harry expressed a good point of view; that gangs practiced the method of making it rough on a member that dropped out and that such methods were not in keeping with the generally accepted way of doing things. Frank summed up the discussion with the statement that it seemed generally agreed to have Kenneth appear before the club and resign in person, and asked Louis to convey this message from the club to him.

Frank renewed the issue of T-shirts. This began a discussion on the matter. Wilfred felt it was now too cold to think about buying T-shirts. George thought the club should put it off until next spring or summer. Frank, too, felt it would be better to wait and possibly order them early enough in advance so that they would have them by spring. Ned made a motion that the club now buy sweatshirts instead. The idea was well received. Discussion about the color and the kind of emblem followed. The boys agreed that the shirts should be white, and have the name "Cadets" stenciled on them. The vote was unanimous that such sweatshirts be purchased. Frank appointed Ned and Louis as a committee of two to investigate where they could be obtained and the price.

Frank announced the coming volleyball tournament at the agency. With little discussion, the fellows voted unanimously to enter a team. Frank appointed Ned as team manager. Ned was a bit reluctant to accept, saying that he didn't know anything about volleyball and probably wouldn't be playing on the team. Most of the fellows voiced the opinion that Ned should be manager. Worker added that because he wouldn't be on the team was all the more reason that he should be manager and, whenever necessary, Worker would work on it with him. He finally accepted.

Frank then called for suggestions for improving the club. Wilfred thought that we should try to get more members down to the meetings and, too, that we should try to get new members. George also felt that we should attempt to get more fellows down to the meetings. Worker asked him how he thought this could be done. George suggested that the fellows be visited personally and also that we should try to have better meetings. Worker indicated that this was a very good suggestion.

Frank then called on Worker, who said that they might adjourn the meeting, gather around in a small circle and put their heads together to decide what was wrong with the club, and what could be done to get things rolling. Frank proceeded to push the table out of the way, saying, "We won't need this." Wilfred and George pulled their bench up into a smaller square and in about ten seconds flat the group was ready to get down to business.

Harry asked Worker if he could be excused as he wanted to attend the meeting of the Landers to see how they ran their meetings. Worker said, if he would mind staying a few minutes, and Harry obligingly said, sure, he'd stay awhile. George indicated that he too would only stay awhile as he had a long way to go to get home.

Worker opened the discussion. He told the fellows that he had been with them now for four meetings and still was unable to recognize clearly the organization of the club, the various committees and their respective jobs, as well as just who the various officers were and how they fitted into the club structure which did exist. George proceeded to give Worker an answer to his questions. He pointed out that there was a president, vice-president, secretary, treasurer and two committees. Worker asked him to indicate who the various officers were. Freddy was president; Frank, vice-president; Paul, treasurer; Harry was secretary; Frank was also chairman; and Mike was athletic chairman.

Worker then asked the fellows what they thought was wrong with the club. George said that they used to have a good club. Worker asked him what made it a good club at the time. He indicated that they used to do a lot of things—teams in every sport that was going on—and really took an interest in athletics. Worker commented that it seemed, then, that the club was primarily interested in athletics. Alex added that now the fellows seemed to let down and referred to the recent incident where the club had not shown up and had lost a game by forfeit.

Worker interjected a bit of homespun philosophy worded in athletic terminology, to the effect that this business of never seeing things through could easily become a habit; that life was a pretty tough proposition and no one was going to do things for you, especially when you yourself were unwilling to "get in and dig"; that, if being thrown for a number of consecutive losses meant a reluctance to carry the ball, you'd always be back in your own territory watching the other fellow run off with the honors. The boys listened attentively. The reason seemed positive. There was a general expression of determination to do a good job in the coming volley-ball tournament.

Gerald expressed the opinion that the fellows were not only interested in athletics but in socials as well. He suggested having a meeting every other week and the alternate weeks the club could plan some social activity with or without girls. Such things as miniature golf, roller skating, and ice skating were offered as suggestions. The fellows seemed to react favorably to these ideas. Worker thought it a swell idea, and asked, "What you mean is planning a sort of social calendar?" Gerald agreed this was what he had in mind. This aroused considerable discussion. Gerald said, for one thing, the fellows didn't know how to dance. Worker suggested inviting some of the girls' clubs to a social with the Cadets and that the girls would more than likely be willing to teach the fellows to dance, if asked to do so. Gerald said that he knew a girl that belonged to one of the clubs at the agency, and thought that they might be able to get a social with that club. Worker was acquainted with this club, said they were a nice group of girls, and thought they would not only agree to a social with the Cadets but would be willing to teach the boys to dance. Harry suggested asking the girls out for miniature golf or something, as he thought it would be easier to get acquainted, and then later they could plan a social and learn to dance. There was no particular comment on this. Gerald said they should learn to dance right away.

Harry then added that he was more in favor of social activities other than ones where the girls would teach the boys to dance, as he felt that the boys would probably be slow in learning to dance well enough and the girls would get bored and lose interest. Worker suggested that this was not necessarily so, that, if the girls enjoyed the fellows' company, they would be glad to engage in social activities with the Cadets whether the fellows were slow in learning to dance or not.

Worker asked Frank if he had a committee working with him on the club's social program. He indicated that he had had a committee at one time. Worker suggested appointing a committee of two or three now to work with him. Gerald, Alex and Wilfred were appointed. Frank asked if they would stay for a meeting and brought the club meeting to a close.

Meeting of Social Committee

Frank drew up a rough calendar for December and January. It was decided that next Tuesday night they plan for a social with the girls' club instead of a meeting. This night was chosen as it was the night before the first day of the Christmas vacation.

Worker asked how they might inform the rest of the fellows about this and was told that the four of them would spread the word around at school. The boys seemed pleased with the job they had done. They thanked Worker as they left.

Worker saw Ned and suggested that he fill out the application form for the volleyball tournament and turn it into the physical education director immediately. Ned went with Worker to the office, got the form and filled it out, ready for handing in the next day.

QUESTIONS

1. What aspects of the agency setting and functions are important for the worker to understand as he begins to work with this group?
2. What does the worker bring to this group in the way of skill, understanding and insight as revealed by reading his statement of previous experience?
3. What are some of the developmental needs of teen-age youth such as the Cadets?
4. When a new worker begins his work with an experienced group, what must he keep in mind regarding the establishment of a good working relationship?
5. What does the group want to know about the worker in the first meeting?
6. How does the worker show his skill in handling the situation when the group asks him questions about himself?
7. What can we learn about a group when we observe the way in which it admits new members?
8. Where is this group in its development as a group at the conclusion of the first meeting?
9. In what way does the worker give help to the group in its first several meetings?
10. What factors may have influenced the worker's decision to take a positive role in talking with the group during the fourth meeting?

7. The Hospital Discussion Club—Group Discussion Aids Recovery

The group described here is one recently organized by the patients in a general hospital. This picture shows the first two months of the group's existence. During that time over a hundred men have participated in the activities, although average attendance has been between 20 and 25. The shifting group membership, as reflected by these figures, is due to certain factors inherent in the hospital setting. When men are discharged, new ones come in; some go back to bed for further operations.

The group members range in age from eighteen to over thirty. Records show that they come from nearly as many backgrounds and racial groups as there are in America. Almost without exception these men have had military service and had been in the service from two to five years.

The group came into being when a number of patients were talking with the hospital recreation worker after a large dance had been held in the auditorium. They enjoyed this different kind of "bull session" so much that they wanted to do something about getting together regularly just for talk. Meetings are held each Thursday night in the small lounge of the Recreation Building. The program has consisted of discussions, with occasionally an outside speaker to bring some special information, but more often with the leadership coming from within the group. Fun, laughter, and refreshments play a part in the gatherings as well as concentration on a particular subject.

Organization is informal, and the men want to keep it that way. Previous attempts by the staff to channelize interest in an open forum had been unsuccessful because of the patients' feeling that it was required. That was why action had not been initiated in this area until original impetus had come from the men themselves. Three members were elected to take responsibility for planning meetings and conferring with Worker. Membership is definitely open, as it would be in a group with so many changes. If you like to discuss things, you are welcome.

From the very first meeting there was a spirited display of interest. The speaker discussed the facts of the strike situation, and then the floor was open to all. By this time the circle of chairs drawn up had proved too small. Wheelchairs filled each vacant space, and more participants were grouped behind leaning on their crutches. The worker had underestimated attendance, and this problem was used to bring some of the more able-bodied on the fringes more physically into the group as they enlarged the circle and brought in more chairs.

Two of the group, Frank Johns and Tom Alberts, had been prime movers in getting this first meeting together. From possibilities suggested by Worker they decided on Mr. Anderson as a person qualified to give an over-all picture of the strike situation. As a well-informed personnel man, he fulfilled the requirements of being expert, objective, and not connected with the service. Announcements about the meeting had been made by some ingenious typed notices in the hospital corridors, a write-up in the hospital newspaper, listing in the weekly program that went to each ward, and also by that old "talk it up" grapevine system among the small group of men who had initiated the idea.

The enthusiasm of the group seemed definitely to indicate continuance of such meetings. Worker threw out the question of what subjects the men would like to plan programs around and whether they wanted an organization. "We need a chairman," seemed to be of general acceptance, and several men's names were proposed—Alberts, Harris (a tall good-looking bilateral leg amputee), and Garcia (a more articulate member of the close-knit Mexican-American subgroup). Since voting was quite close, Blakeman suggested that all three men be on the committee with Alberts, who had received the most votes, in charge. This was approved immediately. Alberts, pounding on the floor with his crutch, asked what the group would like to discuss next Thursday. Quite a few ideas were thrown out, but many centered around supply-and-demand problems. Why can't you buy a car? What are we going to do about civilian clothes? How come things cost so much more if you can find them to buy? Worker's inquiry as to whether they would like to use the resources of their own members on a panel or again look for someone outside for a presentation caused some disagreement. Consensus leaned toward having patients do some research and present the problems and the committee was to find some hospital experts.

This meeting seemed to show the group's progress toward cohesion as a group because it wanted to continue meeting on a regular basis. Because of the maturity of the group members and also their reaction against au-

thoritarianism in any form, Worker endeavored to leave direction as much
as possible to the men themselves. There were the confusion and disorder
of sometimes three persons talking at once at this meeting, but the advantages of discipline growing out of the group appeared more desirable than
more attention to procedure.

Already individual personalities are playing a part. Alberts is better educated than many of the men, but his sense of humor and real interest in
other people makes him very much "one of the boys." Johns, the aggressive
intellectual who was instrumental in starting the group, does not want to
have any official leadership position but wishes to feel completely free to
criticize.

Garcia realizes that he does have a position in relation to one group
of patients. His army promotions and decorations have given him a status
that he brings with him to the group. He has little formal education, but
his obvious competence has been recognized in reality situations. He feels
a sense of responsibility because of the respect given him. Harris accepts
as fitting that his good looks and "line" should earn him a prominent place
and sees himself as representing a special group—the whole ward of bilateral amputees.

During the week the committee met in the office to talk over plans with
Worker. Garcia was encouraged to take a more active part. He seized on
the idea of getting some of his friends to make posters for this week's meeting. Harris said he'd see about publicity in the hospital paper. Alberts had
some of the men lined up for a panel discussion and was only hoping that
they wouldn't go to surgery between now and Thursday.

Among the men in the lounge before the next meeting were two new
patients. Worker had noticed them as men who came in not to read, talk,
or play cards, but to sit and stare at space. She asked if they would mind
helping her to arrange the room. Kraft got up immediately and started to
move the furniture. After several minutes Hill began to help too. There
seemed to be different views about how much room should be left by the
door so that wheelchair patients could get in without difficulty. After trying
it two ways, it was worked out satisfactorily to both men. Kraft inquired
whether there was something else they could do, and Worker explained
about the popcorn machine that was to be used. They brought it in, set it
up, and wanted to know about its operation. When someone was needed to
run it later in the evening, they would like to take it over.

There was not quite so large a turnout for this meeting as the first, but
those coming gathered more promptly. Alberts telephoned to report that
instructions to see his doctor might delay his arrival; however, he did get
there only a few minutes after seven. He seemed to have quite a sense of
responsibility for this meeting. The panel discussion had attentive listeners.
One of the panel members was a new patient, Keller, rather reserved but
quite sure of himself. Older than most of the patients, he had been in busi-

ness for himself before entering the service, and his common-sense opinions based on experience had weight with the group.

Alberts had relatively good control of the group as far as giving everyone a chance at the floor. However, Henderson, a quite upset younger patient, wanted more than his share of talking time. His contributions "had nothing to do with the case," but he definitely wanted the center of the stage. The other men mostly understood that he was disturbed. Though they were patients, there was a definite possibility of disruptive influence. Worker found an unobtrusive way to enlist his help in selling the popcorn made by Kraft and Hill. At this meeting the several bilateral amputees who had stayed in the background as noncontributing members took part in the discussion. They became part of the group instead of unassimilated men on the edge.

Over the popcorn, informal talk of what was of greatest interest came up, as several subjects were in the air. Alberts asked for a vote on what the majority wanted. Information on health and medical care had the largest representation. Harris thought that some accurate factual information ought to be presented, as there were such widely varying ideas. Garcia suggested that one of the doctors on the staff might outline the proposed federal legislation. There was opposition not to this idea as a whole but disagreement around the point of which doctor on the staff should be asked. Smith tentatively proposed that he knew a doctor patient who was interested and a "good Joe." Worker also knew this Captain Meyer, and he seemed a most acceptable choice of the group. Smith was advised to approach him. The meeting had lasted late and several of the men stayed on to help clean up and lock up.

At the third meeting, Harris took over, as Alberts was back in traction. He expressed some anxiety about being in charge, but talking with Worker beforehand and being sure of her assistance and presence reassured him. Harris introduced the speaker with apparent ease, though Worker realized this was difficult for him. Incidentally, this evening he wore both of his prostheses for the first time. There seemed to be a double significance in this. The meeting served as an impetus for him to use his new limbs, and his justified pride in this accomplishment gave him more confidence in taking over a leadership role. Group was very much absorbed in the doctor's presentation of both sides of the case for improved medical care. Captain Meyer was responsive to answering numerous questions. There were differences of opinion, but, for the most part, argument was not on a personal but on a constructive level.

Garcia stated, "We ought to have a name." His suggestion provoked lively interchange with many facetious side remarks. "The Cracker Barrel Philosophers," "Carping Critics," "Round Table," "Cuss and Discuss Club" were some of the ideas. The last name was decided on because its slangy phrasing fitted something in the men's mood. From this talk around a name other ideas materialized; for instance, clippings and articles of interest relating to this week's discussion topic might be displayed on the bulletin board space. Other small interest groups using the building did this, and now this group, assuming an entity of its own, asked for this kind of recognition.

The following weeks saw several developments. Alberts' enforced absence from the group brought Smith more to the fore as a leader. He was young but had much enthusiasm. When Garcia went on leave, Smith was elected a committee member and, because of his more definite sense of direction, made a good balance with Harris. Keller remained as a stabilizing person amid more volatile personalities. Jiminez, given to a rather violent expression of opinion, has the ability to speak vividly if ungrammatically and, just because of his own emotion, to carry the group with him temporarily. Though he wasn't able to come to meetings, Alberts kept an active interest in the group. New patients on his ward were made aware of the "Cuss and Discuss Club."

The meetings must have real meaning, since despite counterattractions, the nucleus group attends regularly. When a name band was playing at the hospital an earlier meeting was agreed upon as men did not want to postpone the meeting. This group is still not highly organized, and its three-person committee, which meets for planning with the group worker, is felt to be sufficient. Planning, however, has moved on to the stage of program scheduling for more than a week ahead. Content of program is now headed toward subjects in relation to the time when the men will be discharged, such as budgeting, housing, etc.

QUESTIONS

1. What peculiar conditions of a hospital setting must be kept in mind by a worker with a group such as this?
2. Which individuals stand out in this group, and how are they using the group to meet personal needs?
3. How does this group seem to be changing as a result of the successful meetings they have had?
4. What contributions can a group such as this make to the men as a help to their recovery and return to normal community life?

8. A Guide for Foster Parent Group Education

Increasingly the group method is being used in the education of foster parents. The excerpt which follows is a clearly expressed summary of the important role of the worker who has responsibility for providing leadership to foster parent groups. Readers should quickly see how much basic group work theory is pertinent to this particular kind of project.

Role of the Leader (Foster Parent Educator) *

A. The Beginning Sessions

In the first group sessions members and leader begin to become acquainted with each other and to establish a working agreement. To become acquainted the leader introduces himself and briefly describes his background and area of competence. He asks members to introduce themselves and to give the names and ages of their foster and natural children.

Then the members' ideas and feelings about being chosen to participate in the group should be expressed. Invariably, some members will be ambivalent about participating in the group. The leader encourages them to discuss their feelings, and thus conveys his interest in the members' thinking and feelings, and gives focus and purpose to the group.

B. Working Agreement

a. Acceptance of the agency's and the group's purpose for foster parents to learn about their role as foster parents, to increase their understanding of foster children, and increase their skill in providing services for children. It is important to stress that the agency's primary purpose in conducting foster parent education groups is to increase the effectiveness of foster family care services.

b. Acceptance of the day, hour and length of sessions, and agreement that additional members will not be admitted after the first session because of the limited number of sessions planned.

c. Acceptance of responsibility of regular and prompt attendance and termination at the end of each session.

d. Acceptance of responsibility to participate in group discussions; to share their thinking and experience; to listen, reflect, and react to each other's contribution; and to help formulate areas for study. In this way, the foster parents will learn from each other as well as from the leader.

e. Acceptance of the leader's responsibilities as follows: to give focus to the discussion, to clarify and to direct their thinking, to contribute his knowledge for their consideration, and to teach principles of parenting and child development.

f. The working agreement is established through a discussion process. The leader is sensitive to the members' reactions by noting body actions, facial expressions, etc. He welcomes questions and invites comments— indicating his interest in their thinking. He encourages members to give the discussion method a try. In addition, the leader must be aware that there will be attempts to change the working agreement and he must be prepared to help the group abide by its limitations for the best use of his leadership. However, the focus of group discussion is flexible within the framework of the specific objectives and purpose of course.

C. Principles of Leadership

a. The leader is a composite teacher and helping person who uses himself and his knowledge to promote relationships which foster learning.

* Albert F. Hanwell *et al., A Guide for Foster Parent Group Education* (Boston College Graduate School of Social Work, 1970) pp. 15–19. Used with permission.

Through his leadership and interaction between group members and leader, the climate and guidance for learning are established.

    b. The leader contributes to the development of positive and constructive interaction within the group by conveying positive feelings for each member, by developing self-awareness so that he can responsibly control his own interactions in the group and by avoiding favorites in the group.

    c. The use of authority is an important tool in leadership. For example, the leader must set limits to prevent a waste of group time and effort and to give opportunity for more concentrated attention and study. Limits convey the leader's interest, understanding, and faith in the members, and create a situation of comfort and security necessary for the members to concentrate on their work.

    d. The leader's interaction with group members provides a model for the group interaction and contributes to melding the group into a working team. As members develop a relationship with the leader, they observe and take on some of his attributes toward other members and start to relate effectively to them.

D. Promoting the Work of the Group

    a. The leader directs the group toward its objectives through providing each member with an opportunity to talk about his experiences, problems and questions.

    b. The leader develops a variety of techniques to focus and facilitate discussion, to insure participation, to set limits and to cope with those members who interfere with discussion.

    c. The leader gives focus to the discussion by translating a member's concern to a universal problem or by searching for an area of common interest so all members will have a chance to participate. This area may be identified by grouping several areas of expressed interest all of which have a common denominator. Through this approach, the leader demonstrates that the purpose of the group is for the members to learn new ideas in problem solving rather than for each individual to obtain specific help with his or her unique problems.

    d. The leader utilizes recent experiences of group members to teach specific content, and should depart from the course outline to make most effective use of these experiences. For example, a foster parent may bring to the group his concerns about a foster child's recent contact with his parents. Although this is an area to be covered by the course, it may be brought up in a session which has a different subject as its focus. Flexibility in dealing with material as it emerges is essential.

E. Teaching Techniques

    a. The leader asks questions or makes comments to advance the group's work.

    b. The leader teaches by confirming an idea or part of an idea that a member of the group advances, and the leader may give his reasons for confirming the idea.

    c. The leader refrains from giving information too quickly, or from communicating the feeling that something a member says is wrong. As a consequence, the foster parents must use their own thinking, knowledge, and intuition to develop the answers. Repeated experience in learning to solve problems in the group is essential to achieve the purpose of helping parents to solve problems in relation to their children's growth and development.

d. The leader deals with the members who interfere with the functioning of the group. For example, a monopolizer or a dominant member may tend to take over the group by talking. These kinds of behaviors are motivated by feelings of inadequacy or fears of being rejected, disliked, or excluded. The leader might respond with warmth to such a member and suggest that they will come back to the point, or the leader might universalize the problem and obtain the group's interest in it.

e. The leader is alert to the shy, quiet members of the group and attempts to encourage their participation through supporting comments they make or ask them to share their experience.

f. Resistance to learning is inevitable. Foster parents tend to manifest resistance through avoiding a focus on their role as parents and putting emphasis on problems with agencies and natural parents. The leader may deal with resistance through accepting opposition and negative feelings and communicating his confidence in the members' wish and ability to learn.

9. The Get-Acquainted Club—Adults Need Groups Too

The idea of a Get-Acquainted Club was first thought of early in December. For a month Worker had been keeping a record of the single girls employed in the industrial plants near our agency. They had been coming to us for a variety of services, and Worker thought the time was right to try to organize a group. Another agency in a nearby industrial community had a similar club, so Worker visited it and got ideas. It was necessary for Worker to do the promotional work connected with starting a new group. She prepared an attractive dodger, a letter and newspaper announcements. The letter was sent to a selected list of girls residing in close proximity to the agency. It read: "Dear——: When the new year rolls around we are launching something new and different. It's the Wednesday Get-Acquainted Club. You are cordially invited to become a charter member by coming to the first meeting next Wednesday night at the (Agency). Tell your friends about this new club and invite them to attend. You will have a grand opportunity to make friends, develop new interests and hobbies. We will serve a topnotch dinner for a modest price. We propose to have outstanding guests, varied entertainment and your favorite hobby group. We would like to hear suggestions from you, too, for the program of this new club." Inadvertently the newspaper announcements said that *both* men and women were invited to become members of this club and, though the agency did not expect to get any calls from men, sure enough, several turned up for the first meeting.

First Meeting. Seventeen came for the first meeting. This was considered a good number. The program had been planned a long time in advance by Worker and it went very smoothly. She had to take a more active role than she wished, leading a mixer game before dinner, pouring the appetizer juice, filling in name cards, greeting people, watching the checkroom, etc. Since some of the people came early they were brought in to help. Worker acted as chairman for the first meeting and introduced the speakers who told about hobby groups meeting in the agency that night. Temporary officers, president and secretary, were chosen by the group. Worker had to make the nominations because no one knew the others well enough to make suggestions. It was agreed that the regular election would be held at the fourth meeting. The group seemed to enjoy the supper and talked about the hobby groups they were going to attend.

Second Meeting. Including Worker, fifteen were present. Lily, aged twenty-one, attractive girl, works in automobile factory, enjoys meeting new friends. Thought club was for girls only, but came back, anyway. Alice, thirty, PBX operator in packing plant, jolly, friendly girl, separated from husband, lives with mother and two children. Likes to dance. Roy, thirty, employed as lead man in shipyard, engaged to be married, good friend of temporary president. Veva, twenty-two, very pretty girl, secretarial employee. Lea, twenty-three, employed in same office as Veva. Dick, twenty-eight, employed in airplane factory, hobby photography, physical disability of some sort. Mary, twenty-six, works in bakery, husband overseas, supports two children, eldest eight years. Club secretary, hard worker. Albert, forty, unmarried, chemist, photography hobby, physical disability. Louise, twenty-two, works as a dentist's assistant. Husband overseas. Needs companionship. John, twenty-two, service dischargee, three years overseas, in hospital six months after crash, wife divorced him while overseas. Needs companionship, reassurance. Cora, thirty-five, executive secretary of Property Owners Association. Very active person. Grace, twenty-three, divorced, engaged to soldier overseas. Ned, twenty-six, discharged veteran, now working in a factory, lives with his sister. Chosen temporary president of club.

John was the first member to come, arriving two hours before supper. He had not been drinking, for the first time in weeks of coming to our building. He said he just stopped to say "Hello" and was going downtown but would be back for dinner. Worker stopped desk job she was doing and asked John if he would mind helping her instead of going in to town. Together they went to the yard to gather leaves and green things for the table. John had his arms loaded although, before he came along, Worker had planned to use some flowers already gathered and in the hall. Worker then asked John to help her move the furniture and set the tables and decorate the clubroom. A high school girl usually comes to do the table setting but John asked, "What can I do now?" He rigged up the loudspeaker too and selected the records to play before dinner.

Ten minutes before assembling time, Mary came directly from work. She was dressed in a pants suit, said "Hi!" to John and told him she had some pictures to show him. She picked up a glass of tomato juice and took it back to the showers with her, saying she was half-starved. Roy and Dick came in next. Since Roy had taken some pictures at the first meeting, the three men were soon engaged in an animated discussion of cameras, photography and pictures generally. John told of taking pictures from a bomber over enemy territory. This is the first time Worker has heard him mention his military service. The men did not go into details but stuck to photography. Ned, Lea, and Veva came in next, and Mary, fresh from her shower, was busy serving tomato juice. Soon all were present. Prior to being seated for dinner, Worker and Ned had planted clues in the dining room. It was Murder Night, and couples had been paired to write up the crime. A necktie, hair ribbon, toothbrush, sleeping potion, knife, etc. were planted, and members had to find all the clues. This caused a lot of talk, and Worker was kidded about the anemic-looking blood (beet juice) on the knife and napkin. At the dinner the conversation ranged from possible solutions of the crime to plans for a membership drive.

After eating, Ned called the meeting to order and Mary, the secretary, read the minutes, took roll call, and collected supper money. Ned asked for ways of building up the membership, and several gave opinions. Cora agreed to telephone every member who missed a meeting and tell them the program for the next week. Louise suggested that the club should do something for others, not just for themselves. The March of Dimes campaign, for example, should receive their support. Grace brought up the idea of contributing to the Center Campaign. Some discussion was held, and Ned put it to a vote. It was decided to bring money next meeting and divide it between the two. Cora said that they ought to have some club stationery so that organizations would get to know them. She was asked to look into costs. It was near 7:30 and another club would want the room, so Worker told Ned they would have to hurry. A ten-minute limit was put on writing the murder story. Much laughter greeted the winning team, Dick and Veva. They received candy as a prize. Since the waitress had left, Worker asked for volunteers to clear the tables. They pitched in willingly and in a short while left for the hobby groups meeting throughout the agency.

QUESTIONS

1. When an agency decides to form a new group what are some of the conditions that might motivate such a decision?
2. What are some of the things the group worker should do in preparation for the first meeting with the group?
3. After the first few meetings of a group what might we be expected to know about them if we have been alert and observant?
4. Individuals go to groups for different reasons. What satisfactions may the members of this group be seeking?
5. How might the past group experience of a person influence his adjustment in and use of a group?
6. What considerations about newly formed groups are influential at the point of program decisions?

10. The Newcomers—They Don't Want Us Here

The Newcomers' Club is composed of seventeen girls, aged fourteen and fifteen years. They live in Garden Homes, a new housing development a mile and a half from a city of over two hundred thousand. Their club is sponsored by a private agency in this city. The group worker is a staff member who has devoted most of her time to these housing projects. Ten states are represented in the membership of the Newcomers; some girls had moved here from far away. No one of the club has lived in this community longer than a year. The club has been meeting for four months, one afternoon each week, at the housing project. Members attend school in the city, but some feel the welcome has been cool. As one girl put it, "The Girls' Athletic Association at the high school is high-hat and doesn't want us." Most of the girls' mothers are employed, as are their fathers. Several girls have said they would like to have their mothers meet their boy friends, but, "Mother is never home anymore!" Though the houses are adequate the girls feel strange and remark, "I don't think I'll ever like it here. It's nice but I miss the blocks. Without streets and square blocks I can't tell where anybody lives. I'm lost all the time!"

The club program has gone well for these first few months. The initial enthusiasm wanes. Louise, who was the first president, moves away. Great unrest and arguing ensue when Helen, vice-president, moves up. Attendance is irregular. Because no programs are offered for boys, a gang of about fifteen boys hang around outside the meeting place each time the Newcomers meet. They make a disturbance every chance they get. The girls are naturally interested in this attention. A great amount of boy and girl pairing occurs after each meeting. Worker wonders if this is the time to launch a larger program of boy and girl activities on a joint basis. Some of the parents are interested in the problem. Much publicity about a Teen-Age Center in a nearby community stimulates interest in such a possibility. When Worker mentions it rather casually to several of the Newcomers, they become most enthusiastic.

QUESTIONS

1. When the members of a group, such as the Newcomers, have moved around a great deal, how might this influence their adjustment in the group?
2. What conditions might determine the extent to which an agency should do extension work in locations such as a housing development?

11. The Hi-Workers—A Group Seeks an Agency

This is a group of sixteen- and seventeen-year-old girls, eleven in number. For seven months they have been meeting in the homes of the members. They recently asked to be admitted to the Jones Community Center, informing Worker that they wanted to be a Center club because it was a central place to meet. They said that all of them went around together. In addition to attending high school they all have part-time jobs after school and Saturdays at the Fisk Department Store. Eleanor T., the president, did most of the talking for the group. Worker explained that each Center club had an adult adviser and that she would be glad to introduce Miss W. to the group to see whether or not they thought she would be a helpful adviser. A date was set for the following Monday night.

The Hi-Workers' Club arrived en masse, all eleven of them. Miss W. was presented by the Worker. Eleanor introduced the members; they greeted Miss W. loudly. Eleanor took charge of the meeting and asked each girl what she had done during the week to publicize the club. She seems very anxious to get the name of the club before people and asked if the club could run announcements in the Center bulletin. Miss W. said the Center would be happy to include its copy. Eleanor then announced that the officers would meet at her house on Wednesday. Significantly, Miss W. was not invited to the meeting of the officers. After the meeting was over, Miss W. offered to show the girls through the Center and point out the different things they could do there. During the tour Miss W. tried to talk with different girls, but Eleanor always crowded right next to her and would not let the others speak. She told Worker they had been a club for seven months. They had had a party each month.

QUESTIONS

1. Why do some groups seem to want to be a part of an agency but simultaneously seem to reject the agency, as in the case of Hi-Workers?
2. When an individual member seems to dominate and control a group, what may this suggest to the worker from the standpoint of establishing a relationship?
3. When the worker is excluded from group affairs, such as the officers' meeting at Eleanor's home, what are the possible meanings?

12. Group Services in the Michigan Department of Social Services

Increasingly state and local departments of social services and welfare are using group services as a part of their program. The following material is a realistic presentation of the many factors involved in such a program.

Group Services in the Michigan Department of Social Services *

My particular segment of this session has to do with the use of groups as a special skill in providing service to clients. In pursuit of this, I find myself in the unenviable position of perhaps being at odds with the title of this panel in that, in my view, group service is definitely not in a special skill area, but is one of several alternative methods of providing services to our clientele.

* By James Theodore Jones, Administrative Assistant for Group Services, Michigan Department of Social Services. Presentation at American Public Welfare Association Central States Regional Conference, May 1969.

In our state, group activity has been an ongoing part of service, dating back to the middle 50's. However, as some of you may recall, that time period was not necessarily as enlightening a one as we have today; so that group service was a kind of activity in which you went ahead and did, but didn't talk about because if you asked permission to do it, such permission would be denied. Let me hasten to add, however, that these early starts in group service were invaluable in terms of the later emerging program in Michigan in the 60's, when the scope of group activity was initiated on a planned statewide basis.

Now, in setting up a planned service, one of the first questions that must be asked is who is going to do it? Does this represent an area of activity to be handled by specially trained staff, or will the use of groups be seen as an appropriate vehicle for providing service that can be utilized by all staff whose training and experience has been related to more traditional ways of providing service?

After a very careful review of the options before us, we came to the conclusion that our best hope for success lay in developing a broad framework under which group services could be provided. In other words, a sort of service umbrella that would define the outside boundaries of group activity in our department, as opposed to other forms of group treatment or, if you will, group therapy. Therefore, in Michigan we set about promoting the expectation that group services would be provided in three general areas related expressly to how we provide service to our clients.

I. The first of these general headings is that of orientation. We believe that all clients deserve an equal orientation as to what the Department can provide and to their maximum discovery and use of all service resources available to them. Expressly, we felt our clients' need to know what the agency will do, what they can expect from us, and what in turn are their responsibilities and what are our general expectations of them. So, whether we are talking of an applicant for financial assistance, a foster parent, a person requesting a license or a ward committed to us, each of them deserve the best kind of orientation as to what services can be expected and will be provided.

II. The second area of general group activity has to do with that of provision of specific information and learning opportunities to both clients and providers of service. (By way of definition, let me say here that we define providers of service as being those individuals whom we recruit to give service to other recipients. These, of course, are foster parents, volunteers, licensed applicants, nursing home operators, and the like.) Over and over again, experience of workers indicates that many of the situations our clients find themselves in are definitely related to the fact that alternative solutions are unknown to them, so that our information and education groups are really designed to handle those situations that could be prevented or corrected if the information were readily at hand.

Our education and information groups are designed to deal with those areas of service need that exist and are unresolved because of ignorance. The focus of such groups is to instruct and to share experiences and alternate techniques which may lead to a more profitable resolution. The area of need may be homemaking, child management, employment preparation, family planning, or a host of other groupings which would seek improved functioning through the utilization of expertise, and the inter-action of participants toward a determined goal.

III. The next area of general activity is a much more complex one which has to do with the whole area of resolution of complex social problems, which, by virtue of their intensity and duration, have almost succeeded in overwhelming our client to the point where he is no longer able to function at optimum capacity.

In this phase of activity, we do not expect that the use of groups is going to open up new frontiers in providing help, or that this service alternative is our next panacea. We do view this as one more tool or weapon, if you will, in which we can provide insight into where the problems lie, which can provide testing of means of effecting change, and which can assist in maintaining the dignity of the individual through the helping process.

Now, at this point, all of the aforementioned rationale sounds great and wonderful, but it is still conceptual material which can only come alive when it is personalized to the service plan developed for a particular client or client family. The framework has to be made real and concrete to deal with the particular situation; for example, a mother overwhelmed by debt, or a family that has stretched its budget to the limits of flexibility and still finds it inadequate to meet needs, or an unemployed person who carries the burden of failure in repeated attempts to be effective in the labor force, or an incapacitated parent who must stand under the accusing judgment of his children in terms of his ability to provide, or a child in foster care removed from whatever roots are known and meaningful to him, or the volunteer, eager to be helpful but overwhelmed by the complexity of administrative procedure which tends to inhibit usefulness. These and many more examples are the everyday concrete realities of service needs. These service needs are not unique to Michigan and represent the day-to-day examples of the situations in public welfare that demand our immediate attention, despite the reams of paper work and admin-istrative procedures that slow down our service responsibilities.

We are fortunate in this state to have the use of group means as a service alternative in 85 per cent of our counties, both large and small, reflecting many local utilizations in keeping with the broad outlines that we have defined.

To achieve such a result has not been easy and there have been specific myths about group service that have had to be overcome. First and foremost is the myth that group service activity is going to save you time. I think a legitimate question in relation to this is, save time for what? Because the job of service is ongoing, what the use of groups has really done is offer consolida-tion both in numbers and content in the helping process. But in just as many instances where the use of groups gives a solution to a problem, the group milieu provides additional diagnostic information to lead workers into other areas of service activity: the end result being that service is expanded with accruing benefits to the client, yet time is not saved.

The second great myth has to do with the idea that an effective group leader is a special kind of personality—a sort of instant energized, self-propelled, homogenized extrovert—to be successful in leadership. It is quite true that certain forms of group service require an investment of experience and training on the part of personnel leading groups. However, the layers of opportunity are so vast in group services that an entry point can be found for almost anyone. The worker who professes fear in confronting a group of twenty persons may find that an interview with an extended family poses no threat and is a working reality with which he can easily deal. At the same time, the worker who feels terrified in terms of what the clients may think of him collectively in a group situation soon discovers that the client is too busy being concerned over what the worker and his peers think of him to let it matter very much. All of this, of course, has its implications for staff development so that we have present elements of knowledge, as well as that of doing. What we have found is that the only elements in terms of special personality necessary for group leadership is a sincere and dedicated interest in our clients and a willingness to move into the doing areas, for when this happens the worker is too busy and too involved in the process to be concerned as to what is happening to him individually.

The third great myth is what I call the "total attendance syndrome" and it seems to be the situation where workers feel that they are social work failures and lousy practitioners when *everyone* invited or solicited for a group meeeting does not appear. We tend to forget that the network of human relationships with which we deal offers so many possibilities for other concerns to intervene—the car will not start, the baby sitter does not show up, the weather is bad, or the person may consider what you have to offer as being not as important as something else he wants to do.

As a result, we then overcompensate in the other direction. We say that we have to invite forty people in order to get ten—then when forty people show up, we have clients in the hallways, clients in the john, clients everywhere.

Somewhere between these extremes lie the reality that services is an individual matter, and the group is merely the vehicle by which this gets done, and that each meeting is only a stepping-stone in a much wider scheme of delivering services and is also a learning experience in how we do this. It is not an end result in itself.

I have sketched for you, very briefly, the ways in which group services have been utilized effectively in Michigan; and in this brief summary, it is my hope that more questions have been raised than have been answered. This is as it should be, for we are dealing with a means of providing service and participation such as we would hope from the question and answer period is the ingredient that would make our group services discussion come alive.

The material which follows is taken from a brochure published by the Michigan Department of Social Services and distributed to persons receiving assistance from the agency.

What Are Group Services?

Group Services is the name given to meetings held with groups of people who want services from the Michigan Department of Social Services. These meetings are set up to determine ways in which the Department may assist people live a more satisfying and productive life for themselves and their families.

But Why Have Group Meeting?

In order to answer this question, we must first look at what the Department does. The Department does two things:
1. It helps people by providing them with money to take care of their needs.
2. It helps people by providing them with non-money services.

Some people only need help in the form of money. But others need both money and certain services that will help them solve problems in their daily life. People who need both kinds of help might include:
1. Single parent families.
2. Unemployed fathers who want to provide for their families.
3. Couples who wish to adopt a child.
4. Working mothers needing day care for their children.
5. Teen-agers who want somebody to listen to them.
6. Older people who want information about medical, legal, and social benefits.
7. Mothers who wish to acquire further homemaking skills.

What Do Group Meetings Try to Do?

Group meetings help people who have the same kind of problems get together to talk with one another and, together, find new ways to solve their problems. Successful groups are those in which the people who are present become comfortable enough with each other to talk freely about a problem or a situation, and to accept from each other honest and realistic answers or directions about what could be done to solve the problem or better the situation.

What Is Expected of Me?

What is expected of a person in a group depends on what kind of group it is. In groups that meet to get *information* about something, you would be expected to listen to what is being said, to take notes if you wish, and to decide whether or not the meeting has been helpful to you. In groups that meet to *discuss* some problem or situation, participation by you is most important. Here, you would be expected to share your experiences as best you can, but if some part of the discussion makes you uncomfortable, you would not be expected to talk about it.

Who Will Be At These Meetings?

The people who will be at the group meetings might be your neighbors, your friends, or other people who, like yourself, want to learn from and help each other.

Will my grant be affected? Group meetings are set up to help people who need this service, and whether you attend or not will not affect your grant.

How do I get there? In some cases, where the group is going to be very large, transportation may be arranged for you by MDSS or other agencies. If the group meeting is planned for a smaller number of people, arrangements might be made with volunteers to get you there. If transportation is a problem for you, talk with your social worker or call your county department.

What about my children? Some meetings will be arranged so that babysitting is provided. In other situations where you are unable to make your own child care plan, your social worker will assist you.

When do these groups meet? Group meetings are held at those times in the day that will be convenient for most people who are invited to attend.

Who leads these groups? Group meetings are usually led by a skilled social worker although other skilled resource people who have information useful to you may also be present.

13. Ruth—A Group Member who Needs Individual Help

Ruth J. is a small, plain-appearing, fair-haired girl, sixteen years of age, new in the community of Woodly. Her father is deceased; her mother is employed. Ruth attends the senior high school and is responsible for the care of her sister Jane, ten years old. A month after settling in Woodly, Ruth began to attend the group work agency, dropping in to play and listen to records in the game room. She tried hard to make friends, but the girls did not respond because she was too loud, and the boys backed away because her overtures were aggressive and pronounced. Worker helped her to get acquainted with Sally T., who tried to be friendly and invited her to attend a meeting of the Blue Jewels girls' club. Ruth wanted to become a club member and asked Sally to submit her name. The girls refused to admit her, saying, "She is too loud; she has a bad reputation with the boys. We don't want her." Sally could not break the news, so Worker discussed the matter, suggesting that Ruth was trying too hard to put herself over with the other youths. Worker explained that there were other things besides clubs and suggested that Ruth attend the Friday night Teen-Age Dances.

This worked out fine the first night; the second night Ruth and a boy slipped away and were observed in his car parked in the lot next to the agency. The Youth Committee in charge of the dances had made a strict rule against this, and Ruth and the boy were warned but no action taken. The same thing happened again the following Friday. The chairman of the Teen-Age Dance Committee reported it to Worker, and Ruth was asked to leave and return the next day for a conference with Worker. She said she could not come the next day but could the day after. Since this would be a Sunday, Worker said to come on Monday after school.

In staff conference the matter was discussed, and it was brought out that Ruth had been reported as being difficult in school and had been noticed out on the streets at very late hours. It was agreed that Worker should assume responsibility for trying to help her. The Teen-Age Dance Committee applied its rule of suspension from dances for three weeks. Worker did not protest this decision but remarked that Ruth was a very unhappy girl in need of help and that she would appreciate it if the Committee would just let the matter rest with her. Worker then called Mrs. G., caseworker with the Family Agency, and explained the situation. Mrs. G. said that she would be glad to try to help Ruth but that Ruth would have to come to the Family Agency for the first conference. Worker had hoped Mrs. G. would see her at the group work agency, but Mrs. G. said this would be undesirable.

Before Worker could compose her thoughts, the phone rang. It was Ruth's mother in a rage because the agency was "mistreating" her daughter. Worker asked Mrs. J. to come by Monday morning on her way to work. When Mrs. J. came in, she launched a tirade against the agency, the people of the community, and the agency workers. She expressed great unhappiness at being in Woodly and wished she had never come. Worker said she was interested in helping Ruth and wondered if Mrs. J. would encourage her to visit Mrs. G. at the Family Agency, because it might help her. Mrs. J.'s response was, "You think my girl ain't normal?" Worker said it was not that, but sometimes people had problems which could be worked out with the help of experienced people. She went on to relate an instance of such a nature, and Mrs. J. seemed to relax. At the close of the story, she said, "You know, after Mr. J. died I had to place Ruth and Jane in my sister's house because I had to go to work. I found out that they were cruel to my girls and I took them away. We tried lots of different arrangements after that but none seemed to work very good." At the end of the interview, she said she would encourage Ruth to visit the Family Agency worker.

Ruth came in to the group work agency, and Worker again explained that they wanted to help her and that the caseworker might be able to do so. Ruth said, "There isn't anything wrong with me. I didn't do anything. Anyway, how can a lady help me by just talk?" The conference continued, with Ruth saying that she was lonely and unhappy. Finally, she said she would try a visit to Mrs. G. Worker telephoned for an appointment. It was set for 4:30 on Tuesday. Worker invited her to accompany her to the costume closet and help do some minor repairs on garments needed for a rehearsal that night. Ruth worked silently for about fifteen minutes and then said she had to return home.

QUESTIONS

1. When a new person comes to the agency, what are some of the elements in a sound "intake" or reception procedure?
2. What is the group worker's responsibility in helping a person to gain the admission to the group that she may be seeking?
3. When the member cannot accept the limits imposed by the agency, the worker, the group, or the activity, what are some of the approaches that may be followed by the worker?
4. How should the group worker go about explaining the help that is available from other workers, such as caseworkers, vocational guidance specialists, and others?

5. In preparing a group member for referral, what items should be included?
6. What must be understood by both group worker and caseworker when referrals are made?
7. Are there basic principles of referral that should be followed?

14. Gary—A Boy Who Needs Planned Group Experience

Gary is a little boy for his age, thirteen years. He is an attractive youngster and has a pleasant personality. Tests indicate an I.Q. of 132. Gary lives with his father, who is almost sixty years of age. His mother died when Gary was an infant; the father has been both father and mother to him and seems to be the sole object of his affection. The father is a machinist who works nights. There is usually a family living in the adjoining apartment, and they are supposed to supervise Gary when the father is away. When the case became known to our agency, Gary was ten and a problem in school. He was the leader of a small group of boys involved in several minor stealing episodes. He would lie, alibi, and try to buy the friendship of other boys by giving them money or candy. The school, juvenile officers, and this agency thought Gary needed group activities, such as the Scouts, Y, etc. Gary said he would like to join, but Mr. P. discouraged him from joining. To worker, Mr. P. expressed interest but to Gary it was just the opposite. Arrangements were made to permit Gary to go to a summer camp for a ten-day stay. Mr. P. agreed but at the last minute changed his mind and refused to let Gary go. He explained that he had a job for Gary.

Gary has never attended church regularly, except for a short time a year ago when his father allowed him to attend a downtown cathedral with his aunt. In discussing this experience he said, "That was the one church that I really liked to attend. I was a big shot down there. I was one of the candle boys. But my dad made me quit going." Mr. P. had quarreled with the aunt.

At the present time Gary does not seem interested in attending any group. He says he does not have time, must do the housework, prepare meals for himself and his father. He has a set of machinist's tools and books and his father lets him come to the plant to work there with him. He spends the rest of his time reading. He attends junior high school, does fairly well in school work, but has no friends.

QUESTIONS

1. How do we know the extent to which persons are or are not ready for planned group experience?
2. When the group worker accepts a referral from the caseworker, what information may be considered pertinent?
3. What are some of the things that the group worker must take into account in trying to help a person get started in a group?
4. Are there advantages and disadvantages in certain types of groups as beginning experience for boys like Gary?

15. Outline for Group Analysis*

In writing this description of the group, it is important to include the part which you as the worker played in these various aspects of the group behavior. This will sometimes need to be done in answering a specific question and at other points can be summarized at the conclusion of a section. In describing your relation to the group, it is important to indicate not only what you did but what were your purposes, your assumptions and, so far as you can evaluate them, the results of your part in the process. You should feel free to describe failure as well as success, since the real success of the analysis lies in your ability to see accurately and clearly what was happening.

A. Identifying Information

I. *Group Composition*
Write a brief description of the members (names disguised) of the group. If the group is larger than 15, it will not be possible to do this for all the members. In that case describe those you know best including, if possible, the "natural leaders" and the least accepted. Such descriptions should include factual information as to age, sex, occupation or grade in school, nationality or racial background, general personal appearance and also material on the member's place in the group and any material you have on family background or other pertinent factors in the person's life.

II. *External Aspects*
1. What is the nature of the social setting in which the group is functioning? What kind of agency is sponsoring the service? What are the neighborhood or community characteristics? Describe the relationship that exists between the social agency, institution, ect., and the social cultural environment of which it is a part.
2. What cultural factors are influential in the environment surrounding the group? To what social class do you think most of its members belong? Are there some outside this class? How are they related to the group? How does the ethnic composition of the group affect its behavior? What conceptions of age and sex roles exist? How do these factors relate to group functioning?

B. Developmental Processes

I. *Group Formation*
1. What type of group is this? Describe its fit in its larger social setting, e.g. one of a number of friendship clubs in a social agency, a committee appointed by some outside authority, an autonomous neighborhood, or whatever.
2. If just formed, describe the process of formation in terms of the original members of the group, and their purpose in forming it. How have you helped the group evolve a "contract" or working agreement?
3. Has the group a stated purpose? If so, what is it? Judging by its behavior, what seems to be the dominant purpose of the group? What satisfactions are its

* Prepared by Dr. Albert S. Alissi, Associate Professor of Social Work, University of Connecticut, School of Social Work. Used with permission.

members getting out of it? What needs are being met? What unavowed purposes do you see evident? How are the group objectives influenced by unconscious motivations, in your opinion? How does the agency function affect the purpose of this group? How does the surrounding community affect group objectives?

4. What changes in purpose or membership policies have occurred during the period of the record? Why did these come about? How have you gone about modifying the contract?

5. How is the membership determined? What agency policies affect membership? What individual factors influence the membership?

6. What relation has a worker had to this process of formation, the determining of objectives and membership? What has he aimed to do in this area? What has resulted?

II. *Group Movement*

1. Present a clear and concise statement describing your conception of the group in developmental terms. What stages of development can you identify? What has been its pattern of development? What do you anticipate will be its future course of development? What has been or will be your role in this process? Focus on your own professional impressions, but note also other conceptions and expectations regarding group development as reflected by the agency, group members, institutional representatives, community leaders, etc.

2. What criteria have you applied to measure group movement and change over time? Compare individual change expectations with group change expectations. To what degree does "movement" indicate goal attainment as compared to group intergration and maintenance of "groupness"? What developmental properties of the group need to be encouraged to help bring about goal attainment and adaptation? What would be the worker's role in the process?

III. *Group Termination*

1. What is the nature of the contract in terms of group termination? Are there any specific objectives which, once met, would indicate termination? What expectations are there regarding the group splitting into new groups or combining with other ongoing groups? How do individual or subgroups "terminate" relationships?

2. When is group termination to be handled? How will you go about helping in this process? What would be your involvement with the group or its members after termination? In which ways would you relate the group to the agency, to outside groups, or to other significant persons or workers?

C. *Interactional Processes*

I. *Group Structure*

1. Describe the status and acceptance pattern in the group by making two sociograms, one in the beginning and one at the end of the recorded period used for analysis. Include each of the two sociograms and describe the relations between the members which they depict, giving your estimate of the underlying bases of such relations, positive and negative feelings involved, effect of social factors in determining acceptance, rejection and status, etc. Describe

any changes in acceptance and rejection patterns and give your estimate of the bases for such changes.

2. During the period of the record, how have subgroups affected the way the group has functioned? Note cliques, conflicts between subgroups, leadership subgroups, etc. How have groups based on person congeniality or personal hostility affected the formation or functioning of authorized groups such as committees?

3. Does the group treat any of its members consistently in certain roles such as scapegoats, rebels, clowns, outcasts, or objects of pity to be uplifted by the group? Describe any such situations. How do you account for the attitudes in these cases—both on the part of the group and from the viewpoint of the individual treated in this way? Are the roles generally consistent with statuses? Under what conditions do you go about influencing these and how?

4. What part have you played in this process of acceptance, rejection and status finding? How have you affected the pattern? How have you used this in relation to individuals? To the whole group?

II. *Group Values*

1. What evidence is there of commonly accepted values affecting the behavior of the group? Are these values formulated into a clearly understood code? If so, what does the code require of its members in the way of behavior, what does it forbid? Do these values deviate from the mores of the neighborhood, agency, or institution? If so, how? At what points are they different from those of the worker?

2. If the group has certain accepted standards, how do they affect individual behavior? How are they enforced by the group? What sanctions—rewards and punishments—are utilized?

3. How are the group values related to its selection of indigenous leaders? To its stigmatizing of certain members? To what extent does the elected or natural leader embody the group ideal? (E.g. in popularity with other sex, physical prowess, prominence in a skill, embodiment of a social purpose, etc.) In what ways are its values influenced by those of its indigenous leaders?

4. Does the group indicate rejection of certain values? Does it have an "enemy" outside itself in the form of another group, racial grouping or area? If so, how is this hostility expressed? Does it show evidences of social prejudices, racial, religious, economic, etc.?

5. Does the group think of itself as being in line with community standards or certain of the community subcultures? Is the group reacting against certain values? What are the value conflicts? Does it consider its standards higher than those of the community, agency or institution? How have you as worker dealt with the group's attitudes toward accepted values?

6. How is the agency attempting to affect these values? What does worker do about them? What is his aim in doing this? What has resulted? Give specific instances.

III. *Group Emotion*

1. What is the general social climate of the group in terms of factors such as the following: friendliness or hostility toward each other; opportunity for free expression of opinion and receptive attitude toward one another; attitude

toward authority as represented by the worker, the agency or the indigenous leaders; ability to cooperate effectively for common ends?

2. What outside factors such as physical setting of the group, fatigue, home, school or work situations, have in your opinion affected this climate? If the climate has changed markedly during the period of the record, what has produced this change?

3. How has *esprit de corps* of the group fluctuated during this period? What has produced these fluctuations? How has it been affected by the program, conflicts, interpersonal acceptance and rejection, events outside the group?

4. Do the members vary in their attachment to the group? How does this show itself? What is the pattern of group attachments?

5. Does the group use any symbols or ritual to express its attachment to the group? Where did these come from? What effect do they have on group cohesion? On individual reactions to the group? What effect do they have on the group's standing with other groups in the agency?

6. Where does the worker fit with respect to the emotional aspects of the group? How has this affected his functioning? What have been the results?

IV. *Group Deliberation and Control*

1. Does the group have a formal system of decision making and control embodied in a constitution or set of rules? If not, what means has it of control? If so, how much does the group abide by its own rules?

2. How much control do the officers exercise over the programs and behavior of the group? How much is this affected by total group participation? What limits are set over the power of the officials? How are group problems solved? Describe the process of deliberation involved. What is your role?

3. What committees does the group have and what are their functions? What part have you had in setting up of committees? What were your aims here?

4. How actively do the members participate in decision making? Are there instances of socially inert, passive members, dependent or dominating members? Are there fringe members not actively engaged in the group? If so, describe psychological basis of this position as you see it. How is participation encouraged or discouraged in the indigenous leadership?

5. What kinds of issues have produced conflicts in the group? How does the group react when it cannot get what it wants? Describe use of authority in such situations. What part did you play in such conflicts?

6. Is there any unauthorized group or individual controlling or attempting to control the group? How is this being done? How successful is it? What methods were used?

7. What contribution do the indigenous leaders make which accounts for their rise of leadership? What needs or drives of theirs do you think are reflected in their leadership? How do they deal with their position as leaders in the group? Differentiate the task-centered aspects from the social-emotional.

8. What agency regulations or requirements affect control of the group? How are such controls put into effect? What part does the agency staff other than the worker have in such control?

9. How do attitudes toward authority, neighborhood tradition, class habits, etc., affect the reactions of the group toward authority and self-government?

10. What has the worker done in regard to the control of the group? At what points has he taken control of himself? What methods did he use? What were his aims in doing this? What were the results? Give specific instances. How has he attempted to establish democratic method through indigenous leaders?

D. Worker's Use of Tools

I. *Relationships*

1. During group meetings, are there certain members who are constantly endangering the effective functioning of the group by such behavior as bullying weaker members, refusal to carry their share of work, showing off by noisy or irritating behavior, passivity or daydreaming, acting tough, monopolizing the leader? Define the most common of these in terms of individuals who often behave in this way. What is the relation of worker to these persons? How does he handle his behavior in the group? How has he used the group program or group pressures to deal with this behavior?

2. Are there certain members who are normally helpful to the group by such behavior as making useful suggestions, assuming responsibility, helping or protecting weaker members, quieting noisy members, upholding agency standards, stimulating thinking or control of emotional outbursts of others? Who does this commonly? What is the relation of the worker to these persons? How has he used their behavior to promote group program or group relations? How has he used group program or pressures to develop their capacities? To what extent does the worker work with the officers or committee chairman in planning business meetings or program?

3. Outside of the group meeting, what contacts has the worker had with members of the group? In lobbies, streets, homes, etc., in which he saw the person by himself or with one or two others? How did these contacts arise? What occurred in the interviews of significance to the person or the functioning of the group?

4. Has this group had any relation to other groups inside the agency? How has this group been related to program planned for whole agency? What effect does this have on its own program? What contacts has it had outside the agency? Describe the contact in each case in terms of activities engaged in and effect on the group. What part has the worker played in intergroup activities? What has he aimed to do through them? What has resulted?

II. *Programming*

1. What activities characterize the group? How are activities, programs, and special events planned and arranged? Are there any sequential patterns? How is the agency, membership, and worker involved in the process?

2. What uses do the various programs serve for the group or any of the members? Which kinds of results were anticipated and recognized? What latent significance can be attached to activities in terms of the group and surrounding groups? Which programs are successful or unsuccessful?

3. What is the worker's conception of programming? How is it related to goals? How is it utilized by the worker to affect other group processes?

III. *Analytic Tools*

1. In reality, the above areas are differentiated for analytical purposes only. In reality, there is considerable interrelationship and interdependence. These are extremely complex and in many cases cannot be detected with our present concepts. Any thoroughgoing analysis, however, will seek to point up the nature of the relationships.

2. Increasingly, it will be important to discover additional ways of measuring the variables discussed above. Taken alone, such indicators as enrollment changes, attendance patterns and averages, rates of participation in special programs and events may not be significant. But, when used to interpret the various group processes, they can be insightful. A good analysis experiments with various measures.

IV. *Evaluation*

Prepare a brief summarizing statement (approximately two pages) which highlights your assessment of the significant features of your professional practice with and in behalf of this group. Evaluate the effectiveness of your method of service, point out specific areas of concern and make a set of recommendations regarding future service.

16. The Cardinals—A Worker Studies Her Work with the Group

The junior high school girls with whom I worked gave this reason for wanting a club: "There are so many things that are fun to do, but our parents won't give permission unless we do them in a group with a chaperon!"

These girls were anxious to play outdoor sports, go camping, have parties, and just sit and talk about themselves. Yet at the age of fourteen, it wasn't so much the activities which stood out in their minds as the fact that their parents still required that they do these things in a group and with an older person.

The Cardinal Club was sponsored by one of the churches in the neighborhood. It was one of 700 clubs in the city organized by a youth-serving agency which includes girls between the ages of seven and eighteen years of age in its program. The agency aims at organizing clubs in all parts of the city so that girls may have the opportunity to work and play in small groups with the guidance and help of trained volunteer adult workers. The agency offers suggestions for club activities, but the members and workers are free to plan any activity if it allows no discrimination of class, race, or financial status, and if it meets the health and safety standards of the agency.

These girls live and attend school in an upper-middle-class section of a large city. Their fathers hold such positions as bankers, road contractors, wholesale merchandisers and airplane designers. The mothers of this group do their own housework, but the majority of people in the neighborhood have maid and gardener service. In general, the girls have taken on the air of being financially well-to-do even though their particular families may not benefit from all the privileges and comforts such a status usually affords.

The Cardinal Club was in its fifth year when I began work with its members. They had formed the club as a group of nine-year-olds and originally this was the only club to which each girl belonged. Then, as time went on, the Cardinal Club became only one of several clubs which each member joined.

At the beginning of the year, each member listed on a sheet of paper the three things she wanted most to do in the club. They wanted a program which would include dancing, singing, making things with their hands, going places with boys, hiking, cooking in the out-of-doors and having parties. Since seven of the eight girls belonged to other clubs in the school and community, and those clubs had specific programs, we tried to make our activities of a type less likely to be duplicated by the other groups. In the case of this particular club, our program was guided not by a plan or pattern set up by the agency but by unmet desires of the girls left over after they had participated in the other club programs.

When I started working with the club, the former worker was doubtful whether the girls would want to continue, since they had such heavy extracurricular schedules. From sixteen girls of the previous year, only seven had renewed their memberships and they did so on the basis that they had plans they'd like to carry through, especially in the out-of-doors, which didn't fit so well into the other club programs.

One objective of the agency is to provide opportunities for girls to have group experiences which will help to satisfy girls' needs and capacities for creative expression, for social participation, and for experimenting in ways of adjusting to people and situations. Since we as a group recognized some duplication in community club programs, letting our activities emphasize an unmet need meant we were in line with the goals of the agency.

Brief Sketches of Members

Betty, fourteen years old. Next to Sue, Betty was the tallest and largest girl in the group. When she took the time, she could be very attractive. Other girls in the club tried to help Betty with fixing her hair and choosing color combinations for clothes. Betty wanted to be neat, particularly if that meant being popular. She often forgot this avenue to popularity and tried to compensate by being a leader in skills which sometimes made her more of an outcast. Being part of the group was a constant struggle for Betty. She was the one who had no particular friend; yet the club was her main source of social activity.

Kate, thirteen. Physically Kate was one of the smaller girls. In addition to being a year younger than the others, Kate was a year lower in school grade. She usually gained attention in club meetings by being the center of whatever was going on. The others accepted her play for attention more easily than Betty's attempts because Kate had a more winning way of doing it.

Martha, fourteen. Martha was an attractive brunette, extremely neat, and always had a mischievous twinkle in her eye. She was the artist of the group. She was happier when she could be leader, and when she was the leader she did a good job. However, when Martha was a follower, she sometimes gained attention by being reckless and scatterbrained, which diminished her chances for being a consistent leader. I consider Martha one of the two members who grew the most through her group experience in the club. Martha had always been the one who could paint and draw. Consequently, her status in this group and other groups was attained through things she could create with her hands.

Along with her artistic ability Martha had a lot of physical energy and wanted to be popular with the group because of things she could do other than drawing. On hikes or at the skating rink, she was always in the lead. For the first few months at club meetings, sitting still in a chair for more than five minutes was impossible for her. When she did sit, she was continually playing with a pencil or handkerchief and often talked to her neighbor while the meeting was being conducted.

As time went on, opportunity came for Martha to preside at meetings and she did an excellent job. In the last spring election for officers, Martha wanted to be president and she did extensive campaigning for herself. She overdid it, which defeated her struggle. I suggested to Martha that the other club members knew, as I did, that she could do other things besides draw, but they didn't want to be told how to vote in an election.

The next week Martha was running for president of a chorus group made up of both boys and girls. She was elected.

Audrey, fourteen. Audrey had gotten into the swing of being an adolescent more gracefully than some of the others. In addition to being an attractive blonde, she had a willing attitude, but sometimes a little too willing. When given a chance to work on a committee she never refused because "being on a committee" added prestige. Once Audrey started a job, she needed periodical reminders in order to get the job completed because, if given a chance, she would offer to be on a new committee and leave the first assignment incomplete.

Mildred, fourteen. Mildred was the natural leader of the group when I first started working with them. She was still their leader at the end of the year. During the nine months the group grew and she grew with them. Although she was of the same age as most of the group, Mildred was at first very disgusted at the way the others acted during club meetings and for a while wasn't certain she wanted to spend the time belonging to the club.

Mildred attended a different junior high school. Except for club meetings she seldom saw the other members. It was her seriousness, her reliability and ability to do many things which made her a leader. Lack of patience and the urge to do other people's jobs were two attitudes Mildred worked at changing. She did come out with more patience and understanding of why others weren't as quick as she was.

Sue, fifteen. At fifteen Sue was almost six feet tall. Because of her size, people expected Sue to act twenty but in growing she had not lost the normal desires of a fifteen-year-old. In addition to her size, Sue was a little hard of hearing and she knew she might lose her hearing completely in a few years. Both Sue and her sister, Mary, were ill a great deal with chronic colds. They were accustomed to being given special concessions in school because of illness or because of their interest and time required in practicing music. They expected the same special attention in the club.

Mary, thirteen. Mary was Sue's younger sister. When she remembered, Mary requested that she and Sue always be together on committees and sit next to each other. Once in a while there would be a family argument. Both forgot to attend meetings frequently. When Mary was president of the group she was so overwhelmed with the idea of being president when her older sister was only vice-president that she was open for few suggestions. Mary was right until proved wrong.

Leah, sixteen. Leah was the oldest member of the group in years, but not in experience. Since an early age, she had moved from state to state, living with different relatives and friends of her parents. Both parents had been killed when she was a child. Because of her frequent moving, she was behind in schooling and, with her shy manner, was also behind in general social adjustment.

This club was the only group to which Leah belonged. For her, it helped a great deal in serving as a practice ground for adjusting to her new family and to new school friends. Leah had lived with this family only one month when she started attending club meetings. I noticed that she didn't go on the Christmas shopping trip or on the skating party. It wasn't until we had a mothers' meeting that I found Leah had not asked for permission to go on these trips. From that time on, Mrs. K., with whom Leah lived, made it a point to find out what the club program was going to be and she encouraged Leah to participate.

The K. family had two children, five and eight years old, whom Leah helped to take care of as a way of paying for her board and room and living expenses. Leah had become too conscientious and felt bound to be at home always with no time for social life allowed. Through the help of the club and the mothers' group, this foster mother and daughter were able to work out a more balanced schedule of living for Leah.

Because all the other girls talked about their mothers and fathers, Leah finally started calling Mr. and Mrs. K. Mom and Dad at club meetings. From there she tried using "Mom" at home.

Leah may never be a leader, but her experience in this club helped her to realize her place as an individual in a group—both her family group and the club group.

The club's first major project of the year was fixing up a member's garage into a clubhouse. The girls started this with much enthusiasm and eight different ideas of how the garage should be redecorated. They worked four weeks at getting the garage in shape for more detailed decorating. Then cold weather came and there was no way to heat the building so their interest went to shorter projects with occasional day meetings at the club-house when it was warm enough.

Other plans made and completed during the year were: four cookouts in backyards to try new menus before going on longer hikes; a trip to the observatory; a Christmas project, which included buying and delivering Christmas presents for children in an institution; a roller skating party with boys; a snow trip to the mountains; an outdoor induction ceremony for officers of the club; a community play day with other clubs sponsored by the same agency; a dad-daughter box supper; and club meetings when they "just talked."

This club met once a week while most of the other clubs to which these same girls belonged met once every two weeks. This group seemed to feel they needed a "talking over" kind of meeting almost every two weeks. For five months we met after school from 3:30 to 5:30. The next five months we met in the evening from 7:00 to 9:00 P.M.

At meetings after school they discussed teachers, classes and activities of other clubs. In the evening there was more talk about family plans or the TV program that was on when they left the house. There were always comments on the latest Coke date or "the" way to fix your hair. What happened at those jam session meetings gave me good clues to the kind of relationship I had with the group.

As far as self-analysis goes, I think they looked to me as a friend in whom they had confidence. After testing me they found that what they called "strictness" was lacking. They saw plans fail because they did not recognize that my substitute for strictness was a belief in a club member's obligation to do a job—not a belief in the worker's obligation to see that members were made to perform with fear of punishment as incentive for working.

Although their way of thinking, their actions and decisions were often different from those I would make, because of this difference I was interested in them not only as club members, but as members of family groups, as schoolgirls and as adolescents.

Describing my role as the worker with this group, I should list the following:

1. Helped advise on way to organize a club.

2. Collected program ideas from the group, added other ideas new to them and helped them decide what to do about the ideas.

3. Worked with individuals in their roles as officers.

4. Experimented with ways of planning both in a large group and with small committees.

5. Helped group to recognize where they were as individuals and as a group so that their plans and ambitions could be scaled to the right dimensions.

6. Helped the group to divide and carry out responsibilities in keeping a club going.

7. Introduced the idea of seeing others as persons with reasons behind their behavior, not just as bad or ignorant people. This was done particularly at jam sessions—when they were always talking about the other fellow.

8. When I thought it necessary, I stepped in to speed things up when group interaction hit a block.

9. Made final decisions when time element was too short for group or committee decision.

10. Tried to help girls understand their relationships to parents, teachers, and other adult friends.

11. Worked at helping to form normal attitudes and relationships with boys.

12. Aided avoidance of same mistakes made in program planning and activities by informal and formal evaluations.

In performing my role as worker with the group I tried to help individuals by learning more about their likes, dislikes, needs, desires, capacities and abilities as persons. Then, knowing what I did, I helped to provide opportunities lacking in the previous experiences of the individual.

With the group as a whole, I tried to learn the same things as I did about each individual and to provide opportunities for needed experiences. As the number of experiences in working together increased, the members gradually began to feel a groupness or a oneness. When questions came up, not one or two but all eight opinions were considered. As the group feeling increased, it was easier to help in planning for the future, even if only the future of one week. And after a year, one or two weeks were about the extent of long-term planning upon which the group could follow through. Over such a period of time this seems like little progress, but from where they were in the scale of experience it was a big step for this group.

The previous four years, this group had been very dependent on its adult leadership. In experience they were at the level of ten-year-olds even though their average actual age was fourteen.

I tried to shift and work at a program of group interdependence, but not dependence on the worker. This idea was so completely new to them that some projects failed because of their lack of experience and initiative. In my role as a worker, I'm sure there were times when I should have permitted the group to be dependent on me and rest up for a new try at going on their own. I believe they would have progressed faster if I had made a practice of offering dependence to balance their struggles at being independent.

This I should do if I were working with them another year. Again, it was the factor of the time it takes to know a group and keep up with the changes which slowed the worker's chances at taking the right step.

QUESTIONS

1. How much would you expect a group that had been meeting together for five years to differ from a group that was newly organized?
2. When group members are active in several other groups, what are the implications for program?
3. What are some of the outstanding differences between the individual members of the group?
4. How would you evaluate the worker's analysis of her role with this group?
5. What do youth of this age need in group experiences as aids to their social development?

17. Group Program as a Therapeutic Tool with Atypical Children

Social group work with children in state hospitals is increasing. This account of how program was developed over a two-and-one-half-year period lends itself to discussion and analysis.

Group Program as a Therapeutic Tool with Atypical Children *

The young atypical child has been the topic of much discussion. The terms "autistic," "symbiotic," and "schizophrenic" are often used to describe some of these children. There is lack of agreement regarding many aspects of the disturbance including definition. The most useful for our purpose is Kessler's by symptom:

"The most important single sign is a severely disturbed relationship with people. This may take the form of a lack of interest in or awareness of people (i.e., autism) or it may take the form of an inability to separate from another person (i.e., symbiosis). From this disturbed relationship with people arise difficulties in communication, inability to initiate or engage in normal play, extraordinary preoccupation with inanimate objects, and clinging to a mechanical, routinized, compulsive, repetitive mode of living." [1]

The literature contains much concerning description and diagnosis, etiology and treatment by psychotherapy.[2] There is little agreement concerning description and diagnosis, etiology is unclear and results of treatment disappointing. Some mention of the "educational approach" or milieu therapy is made.[3] This approach is gaining acceptance and holds some hope of success. Social group work understandings can be applied to this approach.

This paper is an attempt to integrate and conceptualize the knowledge gained in developing a treatment program directed by a social group worker for children who fall in this catergory.

The program developed slowly over a two-and-a-half-year period on the Children's Unit of a large state hospital. Many realities of the setting affected the program's development. Among the most important were: (1) Staff with little understanding of this type of child and no preparation to work with the children. (2) In this stage separation from the total Children's Unit was

* By Louise C. Johnson, ACSW, Assistant Professor, School of Social Work, The University of Iowa. Paper presented to Connecticut Social Welfare Conference, November 17, 1966, published in the *Iowa Journal of Social Work*, Fall 1970. Used with permission.

impossible. (3) Use had to be made of the facilities and equipment readily available. (4) Seeming slowness of change growing out of being part of a large institution. Despite these frustrations a program with goals, themes, and ingredients did develop.

Theoretical concepts drawn on in the program grew out of a social group work frame of reference. Modifications were made to meet the special needs of these children. They included: (1) Assessing developmental levels of the children and providing experiences in program which would aid the children to move to the next level of development. (2) Simplifying the environment so as to remove excess anxiety stimulation thus freeing the child to grow. (3) The concept that more acceptable social behavior which would result in greater acceptance of the child by a larger number of other patients and staff was highly desirable. (4) That learning is facilitated by relationships with others hence relationships with adults and peers was a prime goal. (5) That despite their severe handicap in relating to others these children could be helped by group process stimulated by the use of various program media and adult relationships.

Sixteen children were served in the program. It was structured through the use of small groups of four children. Grouping was based on socialization level. The two lowest groups spent four hours each morning in groups led by graduates of a Child Development sequence. The two higher groups attended school with a special teacher. In each group the children were given individual and group tasks and experiences planned to meet their particular need. All the children ate, slept, dressed in a group where self-help skills were taught and encouraged.

Parents of the children are particularly important as each child needs his parents involved in his life. The goal was to help them be involved with their child on the most constructive level possible. They need help in lessening their guilt and understanding the chid's needs. All parents were seen by social workers either individually or in a group.

These children had mostly come to residential treatment after participation in community programs. They came because they had become destructive to themselves and their families and could no longer be tolerated at home.

Goals

The goal with these children was to help them develop in such a manner that they might live in whatever setting best meets their needs as comfortably as possible. It involved developing the ability to relate to persons on the highest level possible in a more socially acceptable manner.

Themes

Two themes ran throughout the program: reality and timing. For the child to relate to other persons in a more socially acceptable manner he was helped to come in contact with the real world. He learned to understand consequences of behavior and was helped to make the needed changes demanded by society. He learned how the real world functioned and how to function in the real world. The theme of reality orientation was prime.

Timing was also crucial. Because the child finds reality so threatening, he was led to reality-oriented functioning at an imperceptively slow pace. Change can take place when the child is helped to take those steps he is ready to take but not forced to take those still too threatening for him.

Ingredients

The ingredients of the program were the means of helping the child take the steps toward reality. They were the same ingredients which help all children grow in their ability to live in society. Because of his disturbance the young schizophrenic child has missed many steps; he needs a great deal more help in taking these steps.

Structure. The first ingredient and the one upon which all the others were dependent was structure. For the children to be able to respond in any way their need for sameness had to be met. To be comfortable they needed structure. This lowered their anxiety level which usually was very high in these children. It did feed into their ritualistic tendencies but "ritualistic" sameness diminished. They were then able to accept carefully planned "doses" of change and variety in program. In the beginning the program consisted of being in the same place, with the same materials (usually not used by the children) every day at the same time. Initially, the children resisted these limits. Doors had to be locked, anger accepted. Very soon it became evident that this structure was of value to the children. They showed us they wanted it. On days when it was impossible to maintain the program they asked for it and came to go to the area at the scheduled time. When the children no longer needed to be concerned about what would happen, they were able to invest some energy in other activity.

Verbalization. If one of the goals with the children was to bring them into closer touch with reality, then verbalization was a needed ingredient. The real world depends much on verbal communication. It was in this area that normal development was so limited. The children probably had damaged verbalization skills because of deeper damage to their ability to relate. However, verbalization was a method of encouraging relationship. This was done in two ways. First, the child learned to obey simple verbal commands. In the beginning only a very few, well-defined commands such as "sit down" or "you cannot hit" were used and expected to be followed. Reinforcement by punishment or reward was used. The children responded to this and were able to gradually increase their ability to respond to verbal commands in terms of numbers and decreased use of reinforcement. The second area using this ingredient was that of verbalization of feeling. The workers consistently expressed in words how the child was angry or happy or sad. Children who had speech were able to come to express anger in words rather than action. Children without speech expressed their feelings in such ways as asking the worker to hold their hands when they felt like hitting. The worker always verbalized for them. Some of the children just did not seem to understand the meaning of some words. One boy who constantly hit and pinched others came to understand the word "hurt" when the worker used this word every time he hit and pinched at the same time hitting or pinching him just enough to hurt. He soon understood the meaning of "hurt" and then only the word needed to be used. This technique must be used carefully and planfully; never in anger. Some emphasis was also put on encouraging the child to develop speech. He was encouraged to verbalize desires such as milk, cookie, or his name. Initially he received praise for any attempt if only forming lips to make the first letter sound. The child with some speech was helped to overcome tendencies toward ecolia and to verbalize feelings. Care needed to be taken that the matter of speech, important as it was, not be overemphasized. Speech deficiency was only a small part of the children's disturbed functioning. These children slowly and skillfully needed to be led into the world of words and verbalization.

Relationships. As disturbed and bizarre relationships with people is one of the evidences of this disturbance, much emphasis was placed on more normal relationships. The worker was ever sensitive to when the child could tolerate intrusion with relationship on her part and when it was just too threatening. In the early phases this needed to be diluted. For this reason among others, working with the children in small groups seemed more suitable than individually. They seemed less threatened by relationship when they were not the only child receiving an adult's attention. The worker could move from child to child as they were ready to give a small amount of individual attention. As time went on the children demanded "their share of the worker." Rivalry among the children seemed to encourage relationship not only with the worker but with the other children. They seemed to become more aware of all kinds of relationship in this way. This relationship was then used as a means of encouraging much other growth-producing behavior. When they were ready some children progressed to periods of one-to-one relationship for therapeutic purposes.

Relationships with other children came more slowly. However, the very presence of other children and the need to share worker and equipment forced the children to become aware of each other. Often the first relationship with other children was of a negative nature, i.e., hitting, taking a toy. This needed to be handled most skillfully. The child had to be helped to see that he could not hurt others and yet not receive the idea that relating to others was so threatening he would withdraw. The children did come to enjoy parallel play and to be aware that the other children had feelings. They came to be less threatened by relationships.

Four children to each worker proved best. The worker could be aware of each child and meet his needs without being too threatening. The child who was ready to relate to another had an opportunity to find another. This was a sufficient number for a rudimentary group with process evolving around competition for the worker and equipment.

Self-Help. One of the goals was to have these children gain the skills needed to live as comfortably as possible in whatever setting best meets their needs. The ability to care for oneself is of prime importance in meeting this goal; hence routines of daily living were emphasized. A diagnostic appraisal was made of the level on which each child was operating. Gradually each was encouraged to grow at his own pace in a planful manner. This area includes eating, dressing, picking up after oneself, to name a few. One boy progressed to the point that he could walk to and from school alone. The children realized they were different and were proud when they took another step which made them behave more like the other children with whom they lived. This self-confidence gave motivation to try in other areas.

Discourage Bizarre Behavior. As the child grew and learned new ways of behaving he was encouraged to give up his more bizarre patterns of behaving. This took much sensitivity on the part of those working with the children. If this was attempted before the child had gained sufficient means of meeting his needs in another manner it was destructive. However, once the child had these new ways at his command he needed to use the new ways rather than continue in the more bizarre ways. For example: one child exhibited much uncontrolled screaming when displeased. He was told he no longer needed to do this and the worker verbalized his feelings and encouraged him to do likewise. Another child had a fetish of a towel; he was merely told he no longer needed this and instead was given attention or interested in some other activity. The worker must understand the meaning of behavior and the purpose served to be able to make the necessary judgments. Psychiatric consultation was a necessity for determining factors involved.

Play Activity. Erickson[4] has pointed out in an extremely helpful manner that play is a child's work. It is through play that the child learns about himself and his world. The children do not perceive themselves or the world as does the normal child. Their "play" activity was not the same. They often related to objects rather than to persons. When the worker related to the child through play materials he was encouraging interpersonal relationships. He was helping the child understand himself as a person and what he could do, what his body was like. He was helping him explore the real world in which he lived. The more he understood the real world, the more comfortable he was in the real world, the more able he then was to give up his bizarre, fantasy world, the more his "play" activity became like that seen in more normal children. Again to use this ingredient we needed a developmental diagnosis. The child needed to begin with activities of very early childhood and progress as far as he was able through various developmental steps. Large muscle activity had early priority. Toys to be taken apart, put back together and manipulated were essential. The media of paint, clay, water, and crayons were useful. Care needed to be taken that these media were not used by the child as a means to fantasy; rather that the child was exploring touch, smell, color, etc., that he was exploring the world in which he lived. Music always held these children's attention. It was used with body movement, to color to music, to quiet the children when they needed soothing. Physical activity of all kinds helped with body image. Swimming was particularly useful. Later the children liked to be read to and looked at pictures about the real world. Food, cars, boats, objects that had meaning in their lives were most useful. This type of "play" activity was indeed the child's work.

Educational Activity. From "play" activity the child moved into activity with a more formal educational goal: counting, color identification. Then slowly he began a reading readiness program; he learned number concepts in a very concrete manner. He moved into the school setting with a very special teacher. This teacher bridged the gap between the protected group program and the more formal school program. He sometimes began to participate in the special activities of the school: art, music, home economics, industrial arts, physical education with regular school teachers. One child was able to participate in some acedemic classwork while still spending part of the day with his special teacher. At the same time the other ingredients were not neglected. The child's total program was planned to meet his current needs in each area.

In order to meet current needs it was important to start where the child was, understand his behavior and its meaning, and plan a program of restitution; it was essential that an assessment of each child be given considerable emphasis. This evaluation needed to be ongoing as the children grew. All work was based on this evaluation and assessment. It contained a developmental evaluation, a psychiatric evaluation, a social history; in other words, a thorough knowledge of all there was to know about the child.

Program was the heart of the children's treatment. Much more work and study of the techniques and methods is needed. However, this approach does hold promise of aiding the atypical child gain more adequate social functioning. The children worked with in this manner all moved to higher levels of functioning in areas of self-help and use of play materials. Their interpersonal relationships were not as distorted. They displayed less bizarre behavior. They responded to verbal commands and verbalization of feelings. Some used speech more adequately. Some gained academic skills. They were dealing with the world of reality and its demands more adequately.

NOTES

1. Jane W. Kessler, *Psychopathology of Childhood* (Englewood Cliffs, N.J.: Prentice Hall, 1966), pp. 263–264.
2. See James R. Tilton, Marian K. DeMeyer, and Lois Hendricksen Loew, *Annotated Bibliography on Childhood Schizophrenia, 1955–1964* (New York: Grune and Stratton, 1966).
3. *Ibid.*, Chapter VI, Section D, "Other Specialized Approaches in Care, Treatment and Effective Behavioral Change," pp. 114–122.
4. Eric Erickson, *Childhood and Society* (New York: W. W. Norton and Co., Inc., 1950).

18. The Use of Groups in a Training School

The following account is a useful exposition of what is involved in working with girls in a correctional institution. The goals of such work are stated clearly and the problems encountered in trying to achieve these goals are pointed out.

The Use of Groups in a Training School for Juvenile Delinquent Girls *

Within our setting girls are committed by the juvenile courts to the State Department of Public Welfare. The Wisconsin School for Girls is designated as the reception center and school for female delinquents. The school is part of a larger state agency that provides both institution and aftercare services. Aftercare workers are not part of the institution staff but operate in the home

* By Lorraine Davis and Katherine B. Kaminski. Presented in *An Occasional Paper*, No. 6. The School of Social Work, The University of Wisconsin, Madison, 1968. Used with permission.

communities from which the girls are committed. A number of the features found in our setting are also found in the various correctional schools throughout the country: it is an open institution, and there are no walls or fences. As in most other juvenile correctional institutions, population pressures have forced early releases for many who are not ready. The result is a rather rapid turnover and a reduction of the average stay to five months. There is no selection or screening process at intake. Girls between twelve and eighteen may be committed and may be returned or retained through their twentieth year. They are grouped and placed, essentially on the basis of age, in the 10 self-contained cottages that house 25 girls, each in a single room. Staff directly responsible for one cottage includes five counselors, a social worker, and a teacher from the educational program. The clinical services staff is now attempting to provide one participating-consulting psychologist for every two cottages. The social worker has responsibility for the group work, casework, and the coordination of institution and aftercare planning for all the girls in one cottage.

The girls meet as a group for one hour, five days a week. From their inception six years ago, these community meetings were seen as a method of utilizing the peer relationships within the living unit in a more effective and positive way. . . . Regular, structured interaction between the girls and staff of a cottage provides a better opportunity for a more immediate and realistic assessment of situations and problems that arise. The importance of peer group acceptance motivates some of the girls to give up some of their destructive or intolerable behavior. During the meetings, they are encouraged to express themselves freely within certain limits. They may not abuse anyone physically or broadcast discussion material beyond their cottage living group. At first, the situation is viewed with suspicion. Then, as the girls learn that they can express themselves, they may move into a period of testing. When they find that their comments, criticisms, and gripes are accepted with reflection rather than reprisal, they are able to move on to more meaningful material.

In addition to the goals stated—namely providing opportunity for better communication between girls and staff and using peer pressures to promote changes—a number of other goals were set forth. Community meetings were seen as a means of helping the group focus on the cottage structure, as an opportunity to use and discuss authority, and as an opportunity for concrete planning to meet difficulties. It was expected that community meetings would help maintain an acceptable level of control, establish a minimum level of acceptable social interaction, and make some of the participants more accessible for continued help.

After some experience with community meetings, there is a consensus that some of these goals are attainable through the group method. The definite and continuing advantages of the system are that cottage management and control are maintained at a better level; staff is provided with a daily pulse on the situation—on underlying currents and problems that may arise; the daily pressures of close living are relieved through discussion. The meetings also offer additional material for a diagnostic picture of the individual, as patterns of relating to peers and adults and general distortions are re-enacted in the group situation.

However, some distinct disadvantages and limitations to the full achievement of these goals and results have become clear. One of the most obvious problems is the size and turnover of the group membership. With 20 to 25 members, there is a great variation in attention and interest. The continual arrival and departure of members means that only minimum group stability and cohesiveness can be expected over a relatively short period of time. With the majority of the girls' "length of stay" coinciding with the school semesters, the group processes may change every three or four months. Introduction of new members, and a resulting change in structure, forces the group to return to the early developmental phases and processes. Thus, the process is cyclical, almost never developing beyond the transition phases (after which meaningful involvement, commitment, relationships and attitudinal changes might be expected to occur). Within this fluctuating structure relatively little depth or continuity is achieved.

Other factors become obvious. Those girls who exhibit strong "delinquent values" and have strong ties to delinquent subcultures generally have had more experience and success in peer group relationships. This, coupled with their willingness to be openly defiant toward authority figures, and their apparent sophistication and satisfaction with their delinquent values and roles, quickly establishes them as leaders in the group. Often a number of these girls in one living group will form a strong power structure within the group.

As workers began to experiment and form new goals for their work with the groups, the first move was to split the group to enable the staff to work more closely and effectively with a smaller group. Based on the ages and needs of the girls, the goals set, and the orientation and method used by the worker, there were any number of ways that smaller groups could be formed. One worker adapted the "guided group interaction" method for use with younger girls. Another worker, supervising graduate students, had enough staff available to create five small groups in one living unit in the hope of decreasing the negative effects of the power structure upon the group as a whole. This arrangement did, to a degree, reduce the force of the social delinquents in the group and resulted in greater positive participation by all girls.

Another worker obtained administrative cooperation in screening for and admitting the more seriously disturbed or neurotic girls. One of the disadvantages was in attempting to work with these girls without additional staff or without a reduction in the total number of girls. Their emotional needs and demands became more apparent; and the group, in general, was found to be lacking those who could perform stabilizing or leadership roles.

Members of the clinical services staff began to form groups (members drawn from all cottages) with various goals. An unwed mothers' group is being maintained where girls can discuss feelings and problems and receive information specific to their situations. In another instance, a female white psychologist and a male Negro counselor worked with a small group of extremely hostile and antisocial girls who possessed racial and sexual problems. The utilization of a tape-recorded group session with no staff member present is unique in our setting. This group is limited to five members and is drawn from those girls who have been in the living unit longer and who exhibit some maturity. Any communication to the group by the worker is done via tape because the worker conducts another group simultaneously. A recent proposal, not yet used or worked out in detail, has been to use a form of behavior therapy in working with a group of the more seriously limited or socially deprived girls.

There are a number of basic assumptions in this discussion. To the adolescent the peer group is the most important reference group. To the delinquent the peer group can be one of the greatest inhibitors to or motivators of change. Not all adolescents can be helped through the use of groups, but it certainly provides one of the most realistic methods of approaching the delinquent. Delinquents have not responded well to insight therapy but have responded more favorably to varying types of group situations. Pure custodial and routine-oriented programs have not been effective in treating delinquents nor have the traditional therapy methods (individual or group) been effective in producing any significant or lasting changes in modes of behavior. We must be aware that any methods or techniques require careful modification to adjust to and account for different philosophies, staff time, and available money.

19. Group Work in a Prison

Group work in prisons is a developing area of practice. The following example gives the goals of such work and the various approaches that may be used by the worker.

Group Work in a Maximum-Security Prison *

The task of the group worker in a maximum-security prison is to look for ways to bring about some change in the inmate's behavior which will assist him to adjust more favorably within the institution and, more importantly, to be able to return to his community in some way changed so that he is less likely to break the law again.

The ideal goal of group work in this setting might be to produce a well-adjusted, productive member of society. A more realistic goal, however, would be to bring about change in the offender which would assist him to have better control over his deviant tendencies, even though he might remain a somewhat conflicted, uncomfortable person.

While our expectations may be somewhat limited, the challenge of group work in this setting is to bring a number of offenders together in one room to try to effect some favorable change in their behavior, even though many may not have the desire to change. The fact that the setting within which this takes place is artificial and oppressive increases the challenge.

In attempting to bring about some favorable change in client behavior through group work, the following issues may be particularly relevant in a maximum-security institution and might be thought of as limited goals:

(1) Replacing acting out behavior with talking out; that is, verbally expressing angry feelings in preference to physical violence, and thereby precluding disciplinary action by the custodial staff;

(2) Learning how to relate with other persons and acquiring social skills so that one might become more effective in his social interactions;

* By Gerald J. Forthun and Ronald Nuehring. Published in *An Occasional Paper*, Number 6, The School of Social Work, The University of Wisconsin, Madison, 1968. Used with permission.

(3) Learning to deal with the reality of the present, here-and-now situation whether in prison or free society, which might include learning new ways of perceiving a given situation and different ways of reacting to it;

(4) Learning about the connection between one's feelings, one's talking, and one's actual overt behavior;

(5) Accepting responsibility for one's behavior, in spite of the limited opportunities for self-determination in a maximum-security institution.

These issues seem to be particularly relevant in a maximum-security institution because they often take the form of resistances which inmates exploit to avoid changing something about themselves. That is, the inmate might avoid the idea of changing himself by claiming that so many things are unfair in the institution that he has been victimized. He might also claim that he cannot change because he is somewhat of a helpless pawn, that everything within the institution is so structured that he does not have the opportunity to practice making his own decisions.

It is not surprising, then, that one of the most important practical issues with which group workers in correctional settings have to deal is the resistance of the inmate to becoming really involved in treatment. This section of the paper will be concerned with a discussion of some of the forms of resistance often seen and various treatment techniques for meeting these situations.

"The World Is Unfair"

In view of the oppressive nature of most prison settings, it is quite common for a group meeting to develop into a "gripe" session. In fact, group work was first initiated at this institution as a method for allowing some of the inmates to vent their anger in a more acceptable way than by fighting or other disruptive behavior. In this sense, it could be said that a gripe session is a healthy and perhaps necessary reaction to a prison. Frequently during group meetings, however, the griping becomes an end in itself. As a consequence, little is accomplished other than emotional release.

In some cases, griping may be an effective method for the inmate to avoid facing some of his own problems and limitations. It is certainly much more stress-producing for the inmate to begin looking at his personal problems than to complain about prison food, his monotonous job, or other factors outside of himself. The inmate may be joined by other group members in a kind of alliance so that no one asks embarrassing or confronting questions of another group member.

One technique that a group worker might use to meet this type of resistance is a direct confrontation in which he gives his interpretation of what the men in the group are actually doing. Although this method often mobilizes the group's defenses against the worker, it is effective in bringing about at least a temporary shift of attention to the group itself.

The following example is taken from a group meeting of convicted sexual offenders. The last several meetings had consisted primarily of gripes about the way the institution was being run, the inequities of the law, and other conflicts of this nature. The worker handled the situation in this way:

Therapist: I'd rather have you argue a little bit than keep on the way you have been.

Mr. O.: In other words, you'd like to see your members in a session of that nature like many weeks ago.

Therapist: Yes, I'd rather see that than have you sit and bitch about the institution.

Mr. B.: Do we always have to disagree?

Therapist: You don't have to disagree. I'm saying explore. Explore places where you agree and places where you disagree. You spent six months agreeing that you hate the place. What the hell, there are some things that I don't like about this place either. I can agree that some things should be changed, but that doesn't get us anywhere, you see. Everyone sits around and agrees that it's terrible. It's like talking about the weather. Gee, it's a lousy day, and everyone *agrees* it's a lousy day. So what?

Mr. H.: That ain't going to change the weather, huh?

Therapist: No, that's not going to change the weather. That's not going to change *this* place either.

Mr. O.: If you ate any of that steak this noon, you'd probably have something to beef about.

Mr. H.: Say, I want to know, like you said we don't disagree, but we don't know how to approach this thing to really get started, you know.

Mr. L.: Speak for yourself.

Mr. H.: All right, I'll speak for myself.

Therapist: Good point, Mr. H.

Mr. N.: We had a nice discussion going last week, and we got to talking again about the joint and that this was all brought up before several times. But nothing had happened, so why keep bringing it up?

Therapist: Why didn't you say that?

Mr. N.: What?

Therapist: Just what you said. Why didn't you break in and say that?

Mr. N.: Because—ah—I didn't know how the other guys in here felt. You showed me how you felt when I brought up about that conduct report I had a couple weeks ago, so I learned to let it go, you know. I don't want to hear any more about it, you know, about the joint because I know how it is and why bring it up in the group? We're here to help ourselves and bring out our problems. Like you say, we try to avoid that.

In this particular case the worker's direct intervention was effective in reducing the amount of griping in subsequent meetings. An important reason why this approach worked here is that some of the group members were also getting tired of the idea that group meetings were merely gripe sessions. They evidently wanted to accomplish something more constructive.

The worker is actually doing several things here to meet the group's resistance. In a sense he is attempting to promote some dissonance within the group. He is trying to develop anxiety, which is probably a necessary prerogative to change. He is also rewarding those members who show an inclination toward bringing the group to a more constructive discussion.

"Let's Talk about the Weather . . . or Him!"

The idea behind this form of resistance is to talk about something that doesn't make one uncomfortable or perhaps talk about someone else's problems. When group meetings are beginning to become less productive because the members are avoiding personal issues, it may be helpful to review the group's goals and the responsibility of its members to keep the sessions focused on relevant topics.

We have found it helpful to tape-record these discussions of the purposes of group work and to replay the tape at the beginning of the next session. The playing back of the tape seems to have an impact. Individual members, after hearing themselves discuss the purposes, will sometimes become more solidly committed to making the group meetings more productive.

Recording and replaying the group's discussion of the purposes of group work was used in this case when the sessions were becoming less productive. After hearing themselfves on the tape, the group reacted as follows:

Mr. W.: Did you notice how Mr. K said he didn't understand a thing I said? Then five minutes later, he came back and said word for word what I had said.

Mr. B.: First of all, Mr. W, the man said, "What is group therapy?" What you said was not even related. You talked about two people in the street in Chicago or Milwaukee.

Mr. W.: I was under the impression he was asking what group therapy *should* be.

Mr. B.: He didn't say that. He said, "What is group therapy?" What does group therapy mean to you?

Mr. W.: To each one it should mean a different thing.

Mr. E.: What does it mean to *you*? Basically, what does this group mean to you? Time to get out of the shop, or what?

Mr. W.: I think it's soul-searching.

Mr. B.: What does *that* mean?

Mr. W.: What makes you what you are, and where you are going to go from there.

Mr. E.: No, no, not how it relates to all of us. How does it relate to you? I want to know what *you* think of this.

Mr. W.: Well, ah, that question you asked me, it isn't specific enough.

Mr. B.: Don't evade the question. He said, "What does it mean to you?"

Mr. W.: I can't answer that.

Mr. J.: What do you think group therapy is? What does this group mean to you?

Mr. W.: I think this group is, ah . . .

Mr. B.: You're in a bind.

Mr. W.: I'm in a bind.

Mr. B.: You don't know.

Mr. W.: I don't know. Can you help me out?

Mr. E.: No. Nobody's going to help you out.

Mr. W.: Maybe no one else knows either.

Therapist: It sounds like some of the guys are saying that you have a hard time talking about you.

Mr. W.: No, no. I've talked about myself so often, I'd like to give someone else a chance.

Mr. J.: When and where? Where did you talk about it so often?

Mr. W.: In here.

(short silence)

Mr. J.: Where have I been? I haven't heard you very much.

Mr. M.: Well, maybe you were in a different group, Mr. W. I don't know—I haven't heard you either.

In this example the worker's specific intervention was to add structure to the group meetings by reviewing the purpose of the meetings, and more specifically, by tape-recording and replaying the group's discussion of this issue. The worker, in effect, has encouraged the group to take an active part in meeting the resistance of individual members. Many of the members solidly confront the resistive member in an attempt to get him to talk about himself.

"I Can't Change Because . . ."

One important limitation of a maximum-security prison, in terms of treatment, is that behavior is so structured that inmates actually have few ways of showing responsibility. This is unfortunate because many of the men committed to such institutions, particularly men committed under the Sex Crimes Law, are extremely passive, nonassertive, and dependent before they reach the institutions, this being one of their important personal problems.

Many inmates latch onto the fact that prisons foster dependency as a justification for their own passivity. They will say, in so many words, "What happens to me really depends on those other people. I don't have any responsibility for making decisions myself." In this way inmates are able to resist the idea that *they* may have to change something about *themselves*.

"I Can't Change until I'm on the Streets Again Faced with Real-Life Problems"

A variation of the "I Can't Change Because . . ." form of resistance is one in which inmates resist changing by claiming they have accomplished as much as they can while in the institution. In group work one approach to this resistance is to focus very definitely on the immediate day-to-day problems confronting persons *in* the institution. One important area is how well an individual is able to relate with others around him and whether he has been able to change this in any way since being in the group. The individual can also examine whether he has become more assertive in his work or if he has been able to take positive steps toward improving himself through education, recreation, or hobbies.

The worker in the following excerpt from a group meeting is trying to work through this form of resistance by encouraging the group to focus explicitly on the individual's behavior within the institution:

Therapist: I realize you are kind of limited in the things you can do here, but perhaps you men in the group could give Mr. W some suggestions on how he could practice being more assertive while here in the institution.

Mr. B.: (To Mr. W) I think you should try to mix with other people more.

It looks to me like you are always wanting to be by yourself. It looks like you are afraid people are going to take advantage of you or something.

Mr. M.: I think he should pick out a guy that's hard for him to talk to and make a point out of going up to him every so often.

Mr. W.: Well, it's simply just because I'm not interested in sports or any of that stuff that all the people here talk about. I just love lectures and concerts and . . .

Mr. M.: For Chrissake, get back in here. You're in prison. You know they don't have any of that stuff in here. When I first came in here, I didn't like basketball either, and I told myself that I really wasn't interested in it. But later I decided to try it, because I wanted to do *something*. So I did, and I kind of goofed at first, but I began to like it, and now I really enjoy it.

Mr. W.: Well, I like swimming and if . . .

Mr. M.: W, will you get back here with us? You're in prison. Can't you get that through your head?

Mr. B.: I think you are just trying to avoid mixing with people.

Therapist: Is there any kind of activity, Mr. W, that you might want to try during this next week? You can try it and see how you do, and then we will talk about it again at our next meeting.

Mr. W.: Well, maybe I could try shuffleboard, or something like that, but I'm really not interested in anything they have here.

In this example the worker is attempting to bring about behavior change by making the goals more concrete and immediate. The group in this case helps to keep the discussion reality-oriented. It might be noted also that small goals are obviously more easily reached, and that the positive reinforcement of success is very beneficial to one who has not experienced much success in any of his previous undertakings. This particular inmate subsequently was somewhat successful in reaching his limited goal, and he was later rewarded by the group.

"I Broke the Law Because of My Traumatic Childhood Experiences— You Change Me!"

A special kind of resistance is encountered with some clients who have had considerable exposure to formal treatment programs and who resist changing their behavior by using psychological theory to justify this lack of change. They tend to have the attitude that individual or group psychotherapy is a process in which they discuss exclusively their past lives and attempt to isolate various childhood experiences which have had undesirable influences upon the development of their personalities.

Such clients appear to hold two basic assumptions concerning treatment: (1) that once a person has found the "cause" of his objectionable behavior by delving into past childhood conflicts, this behavior will somehow disappear with very little effort or discomfort on his part; and (2) that *unless* the client finds the "key" or cause of this behavior back in his infancy or childhood, he cannot change his behavior. This form of resistance can be carried even further by the client claiming he cannot change his present behavior because he cannot remember his childhood conflicts and, therefore, that it is the staff's responsibility to bring out these painful experiences through the use of hypnotism, drugs, and other aids to psychotherapy, even though the setting may preclude the use of such aids.

In attempting to work through this form of resistance, the therapist or group worker might want to raise the question of whether understanding the conflicts resulting from one's earlier experiences is *all* that is necessary for changing present behavior or if it is even a necessary prerequisite.

The following excerpt from a group meeting illustrates this form of resistance and what steps were taken by the worker to meet it. One member of the group had earlier been complaining that he was not getting anything out of the group treatment. He went on to talk about his past treatment in other institutions and his feeling that he had made much more progress by being involved in some hypnosis. As it later appeared, his idea of making progress was associated with a psychotherapist being interested in him and giving him a lot of attention rather than any measurable behavior changes on his part.

Mr. B.: I think hypnotism would be more helpful than group therapy, because a man who's trained with hypnosis, ah, can get right through to find out the real you. There's a lot of things that you ain't gonna remember because your mind has buried it so far back that it might take you a hundred years of therapy to really bring it out—to see it, to notice and to be able to bisect it and see what the hell it is.

Mr. O.: Yah, but there ain't enough psychiatrists to take care of the people the way it is, let alone try to use hypnosis with everyone.

Mr. W.: You make it like your mind is so complicated that you could never understand it.

Mr. B.: I think everybody's mind is complicated—the most complicated thing you can find—and we're just scratching the surface. We shouldn't really expect too much anyway. I think there is a lot of things that I could remember about if I wanted to, but they are buried so damn far and it's doggone threatening to me that I don't even scratch the surface as far as getting to them.

Therapist: I guess what you have been saying today is that the only way that you will be able to change is if you can bring all those memories back, to know everything or to know a lot of things about your past life. And once you have reached this point where you understand the reasons for your problems, then all of your present behavior is going to change and you won't have any further problems.

Mr. B.: I'm not saying the behavior is going to change immediately—no, but the more you know about your childhood, the better off you are. What I am saying is that I just can't remember some things that have happened that I just don't want to remember. . . . Don't you think it would be a good idea to get these dang things too—to have a look at them?

Therapist: Sometimes, yes, but realistically we can't expect to understand ourselves completely or to know everything that has happened in our childhood.

Mr. B.: No, I'm not saying that from therapy you are going to know everything about yourself, but you should learn some things about yourself which can be important.

Therapist: I'm not denying this at all. I guess what's happening to me is that I'm getting angry. Let me explain why. Because it sounds to me like you are blocking the whole idea of being able to change because you can't find these keys in your childhood, whatever they might be, that have given you some trouble or conflict. You are putting a block in there and, in effect, you are saying, "I can never change until I find out all these things about myself from my childhood." And then it seems as if you are going further by asking, "Well, I'm not receiving the right kind of treatment, such as hypnotism or drugs, or what not." What I'm saying then, at least the way it looks to me, is that you are blocking out the possibility that you might be able to change your behavior.

Mr. B.: I'm not blocking everybody's view of it. I'm just blocking my own view.

From this point the group moved into a lively discussion about whether one has to understand his earlier life conflicts or know the cause of his objectionable behavior in order to change that behavior. Then one group member described how he had been able to make some changes in his present life, even though he did not understand a lot of things about himself. The following resulted:

Mr. B.: Maybe I'm just raising a big bitch session—I'm just so goddam mad with that psychiatrist—just rejected what I talked about without even analyzing it. That bugged me. I just believe there's somethin' out there. I suppose I'm a little bit like the guy who's lookin' for the wonder drug cure for cancer.

Mr. O.: Well, that's natural. I'd like to go over to the State Hospital and get shock treatment; have all this past shame and stuff knocked out of me, too. But it's impossible to do, because they're not gonna let you. Let's put it that way . . . I mean, everybody would want hypnotism or shock treatments sure, but why do *you* want this, Mr. B? Is it because you think you would get more help that way or is it just because it is easier?

Mr. B.: I really think I can get more help that way, not just because it's easier. I've seen these changes take place in other people because . . .

Mr. O.: Well, then, we've got it down then that you honestly believe it would be easier?

Mr. B.: Well, let's put it this way . . . when you come right down to it, it would be easier, yah.

Mr. O.: Now comes the fact, or can you accept the fact that you're just not gonna get it?

Mr. B.: I guess I'll have to, even though I don't like it.

Mr. O.: Yah, see this is what I'm gettin' at; here's where the upset comes in . . . Once you get to the point where you accept the fact that you're not gonna get the damn stuff, you got control over something, see? A minor thing, maybe it's a big thing—who knows? But you get control over one thing; then you can go on to the next thing.

In this example the worker is attempting to clarify what he feels is the main issue under discussion and to confront what appears to be a resistance to change. At that point the worker becomes more frustrated by the continued resistance and begins to show anger. He acknowledges his anger and explains his feelings. As it turns out, this show of affective honesty seems to have a beneficial influence on the group members, as they subsequently became increasingly honest with their own feelings and motivations.

20. Social Work in an Outpatient Psychiatric Setting

The contributions of group work to adults who are outpatients in a psychiatric setting are brought out in this descriptive analysis of a Day Treatment Center which has several active groups.

Social Work with Groups in an Outpatient Setting *

The Day Treatment Center is an arm of the Outpatient Clinic. The veterans who participate in this program are in good enough remission to live in the community, but are unable to work and/or adjust satisfactorily to community life. The Center is open Monday through Friday from 8:15 A.M. to 4:45 P.M. and provides a social, recreational and therapeutic milieu for the veterans. When faced with psychiatric patients who are able to relate on such a minimal level, the social worker who wants to reach them by the use of group must approach the problem in a nontraditional manner. There are actually several groups active in the Day Center. All of the veterans belong to the greater group—the Center. Most participate in some smaller activity groups, such as work incentive therapy, crafts, music and art classes, and patient government. As such, the Center provides a resocialization experience. From the literature the rationale for this kind of an approach can be formulated. Discussions may not be helpful in working with the psychotic patient who does not appear to share a common faith with physicians or others to a sufficient extent for a ready working partnership. If approached for congenial activity, such patients may respond by participation, and the interest aroused by such patients may be of considerable dynamic importance in fostering an enjoyment of normal functioning and a resumption of socially directed and socially rewarding effort. The social worker might offer a group of schizophrenic patients a social and activity program which would be acceptable to them and yet provide them with the therapeutic potential of reinvesting themselves in an interpersonal relationship of significance. Discussions and help in coping with certain kinds of situations can more appropriately be introduced at a later stage. As a result of the relatively casual means of using groups, the social worker is able to evaluate the strengths and weaknesses of each veteran. In order to assure that the more structured discussion type of group is limited to those veterans who could be worked with toward personality change, the worker chooses the members, but allows some to sit in if he is fairly sure it will not be a detrimental experience for them. Thus, the group is formed on the basis of a combination of compulsory and voluntary selection.

The Community Residence program affords several more opportunities for using groups. When there are common problems or information to be dis-

* By Patricia Sherman, Clinical Social Worker, Veterans Administration Out-Patient Clinic, Newark, New Jersey. Published in *Social Work with Groups*, Proceedings of a Seminar Conducted at Leech Farm V.A. Hospital, Pittsburgh, Pa., April 1968. Used here with permission.

seminated, groups are frequently most effective. Sponsors' groups are used to inform them of various procedures, teach them health and dietetic practices and help them ventilate some of their fears and questions with respect to having mental patients in their homes. Because of the many practical issues involved, the sponsors can get mutual support and advice.

Community Residence patients, too, can be helped by groups in much the same way. The problems which they face in trying to adjust to community life after (usually) long periods of hospitalization are common to all. Solutions found effective by one veteran may be useful to another. As in the Day Treatment Center, these veterans frequently are unable to relate on a one-to-one basis with an authority figure, but in the hospital have learned to relate at some level to each other. They can continue to cultivate this relationship while in the Community Residence program. A social worker quite possibly could not be able to reach these patients as effectively as their own peers. This is not to say, however, that as the group progresses there will not be an attempt to involve the patients in some efforts at personality change or modification. Those veterans who seem amenable to this type of therapy may be switched into a more dynamic group either during or after their participation in the Community Residence program. This would depend upon both the needs of the individual and the group. Sometimes members are kept in a particular group because they provide stimulation for the other members of the group.

21. Social Work in a General Medical and Surgical Setting

Social Work with Groups in a General Medical and Surgical Setting *

I will focus on comments on group work in the General Medical and Surgical Veterans Hospital; specifically, the 471-bed teaching hospital in Syracuse, New York. This hospital serves an 18-county area in Central New York, extending in the south from the Pennsylvania border northward through the Auburn, Syracuse, Herkimer area to the northern extremity of the Massena-Plattsburg area. It includes both metropolitan and predominantly rural areas with an estimated population of 265,000.

I will discuss some of the major treatment demands on social workers in the General Medical and Surgical Hospital. Some of the groups we have organized will be briefly discussed in light of predominant characteristics of our clientele. I will try to identify some of the effects client characteristics have had on the organization and operation of our groups, as well as what effects our treatment approaches have had on our clients.

Our staff consists of seven full-time workers with master's degrees, five part-time master's workers, one of whom is a group worker, nine graduate students from Syracuse University School of Social Work, two Neighborhood Youth Corps enrollees, and five undergraduate volunteers.

Nearly all our referrals for treatment request evaluation of family dynamics.

* By Judith S. Lewis, Clinical Social Worker, Veterans Administration Hospital, Syracuse, New York. Published in *Social Work with Groups,* Proceedings of a Seminar Conducted at Leech Farm V.A. Hospital, Pittsburgh, Pa., April 1968. Used here with permission.

Treatment demands, based primarily on referrals from doctors, fall largely into three categories: (1) Requests for services related to discharge planning for medical and psychiatric patients. This type of service involves planning for nursing, proprietary and boarding homes, rooming houses or home care. (2) Requests for rehabilitation, vocational or educational counseling. This group consists largely of psychiatric patients, and some medical patients. (3) Requests for counseling of those patients with special problems such as alcoholism, or marital or financial difficulties. These referrals come most frequently from psychiatric service, although, ever since veterans were ruled eligible for hospitalization, specifically for alcoholism, medical service refers any alcoholics to Social Work Service.

Frequently, the treatment demands stated in the referrals are met long before a patient is actually discharged. For example, this situation frequently arises with patients for whom nursing home placement is prescribed, when placement may not be available for weeks or months after the actual planning is completed. Consequently, it is largely a social work decision whether or not additional treatment will be rendered, and, if so, what kind. Therefore, social workers have not only the choice of treatment method to make, but also the responsibility to identify additional treatment demands, and meet them as time and staff permit.

With this general framework for treatment in mind, I will examine some of the characteristics of our clientele as they relate to the formation of treatment groups in the hospital. I will refer to four characteristic patient groups. I do not see them as mutually exclusive, but will use the patient's major problem as seen by social service as a guide in determining these general groupings. I will also discuss each patient group in light of three aspects of group functioning: (1) goals of groups; (2) worker's techniques, and (3) programs used in groups. I will not discuss the aspect of selection of group members in regard to each patient group, because our selection process is uniform for all groups. Generally, our selection policy is lenient. We exclude only those patients who are too severely mentally or physically disabled to communicate in a group, or who would obviously be destructive forces in the group. . . .

The first and largest group of our clientele are those veterans over sixty-five. Many of them are alone since family members have either died, are too infirm to be of assistance, or have deserted them. Even those who are married often cannot return to their own homes and, therefore, placement planning is the major problem with this group. Although the hospital is designed as an acute care facility, many of these patients have long-term stays ranging from several months to over a year. As community care facilities become more and more crowded, this trend has continued. These patients often become depressed and discouraged about their long hospital stays and the uncertainty of their future plans. Several of our groups have been designed for this segment of our clientele and could be given the general term "pre-discharge" groups.

I will turn now to discussion of these patients in regard to the aspects of group functioning, goals, worker's techniques and programs. The goals of our groups are naturally dependent to some extent on the nature of our hospital and the characteristics of our clientele. Since our hospital is designed to serve acute care patients, long-term treatment goals are almost always unrealistic.

I say "almost" because as I mentioned before, some patients will have long-term hospitalizations. Even so, since the patients are involved with many other services in the hospital, we cannot always count on stable group membership or what is called a "captive" clientele. Of course, group goals must also be in accord with the over-all medical goals for the patient.

Many of our aged veterans are quite disabled physically and emotionally. They are often overwhelmed by their loss of function and have little self-confidence or desire to socialize. At the same time, they are lonely and afraid in an atmosphere which often seems impersonal and uncaring. Goals for these patients have been aimed at support, socialization and identification of concerns which could be faced by the group through use of program.

The worker takes an active role in a group with these patients, although patients are given much encouragement to enter into the activity. Once patients are talking in the group, the worker must use positive directive techniques since conversations among elderly patients awaiting nursing home placements often tend to gravitate toward illness or death of family and friends, or the hopelessness of the future.

Program selection with groups of elderly patients must be done very carefully. For instance, in a geriatric group presently going on, movies and physical activities cannot be considered due to some visual impairment and other physical disabilities of the members. The group is more interested in hearing a speaker and making some large checkers which all the members can see and use on the ward.

The second characteristic patient group consists of those World War II veterans whose primary problems involve family life, marital discord, vocational and financial problems. Many of these patients are on Psychiatric Service and are usually in the hospital longer than one or two months. Frequently, these patients are seen with their families by caseworkers, or are involved in group psychotherapy on their wards. However, some of these patients have been involved in a group called the social service committee which is a branch of the larger patient government organization on open-ward Psychiatric Service. Through this group the patients improve social and problem-solving skills in the context of ward life. The group helps orient newcomers to the ward, informs fellow patients of community resources and hospital departments which can assist them or their families, plans some programs, and acts as a liaison and referral body for the ward and Social Service Department.

These patients often have families to support and they are concerned about community resources for employment, rehabilitation and retraining. Their needs indicate group goals of a more specific task-oriented nature. Testing problem-solving and social skills in the social service committee can be a step toward more adequate functioning in the work world and with family members.

The worker with this type of group can usually take a less aggressive role at first since these patients are frequently more vocal than most of the aged veterans. However, the worker must guide these patients in keeping discussion relevant and purposeful. As the patients become more productive as a group, the worker should be able to assume more of an advisory rather than leadership capacity.

Programs can cover a wide range with this type of group. Patients can be very active in planning activities on or off the ward. Activities which stimulate interaction on social and problem-solving levels among patients and non-patients are best in terms of goal achievement. For example, finding out from their fellow patients what kinds of problems they need help with, e.g. legal or financial, allows the committee to experience a feeling of usefulness and achievement when community resource people from a legal services agency or the department of Social Services enter the hospital and discuss specific problem areas with interested patients.

The third characteristic patient group consists of those patients with special problems such as alcoholism. These patients run the gamut from long- to short-term hospitalization depending on their primary reasons for being in the hospital. They represent all ages and all wards of the hospital. When a group of patients with such specific needs is identified by our department, the group method is usually considered. . . .

Group goals for these patients involve use of interpretation and feedback from peers, in a supportive but reality-oriented atmosphere. Goals also include education about health problems related to drinking, discussion of and referral to community resources.

With these patients, the worker must be clearly accepting of the patient as a worthwhile person, but also firm in his or her persistence in focusing on reality. Controlling the reality focus on discussion is usually more demanding of the worker than encouraging discussion. The worker may also need to pay special attention to protecting some of the less aggressive members who may be scapegoated by the others.

Programs used with this group of patients have included speakers such as doctors, nurses, and dietitians from the hospital, as well as from outside agencies, in addition to movies, and discussions planned by the patients themselves. Turnover is great among these patients, so the group is open-ended, allowing a patient to attend as soon as he is ready. Consequently, flexibility of program as well as worker's role is especially important.

The final group of patients, who seem to have common characteristics, are those veterans about thirty-five years old and younger, some of whom are Vietnam veterans. Many of these patients are restless, bored, and alienated from the majority of the patient population. With some exceptions they seem to have fairly short hospitalizations, and so far have indicated only minimal concern about vocational or educational problems. Through some individual casework contacts, our department has gradually become aware that this group of patients may have particular needs which the past patient populations have not exhibited. Many of these young veterans are returning to unstable family units which do not seem ready to cope with additional problems. The reticence of these patients has so far kept us from discovering what their real concerns are. It remains to be seen how clearly we will be able to identify the special needs of these patients, and by what method we will attempt to meet them.

These patients have only recently been thought of as possible candidates for an additional type of group. Tentatively, goals might be aimed at increased and more meaningful involvement among these patients, and between them and staff during hospitalization. There is a need for organized socialization and activities, as well as opportunity to discuss more serious problems about future plans.

Judging from preliminary group attempts with this group, it seems as though the worker needs to find and maintain a reasonable balance between the role of serious discussion leader and that of coordinator of social activities. Indications so far are that an improper balance of the two would result in group disintegration. Socialization is now seen as the greatest need by these patients, though we feel that there are other needs which these patients are not ready or able to express to us now.

Summary

I have no doubt that social group work belongs in a general, medical and surgical hospital. However, this particular setting requires special attitudes and approaches of the worker. First of all, the group worker in this setting must be willing to give up the traditional idea of long-term treatment as a goal for groups. I think many social workers believe that if one cannot have a long-term stable group, treatment is impossible. I have no evidence that this is true. In fact, I think we have some evidence that short-term groups can be just as therapeutic as the more traditional group is supposed to be.

Secondly, the necessity of great flexibility on the part of the worker is extremely important in this setting. The worker must plan meetings in coordination with many other hospital personnel as well as patients. The worker's role with the patient is but a minor part of his total hospital treatment and, therefore, there are many obstacles to a patient's regular attendance in the group. If necessary, a worker should be prepared to hold a meeting even if most of the patients are absent. There will always be many factors which the worker cannot control in this host setting.

Thirdly, the group worker in this setting must be committed to the cause of teaching other hospital disciplines what group work is all about. If there is poor understanding of group work by other disciplines, group formation, let alone group progress, will be very difficult.

Finally, the group worker in this setting must have an unusual amount of enthusiasm for her work. This is true because the hospital is in many ways a depressing place. Patients are easily caught up in depression about their own conditions and the impersonal nature of the institution. They cannot be expected to jump with enthusiasm at the thought of a group the way teen-agers in a settlement house do. Yet, a positive, enthusiastic, or at least curious, attitude is needed to get a group together. In the hospital, most of that feeling must come from the worker, at least in the beginning. None of these four approaches is complicated or new, but I feel that they are not stressed sufficiently as basic ingredients for group work in the general hospital.

In evaluating the groups in our hospital, it seems that the more successful ones have involved the best use of these four approaches. Success seems less related to the types of patients, specific techniques or programs included. Perhaps as we gain more skill in application of these basic approaches, specific differences in techniques will become more important.

22. Social Work in Veterans Administration Mental Hygiene Clinics

Mental hygiene clinics are making more and more use of group methods to help patients. This account of one such situation is evidence that with clear goals much can be accomplished.

Social Work with Groups in Veterans Administration
Mental Hygiene Clinics *

Our Mental Hygiene Clinic is located in the VA Hospital, Cleveland, Ohio, a GM&S hospital. . . . Our clinic operates during the customary business hours Monday through Friday, plus one evening a week. We usually have three or four groups going, all meeting in the evening. It is, of course, significant that our group therapy flourishes with patients who, upon the whole, hold steady jobs in daytime and can only come to evening clinic.

My group is a so-called open group, i.e., there is no time limit, new patients are invited in and old patients drop out. Such a group can go on forever, and this one—it will surprise some of you to hear that—has gone on for fourteen years. We have had a total of 70 or 80 patients in the group at one time or other.

The organization of the group is most simple. It meets once a week at a fixed time, for one and a half hours. I usually have about a dozen patients on the roster, but the average attendance is only half that. In outpatient clinics we distinctly do not have a captive audience.

But enough of that. I cannot expect you to want to get from me a detailed description of my group. You want to hear how we select our patients for group therapy, what goals we set, what methods we use to achieve them, what group therapy demands of the worker, and what it does both to worker and patients. What, you will ask, is the purpose of this program? What are the hoped-for results that should justify the effort? We generally do not propose to a patient that we have group therapy as the sole or principal modality of treatment. When we suggest group therapy, we offer it as a supplement, rather than as an alternative, to individual interviews. Depending on the patient's condition and situation, we expect one or more of the following benefits:

1. *Socialization.* Some of our patients are social isolates, they want and need companionship but are unable to find it on their own. The therapy group, being a controlled environment, can sometimes supply that. If the patient has never learned, or had unlearned, the art of moving freely in a circle of peers, he can make a new beginning.

2. *Self-Understanding.* The group provides standards for the patient to measure himself by. Observing how others have the same problems, or else different ones, how some are more, some less disturbed than he is, noting how they deal with their difficulties, where they succeed and where they fail, he can get a clearer understanding of his own mind and of his place in the world.

* By Robert Plan, Supervising Social Worker, Mental Hygiene Unit, V.A. Hospital, Cleveland, Ohio. Published in *Social Work with Groups,* Proceedings of a Seminar Conducted at Leech Farm, V.A. Hospital, Pittsburgh, Pa., April 1968. Used here with permission.

3. *Support*. This is perhaps the most important aspect. Experience shows that the group tends to side with the patient in his conflicts with his environment, and also with his ego in his internal conflicts. The patient finds an acceptance which the world at large denies him.

4. *Dependency*. There are patients who are reluctant to come to the clinic even once a month, and others who would scarcely be satisfied if they came every day. The individual therapist may not have the time or the energy to gratify these needs, and it might not be desirable if he did. Group therapy here can supplement individual therapy by offering an additional outlet, and as this satisfaction of dependency needs is provided by peers it would be less debilitating.

With these goals in mind, how can we go about selecting patients? We use what we call clinical judgment—and you know that this term comes in handy whenever we have failed to arrive, as yet, at any clearly formulated criteria. We also have to pay attention to practical considerations.

It has been said by a masterful practitioner that politics is the art of the possible. I'd think that the same goes for social work and for psychotherapy. The patient may need this or that treatment, but will he be willing to undergo it? Will he and we have the time for it? This will be particularly marked with regard to group therapy. Many patients reject it outright. Others accept it verbally, but never come. Others are not free at the time the group meets, or it is impossible to squeeze both individual and group therapy into the available time.

Since the group, in order to be therapeutic, needs to be a peer group, we look for patients on a fairly similar level of education and especially intelligence. They all must be able to carry on a good and lively discussion. We try to eliminate those who would be too disruptive, as well as those who would be overstimulated or in whom group therapy would mobilize too much anxiety. Since the group should widen the participants' horizons, we try for variety in other respects: socioeconomic level, religious background, family status. We do not select by diagnosis, and have both neurotics and psychotics who are well enough to function like neurotics.

So we have the goals set and principles of selection established. It may seem to you that the methods can be deduced from these premises. To a certain extent, I think they can. If self-understanding is only one of the goals, and not a crucial one, it would follow that it doesn't matter too much what topics are discussed in the group. Patients often criticize themselves and each other for talking about subjects that are far removed from their personal problems, such as the war in Vietnam, or the latest baseball game. But for the purposes of socialization and satisfaction of dependency needs, this is just as much grist for the mill as any more personal and portentous topic. Similarly, considering that it is the group as such, rather than individual relationships within the group, from which we expect a therapeutic effect, you may conclude that the performance of the leader is not terribly important. I have found indeed that the better the discussion on a given evening, the less I talk—or perhaps vice versa—though here I may be slighting the important problem of trans-ference.

In any case, none of us have derived an arsenal of methods from systematic application of scientific principles but we have arrived at the methods we use through practice, be it by intuition, by doing what comes natural to us individually, or simply by responding to pressures and counterpressures. I should also add that all I am saying are my personal impressions and opinions—none of it expresses the policy of my station or of any station. . . .

Having thus reviewed goals, selection, and methods, we have to consider what the demands are that group therapy makes on the worker. I do not think this type of group therapy requires anything rare or extraordinary. If we try to list the qualities and skills that the group therapist needs, we are apt to come up with an inventory quite similar to that of a caseworker; such abilities as to listen, to relate, to employ his professional self and to submerge his personal self, to accept without being shocked, to limit himself to the minimum of intervention still consistent with the job at hand. I do not think, though, that a caseworker should act as leader of a therapy group without some preparation. The best form of training is probably an appenticeship as assistant to an experienced group leader.

Finally, what the group does for patients can be measured in terms of how far it achieves our goals. Experience shows they are rarely, if ever, reached completely. They are achieved to a larger or lesser extent, or sometimes not at all. Not so much, however, in the sense that some groups achieve more than others, but rather in the sense that some patients profit more than others; and some do not profit. This points up that our methods of selection and operation need to be improved. Also, that evaluative research, in this as in other fields, is still pretty much in its infancy.

It is easier to say what the group does for the worker. I myself have always found it a stimulating, invigorating experience. It has above all very much enhanced my respect for the patients with whom I work. I am here to give you information about group therapy, not to make propaganda for it; but I can hardly forbear telling you that if I were sure that group therapy has done as much for our patients as it has for me I would be well satisfied.

23. Social Group Work with Expectant Mothers in a Hospital Residential Setting.

Harper Hall is a temporary residential unit in connection with a general hospital. Expectant mothers are admitted to this unit usually in the latter stages of their pregnancies. Referrals to the unit are made by a state department of social services in cooperation with the maternity and infant care division of the state health department. The unit has a capacity of forty. Most of the women are in their late teens or early twenties. Few have completed high school. About half of the women are married, although some have been deserted by their husbands. About half are unmarried. The social service department of the hospital provides casework services to patients referred by doctors, nurses, relatives, other agencies or by the women themselves.

The experimental group work program was offered by the social service department with the goal of stimulating individual and social development through craft activity. By trying out the program for two months it was hoped that some evidence could be gathered to help the department determine if such a service would be helpful to the women involved.

It was agreed that the Harper Hall group would be voluntary, informal, open-ended and activity focused. The general purpose was stated as follows: 1) to use activity as a means of helping expectant mothers to relate to one another on a level which might encourage individual growth; 2) to provide an experience in social relationships and cooperative sharing; 3) to enable the group worker to learn about the concerns of the women and to refer this information to the social service staff. Hopefully, the small group setting will increase mutual support and give the young women a chance to discuss things that are bothering them. Hopefully, the activity experience will teach skills as a way of bolstering self-esteem and self-confidence.

It was planned to have the group meet once each week in the dining room after the evening meal for an hour and a half. A poster was put on the bulletin board and announcements were made in the dining room as ways of recruiting persons into the group.

First Meeting, September 22—Number present 14

Betty Evans, Hilda Jackson, Ruth Kingsley, Louise Lawrence, Kathie Minor, Carla Morrison, Janice Myer, Sally Newman, Mary Ordway, Cele Parsons, Beth Simpson, Ellen Smith, Shirley Stallings, one girl whose name I did not get.

Summary recording. Girls greeted initial announcement at dinner with some suspicion. Very few girls signed up for group when sign-up sheet was passed around. Alice, the matron, asked me afterwards if she might say something to the girls. In a few minutes she returned with the sheets which now had sixteen names. I decided that I would not exclude anyone from the group who wished to come this first time. After supper one of the girls stopped to chat and said she knew how to make bunnies. I expressed an interest in this and she said she would show me how. Soon she returned with materials and we sat at a small table in the dining room. Soon two other girls joined us. The conversation centered on their initial distrust of me because I was a social worker and the girls told about some negative experiences they had had with social workers. They talked about their loneliness and their boredom and how anxious they were for their babies to arrive. The bunny project drew an increasingly large circle of observers and served to introduce me to the girls in an informal way.

At 5:30 I pulled two tables together and girls pulled up chairs. The initial count was twelve girls and included Mary Ordway who earlier had shaken her head when I asked her if she would like to join the group. (I had made a point of approaching her since she had been eating alone at a small table.) In a few minutes Alice came with Cele Parsons who she said was feeling very sad tonight (Cele indeed looked on the verge of tears) and could she join us? The girls were asked to make out name tags which proved very helpful to me. Meanwhile there was quite an audience at neighboring tables who viewed what was happening with considerable interest. The girls responded very enthusiastically to the project, particularly enjoying the beauty of the array of colored papers. There was a happy response to the rather spectacular results they got. Every girl was able to make a flower and several girls continued to make flowers until all the supplies were exhausted. They talked about taking flowers to girls at the hospital and home to their children. They planned various ways they could use them and how they could modify the original instructions.

Evaluation. This was a successful evening. Even those who did not participate seemed to share in the almost joyous spirit which abounded. Cele was smiling when she left with several flowers and a vase she had decorated. Mary beamed as she sat and looked at the lovely flower she had been able to make. Nearly every girl who participated verbalized her pleasure in the experience. Although there was no significant conversation during the flower project I believe there was real value in the girls' feeling that someone cared enough about them to be there. Several expressed a wish that it could happen every night or at least twice a week. I believe my decision to include all fourteen girls was a valid one, particularly this first evening when it was important to prove my good will. All thirteen girls said they would like to come again if they are here next week.

Second Meeting, September 29—Number present 15

Kate Brown, Paula Carter, Elsie George, Ruth Kingsley, Louise Lawrence, Kathie Minor, Janice Myer, Midge Porter, Barbara Robbins, Hazel Sanders, Inez Sawyer, Grace Scully, Ellen Smith, Helen Vickers, Robin Simmons, Laurie Lebeck, Phyllis Malcom, Connie Petersen, Sandra Reynolds, Kathy Ryther and Sharon Zaruba.

Project. Making a variety of animals from washcloths. Providing instructions for various types of animals allowed for the differing skills of the girls. Girls seemed to enjoy choosing individual projects and colors of cloths. Many of the girls made a couple of kinds of toys. They were able to share equipment and materials without long waits since they didn't all begin with the same projects. The level of skills required were about right for the group.

Summary recording. When I came in this week several girls greeted me cordially. One girl introduced me to some others, "She's our social worker!" There did not seem to be any hostility when I made my announcement at dinner. After a little bit one of the girls brought me the lists which contained seventeen names. To provide opportunity for interaction in a smaller group I announced that I would appreciate some help before the group started with making some patterns. Three girls came to help. This was a comfortable happy group but the conversation was not too meaningful. One girl who came the week before talked about how much the program meant to her. At 5:30 I pulled the tables together and immediately they were filled. Three girls sat at a neighboring table. A couple seemed afraid they would be left out and assured me that they had signed up at dinner. The girls seemed to enjoy the project and though there were a few "bugs" to be worked out in the carrying out of the projects every girl stayed to the very end and left with a completed or nearly completed animal. Meaningful conversation around anxieties did not seem to be taking place although there is always considerable conversation about when they will "go over." The married women talk a good deal about their children at home. Alice felt that Hazel Sanders particularly needed the group and although she didn't sign up she came in response to a special invitation from us both. Several girls drew up and became a part of the group although they did not make anything or identify themselves.

All the girls involved in the project filled out questionnaires. Thirteen of the seventeen girls who signed up came to the group. Two came who did not sign up including one identified as having special needs. Seven of the thirteen girls who came the previous week were still on the census. Five of those seven girls came this time.

Evaluation. This seemed to be another successful week. Fifteen seems to be about the maximum number I can comfortably handle. If more than this had shown up I had expected to have the girls draw lots. It is hard to know how to handle the attendance problem since the sign-up sheet doesn't reflect accurately the girls who will come. I believe something important happens in the way of shared experience. Several girls expressed the idea of how much it mattered to them to know someone cared enough about them to come and provide this activity. With a couple of exceptions evaluation sheets were all checked in the "yes" column with a total of two "no" responses.

Third Meeting, October 6—Number present 11

Bernice Allen, Madge Arthur, Frances Bloom, Jackie Dobson, Betty James, Sally Johnson, Louise Lawrence, Susan Pope, Grace Scully, Roberta Small, Audrey Wood.

Project. Making yardstick holders. The level of the project seemed about right for the girls. All were able to cut out and assemble correctly the many colors and shapes of felt. They responded positively to the finished product and many planned to make more at home. The advantage this project had over earlier projects was that after assembly of the units there was a long period where we all sat and sewed which freed members for non-craft-related conversation.

Summary recording. This time when I arrived I found that the posted sign-up sheet already had half a dozen names on it. My announcement at dinner was greeted with interest with several of the girls feeling free to ask questions and several of the girls greeting me. Half a dozen girls responded to my request for some girls to help me cut out patterns. I did not track down some of the girls that I had thought might benefit from the smaller group. For example, Hazel Sanders had signed up ahead but when I asked about her the girls said they thought she had "gone over" so I did not seek her out as planned.

The girls seemed to enjoy the project and there was much more conversation than on previous occasions which dealt with the unit and their anxieties. There was some talk about the amount of pain to be expected, the length of labor, whether or not they were likely to be induced, the process of scraping membranes, talk about one baby that had died, joy or regret about having this particular baby with giving credit to God and others assuring the group it was their decision or responsibility that they were having the baby. At times some girls seemed to be deliberately encouraging anxiety among others, at which times I spoke reassuringly about the quality of care each would receive or that most of them would find their deliveries pretty normal and without complications.

Fourteen girls signed up, three of whom did not come. I discovered later that Hazel signed up at dinner as well as on the preliminary sign-up sheet. All the girls who were in the unit the previous week and had come to the group came again except Hazel. Some girls who had been observers the previous week participated this time like Roberta. The census was unusually low with just 30 girls in the unit.

Evaluation. This was a successful evening which provided the kind of opportunity for discussion which I had hoped for in my original planning. The girls also seemed to feel real satisfaction with what they had accomplished. They also displayed a high level of cooperation in sharing patterns, materials and equipment. There was not quite the exhilaration I had felt in the earlier group meetings but girls seemed pleased and happy to be there. . . .

Fourth Meeting, October 27—Number present 17

Violet Axtel, Sally Blackstone, Cynthia Dawson, Dot Douglas, Betty James, Paula Johansen, Laura Johnson, Jean Gibson, Samantha Kelly, Ruth Kingsley, Dorothy Lindstrom, Gladys Lewis, May Ann Nelson, Winifred Powers, Tina Roberts, Alberta Timmons, Lisa Varney.

Project. Making stuffed animals. This project which required a lot of sewing should have freed the girls to relate to one another on a meaningful verbal level. This did not seem to happen. The finished products were attractive and apparently satisfying to the girls. There was a lot of interest in the patterns and several of the girls spent another hour tracing and cutting patterns to take home with them.

Summary recording. I arrived a little later than usual and some of the girls expressed concern that I was not coming. Soon after I arrived Alice told me that Betty's mother had died that morning. I went down to her room to express my concern and found her distraught. She said her conscience had told her that her mother would never live through Betty's pregnancy and now she was dead. I was glad to learn the priest from St. Thomas' was to come to see her today. I trust he can help her deal with her guilt.

In the interval between supper and the group, several girls brought me patterns and samples of crafts they had written home for or brought back from weekend visits. A former resident had mailed patterns and samples to me. About a dozen girls gathered ahead of time to cut patterns and otherwise prepare for the group. Dorothy went down to Betty's room and encouraged her to join the group. She came and seemed helped by being a part of it. This time we arranged two sets of double tables since I was expecting about 20 girls. Helen Lyons and Lucy Star signed up but did not come. The married women were much freer in expressing their anxieties than the unmarried girls. These anxieties centered around being away from their families. One girl brought snapshots of her children to share. Jean used the exact words I heard last week: "I could just bawl I miss my children so much." Winifred Parsons seemed to be particularly restrained. Susan and Betty on different occasions shared the anxiety they were feeling about members of their families who were here in the city and about to undergo surgery. Sally expressed the anxiety with an almost endless monologue to which few of the group responded. Tina was very quiet and very reluctant to leave. In fact, many of the girls were very reluctant to leave and it was nine o'clock before the final eight or ten girls gathered together their projects. Several women helped wipe tables and sweep up the foam rubber which was scattered about.

Two-thirds of the girls had been in the group before and one-third of the girls were coming for at least the third time. The group thus has considerably more continuity than we had expected. Each week a few girls come who have observed the previous week and decide they want to be a part of it this week. Carolyn Myers and Martha Dark both joined the group for awhile but did not participate in the activity.

Evaluation. I felt that a little less was happening than on some of the other occasions; however, I think my own fatigue may have lessened my sensitivity. Sharing materials, ideas and mutual help seem an important part of what is happening. Since competing *Mod Squad* changed the minds of two or three girls who had planned to come we would have done better with a double and a single table. The girls were quite spread out at the second table and this seemed to separate them emotionally as well. This week Fran, a social work student, came to assist me. This was a great help to me not only in distributing materials and assisting individuals with their work but it helped me to know that somebody else was also observing interaction and available to relate to some of the girls in the group.

Fifth Meeting, November 3—Number present 21

Bess Baker, Cynthia Dawson, Jean Gibson, Samantha Kelly, Margo Kennedy, Ruth Kingsley, Francelia Kronick, Freida Hendricks, Gladys Lewis, Helen Mack, Susan Montclam, Joy Marshall, Carla Murphy, Dot Meyerson, Theresa Munoz, Sally Newson, Janice Ord, Fritzi Phillips, Alberta Timmons, Charlotte Tompkins, Lisa Varney.

Project. Making scissor and ruler holders. This project was somewhat less structured than on some previous occasions since the girls were allowed to develop their own designs if they were so inclined. A few simple patterns were provided for those who did not choose to be original. Even with patterns the girls were free to use them as they chose. Most of the girls responded quite positively to this freedom; developing, in some cases, very unique and attractive designs. This seemed to provide a special satisfaction to them. There were a few who would have done better with a more structured activity and may not have been quite so satisfied with their product.

Summary recording. This week I did not have patterns for the girls cut out ahead. When I went to the dining room at 5:30 four tables full of girls were waiting to begin. As was done last week, we pulled together tables to make two large tables. This time all the seats were taken. In fact, I believe I counted 23 girls at one point. . . . Fran came to help me again and I wonder how I have managed without her. A group of this size requires at least two people to distribute materials and help with crafts as well as to be available to respond as appropriate to group interaction. Betty James came to the group but left. When I sought her out afterwards to express my concern she said she felt she had been ostracized and couldn't come to the group anymore. Neither Fran nor I had been aware of what was happening in that corner. Betty has been the scapegoat so long she may be overly sensitive.

One table started with colored felt and the planning of their flower designs. The other table began with the white plastic lawn chair type and sewing. The table which began with color and design seemed much freer to interact while the group with the white materials was much more restrained until the girls started on their designs. Interaction across the table and between tables for the most part had to do with sharing supplies. On the other hand groups of two and three were intimately involved in what the others in their own group were doing. There was more helping each other than occurred in the more structured craft projects. As on previous occasions every girl finished her project and many continued to work in the group until nearly nine o'clock or simply remain to be a part of what was happening after they were through.

Many of the girls seem eager to share very deep personal concerns with Fran and me when there is opportunity to sit beside them. Many of these concerns are such that there would need to be more group continuity and trust before they could be shared with a broader audience. The married women share their anxieties in most cases more readily than the unmarried, perhaps because it is more "permissible" to express lonesomeness from one's husband and children than to talk about the anxieties surrounding releasing or keeping a baby.

Janice Ord seemed particularly needy, apparently quite lonesome and she had considerable difficulty in relating to others. However, she was responsive to Helen Mack when she discovered they shared some of the same concerns. This was the first time Helen came to the group although each week she was drawn a little closer as an observer, last week actually bringing her chair up to the table but refusing materials. Francelia after three or four weeks in the unit came this time. She talked with me at some length about her baby to come. With the baby this will make five children and she is just twenty-one. I wondered about the anxiety she must be feeling as well. Joy and Charlotte asked if I could get them material so they could make stuffed animals like the girls did last week. Several of the new girls came requesting animal patterns because it helped so much if they had something like sewing to do. Fritzi Philips seemed quite engrossed in what she was doing and related well to the girls she was sitting with.

Evaluation. The group seems to be a meaningful experience for the girls who participate. Alice says on other evenings there is much bickering and expressions of unhappiness. On Tuesdays the girls are happy with what they have accomplished. I get the feeling that for many girls this is the first time they have sat around a table sharing in joint enterprise.

Sixth Meeting, November 10—Number present 30

Catherine Alexander, Betty Anderson, Martha Blake, Melbar Carter, Grace Darwin, Cynthia Dawson, Jean Gibson, Patricia Delong, Jean Traxler, Darlene Elkins, Georgia Hampton, Freida Hendricks, Betty Kind, Priscilla Lewis, Gladys Lewis, Susan Montclam, Joyce Parker, Janice Ord, Fritzi Phillips, Carla Penders, Ruth Kingsley, Ann Royal, Laura Richards,

Theresa Munoz, Alberta Timmons, Harriet Wilton, Lisa Varney, Terry Rule, Dot Meyerson, Beverly Lumpkin.

Project. Making art-form birds, butterflies and owls. This project was well-liked and requires considerable interaction sharing supplies and equipment. Each girl had a choice of patterns and colors and some made their own patterns. This provides structure for those who need it but still considerable latitude. Most of the girls also made milkweed pod mice which was an extra "just for fun."

Summary recording. The group is becoming too big to handle even with Fran's help. The girls gather for the group the minute dinner is over about 4:45 and are eager to start. About ten helped with patterns while at least an equal number just waited for 5:30 to come. We filled two double tables and a single table. More was happening dynamically at the single table where the girls could talk more intimately. Laura asked if only unmarried girls could see social workers, that she had been here three weeks and would really like a chance to talk to one. Harriet wished she had come to the group the other weeks she was here because it made her feel less lonely but she was "chicken" to come before, afraid she wouldn't do well. Janice Ord was much more a part of the group this time and seemed quite well accepted. Cynthia Dawson had more confidence this time and developed her own pattern for a baby owl. Fritzi Phillips as previously showed enormous imagination and talent and was very engrossed in what she was doing. Beverly Lumpkin did not sign up this time and left immediately after dinner.

Evaluation. If the group were to be continued we should think about dividing it into two sessions since it is impossible to be sensitive to what is happening to so many girls even with a helper. This is probably reflected in the check sheets.

There were 26 girls who filled out check sheets. All said they would like to come again but just two-thirds of them said they talked about something that mattered, that they were happier than before they came and that they felt closer to other members of the group now. However, 15 checked all yeses and many of these wrote about looking forward to the group.

Twelve girls who were in the group last week were still in the unit and all of them came to the group this time.

Seventh Meeting, November 17—Number present 25

Catherine Alexander, Betty Anderson, Wanda Bekins, Sue Collins, Grace Darwin, Helen Duncan, Patricia Delong, Pam Anderson, Darlene Elkins, Kay Hanson, Freida Hendricks, Harriet Helms, Elli Johnson, Priscilla Lewis, Regina Hartford, Greta Gunderson, Carla Penders, Dot Myerson,

Joyce Phillips, Thelma Walker, Theresa Munoz, Janice Ord, Pam Larkins, Fay McFarlane, Ursilla Small.

Project. Washcloth and soap candles and rickrack candy canes. The candles were fun for the girls but were too quickly done. The candy canes were too intricate and anxiety producing. This is the first project that some of the girls left unfinished since the group began. The tiny stitches and the high degree of structure did not allow for the variety of competencies or an expression of individual taste.

Summary recording. The girls had the tables pulled together and were seated when Fran and I arrived at 5:30. One table was completely full. I should have asked one girl to go to the other table to make room for me because I was not a part of the group sitting on a chair just pulled up at the corner of a table. One of the first things I told the girls was that this would be the last meeting of the group. There was little reaction to this since I guess they all are expecting to have their babies this week anyway! The table where I was sitting seemed to have little going on. The girls were very subdued. I was subdued myself and I think the girls to some degree respond to my mood. I cut the ribbon for the candles the wrong length and apologized for this saying I thought I had it all checked out and then I made a mistake. Catherine spoke up and said that was okay. That was why they were all here. They had done the same thing. Everybody seemed to enjoy that! Fran saw a lot more happening at her table which was a similar group. There was considerable discussion about delivery and also sharing and helping one another.

Sue Collins stayed afterwards and talked about her experiences with the social worker in her home community and her anxiety about her little boy who was taken from her by court order. Joyce Phillips also stayed after the group was over discussing her anxiety about getting a job so she can support herself and her baby. Both expressed a lot of hostility toward county officials with whom they have had to deal. Both Fran and I talked with the girls about the HELP program and other resources which might be available to them. Theresa Munoz joined in the conversation when we considered how each of the girls might best earn her high school diploma since they had all quit school. They seemed grateful to have the chance to discuss their concerns and consider some of the alternatives available to them.

Pam Larkin is apparently feeling pretty unhappy since she checked "no" to all the questions on the check sheet except wishing to come again. Greta Gunderson also felt the group experience hadn't helped things very much for her.

Evaluation. Some of the girls decided that another time they would prefer to sit at individual tables like they do at dinner. Of course, this would mean we would have four groups instead of two. Perhaps this would allow them to more comfortably air their anxieties. It would also be hard for the worker to keep track of what was happening. Girls would probably sit in the friendship groupings and not interact with a broader group which is an advantage of the present arrangement.

Overall Evaluation

At the conclusion of each meeting participants were asked to complete a checklist. From a total of 111 respondents all said they would like to come again if they were here next week; 107 said they enjoyed the group because they were making something; 99 said they felt closer to other members of the group now; 96 replied that it was easier to talk because they were making something; 94 said they felt happier than before they came and 84 said they talked about something that mattered to them that evening.

Participants indicated their enthusiasm and appreciation for the group experience by their written comments: "I feel this is good to break the boredom and even though it is something small, you feel you have accomplished something in the end and it made me feel good inside." "This helps to pass the time and it helps to relieve some minds and gets us away from our problems for awhile." "The stuffed animals are really nice, especially for those of us who have little ones at home to give them to. Kinda makes up for being gone." "This project, I believe, is good for us because not only are we learning new things, we are learning to help others." "It takes concentration and in this way keeps our minds off of our problems." "I feel this is a good idea to have something different to look forward to each week. Being away from your family gets lonely and the class helps to make you a little happier." "You learn something about the people you are sharing this experience with." "I think this group is real nice for us girls. It gives me a good feeling to know I have accomplished something."

Although the women are quick to recognize that the group relieves their boredom, as a group worker I have seen much more than this happen. They have shown mutual concern for one another by sharing materials or letting an emotionally needy girl have a special color or pattern; a sad girl has been comforted; or an inept girl has been helped with her project. They have talked about their loneliness; how they miss their children and their anxiety about delivery. When they leave the group carrying a finished product which they have made many of the girls just "glow" with the satisfaction they feel about what they have been able to do. It seems apparent that they are happier and feel better about themselves. On several occasions an isolate has taken the courage to come to the group and then expresses the feeling of "belonging now."

The matron says the quality of the evening is different; the girls are not bickering as they usually do and many of them continue with similar projects all week which means they share patterns, materials, equipment.

Referrals have been made regularly to the social service staff on the basis of observation and expressed concerns. My experience with this group strongly suggests it meets many social and psychic needs of the patients and that it should be continued.

QUESTIONS

1. What are some of the important factors in this setting that must be considered by the worker as she gets underway with he group?
2. What are some of the needs of these young women that might be met by group experience?
3. How do you account for the increase in attendance as the group goes on?
4. What do you think of the choice of craft projects for this kind of short-term group with built-in turnover of members?
5. How can these girls help one another through group experience?
6. In what ways can the worker give help to the girls?
7. How would you evaluate this project? Do you agree that it should be continued?

Bibliography of Selected Readings

The literature of social group work has grown tremendously in the past two decades. This growth represents the vigor of the field and the increased willingness of practitioners to share their views and experiences with others. At the same time many of the early writings about group work continue to be of great value for the student. This bibliography of selected readings is an attempt to combine the early and basic material with the new writings. An effort has been made to offer a wide range of publications. Thus students who may have missed some of the early publications will find references to them here. For others who are familiar with the earlier works the more recent references will be of special value.

ACKLEY, EDITH, and FLIEGIL, BEVERLY. "A Social Work Approach to Street-Corner Girls," *Social Work,* October 1960.

ALLEN, RUTH E. "A Study of Subjects Discussed by Elderly Patients in Group Counselling," *Social Casework,* July 1962.

ALISSI, ALBERT S. "Social Influence on Group Values," *Social Work,* January 1965.

APAKA, T., HIRSCH, S., and KLEIDMAN, S. "Establishing Group Supervision in a Hospital Social Service Department," *Social Work,* October 1967.

ARONOWITZ, EUGENE. "Ulterior Motives in Games: Implications for Group Work with Children," *Social Work,* October 1968.

——— and WEINBERG, DENISE. "The Utilization of Reinforcement Theory in Social Group Work Practice," *Social Service Review,* December 1966.

AUSTIN, DAVID. "Goals for Gang Workers," *Social Work,* October 1957.

AVES, GERALDINE M. *The Voluntary Worker in the Social Services.* Beverly Hills, California: Sage Publications, 1969.

BAILEY, MARGARET B. "Al-Anon Family Groups—as an Aid to Wives of Alcoholics," *Social Work,* January 1965.

BAKER, J. "Male Adolescent Inmates' Perception of Helping Persons," *Social Work,* April 1965.

BAKER, LAURA NELSON. *Those Who Care.* Boston: Little Brown and Company, 1964.

BALES, ROBERT F. *Interaction Process Analysis: A Method for the Study of Small Groups.* Cambridge, Mass.: Addison-Wesley Press, 1951.

BARCLAY, LILLIAN E. "A Group Approach to Young Unwed Mothers," *Social Casework,* July 1969.

BARNWELL, JOHN. "Group Treatment of Older Adolescent Boys in a Family Agency," *Social Casework,* May 1960.

———. "The Mothers Club as a Setting for Group Counselling," in Norman Fenton and Kermit Wiltse, editors, *Group Methods in the Public Welfare Program.* Palo Alto, California: Pacific Books, 1963.

BARTLETT, HARRIET. "Towards Clarification and Improvement of Social Work Practice," *Social Work,* April 1958.

BATTEN, R. T. *The Non-directive Approach in Group and Community Work.* London: Oxford University Press, 1967.

BAUMGARTEL, HOWARD. "The Concept of Role," in Bennis, Benne, and Chin, *The Planning of Change.* New York: Holt, Rinehart, and Winston, 1961.

BELL, COURTNEY W., and KAPLAN, HARVEY L. "Public-Voluntary Sponsorship of a Mother's Group," *Social Casework,* January 1964.

BENNIS, WARREN G., SCHEIN, EDGAR H., BERLEW, DAVID E., and STEELE, FRED L. *Interpersonal Dynamics: Essays and Readings on Human Interaction.* Homewood, Illinois: The Dorsey Press, 1964.

BERELSON, BERNARD, and STEINER, GARY A. *Human Behavior: An Inventory of Scientific Findings,* New York: Harcourt, Brace, and World, 1964.

BERNE, ERIC. *Principles of Group Treatment.* New York: Oxford University Press, 1966.

———. *The Structure and Dynamics of Organizations and Groups.* New York: Grove Press, 1963.

BERNSTEIN, DANIEL R. "A Nine Year Old Finds Himself," *The Group,* January 1951.

———. "Social Group Work: A Diagnostic Tool in Child Guidance," *American Journal of Orthopsychiatry,* April 1965.

BERNSTEIN, SAUL. "Charting Group Progress," in Dorothea Sullivan, editor, *Readings in Group Work.* New York: Association Press, 1952.

———. "Values and Group Work," in Saul Bernstein, editor, *Further Explorations in Groups Work.* Boston University School of Social Work, 1970.

———, editor. *Explorations in Group Work—Essays in Theory and Practice.* Boston University School of Social Work, 1965.

BIDDLE, BRUCE J., and THOMAS, EDWIN J. *Role Theory—Concepts and Research.* New York: John Wiley and Sons, 1966.

BLACKEY, EILEEN A. *Group Leadership in Staff Training.* Washington, D.C.: U.S. Department of Health, Education, and Welfare, Children's Bureau Publication No. 361, 1964.

BLUM, ARTHUR. "Peer-Group Structure and a Child's Verbal Accessibility in a Treatment Institution," *Social Service Review,* December 1962.

———. "The Social Group Work Method: One View," in *A Conceptual Framework for the Teaching of Social Group Work Method in the Classroom.* New York: Council on Social Work Education, July 1964.

BORGATTA, EDGAR F. "What Social Science Says About Groups" in *Social Welfare Forum, 1957.* Published for the National Conference on Social Welfare by Columbia University Press, New York: 1957.

BOSWELL, LUADA. "A Report on Two Girl Scout Pilot Projects" in *New Perspectives on Services to Groups, 1961.* New York: National Association of Social Workers, 1961.

BRAGER, GEORGE. "Improving Service for Street-Corner Youth" in *Social Work Practice, 1962.* Published for the National Conference on Social Welfare by Columbia University Press, New York, 1962.

BRAVERMAN, SHIRLEY. "The Informal Peer Group as an Adjunct to Treatment of the Adolescent," *Social Casework,* March 1966.

BRIAR, SCOTT. "The Family as an Organization," *Social Service Review*, September 1964.

BRIGHT, SALLIE E. "Letting the Public in on Group Work Objectives," *The Group*, October 1948.

BRODSKY, IRVING. "The New Role of the Community Center," in *Social Welfare Forum, 1964*. Published for the National Conference on Social Welfare by Columbia University Press, 1964.

BROWN, LOUISE, and HARTFORD, MARGARET E. "Effecting Value Change in Race Relations Through Group Service Agencies," in *Social Work Practice, 1965*. Published for the National Conference on Social Welfare by Columbia University Press, New York, 1965.

BRUCK, MAX. "An Evaluation of the Use of Group Treatment for 'Hard-to-Reach' Latency-Age Children in a Community Guidance Clinic," *Child Welfare*, July 1966.

——. "Behavior Modification Theory and Practice," *Social Work*, April 1968.

BRUSSEL, BENJAMIN B. "The Educational and Therapeutic Effects of the Group Process Experience," *Mental Hygiene*, October 1967.

BURKE, P. J. "Authority Relations and Disruptive Behavior in Small Discussion Groups," *Sociometry*, September 1966.

BURNS, MARY E., and GLASSER, PAUL H. "Similarities and Differences in Casework and Group Work Practice," *Social Service Review*, December 1963.

CARLETTI, JUNE A. "Group Treatment of Chronic, Regressed Psychiatric Patients," *Social Casework*, February 1963.

CARTER, WOODROW W. "Group Counselling for Adolescent Foster Children," *Children*, January–February 1968.

CARTWRIGHT, DORWIN. "The Nature of Group Cohesiveness" in Dorwin Cartwright and Alvin Zander, editors, *Group Dynamics—Research and Theory*. Third Edition. New York: Harper and Row, 1968.

CARTWRIGHT, DORIN, and ZANDER, ALVIN. "Leadership and Performance of Group Functions: Introduction," in Dorwin Cartwright and Alvin Zander, editors, *Group Dynamics—Research and Theory*. Third Edition. New York: Harper and Row, 1968.

——. "Pressures to Uniformity in Groups: Introduction," in Dorwin Cartwright and Alvin Zander, editors, *Group Dynamics—Research and Theory*. Third Edition. New York: Harper and Row, 1968.

——. "The Structural Properties of Groups: Introduction," in Dorwin Cartwright and Alvin Zander, editors, *Group Dynamics—Research and Theory*. Third Edition. New York: Harper and Row, 1968.

——, editors. *Group Dynamics—Research and Theory*. Third Edition. New York: Harper and Row, 1968.

CELLI, VINCENT F. "Using Groups for Study of Prospective Adoptive Couples," *Public Welfare*, July 1969.

CHAPPELEAR, EDITH M., and FRIED, JOYCE E. "Helping Adopting Couples Come to Grips with Their New Parental Roles," *Children*, November–December 1967.

CHILMAN, CATHERINE S., and KRAFT, IVOR. "Helping Low-Income Parents Through Parent Education Groups," *Children*, July–August 1963.

CHURCHILL, SALLIE R. "Prestructuring Group Content," *Social Work*, July 1959.

——. "Social Group Work—a Diagnostic Tool," *American Journal of Orthopsychiatry*, April 1965.

COLE, MINERVA G., and PODELL, LAWRENCE. "Serving Handicapped Children in Group Programs," *Social Work*, January 1961.

COLLINS, BARRY E., and GUETZKOW, HAROLD. *A Social Psychology of Group Process for Decision-Making.* New York: John Wiley and Sons, 1964.

CONKLIN, LLOYD T., *et al.* "Use of Groups During the Adoptive Post-placement Period," *Social Work,* April 1962.

CONOVER, MERRILL B. "Group Services," in *Encyclopedia of Social Work, 1965.* New York: National Association of Social Workers, 1965.

CONRAD, GERTRUDE, and ELKINS, HARRY. "The First Eighteen Months of Group Counselling in a Family Service Agency," *Social Work,* March 1969.

COOMBS, R. H. "Social Participation, Self-Concept, and Interpersonal Valuation," *Sociometry,* September 1969.

CORTAZZO, ARNOLD D. "Increasing Sociability for the Retarded Through Activity Programs," *Journal of Rehabilitation,* March–April 1964.

COX, RACHEL. "Social Work in Elementary Schools: Techniques and Goals," *Social Work,* April 1963.

COYLE, GRACE L. "Concepts Relevant to Helping the Family as a Group," *Social Casework,* July 1962.

––––––. *Group Experience and Democratic Values.* New York: Woman's Press, 1947.

––––––. "Group Work in Psychiatric Settings: Its Roots and Branches," *Social Work,* January 1959.

––––––. *Group Work with American Youth.* New York: Harper and Brothers, 1948.

––––––. *Social Process in Organized Groups.* New York: Richard R. Smith, Inc., 1930.

––––––. "Some Basic Assumptions about Social Group Work" in Marjorie Murphy, editor, *The Social Group Work Method in Social Work Education,* Vol. XI, *Curriculum Study.* New York: Council on Social Work Education, 1959.

––––––. *Studies in Group Behavior.* New York: Harper, 1937.

––––––. "What Is This Social Group Work?" *The Survey,* May 1935.

––––––, and FISHER, RAYMOND. "Helping Hospitalized Children Through Group Work," *Children,* March–April 1952.

CROWTHERS, VIRGINIA L. "The School as a Group Setting" in *Social Work Practice, 1963.* Published for the National Conference on Social Welfare by Columbia University Press, New York, 1963.

CUDABACH, DOROTHEA, and KAHN, R. DAVID. "A Therapeutic Social Club for Post-hospitalized Psychiatric Patients" in *Social Work with Groups, 1959.* New York: National Association of Social Workers, 1959.

CYRUS, ADA SHEW. "Group Treatment of Disadvantaged Mothers," *Social Casework,* February 1967.

"Definition of the Function of the Group Worker," *The Group,* May 1949.

DILLON, VERA. "Group Intake in a Casework Agency," *Social Casework,* January 1965.

DILLOW, LOUISE B. "The Group Process in Adoptive Home Findings," *Children,* July–August 1968.

DIMOCK, HEDLEY S., and TRECKER, HARLEIGH B. *Supervision of Group Work and Recreation.* New York: Association Press, 1949.

DUBOIS, RACHEL DAVIS, and MEW-SOONG LI. *Reducing Social Tension and Conflict Through the Group Conversation Method.* New York: Association Press, 1971.

DOLL, ADOLIN G. "Group Learning for Foster Parents II—In a Public Agency," *Children,* September–October 1967.

DURFEE, ELIZABETH, *et al.* "An Adoptive Parents Group," *Child Welfare,* February 1965.

DURKIN, HELEN E. *The Group in Depth.* New York: International Universities Press, Inc., 1964.

Educational Developments in Social Group Work. New York: Council on Social Work Education, 1962.

EATON, JOSEPH. "A Scientific Base for Helping" in Alfred J. Kahn, editor, *Issues in American Social Work.* New York: Columbia University Press, 1961.

EISEN, ARNOLD. "Group Work with Newly Arrived Patients in a Mental Hospital," in *Social Work with Groups, 1958.* New York: National Association of Social Workers, 1958.

————, et al. "Group Processes in a Voluntary Psychiatric Hospital," *American Journal of Orthopsychiatry,* July 1963.

EISENSON, JON, AUER, J. JEFFREY, and IRWIN, JOHN V. *The Psychology of Communication.* New York: Appleton-Century-Crofts, 1963.

ELIAS, ALBERT. "Group Treatment Programs for Juvenile Delinquents," *Child Welfare,* May 1968.

EMERSON, R. M. "Mount Everest: A Case Study of Communication Feedback and Sustained Group Goal Striving," *Sociometry,* September 1966.

EMPEY, LE MAR T. "Sociological Perspectives and Small-Group Work with Socially Deprived Youth," *Social Service Review,* December 1968.

EPSTEIN, HOWARD V. "Group Work to Help Older Adults Fulfill Citizen Roles," in *Social Work Practice, 1965.* Published for the National Conference on Social Welfare by Columbia University Press, 1965.

ESHBAUGH, MARK, and WALSH, JAMES. "A Group Approach to Parents of Children in Trouble," *Children,* May–June 1964.

FAIL, NAOMI W. "Group Therapy in a Home for the Aged," *Gerontologist,* September 1967.

FALCK, HANS. "Social Group Work and Planned Change," in *Social Work Practice, 1964.* Published for the National Conference on Social Welfare by Columbia University Press, New York: 1964.

————. "The Use of Groups in the Practice of Social Work," *Social Casework,* February 1963.

FARRAR, MARCELLA, and FERRARI, NELIDA. "Casework and Group Work in a Home for the Aged," *Social Work,* April 1960.

FELDMAN, RONALD. "Determinants and Objectives in Social Group Work Intervention," in *Social Work Practice, 1967.* Published for the National Conference on Social Welfare by Columbia University Press, New York, 1967.

————. "Group Integration, Intense Interpersonal Dislike, and Social Group Work Intervention," *Social Work,* July 1969.

————. "Group Services Programs in Public Welfare: Pattern and Perspectives," *Public Welfare,* July 1969.

FENTON, NORMAN, and WILTSE, KERMIT T. *Group Methods in the Public Welfare Program.* Palo Alto: Pacific Books, 1963.

FEIT, MARVIN. "The Need for a Shift in Emphasis in Research Relevant to Social Group Workers," *Journal of Jewish Communal Service,* Summer 1969.

FINGER, SALLY. "The Group Method in Services to Unmarried Mothers and Their Parents," *Child Welfare,* December 1966.

FISHER, RAYMOND. "Use of Groups in Social Treatment by Caseworkers and Group Workers," in *Use of Groups in the Psychiatric Setting.* New York: National Association of Social Workers, 1960.

FORMAN, MARK. "Conflict, Controversy, and Confrontation in Group Work with Older Adults," *Social Work,* January 1967.

FOX, E. F. "The Termination Process: A Neglected Dimension in Social Work," *Social Work,* October 1969.

FRANK, DONALD S. "Group Counselling Benefits Jobseekers with Epilepsy," *Rehabilitation Record,* January–February 1968.

FRANKEL, GODFREY. "Acceptance and Rejection in Membership," *The Group,* June 1954.

FREEMAN, DOROTHY R. "Counselling Engaged Couples in Small Groups," *Social Work,* October 1965.

FREY, LOUISE A. "A Social Group Work Approach to Socially Disadvantaged Girls in a School," *Child Welfare,* December 1965.

———. "Support and the Group: A Generic Treatment Form," *Social Work,* October 1962.

———. "Social Group Work in Hospitals," in *New Perspectives on Services with Groups.* New York: National Association of Social Workers, 1961.

———, editor. *Use of Groups in the Health Field.* New York: National Association of Social Workers, 1966.

———, and KOLODNY, RALPH L. "Illusions and Realities in Current Social Work with Groups," *Social Work,* April 1964.

———, and MEYER, M. "Explorations and Working Agreement in Two Social Work Methods," in Saul Bernstein, editor, *Explorations in Group Work.* Boston University School of Social Work, 1965.

GANTER, GRACE, and POLANSKY, NORMAN A. "Predicting a Child's Accessibility to Individual Treatment from Diagnostic Groups," *Social Work,* July 1964.

GARLAND, JAMES A., and FREY, LOUISE A. "Application of Stages of Group Development to Groups in Psychiatric Settings," in Saul Bernstein, editor, *Further Explorations in Group Work.* Boston University School of Social Work, 1970.

GARVIN, CHARLES D., and GLASSER, PAUL H. "Social Group Work: The Preventive and Rehabilitative Approach," in *Encyclopedia of Social Work,* Sixteenth Issue, Vol. II. New York: National Association of Social Workers, 1971.

GERSHENSON, SIDNEY, and SCHREIBER, MEYER. "Mentally Retarded Teen Agers in a Social Group," *Children,* May–June 1963.

GILMAN, MARRIT, and GORLICH, ELIZABETH. *Group Counseling with Delinquent Youth.* Washington, D.C.: U.S. Department of Health, Education, and Welfare, Children's Bureau Publication No. 459, 1968.

GOLDSTEIN, HARRIET. "Group Learning for Foster Parents I—In a Voluntary Agency," *Children,* September–October 1967.

GLASSER, PAUL H. "Group Methods in Child Welfare: Review and Preview," *Child Welfare,* May 1963.

———. "Social Role, Personality and Group Work Practice," in *Social Work Practice, 1962.* Published for the National Conference on Social Welfare by Columbia University Press, New York, 1962.

GOLDBERG, THEODORE. "Group Work Practice in a Juvenile Detention Center," in *Social Work Practice, 1965.* Published for the National Conference on Social Welfare by Columbia University Press, New York, 1965.

GOTTSEGM, MONROE G. "The Role of an Assessment Group in a Hospital Setting," *American Journal of Psychotherapy,* January 1963.

GROB, HARRY E., JR., and VAN DOREN, ERIC E. "Aggressive Group Work with Teenage Delinquent Boys," *Children,* May–June 1969.

GRODOFSKY, DANIEL. "Values: Implications for Current Practice," *Journal of Jewish Communal Service,* Summer 1969.

Group Method and Services in Child Welfare. New York: Child Welfare League of America, 1963.

"Group Services in Public Welfare Settings," *Public Welfare,* October 1968.

Group Treatment in Family Service Agencies. New York: Family Service Association of America, 1964.

"Group Work in the Division of Rehabilitation, District of Columbia," *Rehabilitation Record,* January–February 1970.

GURTSMA, ROBERT H. "Group Therapy with Juvenile Probationers and Their Parents," *Federal Probation,* March 1960.

GUST, TIM. "Group Counseling with Rehabilitation Clients," *Rehabilitation Record,* January–February 1970.

HAGBERG, K. L. "Combining Social Casework and Group Work Methods in a Children's Hospital," *Children,* September–October 1969.

HALL, SELMA B. "Understanding of Development Goals of Older Adults as an Imperative in Social Group Work Practice," in *Social Work Education for Better Services to the Aging,* Vol. II. New York: Council on Social Work Education, 1959.

HANWELL, ALBERT F. *A Guide for Foster Parent Group Education.* Boston: Boston College Graduate School of Social Work, 1969.

HARE, PAUL A., *et al,* editors. *Small Groups: Studies in Social Interaction.* New York: Knopf, 1965.

HARLOW, MINNIE. "Content of the Group Experience in a Psychiatric Hospital," in *Social Group Work with Older People.* New York: National Association of Social Workers, 1963.

HARM, CARL S., and GOLDEN, JOSEPH. "Group Worker's Role in Social Process in a Medical Institution," *Social Work,* April 1961.

HARRIS, ELIZABETH T. "Parents Without Partners, Inc.: A Resource for Clients," *Social Work,* April 1966.

HARTFORD, MARGARET E. "The Preparation of Social Workers Competent to Practice with People in Groups," *Journal of Social Work Education,* Fall 1967.

————. "Social Work in Group Services—Changing Approaches in Practice Theory and Techniques," in *Trends in Social Work Practice and Knowledge.* New York: National Association of Social Workers, 1966.

————. "Use of Social Group Work in Helping Members Accept Difference," in *Social Work Practice, 1964.* Published for the National Conference on Social Welfare by Columbia University Press, New York, 1964.

————, editor. *Working Papers Toward a Frame of Reference for Social Group Work.* New York: National Association of Social Workers, 1964.

HESLIN, RICHARD, and DUNPHY, DEXTER. "Three Dimensions of Member Satisfaction in Small Groups," *Human Relations,* May 1964.

HESS, ROBERT D., and HANDEL, GERALD. "The Family as a Psychosocial Organization," in Gerald Handel, editor, *The Psychosocial Interior of the Family.* Chicago: Aldine Publishing Company, 1967.

HILL, WILLIAM. "Two Approaches for Analyzing Family Group Interaction," in *Social Work Practice, 1964.* Published for the National Conference on Social Welfare by Columbia University Press, New York, 1964.

HOMANS, GEORGE. *The Human Group.* New York: Harcourt, Brace, and World, Inc., 1950.

JACOBS, JOSEPH. "Social Action as Therapy in a Mental Hospital," *Social Work,* January 1964.

JOHNSON, ARLIEN. *School Social Work.* New York: National Association of Social Workers, 1962.

JOHNSON, MARTHA. "A Child Welfare Worker Uses the Group Method with A.D.C. Families," *Child Welfare,* January 1963.

KAISER, CLARA A. "Characteristics of Social Group Work," in *Social Welfare*

Forum, 1957. Published for the National Conference on Social Welfare by Columbia University Press, New York, 1957.

——. "The Social Group Work Process," in Marjorie Murphy, editor, *The Social Group Work Method in Social Work Education*, Vol. XI, *Curriculum Study*. New York: Council on Social Work Education, 1959.

——. "The Social Group Work Process," *Social Work*, April 1958.

KAPLAN, IRVING H. "Some Aspects of Group Work in a Psychiatric Hospital," *Social Work*, July 1960.

KATZ, ROBERT L. *Empathy: Its Nature and Uses*. New York: The Free Press of Glencoe, 1967.

KEVIN, DAVID. "Group Counselling of Mothers in an A.F.D.C. Program," *Children*, March–April 1967.

KIESLER, CHARLES. "Conformity and Commitment," *Transaction*, June, 1967.

KLEIN, ALAN F. "Exploring Family Group Counselling," *Social Work*, January 1963.

——. "Individual Change Through Group Experience," in *Social Welfare Forum, 1959*. Published for the National Conference of Social Welfare by Columbia University Press, New York, 1959.

——. *Social Work Through Group Process*. Albany: State University of New York at Albany, School of Social Work, 1970.

——. *Society—Democracy and the Group*. New York: Whiteside, 1953.

KLEIN, JOYCE G. "Social Group Treatment: Some Selected Dynamics," in *Use of Groups in the Psychiatric Setting*. New York: National Association of Social Workers, 1961.

KLEIN, MALCOLM. "Juvenile Gangs, Police and Detached Workers: Controversies about Intervention," *Social Service Review*, June 1965.

KOLODNY, RALPH L. " A Group Approach to the Isolated Child," *Social Work*, July 1961.

——. "The Handicapped Child and His Peer Group: Strategy for Integration," in Saul Bernstein, editor, *Further Explorations in Group Work*. Boston University School of Social Work, 1970.

——. "The Impact of Peer Group Activity on the Alienated Child—Experiences of a Specialized Group Work Department," *Smith College Studies in Social Work*, February 1967.

——, and WALDFOGEL, SAMUEL. "Modifying Tensions Between the Handicapped and Their Normal Peers in Group Work with Children," *Child Welfare*, January 1967.

KONOPKA, GISELA. *Group Work in the Institution*. New York: Association Press, 1970. Revised Edition.

——. *Social Group Work: A Helping Process*. Englewood Cliffs, N.J.: Prentice-Hall, 1963.

——. "Social Group Work: A Social Work Method," *Social Work*, October 1960.

——. "The Role of the Group Worker in the Psychiatric Setting," *American Journal of Orthopsychiatry*, January 1952.

——, and CZAKY, VERNIE-MAE L. *An Approach to the Evaluation of Change Through the Use of Group Work Method*. School of Social Work, University of Minnesota, October 1965. Mimeographed.

KRUSCHKE, DOUGLASS, and STOLLER, FREDERICK H. "Face to Face with the Drug Addict: An Account of an Intensive Group Experience," *Federal Probation*, June 1967.

LAIBMAN, ERWIN M. "Group Counselling with Parents in an Agency Serving Adolescents," *Social Work*, April 1961.

LANE, DOROTHEA. "Psychiatric Patients Learn a New Way of Life" in *New*

Perspectives on Services to Groups: Theory, Organization and Practice. New York: National Association of Social Workers, 1961.

LEADER, ARTHUR L. "The Role of Intervention in Family-Group Treatment," *Social Casework,* June 1964.

LEICHTER, ELSE. "Scope and Versatility of Group Counselling in Family Casework," in *The Use of Group Techniques in the Family Agency.* New York: Family Service Association of America, 1959.

LERMAN, PAUL. "Group Work with Youth in Conflict," *Social Work,* October 1958.

LEVINE, BARUCH. *Fundamentals of Group Treatment.* Chicago: Whitehall Company, 1967.

————. "Principles for Developing Ego-Supportive Group Treatment Service," *Social Service Review,* December 1965.

————, and SCHILD, JUDITH. "Group Treatment of Depression," *Social Work,* October 1969.

LEWIN, KURT. *Resolving Social Conflicts.* New York: Harper and Brothers, 1945.

LIFTON, WALTER. *Working with Groups: Group Process and Individual Growth.* New York: John Wiley and Sons, Inc., 1966.

LIPPITT, RONALD. "Unplanned Maintenance and Planned Change in the Group Work Process," in *Social Work Practice, 1962.* Published for the National Conference on Social Welfare by Columbia University Press, New York, 1962.

LIPPMAN, HYMAN. "Diagnosis and Treatment of Children in Groups," in *Use of Groups in a Psychiatric Setting.* New York: National Association of Social Workers, 1960.

LINDBERG, DWAINE, and WOSMEK, ANNE W. "The Use of Family Sessions in Foster Home Care," *Social Casework,* March 1963.

LINDSAY, ANNE W. *Group Work Recording—Principles and Practices.* New York: Whiteside, 1952.

LOWY, LOUIS. "Goal Formation in Social Work with Groups," in Saul Bernstein, editor, *Further Explorations in Group Work.* Boston University School of Social Work, 1970.

————. "Meeting the Needs of Older People on a Differential Basis," in *Social Group Work with Older People.* New York: National Association of Social Workers, 1963.

————. "The Group in Social Work with the Aged," *Social Work,* October 1962.

MAAS, HENRY. "Group Influence on Client-Worker Interaction," *Social Work,* April 1964.

MABLEY, ALBERTINA. "Group Application Interviews in a Family Agency," *Social Casework,* March 1966.

MAIER, HENRY W. "Application of Psychological and Sociological Theory to Teaching Social Work with the Group," *Journal of Education for Social Work,* Spring 1967.

————. "Group Living: A Unique Feature in Residential Treatment," in *Social Work with Groups.* New York: National Association of Social Workers, 1961.

————, editor. *Group Work as a Part of Residential Treatment.* New York: National Association of Social Workers, 1965.

Making Democracy Work—a Study of Neighborhood Organization. New York: National Federation of Settlements and Neighborhood Centers, 1968.

MANDELBAUM, ARTHUR. "The Group Process in Helping Parents of Retarded Children," *Children,* November–December 1967.

MATSUSHIMA, JOHN. "Group Work with Emotionally Disturbed Children in Residential Treatment," *Social Work,* April 1962.

————, and BERWALD, CATHERINE. "The Group Worker's Contribution in Residential Treatment of a Boy," *Social Service Review,* September 1965.

MAXWELL, JEAN M. "Group Services—Well-being for Older People" in *Social Work with Groups.* New York: National Association of Social Workers, 1960.

————. "Helping Older People Through Social Group Work," in *Potentials for Service Through Group Work in Public Welfare.* Chicago: American Public Welfare Association, 1962.

McCOY, JACQUELINE, and DONAHUE, JACK M. "Educating Foster Mothers Through the Group Process," *Child Welfare,* March 1960.

McGRIFF, DOROTHY. "Working with a Group of Authoritative Mothers," *Social Work,* January 1960.

MIDDLEMAN, RUTH R. "Social Group Work in a Maternity Home," *Child Welfare,* February 1959.

————. *The Non-verbal Method in Working with Groups.* New York: Association Press, 1968.

MILLS, ROBERT B., *et al.* "Introducing Foster Mother Training Groups in a Voluntary Child Welfare Agency," *Child Welfare,* December 1967.

MILLS, THEODORE M. *The Sociology of Small Groups.* Englewood Cliffs, N.J.: Prentice-Hall, Inc., 1967.

MONTELIUS, MARJORIE. *Helping People in Groups.* Six Background Papers from the Workshop on Group Services, April 1965. Washington, D.C.: U.S. Department of Health, Education, and Welfare.

————. *Working with Groups: A Guide for Administration of Group Services in Public Welfare.* Washington, D.C.: U.S. Department of Health, Education, and Welfare, 1966.

NEWMAN, CARL, and GLOVER, LAURICE. "Group Psychotherapy and Social Group work: A Clinical Comparison," *Mental Hygiene,* October 1967.

NEWSTETTER, W. I. "What Is Social Group Work?" in *Proceedings of the National Conference on Social Work.* Chicago: University of Chicago Press, 1935.

NORTHEN, HELEN. "Evaluating Movement of Individuals in Social Group Work," in *Group Work Papers, 1957.* National Conference on Social Welfare. New York: National Association of Social Workers, 1958.

————. "Interrelated Functions of the Social Group Worker," *Social Work,* April 1957.

————. *Social Work with Groups.* New York: Columbia University Press, 1969.

OLMSTEAD, MICHAEL S. *The Small Group.* New York: Random House, 1959.

ORTOF, MURRAY. "Group Services to Families Receiving A.D.C.," *Child Welfare,* March 1962.

————. "The Small Group and Agency Goal Attainment," *Journal of Jewish Communal Service,* Winter 1963.

O'ROURKE, HELEN, and CHAVERA, FAYE. "The Use of Groups with Unmarried Mothers to Facilitate Casework," *Child Welfare,* January 1968.

OTTAWAY, A. K. C. *Learning Through Group Experience.* London: Routledge and Kegan Paul, 1966.

PAPELL, CATHERINE, and ROTHMAN, BEULAH. "Group Work's Contribution to a Common Method," in *Social Work Practice, 1966.* Published for the National Conference on Social Welfare by Columbia University Press, New York, 1966.

————. "Social Group Work Models: Possession and Heritage," *Journal of Education for Social Work,* Fall 1966.

PARADISE, ROBERT. "The Factor of Timing in the Addition of New Members to Established Groups," *Child Welfare,* November 1968.

————, and DANIELS, ROBERT. "Group Composition as a Treatment Tool with Children," in Saul Bernstein, editor, *Further Explorations in Group Work.* Boston University School of Social Work, 1970.

PHILLIPS, GERALD M., and ERICKSON, EUGENE C. *Interpersonal Dynamics in the Small Group.* New York: Random House, 1970.

PHILLIPS, HELEN. *Essentials of Social Group Work Skill.* New York: Association Press, 1951.

————. "Group Services to Clients: Purpose and Process," *Child Welfare,* June 1963.

————. "What Is Group Work Skill?" *The Group,* June 1954.

PEIRCE, FRANK J. "Social Group Work in a Women's Prison," *Federal Probation,* December 1963.

Potentials for Service Through Group Work in Public Welfare. Chicago: American Public Welfare Association, 1962.

PREININGER, D. R. "Reactions of Normal Children to Retardates in Integrated Groups," *Social Work,* April 1968.

RANK, BETTY JANE. "Content of the Group Experience in a Day Center" in *Social Group Work with Older People.* New York: National Association of Social Workers, 1963.

RATHBUN, CONSTANCE, and KOLODNY, RALPH L. "A Group Approach to Cross-Cultural Adoptions," *Children,* May–June 1967.

REDL, FRITZ. "The Art of Group Composition," in Suzanne Schulze, editor, *Creative Group Living in a Children's Institution.* New York: Association Press, 1951.

REISTROFFER, MARY. "A University Extension Course for Foster Parents," *Children,* January–February 1968.

RIEGEL, BARBARA. "Group Meetings with Adolescents in Child Welfare," *Child Welfare,* July 1968.

RIESSMAN, FRANK. "The Helper Therapy Principle," *Social Work,* April 1965.

ROBBINS, HAROLD W., and SLAWSON, ROBERT W. "Program Curriculum, Means or End—Another Look," *Journal of Jewish Communal Service,* Fall 1960.

ROGERS, CARL R. *Freedom to Learn.* Columbus, Ohio: Charles E. Merrill Publishing Company, 1969.

ROGERS, MURIEL NELSON. "A Group Educational Program for Marginally Adjusted Families," *Social Casework,* April 1962.

ROSE, SHELDON D. "A Behavioral Approach to Group Treatment of Children," in *The Socio-Behavioral Approach and Applications to Social Work.* New York: Council on Social Work Education, 1967.

————. "A Behavioral Approach to the Group Treatment of Parents," *Social Work,* July 1969.

ROSTOV, BARBARA. "Group Work in the Psychiatric Hospital: A Critical Review of the Literature," *Social Work,* January 1965.

RYAN, FRANCIS J. "Clarifying Some Issues in Family Group Casework," *Social Casework,* April 1967.

SACKS, GERDA G. "The Group Method in Services to Foster Parents of Pre-adoptive Children," *Child Welfare,* December 1966.

SALOSHIN, H. E. *Development of an Instrument for the Analysis of the Social Group Work Method in Therapeutic Settings.* Ph. D. Dissertation, School of Social Work, University of Minnesota, 1954.

SARRI, ROSEMARY, and GALINSKY, M. J. "A Conceptual Framework for Teaching Group Development in Social Group Work," in *A Conceptual Framework for the Teaching of the Social Group Method in the Classroom.* New York: Council on Social Work Education, 1964.

SARRI, ROSEMARY, et al. "Diagnosis in Group Work," in Robert Vinter, editor, *Readings in Group Work Practice.* Ann Arbor, Michigan: Campus Publications, 1967.

SAUL, SHURA, SEGAL, ARTHUR, and SAUL, SIDNEY R. "The Use of the Small Group in Orienting New Residents to a Home for the Aged: The Admission Group," *Journal of Jewish Communal Service,* Spring 1962.

SAUL, SIDNEY R., EISMAN, NADINE, and SAUL, SHURA. "The Use of the Small Group in the Helping Process," *The New Outlook for the Blind,* April 1964.

SCARPITTI, FRANK, and STEPHENSON, RICHARD M. "The Use of the Small Group in the Rehabilitation of Delinquents," *Federal Probation,* September 1966.

SCHEIDLINGER, SAUL. "Social Group Work and Group Psychotherapy," *Social Work,* July 1956.

———. "The Concept of Latency: Implications for Group Treatment," *Social Casework,* June 1966.

SCHEIN, E., and BENNIS, W. G. *Personal and Organizational Change Through Group Methods.* New York: John Wiley, 1966.

SCHWARTZ, WILLIAM. "Group Experience in Resident Camping," *Social Work,* April 1960.

———. "Group Work and the Social Scene," in Alfred Kahn, editor, *Issues in American Social Work.* New York: Columbia University Press, 1959.

———. "Group Work in Public Welfare," *Public Welfare,* October 1968.

———. "Neighborhood Centers and Group Work," in Henry S. Maas, editor, *Research in the Social Sciences: A Five Year Review.* New York: National Association of Social Workers, 1971.

———. "Small Group Science and Group Work Practice," *Social Work,* October 1963.

———. "Social Group Work: The Interactionist Approach," in *Encyclopedia of Social Work,* Sixteenth Issue, Vol. II. New York: National Association of Social Workers, 1971.

———. "Toward a Strategy of Group Work Practice," *Social Service Review,* September 1962.

———, and ZALBA, SERAPIO R., editors. *The Practice of Group Work.* New York: Columbia University Press, 1971.

SHALINSKY, W. "Group Composition as an Element of Social Group Work Practice," *Social Service Review,* March 1969.

SHAPIRO, JOAN. "Group Work with Urban Rejects in a Slum Hotel," in *Social Work Practice, 1967.* Published for the National Conference on Social Welfare by Columbia University Press, New York, 1967.

———. "Single-Room Occupancy: Community of the Alone," *Social Work,* October 1966.

———. *Communities of the Alone: Working with Single Room Occupants in the City.* New York: Association Press, 1971.

SHEPHERD, CLOVIS R. *Small Groups: Some Sociological Perspectives.* San Francisco: Chandler Publishing Co., 1964.

SHERMAN, SANFORD N. "The Sociopsychological Character of Family Group Treatment," *Social Casework,* April 1964.

SHOEMAKER, LOUISE P. "Group Work in Public Welfare," in *Social Work Practice, 1967.* Published for the National Conference on Social Welfare by Columbia University Press, New York, 1967.

———. "Social Group Work in the A.D.C. Program," *Social Work,* January 1963.

———. "The Use of Group Work Skills with Short-Term Groups," in *Social Work with Groups, 1960.* New York: National Association of Social Workers, 1960.

SHORE, HERBERT. "Content of the Group Experience in a Home for the Aged," in *Social Group Work with Older People.* New York: National Association of Social Workers, 1963.

SHORT, JAMES F., JR., and STRODTBECK, FRED L. *Group Process and Gang Delinquency.* Chicago: University of Chicago Press, 1965.

SHULMAN, LAWRENCE. *A Casebook of Social Work with Groups: The Mediating Model.* New York: Council on Social Work Education, 1968.

———. "Scapegoats, Group Workers and Pre-emptive Intervention," *Social Work,* April 1967.

SIDMAN, JACK, and SIDMAN, LEONA KAY. "Community Volunteers as Discussion Leaders for Juvenile Probationers," in *Volunteer Programs in Courts.* U.S. Department of Health, Education, and Welfare, Social and Rehabiltation Service, Office of Juvenile Delinquency and Youth Development, 1969.

SILVERMAN, MARVIN. "Knowledge in Social Group Work: A Review of the Literature," *Social Work,* July 1966.

SILVERSTEIN, SANDRA. "A New Venture in Group Work with the Aged," *Social Casework,* December 1969.

SLAVSON, S. R. *Creative Group Education.* New York: Association Press, 1937.

SLOAN, MARION. "The Role of the Group Worker in the Adult Psychiatric Hospital," in Harleigh B. Trecker, editor, *Group Work in the Psychiatric Setting.* New York: Whiteside, 1956.

SMALLEY, RUTH. *Theory for Social Work Practice.* New York: Columbia University Press, 1967.

Social Group Work with Older People: Proceedings of a Seminar, June, 1961. New York: National Association of Social Workers, 1963.

SOLOMAN, BARBARA BRYANT. "Social Group Work in the Adult Out-patient Clinic," *Social Work,* October 1968.

SOMERS, MARY LOUISE. "Group Processes Within the Family Unit," in *The Family as the Patient: The Group Approach to Treatment.* New York: National Association of Social Workers, 1965.

SPELLMAN, DOROTHEA C. "Nucleus and Boundaries in Social Group Work: Seven Propositions," *Social Work,* October 1961.

SPERGEL, IRVING. "Selecting Groups for Street Work Service," *Social Work,* April 1965.

———. *Street Gang Work—Theory and Practice.* Reading, Mass.: Addison-Wesley Publishing Company, 1966.

STANLEY, RUTH LIGHT. "The Group Method in Foster Home Studies," in *Social Work Practice, 1963.* Published for the National Conference on Social Welfare by Columbia University Press, New York, 1963.

STEIDEMAN, ETHEA GILL. "Group Treatment with Resistant Family Service Clients," *Social Casework,* January 1964.

STRICKER, MARTIN, and ALLGEYER, JEAN. "The Crisis Group: A New Application of Crisis Theory," *Social Work,* July 1967.

STUART, RICHARD. "Research in Social Work: Social Casework and Social Group Work," in *Encyclopedia of Social Work,* Sixteenth Issue, Vol. II. New York: National Association of Social Workers, 1971.

SULLIVAN, DOROTHEA F., editor. *Readings in Group Work.* New York: Association Press, 1952.

TANAKA, HENRY. "Group Living on a Psychiatric Ward," *Social Work*, October 1962.

TAYLOR, CHARLES W. "An Experiment in Group Counselling with Juvenile Parolees," *Crime and Delinquency*, October 1961.

THIBAUT, J. W., and KELLEY, H. H. *The Social Psychology of Groups*. New York: John Wiley and Sons, Inc., 1969.

THOMAS, CAROLYN. "The Use of Group Methods with Foster Parents," *Children*, November–December 1961.

THOMPSON, SHEILA, and KAHN, J. H. *The Group Process as a Helping Technique*. Oxford: Pergamon Press, 1970.

TINE, SEBASTIAN. "Process and Criteria for Grouping," in *Social Group Work with Older People*. New York: National Association of Social Workers, 1963.

———, HASTINGS, KATHERINE, and DEUTSCHBERGER, PAUL. "Generic and Specific in Social Group Work Practice with the Aging," in *Social Work with Groups, 1960*. Selected Papers, National Conference on Social Welfare, 1960. New York: National Association of Social Workers, 1961.

TOWEY, MARTIN, et al. "Group Activities with Psychiatric Inpatients," *Social Work*, January 1966.

"The Group Method with Clients, Foster Families and Adoptive Families," *Child Welfare*, December 1966.

"The Use of Groups at a Training School for Delinquent Girls" and "Group Work in a Maximum Security Prison," *An Occasional Paper*, Number 6. School of Social Work, University of Wisconsin, 1968.

TRECKER, AUDREY R., and TRECKER, HARLEIGH B. *Committee Common Sense*. New York: Whiteside, 1954.

———. *How to Work with Groups*. New York: Woman's Press, 1952.

TRECKER, HARLEIGH B. *Group Services in Public Welfare: Guide for Administration and Program Development*. Washington, D.C.: U.S. Department of Health, Education, and Welfare, Bureau of Family Services, 1964.

———, editor. *Group Work Foundations and Frontiers*. New York: Whiteside and William Morrow and Co., 1955.

———, editor. *Group Work in the Psychiatric Setting*. New York: Whiteside and William Morrow and Co., 1956.

———. "Social Group Work," in *Social Work Yearbook*. New York: Russell Sage Foundation, 1949.

———. *Social Group Work—Principles and Practices*. Revised and enlarged. New York: Association Press, 1955. Fifth printing, 1957.

TROPP, EMANUEL. *A Humanistic Foundation for Group Work Practice*. New York: Selected Academic Readings, 1969.

———. "Group Intent and Group Structure: Essential Criteria for Group Work Practice," *Journal of Jewish Communal Service*, Spring 1965.

———. "The Further Development of Group Work as a Separate Method," in *Social Work Practice, 1966*. Published for the National Conference on Social Welfare by Columbia University Press, New York, 1966.

———. "Maturity in Social Functioning: The Developmental Goal of Group Work," *Journal of Jewish Communal Service*, Winter 1966.

———. "Social Group Work: The Developmental Approach," in *Encyclopedia of Social Work*, Sixteenth Issue, Vol. II. New York: National Association of Social Workers, 1971.

———. "The Group: In Life and in Social Work," *Social Casework*, May 1968.

TULANE UNIVERSITY SCHOOL OF SOCIAL WORK. *The Use of Group Methods in the Practice of Casework: A Workshop*. New Orleans: Tulane University, 1960.

TYLER, RALPH. "Implications of Research in the Behavioral Sciences for Group Life and Group Services," in *Social Welfare Forum, 1960*. Published for the National Conference on Social Welfare by Columbia University Press, New York, 1960.

VERNER, MAJOR MARY E. "The Group Approach in a Maternity Home," *Child Welfare*, September 1961.

VINIK, ABE. "Role of the Group Service Agency," *Social Work*, July 1964.

VINTER, ROBERT D. *Readings in Group Work Practice*. Ann Arbor, Michigan: Campus Publications, 1967.

———. "Social Group Work," in *Encyclopedia of Social Work*. New York: National Association of Social Workers, 1965.

———. "The Social Structure of Service," in Edwin J. Thomas, editor, *Behavioral Science for Social Workers*. New York: The Free Press, 1967.

———, and SARRI, ROSEMARY. "Group Method for the Control of Behavior Problems in Secondary Schools," in David Street, editor, *Innovations in Mass Education*. New York: John Wiley and Sons, 1969.

———, and SARRI, ROSEMARY. "Malperformance in the Public Schools: A Group Work Approach," *Social Work*, January 1965.

VOGT, HERBERT. "Group Counselling in Juvenile Probation," *Federal Probation*, September 1961.

WALSH, BETTY, and SPITZER, KURT. "A Problem Focused Model of Practice," *Social Casework*, June 1969.

WATSON, KENNETH W. "Preadolescent Foster Children in Group Discussion," *Children*, March–April 1968.

WEINER, HYMAN J. "The Hospital, The Ward, and The Patient as Clients," *Social Work*, October 1959.

———. "Social Change and Social Group Work Practice," *Social Work*, July 1964.

WEISMAN, CELIA. "Social Structure as a Determinant of the Group Worker's Role," *Social Work*, July 1963.

WEISSMAN, HAROLD H., and HEIFETZ, HENRY. "Changing Program Emphases of Settlement Houses," *Social Work*, October 1968.

———. *Individual and Group Services in the Mobilization for Youth Experience*. New York: Association Press, 1969.

WHITE, RALPH, and LIPPITT, RONALD. "Leader Behavior and Member Reactions in Three Social Climates," in Dorwin Cartwright and Alvin Zander, editors, *Group Dynamics*. New York: Harper and Row, 1968. Third edition.

WILSON, GERTRUDE. "The Social Worker's Role in Group Situations" in Marjorie Murphy, editor, *The Social Group Work Method in Social Work Education*, Vol. XI, *Curriculum Study*. New York: Council on Social Work Education, 1959.

———, and RYLAND, GLADYS. *Social Group Work Practice*. Cambridge: Riverside Press, 1949.

WITTES, GLORIANNE, and RADIN, NORMA. "Two Approaches to Group Work with Parents in a Compensatory Preschool Program," *Social Work*, January 1971.

WOLF, ARON S. "Participation of the Aged in the Group Process," *Mental Hygiene*, July 1967.

WOODRUFF, ROBERT R. "Group Work in a Children's Hospital," *Social Work*, July 1957.

WYERS, NORMAN L. "Adaptations of the Social Group Work Method," *Social Casework*, November 1969.

YOUNGMAN, LOUISE C. "Social Group Work in the A.F.D.C. Program," *Public Welfare,* January 1965.

ZENO, FRANK B. "Social Work with Groups of [Hospital] Patients' Relatives," in Claire R. Lustman, editor, *Social Work with Groups.* Veterans Administration Hospital, Pittsburgh, Pa., 1963.

Index